AN INTRODUCTION
TO COUNSELLING

AN INTRODUCTION
TO COUNSELLING

John McLeod

Open University Press
Buckingham · Philadelphia

Open University Press
Celtic Court
22 Ballmoor
Buckingham
MK18 1XW

and
1900 Frost Road, Suite 101
Bristol, PA 19007, USA

First Published 1993

A catalogue record of this book is available from the British Library

ISBN 0 335 19018 9 (pb)

Library of Congress Cataloging-in-Publication Data
McLeod, John, 1951–
    An introduction to counselling / John McLeod.
        p.   cm.
    Includes bibliographical references and index.
    ISBN 0-335-19018-9 (pbk.)
    1. Counseling.   I. Title.
BF637.C6M379   1993
361.3′ 23—dc20   92-40324
                                                        CIP

Typeset by Colset Pte Ltd, Singapore
Printed in Great Britain by Biddles Ltd, Guildford and King's Lynn

To the memory of my mother, Isobel McLeod

CONTENTS

ACKNOWLEDGEMENTS

I would like to acknowledge the generous collaboration of a number of people who have discussed the ideas in this book and have greatly contributed to its relevance, clarity and accuracy: Ida Bentley, David Brazier, Dee Cooper, Pam Horrocks, Maya Patel and Phil Smith. My thanks are also due to Chuck Devonshire, Colin Lago, Elke Lambers, Dave Mearns and Brian Thorne for enabling me to learn counselling, and to Boris Semeonoff who enabled me to learn scholarship. My colleagues Val Davies, Chris Phillipson and Clair Wardle have been highly supportive in the way they have tolerated my preoccupation with this writing task over a very busy period in the department.

My last, and by far my greatest, debt is to my wife Julia, without whose encouragement I would never have attempted this book, and without whose unstinting love and assistance I would never have completed it.

ONE

WHAT IS COUNSELLING?
THE CULTURAL ORIGINS OF
CONTEMPORARY PRACTICE

Counselling is an activity embedded in the culture of modern industrialized societies. It represents an occupation and activity of relatively recent origins. In Britain, the Standing Council for the Advancement of Counselling (SCAC) was formed in 1971, and became the British Association for Counselling (BAC) in 1976. The membership of the BAC grew from 1000 in 1977 to 8556 in 1992 (BAC, 1977, 1992). In the USA the more specialized Division 17 (Counselling Psychology) of the American Psychological Association expanded from 645 members in 1951 to 2695 in 1978 (Whiteley, 1984). These figures indicate only the extent of the growth in numbers of more highly trained or professionalized counsellors in these countries. There are, in addition, many people active in voluntary organizations who provide non-professional counselling and who are not represented in these statistics. And the majority of people now working in the 'human service' professions, including nursing, teaching, the clergy, the police and many others, would consider counselling to be part of their work role. Counselling has been a relatively recent addition to the range of 'human service' professions, and its meaning and place within contemporary culture is still evolving. For example, there can be found contrasting definitions of 'counselling':

> The term 'counselling' includes work with individuals and with relationships which may be developmental, crisis support, psychotherapeutic, guiding or problem solving . . . The task of counselling is to give the 'client' an opportunity to explore, discover and clarify ways of living more satisfyingly and resourcefully.
>
> (BAC, 1984)

Counseling denotes a professional relationship between a trained counsellor and a client. This relationship is usually person-to-person, although it may sometimes involve more than two people. It is designed to help clients to understand and clarify their views of their lifespace, and to learn to reach their self-determined goals through meaningful, well-informed

choices and through resolution of problems of an emotional or interpersonal nature.

(Burks and Stefflre, 1979: 14)

It can be seen from these definitions that counselling can have different meanings. For example, Burks and Stefflre (1979) stress the idea of the 'professional'
relationship, and the importance of 'self-determined' goals. The BAC definition
places emphasis on exploration and understanding rather than action. These
contrasting interpretations arise from the process by which counselling has
emerged within modern society. In this chapter, these definitions will be
explored through an examination of their cultural and historical context.

Counselling is provided under a variety of different labels. To employ a
metaphor from the world of business, there are a range of competing products
which offer the consumer or client more or less the same service. The up-market
version of the product is sold as 'psychotherapy', which is provided by practitioners who are usually very highly trained specialist professionals, often with a
background in medicine. Psychotherapy can be a lengthy process. Although
there is an increasing interest in forms of 'brief' psychotherapy, which may consist of a series of ten or twelve sessions, it is probably fair to say that most
psychotherapists would consider it necessary for clients to be in treatment for a
year or more for beneficial results to occur. The most expensive and exclusive
version of psychotherapy remains classical Freudian *psychoanalysis*.

There has been considerable debate over the difference between counselling
and psychotherapy. Some would claim that a clear distinction can be made between the two, with psychotherapy representing a deeper, more fundamental or
involved process of change with more disturbed clients. Others maintain that
counsellors and psychotherapists are basically doing the same kind of work,
using identical approaches and techniques, but are required to use different titles
in response to the demands of the agencies who employ them. For example,
traditionally psychotherapy has been the term used in medical settings such as
psychiatric units, and counselling the designation for people working in educational settings such as student counselling centres. One significant difference between counselling and psychotherapy is that much counselling is conducted by
non-professional volunteer workers, whereas psychotherapy is an exclusively
professional occupation. However, both counselling and psychotherapy can be
viewed as activities distinct from advice-giving, caring and teaching.

Another term which is increasingly being used is that of *counselling psychologist*.
This refers to a counsellor who has initial training in psychology, and who uses
psychological methods and models in his or her approach. This label explicitly
imports the language of science into counselling, by associating it with a specific
scientific discipline. There are also several labels which refer to counsellors who
work with particular client groups, for example mental health counsellor, marriage counsellor or student counsellor. The distinctive feature of these practitioners is that they will possess specialist training and expertise in their particular
field in addition to a general counselling training.

Finally, there are many instances where counselling is offered in the context of a relationship which is primarily focused on other, non-counselling concerns. For example, a student may use a teacher as a person with whom it is safe to share worries and anxieties. A community nurse may visit a home to give medical care to a patient who is terminally ill, but finds herself giving emotional support to the spouse. In these situations it seems appropriate to see what is happening as being a teacher or nurse using counselling skills rather than engaging in an actual counselling relationship. They are counselling, but not being counsellors. This is a useful distinction to make, because it reserves 'counselling' (or 'psychotherapy') for situations where there is a formal counselling contract and the counsellor has no other role in relation to the client. However, there are many situations where it can become difficult to draw a line between counselling and the use of counselling skills. The nurse in the example above, for instance, might be able to work with the spouse in a counselling mode over a fairly lengthy period, and anyone listening to a tape recording of their sessions might be unable to tell the difference between what the nurse was doing and what a trained bereavement counsellor would have done.

It is probably not helpful to draw rigid lines of professional demarcation which deny that teachers, nurses, probation officers or social workers can ever be counsellors to their clients. Nevertheless, it is also important to recognize that clients can become confused, or damaged, when the people who are trying to help them become enmeshed in role conflicts through attempting to be counsellor as well as, for instance, teacher or nurse. This issue is discussed further in Chapter 10. It can also be damaging for both client and worker if the counselling process moves into areas beyond the training or competence of the helper. The difficulties involved in making clear distinctions between counselling proper and the use of counselling skills have been a matter of much debate (see Bond, 1989).

Even more difficult to define, as varieties of counselling and psychotherapy, are hypnotherapy and a whole range of activities in the area of *healing*. The use of hypnosis as a means of helping people with emotional or behavioural difficulties can be traced back to the eighteenth century. For a variety of reasons, however, hypnosis has never been accepted as part of the mainstream of psychotherapeutic or counselling thinking. Certainly, the training that most people who call themselves 'hypnotherapists' have had would tend not to be recognized or accepted by the main professional bodies in counselling or psychotherapy. Similarly, healing approaches, which may involve techniques such as meditation, prayer and the use of massage and herbal remedies, have generally been regarded as outside mainstream counselling. The theoretical basis and practical techniques associated with both hypnotherapy and healing do not, currently, fit readily into the ways that most counsellors and psychotherapists think and work, although many counsellors are interested in these perspectives and there have been many attempts to bridge this gap (Sheikh and Sheikh, 1989; Graham, 1990).

The diversity of counselling theory and practice

Karasu (1986) reported having come across more than 400 distinct models of counselling and psychotherapy. The fact that this whole field of study is of relatively recent origin means that there has not yet been time for the explosion of new ideas which appeared between 1950 and 1970 to have become integrated into a unified approach. There is some evidence of the emergence of a strong trend towards integration and unification of approaches in the 1980s (see Chapter 6). However, despite the movement in favour of theoretical unification and integration, it is widely recognized that the three 'core' approaches of psychodynamic, cognitive–behavioural and humanistic (see Chapters 2, 3 and 4) represent fundamentally different ways of viewing human beings and their emotional and behavioural problems (Mahrer, 1989).

There also exists a wide diversity in counselling practice, with counselling being delivered through one-to-one contact, in groups, with couples and families, over the telephone, and even through written materials such as books and self-help manuals.

The mix of cultural, economic and social forces which contributed to the emergence of a multiplicity of counselling theories has also given rise to a wide diversity of settings where counselling is practised and client groups at whom it is targeted. There are, for example, many counselling agencies that are funded by, or attached to, organizations which have a primary task of providing medical and health care. These range from mental health/psychiatric settings, which typically deal with highly disturbed or damaged clients, through to counselling available in primary care settings, such as GP surgeries, and from community nurses. There has been a growth in specialist counselling directed towards people with particular medical conditions such as AIDS, cancer and various genetic disorders. Counselling has also played an important role in many centres and clinics offering alternative or complementary health approaches.

One of the primary cultural locations for counselling and psychotherapy can therefore be seen to be alongside medicine. Even when counsellors and counselling agencies work independently of medical organizations, they will frequently establish some form of liaison with medical and psychiatric services, to enable referral of difficult clients.

Counselling also has a place in the world of work. A variety of counselling agencies exist for the purpose of helping people through difficulties, dilemmas or anxieties concerning their work role. These agencies include vocational guidance, student counselling services and employee assistance programmes or workplace counselling provided by large organizations in industry and the public sector. Whether the work role is that of executive, postal worker or college student, counsellors are able to offer help with stress and anxiety arising from the work, coping with change and making career decisions.

There is yet another whole section of counselling practice that is not primarily focused on arriving at solutions to problems, but is instead directed towards the exploration of meaning and the expansion of awareness. This kind of counselling is strongly represented in private practice and 'growth centres'.

A number of counselling agencies have evolved to meet the needs of people who experience traumatic or sudden interruptions to their life development and social roles. Prominent among these are agencies and organizations offering counselling in such areas as marital breakdown, rape and bereavement. The work of the counsellor in these agencies can very clearly be seen as arising from social problems. For example, changing social perceptions of marriage, redefinitions of male and female roles, new patterns of marriage and family life, and legislation making divorce more available represent major social and cultural changes of this century. Counselling provides a way of helping individuals to negotiate this changing social landscape.

A further field of counselling activity lies in the area of addictions. There exists a range of counselling approaches developed to help people with problems related to drug and alcohol abuse, food addiction and smoking cessation. The social role of the counsellor can be seen particularly clearly in this type of work. In some areas of addiction counselling, such as with hard drug users, counsellors operate alongside a set of powerful legal constraints and moral judgements. The possession and use of heroin, for example, is seen by most people as morally wrong, and has been made a criminal offence. The counsellor working with a heroin addict, therefore, is not merely exploring 'ways of living more satisfyingly and resourcefully' (British Association for Counselling, 1984), but is mediating between competing social definitions of what an acceptable 'way of living' entails. In other fields of addiction counselling, such as food, alcohol and cigarette abuse, the behaviour in question is heavily reinforced by advertising paid for by the slimming, drink and tobacco industries. The incidence of alcohol and smoking-related diseases would be more effectively reduced by tax increases than by increases in the number of counsellors, an insight which raises questions about the role of counselling in relation to other means of control of behaviour.

The range and diversity of counselling settings is explored in detail in Dryden *et al.* (1989). This discussion of the place of counselling in society has argued that counselling is not merely a process of individual learning. It is also a social activity that has a social meaning, Often, people turn to counselling at a point of transition, such as the transition from child to adult, married to divorced, addict to straight. Counselling is also a culturally-sanctioned means of enabling adaptation to social institutions. Counsellors are rarely managers or executives who hold power in colleges, businesses or communities. Counsellors, instead, have a more 'liminal' role, being employed at the edge of these institutions to deal with those in danger of falling off or falling out.

The aims of counselling

Underpinning the diversity of theoretical models and social purposes discussed above are a variety of ideas about the aims of counselling and therapy. Some of the different aims that are espoused either explicitly or implicitly by counsellors are listed:

Insight. The acquisition of an understanding of the origins and development of emotional difficulties, leading to an increased capacity to take rational control over feelings and actions (Freud: 'where id was, shall ego be').

Self-awareness. Becoming more aware of thoughts and feelings which had been blocked off or denied, or developing a more accurate sense of how self is perceived by others.

Self-acceptance. The development of a positive attitude towards self, marked by an ability to acknowledge areas of experience which had been the subject of self-criticism and rejection.

Self-actualization or individuation. Moving in the direction of fulfilling potential or achieving an integration of previously conflicting parts of self.

Enlightenment. Assisting the client to arrive at a higher state of spiritual awakening.

Problem-solving. Finding a solution to a specific problem which the client had not been able to resolve alone. Acquiring a general competence in problem-solving.

Psychological education. Enabling the client to acquire ideas and techniques with which to understand and control behaviour.

Acquisition of social skills. Learning and mastering social and interpersonal skills such as maintenance of eye contact, turn-taking in conversations, assertiveness or anger control.

Cognitive change. The modification or replacement of irrational beliefs or maladaptive thought patterns associated with self-destructive behaviour.

Behaviour change. The modification or replacement of maladaptive or self-destructive patterns of behaviour.

Systemic change. Introducing change into the way in which social systems (e.g. families) operate.

Empowerment. Working on skills, awareness and knowledge which will enable the client to confront social inequalities.

Restitution. Helping the client to make amends for previous destructive behaviour.

It is unlikely that any one counsellor or counselling agency would attempt to achieve the objectives underlying all of the aims in this list. Traditionally, psychodynamic counsellors have focused primarily on insight, humanistic practitioners have aimed to promote self-acceptance and personal freedom, and cognitive–behavioural therapists have been mainly concerned with the management and control of behaviour.

Counselling as an interdisciplinary area of study

Although counselling and psychotherapy initially emerged from within the discipline of psychiatry, in more recent times they have come to be regarded as applied sub-branches of the academic discipline of psychology. In some European countries, holding a psychology degree is necessary to enter training in psychotherapy. In the USA, and increasingly in Britain, the term counselling psychology is widely used. Psychology textbooks give substantial coverage to the work of psychotherapists like Freud, Rogers and Wolpe. Being located in psychiatry and psychology has given counselling and psychotherapy the status of an applied science. However, despite the enormous value of psychological perspectives within counselling practice, it is essential to acknowledge that other academic disciplines are also actively involved.

Some of the most important ideas in counselling and psychotherapy have originated in philosophy. The concept of the 'unconscious' had been used in nineteenth-century philosophy (Ellenberger, 1970) some time before Freud began to use it in his theory. The concepts of phenomenology and authenticity had been developed by existential philosophers such as Heidegger and Husserl long before they influenced Rogers, Perls and other humanistic therapists. The field of moral philosophy also makes an input into counselling, through offering a framework for making sense of ethical issues (see Chapter 10).

Another field of study which has a strong influence on counselling theory and practice is religion. Several counselling agencies have either begun their life as branches of the church, or have been helped into existence by founders with a religious calling. Many of the key figures in the history of counselling and psychotherapy have had strong religious backgrounds, and have attempted to integrate the work of the counsellor with the search for spiritual meaning. Jung has made the most significant contribution in this area. Although the field of counselling is permeated with Judaeo-Christian thought and belief, there is increasing interest among some counsellors in the relevance of ideas and practices from other religions, such as Zen Buddhism (Suzuki *et al.*, 1970; Ramaswami and Sheikh, 1989).

A third sphere of intellectual activity which continues to exert a strong influence on counselling is the arts. There is a strong tradition in counselling and psychotherapy of using methods and techniques from drama, sculpture, dance and the visual arts to enable clients to give expression to their feelings and relationship patterns. In recent years psychodrama and art therapy have become well-established specialist counselling approaches, with their own distinctive theoretical models, training courses and professional journals. There has similarly been valuable contact between counselling and literature, primarily through an appreciation that language is the main vehicle for therapeutic work, and that poets, novelists and literary critics have a great deal to say about the use of language. Specific literature-based techniques have also been employed in counselling, such as autobiography, journal writing, poetry writing and bibliotherapy.

Counselling is in many respects an unusual area of study in that it encompasses a set of strongly competing theoretical perspectives, a wide range of practical applications and meaningful inputs from a number of contributing disciplines. The field of counselling and psychotherapy represents a synthesis of ideas from science, philosophy, religion and the arts. It is an interdisciplinary area that cannot appropriately be incorporated or subsumed into any one of its constituent disciplines. An approach to counselling which was, for example, purely scientific or purely religious in nature would soon be seen not to be counselling at all, in its denial of key areas of client and practitioner experience.

The cultural origins of counselling

To understand the diversity of contemporary counselling, and to appreciate the significance of current patterns of practice, it is necessary to look at the ways in which counselling has developed and evolved over the past 200 years. The differences and contradictions within present-day counselling have their origins in the social and historical forces that have shaped modern culture as a whole.

People in all societies, at all times, have experienced emotional or psychological distress and behavioural problems. In each culture there have been well-established indigenous ways of helping people to deal with these difficulties. The Iroquois Indians, for example, believed that one of the causes of ill-health was the existence of unfulfilled wishes, some of which were only revealed in dreams (Wallace, 1958). When someone became ill and no other cause could be determined, diviners would discover what his or her unconscious wishes were, and arrange a 'festival of dreams' at which other members of the community would give these objects to the sick person. There seems little reason to suppose that modern-day counselling is any more valid, or effective, than the Iroquois festival of dreams. The most that can be said is that it is seen as valid, relevant or effective by people in this culture at this time.

Although counselling and psychotherapy have only become widely available to people during the second half of the twentieth century, their origins can be traced back to the beginning of the eighteenth century, which represents a turning point in the social construction of madness. Before this, the problems in living which people encountered were primarily dealt with from a religious perspective, implemented at the level of the local community (McNeill, 1951; Neugebauer, 1978, 1979). In Europe the vast majority of people lived in small rural communities and were employed on the land. Within this way of life, anyone who was seriously disturbed or insane was tolerated as part of the community. Less extreme forms of emotional or interpersonal problems were dealt with by the local priest, for example through the Catholic confessional. McNeill (1951) refers to this ancient tradition of religious healing as 'the cure of souls'. An important element in the cure of souls was confession of sins followed by repentance. McNeill (1951) points out that in earlier times confession of sins took place in public, and was often accompanied by communal admonishment, prayer and even excommunication. The earlier Christian rituals for helping troubled souls were, like the Iroquois festival of dreams, communal affairs. Only later did individual private confession became established. McNeill (1951) gives many examples of clergy in the sixteenth and seventeenth centuries acting in a counselling role to their parishioners.

As writers such as Foucault (1967), Rothman (1971), Scull (1979, 1981b, 1989) and Porter (1985) have pointed out, all this began to change as the Industrial Revolution took effect, as capitalism began to dominate economic and political life, and as the values of science began to replace those of religion. The fundamental changes in social structure and in social and economic life which took place at this point in history were accompanied by basic changes in relationships and in the ways people defined and dealt with emotional and psychological needs. Albee (1977) has written that

> Capitalism required the development of a high level of rationality accompanied by repression and control of pleasure seeking. This meant the strict control of impulses and the development of a work ethic in which a majority of persons derived a high degree of satisfaction from hard work. Capitalism also demanded personal efforts to achieve long-range goals, an increase in personal autonomy and independence . . . The system depended on a heavy emphasis on thrift and ingenuity and, above all else, on the strong control and repression of sexuality.

The key psychological shift that occurred, according to Albee (1977), was from a 'tradition-centred' (Riesman *et al.*, 1950) society to one in which 'inner-direction' was emphasized. In traditional cultures, people live in relatively small communities in which everyone knows everyone else, and behaviour is monitored and controlled by others. There is direct observation of what people do, and direct action taken to deal with social deviance through scorn or exclusion. The basis for social control is the induction of feelings of shame. In urban, industrial societies, on the other hand, life is much more anonymous, and social control must be implemented through internalized norms and regulations, which result in guilt if defied. From this analysis, it is possible to see how the central elements of urban, industrial, capitalist culture create the conditions for the development of a means of help, guidance and support which addresses confusions and dilemmas experienced in the personal, individual, inner life of the person. The form which that help took, however, was shaped by other events and processes.

The historical account pieced together by Scull (1979) indicates that during the years 1800 to 1890 the proportion of the population of England and Wales living in towns larger than 20,000 inhabitants increased from 17 to 54 per cent. People were leaving the land to come to the city to work in the new factories. Even on the land, the work became more mechanized and profit-oriented. These large-scale economic and social changes had profound implications for all disadvantaged or handicapped members of society. Previously there had been the slow pace of rural life, the availability of family members working at home, and the existence of tasks that could be performed by even the least able. Now there was the discipline of the machine, long hours in the factory, and the fragmentation of the communities and family networks that had taken care of the old, sick, poor and insane. There very quickly grew up, from necessity, a system of state provision for these non-productive members of the population, known as the workhouse system. Inmates of workhouses were made to work, under conditions of strict discipline. It soon became apparent that the insane were difficult to control and disruptive of the workhouse regime. As one workhouse report from 1750 put it,

> The law has made no particular provision for lunaticks and it must be allowed that the common parish workhouse (the inhabitants of which are mostly aged and infirm people) are very unfit places for the reception of such ungovernable and mischievous persons, who necessarily require separate apartments.
>
> (Cited in Scull, 1979: 41)

Gradually these separate apartments, the asylums, began to be built, beginning slowly in the middle of the eighteenth century and given further encouragement by the 1845 Asylums Act, which compelled local justices to set up publicly run asylums. This development marked the first systematic involvement of the state in the care and control of the insane in European society.

At first, the asylums were seen as places where lunatics could be contained, and attempts at therapeutic intervention were rare. In a few asylums run by Quakers, for example Tuke at the York Asylums, there evolved what was known as 'moral treatment' (Scull, 1981a). In most institutions, however, lunatics were treated like animals and kept in appalling conditions. The Bethlem Hospital in London, for instance, was open to the public, who could enter to watch the lunatics for a penny a time. During this early period of the growth of the asylums movement, at the beginning of the nineteenth century, the medical profession had relatively little interest in the insane. From the historical investigations carried out by Scull (1975), it can be seen that the medical profession gradually came to recognize that there were profits to be made from the 'trade in lunacy', not only from having control of the state asylums which were publicly funded, but also from running asylums for the insane members of the upper classes. The political power of the medical profession allowed them, in Britain, to influence the contents of Acts of Parliament which gave the medical profession control over asylums. The defeat of moral treatment can be seen as a key moment in the history of psychotherapy: science replaced religion as the dominant ideology underlying the treatment of the insane.

During the remainder of the nineteenth century the medical profession consolidated its control over the 'trade in lunacy'. Part of the process of consolidation involved re-writing the history of madness. Religious forms of care of the insane were characterized as 'demonology', and the persecution of witches was portrayed, erroneously, as a major strand in the pre-scientific or pre-medical approach to madness (Szasz, 1971; Kirsch, 1978; Spanos, 1978). Medical-biological explanations for insanity were formulated, such as phrenology (Cooter, 1981) and sexual indulgence or masturbation (Hare, 1962). Different types of physical treatment were experimented with:

> hypodermic injections of morphia, the administration of the bromides, chloral hydrate, hypocymine, physotigma, caanabis indicta, amyl nitrate, conium, digitalis, ergot, pilocarpine, the application of electricity, the use of the Turkish bath and the wet pack, and other remedies too numerous to mention, have had their strenuous advocates.
>
> (Tuke, 1882, *History of the Insane*, cited in Scull, 1979)

An important theme throughout this era was the use of the asylum to oppress women, who constituted the majority of inmates (Showalter, 1985). Towards the end of the century, the medical specialism of psychiatry had taken its place alongside other areas of medicine, backed by the system of classification of psychiatric disorders devised by Kraepelin, Bleuler and others. Many of these developments were controversial at the time. For example, there was considerable debate over the wisdom of locking up lunatics in institutions, since contact with other disturbed people was unlikely to aid their rehabilitation. Several critics of psychiatry during the nineteenth century argued that care in the community was much better than institutionalization. There was also a certain amount of public outcry over the cruelty with which inmates were treated, and scepticism over the efficacy of medical approaches.

The issues and debates over the care of the insane in the nineteenth century may seem very familiar to us from our vantage point a century later. We are still arguing about the same things. But an appreciation of how these issues originally came into being can help us by bringing into focus a number of very clear conclusions about the nature of care offered to emotionally troubled people in modern industrial society. When we look at the birth of the psychiatric profession, and compare it with what was happening before the beginning of the nineteenth century, we can see that:

1 Emotional and behavioural 'problems in living' became medicalized.
2 There emerged a 'trade in lunacy', an involvement of market forces in the development of services.
3 There was an increased amount of rejection and cruelty in the way the insane were treated, and much greater social control.
4 The services that were available were controlled by men and used to oppress women.
5 Science replaced religion as the main framework for understanding madness.

None of these factors was evident to any extent before the Industrial Revolution, and all are still with us today. They can be seen as fundamental to the way that any industrialized, urbanized, secularized society responds to the question of madness. The French social philosopher Foucault (1967) has pointed out that one of the central values of the new social order which emerged in the nineteenth century was reason or rationality. For a society in which a rational, scientific perspective on life was all-important, the irrational lunatic, who had lost his reason, would readily become a scapegoat, a source of threat to be banished to an asylum somewhere outside the city. Foucault (1967) describes this era as an age of 'confinement', in which society developed means of repressing or imprisoning representatives of unreason or sexuality.

By the end of the nineteenth century psychiatry had achieved a dominant position in the care of the insane, now re-categorized as 'mentally ill'. From within medicine and psychiatry, there now evolved a new specialism of psychotherapy. The earliest physicians to call themselves psychotherapists had been Van Renterghem and Van Eeden, who opened a Clinic of Suggestive Psychotherapy in Amsterdam in 1887 (Ellenberger, 1970). Van Eeden defined psychotherapy as 'the cure of the body by the mind, aided by the impulse of one mind to another' (Ellenberger, 1970: 765). Hypnosis was a phenomenon of great interest to the European medical profession in the nineteenth century. Originally discovered by the pioneers of 'animal magnetism', Johann Joseph Gassner (1727–79) and Franz Anton Mesmer (1734–1815), hypnotism came to be widely used as an anaesthetic in surgical operations before the invention of chemical anaesthetics. During the 1880s, the influential French psychiatrists Charcot and Janet began to experiment with hypnosis as a means of treating 'hysterical' patients. There were two aspects of their hypnotic technique that have persisted to this day as key concepts in contemporary counselling and psychotherapy. First, they emphasized the importance of the relationship between doctor and patient. They knew that hypnosis would not be effective in the absence of what they called 'rapport'. Second, they argued that the reason why hypnosis was helpful to patients was that it gave access to an area of the mind that was not accessible during normal waking consciousness. In other words, the notion of the 'unconscious' mind was part of the apparatus of nineteenth-century hypnotism just as much as it is part of twentieth-century psychotherapy.

The part played by hypnosis in the emergence of psychotherapy is of great significance. Bourguignon (1979), Prince (1980) and many others have observed that primitive cultures employ healing rituals which rely on trance states or altered states of consciousness. The appearance of Mesmerism and hypnosis through the eighteenth and nineteenth centuries in Europe, and their transformation into psychotherapy, can be viewed as representing the assimilation of a traditional cultural form into modern scientific medicine.

The key figure in this process was, of course, Sigmund Freud. Having spent four months with Charcot in Paris during 1886–7, Freud went back to Vienna to set up in private practice as a psychiatrist. He soon turned his back on the specific techniques of hypnosis, choosing instead to develop his own technique of psychoanalysis based on free association and the interpretation of dreams. Freud became, eventually, an enormously powerful figure not only in medicine and psychotherapy, but in European cultural history as a whole. Without denying the genius and creativity of Freud, it is valuable to reflect on some of the ways in which his approach reflected the intellectual fashions and social practices of his time. For example:

1 Individual sessions with an analyst were an extension of the normal practice of one-to-one doctor–patient consultations prevalent at that time.
2 Freud's idea of a unitary life-force (libido) was derived from nineteenth-century biological theories.
3 The idea that emotional problems had a sexual cause was widely accepted in the nineteenth century.
4 The idea of the unconscious had been employed not only by the hypnotists, but also by other nineteenth-century writers and philosophers.

The distinctive contribution of Freud can probably be regarded as his capacity to assimilate all of these ideas into a coherent theoretical model which has proved of great value in many fields of work. The cultural significance of Freudian ideas can be seen to lie in the implicit assumption that we are all neurotic, that behind the façade of even the most apparently rational and successful person there lie inner conflicts and instinctual drives. The message of Freud was that psychiatry is relevant not just for the mad man or woman in the asylum, but for everyone. The set of ideas contained in psychoanalysis also reflected the challenges faced by members of the European middle classes making the transition from traditional to modern forms of relationship. Sollod (1982: 51–2) writes that in Victorian society

> it was quite appropriate to view elders as father figures and experience oneself as a respectful child in relationship to them. In the (modern) secular world, impersonal economic and employment arrangements rather than traditional ties bind one to authority, so such transferential relationships to authority figures could be inappropriate and maladaptive rather than functional.

Freudian ideas had a somewhat limited impact in Britain and Europe during his lifetime, where up until quite recently psychoanalysis was acceptable and accessible only to middle-class intellectuals and artists. In Britain, for example, the early development of psychoanalysis was associated with the literary elite of the 'Bloomsbury group' (Kohon, 1986). It was not until psychoanalysis emigrated to the USA that psychotherapy, and then counselling, became more widely available.

Freud had a great loathing of American society. He visited there in 1909 with Jung and Ferenczi, to give some lectures and receive an honorary degree at Clark University, and was later to write that America was a 'gigantic mistake' (Gay, 1988). But American culture resonated to the ideas of psychoanalysis, and when the rise of fascism in Europe led to prominent analysts like Ferenczi, Rank and Erikson moving to New York and Boston, they found a willing clientele. Compared to Europe, American society demonstrated a much greater degree of social mobility, with people being very likely to live, work and marry outside their original neighbourhood, town, social class or ethnic group. There were therefore many individuals who had problems in forming satisfactory relationships, or having a secure sense of personal identity. Moreover, the 'American Dream' insisted that everyone could better themselves, and emphasized the pursuit of happiness of the individual as a legitimate aim in life. Psychotherapy offered a fundamental, radical method of self-improvement. The psychoanalysts arriving in the USA in the 1930s found that there was already a strong popular interest in psychology, as indicated by the self-help books of Samuel Smiles and the writings of the behaviourist J. B. Watson. There was also a strong tradition of applied psychology, which had been given impetus by the involvement of academic psychologists in the US Army in the First World War. Psychological tests were widely used in education, job selection and vocational guidance, which meant that the notion of using psychology to help ordinary people was generally taken for granted.

The idea of psychoanalysis held a great attraction for Americans, but for it to become assimilated into the culture required an Americanization of Freud's thinking. Freud had lived in a hierarchically organized, class-dominated society, and had written from a world-view immersed in classical scholarship and biological science, informed by a pessimism arising from being a Jew at a time of violent anti-Semitism. There were, therefore, themes in his writing that did not sit well with the experience of people in the USA. As a result there emerged in the 1950s a whole series of writers who reinterpreted Freud in terms of their own cultural values. Foremost among these were Carl Rogers, Eric Berne, Albert Ellis, Aaron Beck and Abraham Maslow. Many of the European analysts who went to the USA, such as Erikson and Fromm, were also prominent in re-framing psychoanalysis from a wider social and cultural perspective, thus making it more acceptable to an American clientele.

One of the strongest sources of resistance to psychoanalysis in American culture lay in academic psychology. Although William James (1890), who had been one of the first scholars to make psychology academically respectable in American universities, had given close attention to Freudian ideas, American academic psychologists had become deeply committed to a behaviourist approach from about 1918. The behaviourist perspective emphasized the use of scientific methods such as measurement and laboratory experiments, and was primarily oriented to the study of observable behaviour rather than obscure internal processes, such as dreams, fantasies and impulses. The behaviourist academic establishment was consequently fiercely opposed to psychoanalysis, and refused to acknowledge it as worthy of serious study. Although some academic departments of psychiatry did show some limited interest in psychoanalysis, most practitioners and writers were forced to work in private practice or within the hospital system, rather than having an academic base. When Rogers, Berne and Ellis developed distinctive American brands of therapy in the 1950s and 1960s there was initially only very limited academic discussion of their work and ideas. One of the distinctive contributions of Rogers was to invent systematic methods of carrying out research into the processes and out-comes of therapy. The effect of this innovation was to reinforce the legitimacy of therapy as a socially acceptable enterprise by giving it the respectability and status of an applied science. In 1947 Rogers became the first therapist to be made President of the American Psychological Association (Whiteley, 1984). The con-firmation of therapy as an applied science was given further impetus by the entry into the therapy arena of cognitive–behavioural approaches in the 1960s, bring-ing with them the language and assumptions of behavioural psychology, and the image of the 'scientist-practitioner' (see Chapter 4).

The development of psychotherapy in the USA represented an enormous expansion of the 'trade in lunacy'. The weakness of the public health system in that country meant that most counselling and therapy was dominated by theories and approaches developed in private practice. The influence and prestige of the private-practice model has been such that even counselling agencies which emerged in the voluntary sector, or in educational settings, have followed its lead. In the field of social work the casework approach has been heavily influenced by psychotherapeutic practice.

The relationship between organized religion and the historical development of counselling and psychotherapy is also worth noting at this point. Halmos (1965) has documented the correspondence in this century in Britain between the decline in numbers of clerical personnel and the rise in numbers of counsellors. He argues that religious faith is being replaced by a set of beliefs and values that he calls the 'faith of the counsellors'. Nelson and Torrey (1973) have described some of the ways in which therapy has taken over from religion in such areas of life as offering explanations for events that are difficult to understand, offering answers to the existential question 'what am I here for?', defining social values and supplying ritual ways of meeting other people.

The story of the early life of Carl Rogers (1902–87), founder of the client-centred or person-centred approach to counselling and therapy (see Chapter 3), contains many of the themes already mentioned. The early background of Rogers (Rogers, 1961; Kirschenbaum, 1979) was that he was brought up in a rural community in the American Midwest, a member of a strictly religious Protestant family in which there was active disapproval of leisure activities such as gambling or theatre-going. As a substitute for forbidden leisure pursuits, Rogers displayed a strong interest in scientific agriculture, by the age of 14 conducting his own experiments on crops and plants. He decided to become a minister, and at the age of 20 in preparation for this vocation was a delegate to the World Student Christian Federation Conference in China. This exposure to other cultures and beliefs influenced him to break away from the rigid religious orientation of his parents, and when he entered theological college he chose one of the most liberal seminaries, the Union Theological Seminary. However, following exploration of his faith in the equivalent of a student-led 'encounter group', Rogers decided to change career and began training as a psychologist at Columbia University, where he was exposed to the ideas of the progressive education movement, which emphasized a trust in the freedom to learn and grow inherent in each child or student.

This account of Rogers's early life shows how the dual influences of religion and science came together in a career as a therapist. The respect for scientific rigour was expressed in his involvement in research, where he was one of the first to make recordings of therapy sessions, and developed a wide range of methods to investigate aspects of the therapy process. The influence of Protestant thought on client-centred theory is apparent in the emphasis on the capacity of each individual to arrive at a personal understanding of his or her destiny, using feelings and intuition rather than being guided by doctrine or reason. The client-centred approach is also focused on behaviour in the present, rather than on what has happened in the past. Sollod (1978: 96) argues that the Protestantism of client-centred therapy can be compared with psychoanalysis, where 'the trust is in the trained reason of the therapist (rabbi) and in his Talmudic interpretations of complex phenomena.'

Following his qualification as a clinical psychologist, Rogers worked mainly with disturbed children and adolescents, and their families, in a child study department of the Society for the Prevention of Cruelty to Children in Rochester, New York. Although he received further training in psychodynamically oriented therapy from Jessie Taft, a follower of Otto Rank (Sollod, 1978), he did not identify himself as a student of any particular approach, and through his years at Rochester (1928 to 1940) largely evolved his own distinctive approach, guided by his sense of what seemed to help his clients. Rogers was, in his clinical work, and earlier in his experience at Columbia, immersed in the values of American culture, and his theory contains many elements of that cultural context. Meadow (1964), for example, has suggested that client-centred therapy has adopted 'basic American cultural norms', such as distrust of experts and authority figures, emphasis on method rather than theory, emphasis on individuals' needs rather than shared social goals, lack of interest in the past, and a valuing of independence and autonomy.

The historical account given here is inevitably incomplete and partial. Relatively little scholarly attention has been devoted to the task of understanding the emergence of counselling and psychotherapy in twentieth-century society. However, from even this limited discussion of historical factors it can be seen that the form and shape of contemporary theory and practice has been strongly influenced by cultural forces (Woolfe, 1983; Pilgrim, 1990; Salmon, 1991). In particular, it becomes evident that the key figures in the history of counselling, such as Freud or Rogers, were not inventors of new theories so much as people who were able to articulate and give words to a way of thinking or working which was beginning to crystallize in the culture around them. A historical account also brings to the surface and illuminates some of the underlying, fundamental issues that cut across all theoretical orientations and all forms of counselling practice. These basic issues concern, first, our understanding of the social meaning of counselling and, second, the image of the person being promoted by counselling theories.

The social meaning of counselling

It was clear from the discussion of the origins of psychiatry that, certainly in the early years, the emphasis in psychiatric care was on the control of individuals who were seen as disruptive to the smooth running of society. Although much has changed in psychiatry, even now in most places psychiatrists have the power to enforce compulsory hospitalization. At the other extreme, humanistic counsellors aim for 'self-actualization' and assume that their clients have responsibility for their own lives and actions. There is a strong tendency for counsellors and counselling organizations to place themselves explicitly at the personal freedom and liberation end of this continuum. In practice, however, there are pressures in the direction of social conformity and control in all counselling situations. Most immediate and concrete are the values and beliefs of the counsellor regarding what behaviour is or is not socially acceptable in a client. Less tangible is the influence of who is paying for the counselling, particularly in counselling settings such as colleges, business organizations or voluntary agencies, where it is not the client who pays. Finally, in extreme cases, where clients threaten to harm themselves or others, there are powerful social pressures and sanctions that urge the counsellor to take control and do something.

Some writers have regarded their approach to counselling or psychotherapy as providing a critique of existing social norms, or even as a means of bringing about social change. The radical psychoanalyst Kovel (1981), for example, has argued that classical Freudian theory represented a powerful tool for political change, and regretted the ways in which second-generation, post-Freudian theorists adapted Freudian ideas, particularly in the USA:

> what was great in Freud – his critical ability to see beneath, if not beyond, the established order – was necessarily jettisoned; while what was compatible with advanced capitalist relations – the release of a little desire, along with its technical control and perversion – was as necessarily reinforced.

The argument that the radical edge of Freudian theory has been lost is also made by Holland (1977), and the idea of counselling or therapy as a vehicle for social change has been evoked by Rogers (1978). Within contemporary practice, the alliance between therapy and social action has been made most effectively by feminist and gay counsellors, and practitioners from ethnic minority groups (see Chapter 7). However, these attempts to radicalize counselling all necessarily confront the same contradiction: that of seeking social change through a medium which individualizes and 'psychologizes' social problems (Conrad, 1981).

Another critical aspect of the social nature of counselling concerns the division of power between client and counsellor. Historically, the counsellor–client relationship has modelled itself on the doctor–patient and priest–parishioner relationships. Traditionally, doctors and priests have been seen as experts and authority figures, and the people who consulted them expected to be told what to do. In the counselling world, by contrast, many practitioners would espouse the ideal of 'empowering' clients and would agree to a greater or lesser extent with the statement by Carl Rogers that 'it is the client who knows what is right'. Nevertheless, the circumstances of most counselling interviews reproduce aspects of the doctor–patient power relationship. The meeting takes place on the territory of the counsellor, who has the power to begin and end the session. The counsellor knows everything about the client; the client knows little about the counsellor. Some counsellors have been so convinced of the unhelpfulness of the counsellor–client power imbalance that they have advocated self-help counselling networks (see Chapter 9) where people take it in turns to counsel each other. It is also relevant to note here that numerically by far the greatest number of counselling contacts are made through telephone counselling agencies, in situations where the client has much more control over how much he or she is known and how long the session will last.

Many writers in recent years have drawn attention to the ways in which power can be abused in the counselling relationship, for example through sexual exploitation of clients. One of these writers, Masson (1988, 1992), has compiled a substantial dossier of instances of abuse of clients. He argues that this kind of abuse does not merely consist of an occasional lapse in ethical standards, but is in fact an intrinsic and inevitable consequence of any therapeutic contract. Masson (1988: 296) has written that 'the profession itself is corrupt . . . The very mainspring of psychotherapy is profit from another person's suffering,' and suggests that the abolition of psychotherapy is desirable. While few would agree with this position of absolute condemnation, it is nevertheless impossible to deny, in the face of the massive evidence he presents, that his arguments deserve serious consideration. The fact that so many of the examples of abuse which Masson (1988, 1992) has uncovered relate to situations of men abusing women invites comparison with the more general social phenomenon of male violence against women, expressed through physical violence, rape and pornography.

The social nature of counselling permeates the work of the counsellor in three ways. First, the act of going to see a counsellor, and the process of change arising from counselling, will always have some effect on the social world of the client. Second, the power and status of the counsellor derive from the fact that he or she occupies a socially sanctioned role of 'healer' or 'helper'. The specific healing or helping role that the counsellor adopts will depend on the cultural context. For example, therapists in hospital settings use the language of science to describe their work, while those employed in holistic or alternative health clinics use the language of growth and spirituality. Third, client and counsellor re-enact in their relationship the various modes of social interaction they use in the every-day world.

These three dimensions to the social or cultural basis of counselling interlock and interact in practice. An example of how these ideas can be brought together to construct an understanding of the way that counselling operates within a social context is provided by the 'status accreditation' model of Bergner and Stubbs (1987). They suggest that therapists are viewed as members in good standing of the community. To be a therapist is to have received endorsement that one is rational, significant, honest and credible. Any attributes or characteristics that the therapist assigns to the client are therefore likely to be believed and accepted. Bergner and Stubbs (1987) point out that in a positive therapeutic relationship the therapist will behave towards the client as if he or she is someone who makes sense, who is worthy of attention, who has the power to choose and who has strengths. The attribution or assignment of these characteristics from a high-status person (such as a counsellor or therapist) has the effect on clients of 'confirming them in new positions or ''statuses'' that carry with them expanded eligibility for full participation in society' (Bergner and Staggs, 1987: 315). Frank (1974: 272) presents the same point of view in writing that 'since the therapist represents the larger society, all therapies help to combat the patient's isolation and reestablish his sense of connectedness with his group, thereby help-ing to restore meaningfulness to life.' From this perspective, therapy can be viewed as a social process which offers people accreditation of their status as sane, worthy members of society. The process can be seen as the opposite of the 'labelling' by which people deemed to be 'mentally ill' are stigmatized as dangerous, irrational outsiders (Scheff, 1974).

The image of the person

At a practical level an approach to counselling such as psychoanalysis or behaviour therapy may be seen to consist merely of a set of strategies for helping. Underneath that set of practical procedures, however, each approach represents a way of seeing people, an image of what it is to be a person. Back in the days of the asylums, lunatics were seen as being like animals: irrational, unable to communicate, out of control. Some of these meanings were still present in the Freudian image of the person, except that in psychoanalysis the animal/id was merely one, usually hidden, part of the personality. The behaviourist image of the person has often been described as 'mechanistic': clients are seen as like machines that have broken down but can be fixed. The image of the counselling client in cognitive approaches is also mechanistic, but uses the metaphor of the modern machine, the computer: the client is seen as similar to an inappropriately programmed computer, and can be sorted out if rational commands replace irrational ones. The humanistic image is more botanical. Rogers, for example, uses many metaphors relating to the growth of plants and the conditions which either facilitate or inhibit that growth.

The question of the kind of world that is represented by various approaches to counselling goes beyond the mere identification of the different 'root metaphors' which lie at the heart of the different theoretical systems. There is also the question of whether the counselling model reflects the reality of the world as we experience it. For example, psychoanalytic theory was the product of an acutely male-dominated society, and many women writers and practitioners have asserted that they see in it little that they can recognize as a woman's reality. Humanistic approaches represent a positive, optimistic vision of the world, which some critics would see as denying the reality of tragedy, loss and death. It could also be said that virtually all counselling theories embody a middle-class, white, Judaeo-Christian perspective on life.

The importance for counselling of the image of the person or world-view represented by a particular approach or theory lies in the realization that we do not live in a social world that is dominated by a unitary, all-encompassing set of ideas. An essential part of the process of becoming a counsellor is to choose a version of reality that makes sense, that can be lived in. But no matter which version is selected, it needs to be understood that it is only one among several possibilities. The client, for example, may view the world in a fundamentally different way, and it may be that this kind of philosophical incompatibility is crucial. Van Deurzen-Smith (1988: 1) has suggested that

> every approach to counselling is founded on a set of ideas and beliefs about life, about the world, and about people . . . Clients can only benefit from an approach in so far as they feel able to go along with its basic assumptions.

The different root metaphors, images or basic assumptions about reality which underlie different approaches to counselling can make it difficult or impossible to reconcile or combine certain approaches, as illustrated by the debate between

Rogers and Skinner on the nature of choice (Kirschenbaum and Henderson, 1990). Historically, the development of counselling theory can be seen as being driven at least in part by the tensions between competing ideologies or images of the person. The contrast between a biological conception of the person and a social/existential one is, for example, apparent in many theoretical debates in the field. Bakan (1966) has argued that psychological theories, and the therapies derived from them, can be separated into two groups. The first group encompasses those theories which are fundamentally concerned with the task of understanding the *mystery* of life. The second group includes theories that aim to achieve a *mastery* of life. Bakan (1966) views the 'mystery–mastery complex' as underlying many debates and issues in psychology and therapy.

Finally, there is the question of the way the image of the person is used in the therapeutic relationship, whether the image held by the counsellor is imposed on the client, as a rigid structure into which the client's life is forced, or, as Friedman (1982) would prefer, the 'revelation of the human image . . . takes place *between* the therapist and his or her client or *among* the members of a group.'

Conclusions

This chapter began with some definitions of counselling. To understand these definitions requires an appreciation of the history of counselling and its role in contemporary society. Members of the public, or clients arriving for their first appointment, generally have very little idea of what to expect. Few people can tell the difference between a psychiatrist, psychologist, counsellor and psychotherapist, never mind differentiate between alternative approaches to counselling that might be on offer. But behind that lack of specific information, there resonates a set of cultural images which may include a fear of insanity, shame at asking for help, the ritual of the confessional, and the image of doctor as healer. In a multicultural society the range of images may be very wide indeed. The counsellor is also immersed in these cultural images, as well as being socialized into the language and ideology of a particular counselling approach or into the implicit norms and values of a counselling agency. To understand counselling requires moving the horizon beyond the walls of the interview room, to take in the wider social environment within which the interview room has its own special place. In the following chapters, this critical perspective will be further developed through an examination of some of the most significant areas of contemporary theory and practice.

Topics for discussion and reflection

1 Select a counselling agency with which you are familiar. What do you know about the historical development of that agency? To what extent can its creation be understood in terms of the themes discussed in this chapter? What is the social role of the agency within its community?

2 Ask people you know to give you their definition of terms such as 'counsellor', 'psychotherapist', 'hypnotherapist' and 'psychiatrist'. Invite them to tell you what they believe happens when someone consults one of these professionals. What are the origins of the images and ideas you elicit?
3 What are the advantages and disadvantages of considering counselling and psychotherapy as being fundamentally branches of applied science?
4 What is the relationship between religious beliefs and counselling in your own life, and in the lives of other counsellors you know or have read about?

TWO

FROM FREUD TO BRIEF THERAPY: THEMES AND ISSUES IN THE PSYCHODYNAMIC APPROACH TO COUNSELLING

Sigmund Freud (1856–1939) is widely regarded as being not only one of the founders of modern psychology, but also a key influence on Western society in the twentieth century. As a boy Freud had ambitions to be a famous scientist, and he originally trained in medicine, becoming in the 1880s one of the first medical researchers to investigate the properties of the newly discovered coca leaf (cocaine). However, the anti-Semitism in Austrian middle-class society at that time meant that he was unable to continue his career in the University of Vienna, and he was forced to enter private practice in the field that would now be known as psychiatry. Freud spent a year in Paris studying with the most eminent psychiatrist of the time, Charcot, who taught him the technique of hypnosis. Returning to Vienna, Freud began seeing patients who were emotionally disturbed, many of them suffering from what was known as 'hysteria'. He found that hypnosis was not particularly effective for him as a treatment technique, and gradually evolved his own method, called 'free association', which consisted of getting the patient to lie in a relaxed position (usually on a couch) and to 'say whatever comes to mind'. The stream-of-consciousness material that emerged from this procedure often included strong emotions, deeply buried memories and childhood sexual experiences, and the opportunity to share these feelings and memories appeared to be helpful for patients. One of them, Anna O, labelled this method 'the talking cure'.

Further information about the development of Freud's ideas, and the influence on his thought of his own early family life, his Jewishness, his medical training and the general cultural setting of late nineteenth-century Vienna, can be found in a number of books (e.g. Wollheim, 1971; Gay, 1988).

Freud's method of treatment is called *psychoanalysis*. From the time his theory and method became known and used by others (starting from about 1900) his ideas have been continually modified and developed by other writers on and practitioners of psychoanalysis. As a result, there are now many counsellors and psychotherapists who would see themselves as working within the broad tradition initiated by Freud, but who would call themselves *psychodynamic* in orientation rather than psychoanalytic. Counsellors working in a psychodynamic way with clients all tend to make similar kinds of assumptions about the nature of the client's problems, and the manner in which these problems can best be worked on. The main distinctive features of the psychodynamic approach are:

1 An assumption that the client's difficulties have their ultimate origins in childhood experiences.
2 An assumption that the client may not be consciously aware of the true motives or impulses behind his or her actions.
3 The use in counselling and therapy of techniques such as dream analysis, interpretation and transference.

These features will now be examined in more detail.

The childhood origins of emotional problems

Freud noted that, in the 'free association' situation, many of his patients reported remembering unpleasant or fearful sexual experiences in childhood, and, moreover, that the act of telling someone else about these experiences was therapeutic. Freud could not believe that these childhood sexual traumas had actually happened in reality (although today we might disagree), and made sense of this phenomenon by suggesting that what had really happened had its roots in the child's own sexual needs.

It is important to be clear here about what Freud meant by 'sexual'. In his own writing, which was of course in German, he used a concept that might more accurately be translated as 'life force' or, more generally, 'emotional energy'. While this concept has a sexual aspect to it, it is unfortunate that its English translation focuses only on this aspect.

Freud surmised, from listening to his patients talk about their lives, that the sexual energy, or libido, of the child develops or matures through a number of distinct phases. In the first year of life, the child experiences an almost erotic pleasure from its mouth, its oral region. Babies get satisfaction from sucking, biting and swallowing. Then, between about two and four years of age, children get pleasure from defecating, from feelings in their anal region. Then, at around five to eight years of age, the child begins to have a kind of immature genital longing, which is directed at members of the opposite sex. Freud called this the phallic stage. (Freud thought that the child's sexuality became less important in older childhood, and he called this the latency stage.)

The phases of psycho-sexual development set the stage for a series of conflicts between the child and its environment, its family and, most important of all, its parents. Freud saw the parents or family as having to respond to the child's needs and impulses, and he argued that the way in which the parents responded had a powerful influence on the later personality of the child. Mainly, the parents or family could respond in a way that was too controlling or one that was not controlling enough. For example, little babies cry when they are hungry. If the mother feeds the baby immediately every time, or even feeds before the demand has been made, the baby may learn, at a deep emotional level, that it does not need to do anything to be taken care of. It may grow up believing, deep down, that there exists a perfect world and it may become a person who finds it hard to accept the inevitable frustrations of the actual world. On the other hand, if the baby has to wait too long to be fed, it may learn that the world only meets its needs if it gets angry or verbally aggressive. Somewhere in between these two extremes is what the British psychoanalyst D. W. Winnicott has called the 'good enough' mother, the mother or caretaker who responds quickly enough without being over-protective or smothering.

Freud suggests a similar type of pattern for the anal stage. If the child's potty training is too rigid and harsh, it will learn that it must never allow itself to make a mess, and may grow up finding it difficult to express emotions and with an obsessional need to keep everything in its proper place. If the potty training is too permissive, on the other hand, the child may grow up without the capacity to keep things in order.

The third developmental stage, the phallic stage, is possibly the most significant in terms of its effects on later life. Freud argues that the child at this stage begins to feel primitive genital impulses, which are directed at the most obvious target: its opposite sex parent. Thus at this stage little girls are 'in love' with their fathers and little boys with their mothers. But, Freud goes on, the child then fears the punishment or anger of the same-sex parent if this sexual longing is expressed in behaviour. The child is then forced to repress its sexual feelings, and also to defuse its rivalry with the same-sex parent by identifying more strongly with that parent. Usually, this 'family drama' would be acted out at a largely unconscious level. The effect later on, in adulthood, might be that people continue to repress or distort their sexuality, and that in their sexual relationships (e.g. marriage) they might be unconsciously seeking the opposite-sex parents they never had. The basic psychological problem here, as with the other stages, lies in the fact that the person's impulses or drives are 'driven underground', and influence the person unconsciously. Thus someone might not be consciously aware of having 'chosen' a marriage partner who symbolically represents his or her mother or father, but his or her behaviour towards the partner may follow the same pattern as the earlier parent–child relationship. An example of this might be the husband who as a child was always criticized by his mother, and who later on seems always to expect his wife to behave in the same way.

It may be apparent from the previous discussion that, although Freud in his original theory emphasized the psycho-sexual nature of childhood development, what really influences the child emotionally and psychologically as he or she grows up is the quality of the relationships he or she has with his or her parents and family. This realization has led more recent writers in the psychodynamic tradition to emphasize the psycho-social development of the child rather than the sexual and biological aspects.

One of the most important of these writers is the psychoanalyst Erik Erikson, whose book *Childhood and Society* (1950) includes a description of eight stages of psycho-social development, covering the whole lifespan. His first stage, during the first year or so of life, is equivalent to Freud's 'oral' stage. Erikson, however, suggests that the early relationship between mother and child is psychologically significant because it is in this relationship that the child either learns to trust the world (if his or her basic needs are met) or acquires a basic sense of mistrust. This sense of trust or mistrust may then form the foundation for the type of relationships the child has in later adult life.

Another writer who stresses the psycho-social events of childhood is the British psychoanalyst John Bowlby (1969, 1973, 1980, 1988). In his work, he examines the way that the experience of attachment (the existence of a close, safe, continuing relationship) and loss in childhood can shape the person's capacity for forming attachments in adult life.

Although subsequent theorists in the psychodynamic tradition have moved the emphasis away from Freud's focus on sexuality in childhood, they would still agree that the emotions and feelings that are triggered by childhood sexual experiences can have powerful effects on the child's development. However, the basic viewpoint that is shared by all psychoanalytic and psychodynamic counsellors and therapists is that to understand the personality of an adult client or patient it is necessary to understand the development of that personality through childhood, particularly with respect to how it has been shaped by its family environment.

The importance of the 'unconscious'

Freud did not merely suggest that childhood experiences influence adult personality; he suggested that the influence occurred in a particular way – through the operation of the unconscious mind. The 'unconscious', for Freud, was the part of mental life of a person that was outside direct awareness. Freud saw the human mind as divided into three regions:

- The *id* ('it') a reservoir of primitive instincts and impulses which are the ultimate motives for our behaviour. Freud assumed that there were two core drives: life/love/sex/Eros and death/hate/aggression/Thanatos. The id has no time dimension, so that memories trapped there through repression can be as powerful as when the repressed event first happened. The id is governed by the 'pleasure principle', and is irrational.
- The *ego* ('I'), the conscious, rational part of the mind, which makes decisions and deals with external reality.
- The *superego* ('above I'), the 'conscience', the store-house of rules and taboos about what you should and should not do. The attitudes a person has in the superego are mainly an internalization of his or her parents' attitudes.

There are two very important implications of this theory of how the mind works. First, the id and most of the superego were seen by Freud as being largely unconscious, so that much of an individual's behaviour could be understood as being under the control of forces (e.g. repressed memories, childhood fantasies) that the person cannot consciously acknowledge. The psychodynamic counsellor or therapist, therefore, is always looking for ways of getting 'beneath the surface' of what the client or patient is saying – the assumption is that what the person initially says about himself or herself is only part of the story, and probably not the most interesting part.

Second, the ego and the other regions (the id and superego) are, potentially at any rate, almost constantly in conflict with each other. For example the id presses for its primitive impulses to be acted upon ('I hate him so I want to hit him') but the ego will know that such behaviour would be punished by the external world, and the superego tries to make the person feel guilty because what he or she wants to do is wrong or immoral. It is, however, highly uncomfortable to live with such a degree of inner turmoil, and so Freud argued that the mind develops defence mechanisms – for example, repression, denial, reaction formation, sublimation, intellectualization and projection – to protect the ego from such pressure. So, not only is what the person consciously believes only part of the story, it is also likely to be a part that is distorted by the operation of defence mechanisms.

The therapeutic techniques used in psychoanalysis

The Freudian or psychodynamic theory described in the previous sections originally emerged out of the work of Freud and others in helping people with emotional problems. Many aspects of the theory have, therefore, been applied to the question of how to facilitate therapeutic change in clients or patients. Before we move on to look at the specific techniques used in psychoanalytic or psychodynamic therapy and counselling, however, it is essential to be clear about just what the aims of such treatment are. Freud used the phrase 'where id was, let ego be' to summarize his aims. In other words, rather than being driven by unconscious forces and impulses, people after therapy will be more rational, more aware of their inner emotional life, and more able to control these feelings in an appropriate manner. A key aim of psychoanalysis is, then, the achievement of insight into the true nature of one's problems (i.e. their childhood origins). But genuine insight is not merely an intellectual exercise – when the person truly understands, he or she will experience a release of the emotional tension associated with the repressed or buried memories. Freud used the term 'catharsis' to describe this emotional release.

There are a number of therapeutic techniques or strategies used in psychoanalytic or psychodynamic therapy, including those that follow.

1 *Free Association or 'saying whatever comes to mind'*. The intention is to help the person to talk about himself or herself in a fashion that is less likely to be influenced by defence mechanisms. It is as though in free association the person's 'truth' can slip out.

2 *Working on dreams and fantasies*. Freud saw the dream as 'the royal road to the unconscious', and encouraged his patients to tell him about their dreams. Again, the purpose is to examine material that comes from a deeper, less defended, level of the individual's personality. It is assumed that events in dreams symbolically represent people, impulses or situations in the dreamer's

waking life. Other products of the imagination, for example waking dreams, fantasies and images, can be used in the same way as night dreams in analysis.

3 *Identifying and analysing resistances and defences.* As the client talks in free association, the therapist may notice that he or she is avoiding, distorting or defending against certain feelings or insights. Freud saw it as important to understand the source of such resistance, and would draw the patient's attention to it if it happened persistently. For example, a student seeing a counsellor for help with study problems, who then persistently blames tutors for his difficulties, is probably avoiding his own feelings of inadequacy, or dependency, by employing the defence mechanism of projection (i.e. attributing to others characteristics you cannot accept in yourself).

4 *Systematic use of the relationship between the counsellor and client.* Psychoanalytic counsellors and therapists tend to behave towards their clients in a slightly reserved, detached, neutral or formal manner. It is unusual for psychoanalytically trained counsellors to share much of their own feelings or own lives with their clients. The reason for this is that the counsellor is attempting to present himself or herself as a 'blank screen' on to which the client may project his or her fantasies or deeply held assumptions about close relationships. The therapist expects that as therapy continues over weeks or months, the feelings clients hold towards him or her will be similar to the feelings they had towards significant, authority figures in their own past. In other words, if the client behaved in a passive, dependent way with her own mother as a child, then she could reproduce this behaviour with her therapist. By being neutral and detached, the therapist ensures that the feelings the client has toward him or her are not caused by anything the therapist has done, but are a result of the client projecting an image of his or her mother, father, etc. on to the therapist. This process is called transference and is a powerful tool in psychoanalytic therapy, since it allows the therapist to observe the early childhood relationships of the client as these relationships are re-enacted in the consulting room. The aim would be to help the client to become aware of these projections, first in the relationship with the therapist but then in relationships with other people, such as his or her spouse, boss, friends and so on.

5 *The use of interpretation.* A psychoanalytic counsellor or therapist will use the processes described above – transference, dreams, free association, etc. – to generate material for interpretation. Through interpreting the meaning of dreams, memories and transference, the therapist is attempting to help clients to understand the origins of their problems, and thereby gain more control over them and more freedom to behave differently. However, effective interpretation is a difficult skill. Some of the issues which the therapist or counsellor must bear in mind when making an interpretation are:

- Is the timing right? Is the client ready to take this idea on board?
- Is the interpretation correct? Has enough evidence been gathered?
- Can the interpretation be phrased in such a way that the client will understand it?

6 *Other miscellaneous techniques.* When working with children as clients, it is

unrealistic to expect them to be able to put their inner conflicts into words. As a result, most child analysts use toys and play to allow the child to externalize his or her fears and worries. Some therapists working with adults also find it helpful to use expressive techniques, such as art, sculpture and poetry. The use of projective techniques, such as the Rorschach Inkblot Test or the Thematic Apperception Test (TAT), can also serve a similar function. Finally, some therapists encourage their clients to write diaries or autobiographies as a means of exploring their past or present circumstances.

Although the number of actual psychoanalysts in Britain is small, the influence on counselling in general of psychoanalysis and the psychodynamic tradition has been immense. It is probably true to say that virtually all counsellors have been influenced at some level by psychoanalytic ideas. It should be acknowledged that the understanding of Freud that we in Britain and the USA have is a version filtered through his translators. Bettelheim (1983) has suggested that the ideas and concepts introduced by Freud in his original writings (in German) have been made more 'clinical' and more mechanical through translation into English.

The account of Freudian theory and practice given here can provide no more than a brief introduction to this area of literature. The interested reader who would wish to explore psychoanalytic thinking in more depth is recommended to consult Freud's own work. The *Introductory Lectures* (Freud, 1917), *New Introductory Lectures* (Freud, 1933) and the case studies of the Rat Man (Freud, 1909), Schreber (Freud, 1910) and Dora (Freud, 1901) represent particularly accessible and illuminating examples of the power of Freudian analysis in action. The writings of Michael Jacobs (1986, 1988) offer valuable examples of the application of psychodynamic ideas in counselling settings.

The post-Freudian evolution of the psychodynamic approach

It is well documented that Freud demanded a high level of agreement with his ideas from those around him. During his lifetime, several important figures in psychoanalysis who had been his students or close colleagues were involved in disputes with Freud and subsequently left the International Association for Psycho-Analysis. The best known of these figures is Carl Jung, who was regarded as Freud's 'favourite son' within the psychoanalytic circle, and was expected in time to take over the leadership of the psychoanalytic movement. The correspondence between Freud and Jung has been collected and published, and illustrates a growing split between the two men which became irrevocable in 1912. The principal area of disagreement between Freud and Jung centred on the nature of motivation. Jung argued that human beings have a drive towards 'individuation', or the integration and fulfilment of self, as well as more biologically based drives associated with sexuality. Jung also viewed the unconscious as encompassing spiritual and transcendental areas of meaning.

Other prominent analysts who broke off from Freud included Ferenczi, Rank, Reich and Adler. Ferenczi and Rank were frustrated with the lack of interest

Freud showed in the question of technique, of how to make the therapy a more effective means of helping patients. Reich left to pursue the bodily, organismic roots of defences, the ways in which the sexual and aggressive energy which is held back by repression, denial and other defences is expressed through bodily processes such as muscle tension, posture and illness. The theme which Adler developed was the significance of social factors in emotional life, for example the drive for power and control, which is first experienced in situations of sibling rivalry.

The disagreements between Freud and his followers are misunderstood if they are regarded as mere personality clashes, examples of Freud's irrationality, or attributable to cultural factors such as the Austrian Jewishness of Freud as against the Swiss Protestantism of Jung. These disagreements and splits represent fundamental theoretical issues within the psychodynamic approach, and although the personalization of the debate during the early years can obscure the differences over ideas and technique, it also helps by making the lines of the debate clear. The underlying questions being debated by Freud and his colleagues were:

• What happens in the early years of life to produce later problems?
• How do unconscious processes and mechanisms operate?
• What should the therapist do to make psychoanalytic therapy most effective for patients or clients?

While Freud was alive he dominated psychoanalysis, and those who disagreed with him were forced to set up separate and independent institutes and training centres. The results of these schisms in psychoanalysis persist to this day, in the continued existence of separate Jungian, Adlerian and Reichian approaches. After the death of Freud in 1939, it became possible to re-open the debate in a more open fashion, and to reintegrate some of the ideas of the 'heretics' into a broader-based psychodynamic approach. It would be impossible to review here all the interesting and useful elements of contemporary psychodynamic thinking about counselling and psychotherapy. However, three of the most important directions in which the approach has evolved since Freud's death have been through the development of a theoretical perspective known as the 'object relations' approach, the work of the British 'Independents', and the refinements to technique necessary to offer psychodynamic counselling and therapy on a time-limited basis.

The object relations school

The originator of the object relations movement with the psychodynamic approach is usually accepted to be Melanie Klein. Born in Austria, Klein trained with a student of Freud, Sandor Ferenczi, in Hungary, and eventually moved to Britain in 1926, becoming an influential member of the British Psycho-Analytical Society. The work of Klein was distinctive in that she carried out psychoanalysis with children, and placed emphasis on the relationship between mother and child in the very first months of life, whereas Freud was mainly concerned with the dynamics of Oedipal conflicts, which occurred much later in childhood. For Klein, the quality of relationship which the child experienced with human 'objects' (such as the mother) in the first year set a pattern of relating which persisted through adult life. The original writings of Klein are difficult, but Segal (1964), Segal (1985, 1992) and Sayers (1991) present accessible accounts of her life and work.

The fundamental difference between the psychoanalytic and object relations perspectives is expressed well by Cashdan (1988):

> Within object relations theory, the mind and the psychic structures that comprise it are thought to evolve out of human interactions rather than out of biologically derived tensions. Instead of being motivated by tension reduction, human beings are motivated by the need to establish and maintain relationships. It is the need for human contact, in other words, that constitutes the primary motive within an object relations perspective.

Before Klein, very few psychoanalysts had worked directly with children. Using drawings, toys, dolls and other play materials, Klein found that she was able to explore the inner world of the child, and discovered that the conflicts and anxieties felt by children largely arose not from their sexual impulses, as Freud had assumed, but from their relationships with adults. The relationship with the mother, in particular, was a centrally important factor. A young child, in fact, cannot survive without a caretaker, usually a mother. Another child psychoanalyst working within this tradition, D. W. Winnicott (1964), wrote that 'there is no such thing as a baby', pointing out that 'a baby cannot exist alone, but is essentially part of a relationship'.

From the point of view of the baby, according to Klein, the mother in the first months is represented by the 'part-object' of the breast, and is experienced as either a 'good object' or as a 'bad object'. She is 'good' when the needs of the baby are being met through feeding. She is 'bad' when these needs are not being met. The baby responds to the bad object with feelings of destructive rage. The first few months are described by Klein as a 'paranoid-schizoid' period, when the baby feels very little security in the world and is recovering from the trauma of birth. Over time, however, the baby begins to be able to perceive the mother as a more realistic whole object rather than as the part-object of the breast, and to understand that good and bad can coexist in the same person. The early phase of splitting of experience into 'good' and 'bad' begins to be resolved.

The next phase of development, according to Klein, is characterized by a 'depressive' reaction, a deep sense of disappointment and anger that a loved person can be bad as well as good. In the earlier phase, the baby was able to maintain the fantasy of the 'good mother' as existing separate from the 'bad'. Now he or she must accept that the bad and the good go together. There is a primitive sense of loss and separation now that the possibility of complete fusion with the 'good' mother has been left behind. There may be a sense of guilt that it was the child himself or herself who was actually responsible for the end of the earlier, simpler, phase of the relationship with the mother.

It is essential to recognize that the infant is not consciously aware of these processes as they happen. The awareness of the child is seen as dream-like and fragmented rather than logical and connected. Indeed, it is hard for adults to imagine what the inner life of a child might be like. In her effort to reconstruct this inner life, Klein portrays a world dominated by strong impulses and emotions in response to the actions of external 'objects'. The assumption is that the emotional inner world of the adult is built upon the foundations of experience of these earliest months and years.

One of the key characteristics of this inner world, according to the object relations perspective (and other psychological theories, such as that of Piaget), is the inability of the child to differentiate between what is self and what is the rest of the world. In the beginning, the child is egocentric in the sense that it believes it has power over everything that happens in its world; for example, that food arrives because I cry, it is morning because I wake up, or Grandad died because I didn't take care of him.

The model of child development provided by Klein can usefully be supplemented by that offered by Margaret Mahler (1968; Mahler et al., 1975), another central figure within the object relations approach. Mahler views the child in the first year of life as being autistic, without any sense of the existence of other people. Between two and four months is the 'symbiotic' stage, in which there is the beginning of recognition of the mother as an object. Then, from about four months through to three years of age, the infant undergoes a gradual process of separation from the mother, slowly building up a sense of self independent from the self of the mother. At the beginning of this process the infant will experiment with crawling away from the mother then returning to her. Towards the end of the period, particularly with the development of language, the child will have a name and a set of things that are 'mine'.

It can be seen here that the theoretical framework being developed by Mahler and her colleagues from the basis of an 'object relations' perspective includes a strong emphasis on the idea of 'self', a concept which was not extensively used by Freud. Where Freud, influenced by his medical and scientific training, saw personality as ultimately determined by the biologically driven stages of psychosexual development and biologically based motives, theorists such as Klein and Mahler came to view people as fundamentally social beings. In Britain, this branch of psychoanalysis is usually called, following Klein, the 'object relations' school. In the USA, influenced by writers such as Kohut (1971, 1977) Mahler et al. (1975) and Kernberg (1976, 1984), similar ideas are referred to as 'self' theory.

By observing both 'normal' and disturbed children, Klein, Mahler and other object relations theorists have been able to piece together an understanding of the emotional life of the child which is, they would assert, more accurate than that reconstructed by Freud through interpretation of the free associations of adult patients in therapy. However, like Freud they regard the troubles of adult life as being derived ultimately from disturbances in the developmental process in childhood. Winnicott used the phrase 'good enough' to describe the type of parenting which would enable children to develop effectively. Unfortunately, many people are subjected to childhood experiences that are far from 'good enough', and result in a variety of different patterns of pathology.

One of the most fundamental of the dysfunctional patterns described by object relations counsellors and therapists is *splitting*, which refers to a way of defending against difficult feelings and impulses that can be traced back to the very first months of life. Klein, it will be recalled, understood that babies could only differentiate between the wholly 'good' and wholly 'bad' part-object of the breast. This object was experienced by the baby as one associated with pleasurable and blissful feelings while feeding, or with feelings of rage when it was absent or taken away. Correspondingly, the psychological and emotional world of the baby at this very early stage consisted only of things that were good or bad; there were no shades of feelings in between. The fundamental insecurity and terror evoked by the feelings of 'bad' led Klein to characterize this as a 'paranoid-schizoid' position.

As the child grows and develops, it becomes able to perceive that good and bad can go together, and therefore it can begin to distinguish different degrees of goodness and badness. When this development does not proceed in a satisfactory manner, or when some external threat re-evokes the insecurity of these early months, the person may either grow up with a tendency to experience the world as 'split' between objects which are all good or all bad, or may use this defence in particular situations.

It is not difficult to think of examples of splitting in everyday life, as well as in the counselling room. Within the social and political arena, many people see only good in one political party, soccer team, religion or nationality, and attribute everything bad to the other. Within relationships and family life, people have friends and enemies, parents have favourite and disowned children, and the children may have perfect mothers and wicked fathers. Within an individual personality, sexuality may be bad and intellect good, or drinking reprehensible and abstinence wonderful.

For the psychodynamic counsellor, the client who exhibits splitting is defending against feelings of love and hate for the same object. For example, a woman who idealizes her counsellor and complains repeatedly in counselling of the misdeeds and insensitivity of her husband may have underlying strong feelings of longing for closeness in the marriage and rage at the way he abuses her, or an underlying need to be taken care of by him coupled with anger at his absences at work. As with the other defences described earlier in the chapter, the task of the counsellor is first of all to help the client to be aware of the way she is avoiding her true feelings through this manoeuvre, then gently encouraging exploration and understanding of the emotions and impulses that are so hard to accept. From a psychodynamic perspective, the reason why the person needs to use the defence is that some aspects of the current situation are similar to painful childhood situations, and are bringing to the surface long buried memories of early events. Although the client may be a socially and professionally successful and responsible adult, the inner emotional turmoil she brings to counselling is the part of her that is still a child, and only has available to it infantile ways of coping, such as splitting. So, in the case of the woman who idealizes her counsellor and scorns her husband, it may eventually emerge that, perhaps, the grandfather who was supposed to look after her when mum was out actually abused her sexually, and she could only deal with this by constructing a 'good' grandad object and a 'bad' one.

The defence mechanism of splitting is similar to the classic Freudian ideas of defence, such as repression, denial and reaction formation, in that these are all processes which occur within the individual psyche or personality. The Kleinian notion of *projective identification*, however, represents an important departure, in that it describes a process of emotional defence that is interpersonal rather than purely intrapersonal. Being able to apply the idea of projective identification is therefore a uniquely valuable strategy for psychodynamic counsellors who view client problems as rooted in relationships.

The concept of 'projection' has already been introduced as a process whereby the person defends against threatening and unacceptable feelings and impulses by acting as though these feelings and impulses only existed in other people, not in the person himself or herself. For example, a man who accuses his work colleagues of always disagreeing with his very reasonable proposals may be projecting on to them his own buried hostility and competitiveness. The counsellor who persists in assuming that a depressed client really needs to make more friends and join some clubs may be projecting her own fear of her personal inner emptiness.

Projective identification occurs when the person to whom the feelings and impulses are being projected is manipulated into believing that he or she actually has these feelings and impulses. For instance, the man who accuses his colleagues may unconsciously set up circumstances where they have little choice but to argue with him, for example by not explaining his ideas with enough clarity. And the counsellor may easily persuade the depressed client that she herself does want to make friends.

From an object relations perspective, the dynamics of projective identification have their origins in very early experience, in the time when the child was unable to tell the difference between self and external objects. In projective identification, this blurring of the self–other boundary is accompanied by a need to control the other, which comes from the early state of childhood grandiose omnipotence.

Cashdan (1988) has identified four major patterns of projective identification, arising from underlying issues of dependency, power, sexuality and ingratiation. He describes projective identification as a process that occurs in the context of a relationship. In the case of dependency, the person will actively seek assistance from other people who are around, by using phrases such as 'What do you think?' or 'I can't seem to manage this on my own.' The person is presenting a relationship stance of helplessness. Usually, however, these requests for help are not based on a real inability to solve problems or cope, but are motivated by what Cashdan (1988) calls a 'projective fantasy', a sense of self-in-relationship originating in disturbed object relations in early childhood. The dependent person might have a projective fantasy which could be summarized as a fundamental belief that 'I can't survive'. The great reservoir of unresolved childhood need or anger contained within this fantasy is what gives urgency and

Table 1 The process of projective identification

Underlying issue	Projective fantasy	Way of relating to others	Response elicited from others
Dependency	'I can't survive'	'Can you help me?'	Caretaking
Power	'You can't survive'	'Do what I say'	Incompetence
Sexuality	'I'll make you sexually whole'	Flirting	Arousal
Ingratiation	'You owe me'	Self-sacrifice ('I work my fingers to the bone')	Appreciation

Source: derived from Cashdan (1988)

force to what may otherwise appear to be reasonable requests for assistance. The recipient of the request is therefore under pressure, and may be induced into taking care of the person. Similar processes take place with sexuality, power and ingratiation, as illustrated in Table 1.

As with any psychodynamic perspective, current problems are viewed as having their origins in childhood experience. In each of these patterns of projective identification, the outcome is to re-create in an adult relationship the type of object relations that prevailed in childhood. The dependent person will possibly have had a mother who needed to look after him or her all the time. The powerful person will have grown up in a family where one of the parents needed to be taken care of. The sexual person will have grown up in a family where closeness was only achieved through sexual contact of some kind. The ingratiating person will have known early relationships based on earning acceptance and acknowledgement for being helpful.

The idea of projective identification provides psychodynamic counsellors with a useful conceptual tool for disentangling the complex web of feelings and fantasies which exist in troubled relationships. The unconscious intention behind projective identification is to induce or entice the other to behave towards the self as if the self was in reality a dependent, powerful, sexual or helpful person. This interpersonal strategy enables the person to deny that the dependency, for example, is a fantasy which conceals behind it a multiplicity of feelings, such as resentment, longing or despair. There may be times when the projection is acceptable to the person on the receiving end, perhaps because it feeds his or her fantasy of being powerful or caring. But there will be times when the recipient becomes aware that there is something not quite right, and resists the projection. Or there may be times when the projector himself or herself becomes painfully aware of what is happening. Finally, there will be occasions in counselling when projective identification is applied to the counsellor, who will be pressured to treat the client in line with fantasy expectations. These times provide rich material for the counsellor to work with.

Defence mechanisms such as splitting and projective identification constitute two of the important building blocks of the object relations approach within the psychodynamic orientation to counselling. It is essential to recognize, however, that in practice the problems and anxieties with which clients present at counselling typically encompass complex sets of fantasies and defences, and that our discussion so far has introduced these process through simplified examples, taken out of context of the whole of the inner life and relationships of a client. It is useful, therefore, to examine two of the contributions of object relations and self theorists to putting the whole picture of the life of a client back together again, by describing the types of adult personality that result from particular disturbances in early object relations. The two personality patterns which have received most attention within contemporary psychodynamic theory are the *narcissistic character disorder* and the *borderline personality disorder*.

The concept of narcissism was originally introduced by Freud, who drew upon the Greek legend of Narcissus, a youth who fell in love with his own reflection. Freud viewed over-absorption in self as a difficult condition to treat through psychoanalysis, since it was almost impossible for the analyst to break through the narcissism to reach the underlying conflicts. Kohut (1971) and Kernberg (1975) initiated a re-evaluation of the problem of narcissism within psychoanalysis. Kohut (1971) argued that the narcissistic person is fundamentally unable to differentiate between self and other. Rather than being able to act towards others as separate entities, in narcissism other people are experienced as 'self-objects', as little more than extensions of the self. Other people only exist to aggrandize and glorify the self. For Kohut, the solution to this lay in the transference relationship between client and therapist. If the therapist refrained from directly confronting the falseness and grandiosity of the client, but instead empathized with and accepted the client's experience of things, a situation would be created which paralleled the conditions of early childhood.

Kohut (1971) argued that, just as the real mother is never perfect, and can only hope to be 'good enough', the therapist can never achieve complete empathy and acceptance. The client therefore experiences, at moments of failure of empathy, a sense of 'optimal frustration'. It is this combination of frustration in a context of high acceptance and warmth that gradually enables the client to appreciate the separation of self and other. Although the model proposed by Kohut (1971, 1977) has much more to say on the matter than is possible here, it should be apparent that the application of concepts from an object relations perspective has made a significant contribution to the understanding and treatment of this disorder.

Another important area of advance has been in work with 'borderline' clients. This label is used to refer to people who exhibit extreme difficulties in forming relationships, have been profoundly emotionally damaged by childhood experiences, and express high levels of both dependency and rage in the relationship with the therapist. One of the meanings of 'borderline' in this context refers to the idea of 'borderline schizophrenic'. Traditionally, people with this kind of depth and array of problems have not been considered as viable candidates for psychodynamic therapy, and have generally been offered long-term 'supportive' therapy rather than anything more ambitious. The work of Kernberg (1975,

1984) and others from an object relations/self perspective has attributed the problems of borderline clients to arrested development in early childhood. These
people are understood to be emotionally very young, dealing with the world as
if they were in the paranoid-schizoid stage described by Klein, where experience
is savagely split between 'good' and 'bad'. The task of the therapist is to enable
the client to regress back to the episodes in childhood which presented blocks to
progress and maturity, and to discover new ways of overcoming them. This type
of therapy can be seen almost as providing a second chance for development with
a special kind of parenting, with the therapeutic relationship acting as a substitute for the nuclear family.

Therapy with borderline clients is often conducted over several years, with the
client receiving multiple sessions each week. The intensity and challenge of this
kind of therapeutic work, and the generally moderate success rates associated
with it, mean that practitioners are often cautious about taking on borderline
clients, or limit the number of such clients in their case load at any one time
(Aronson, 1989).

The British Independents

The psychodynamic approach to counselling in the post-Freudian era has been
marked by the emergence of a range of different writers who have developed the
theory in different directions. One of the significant groupings of psychodynamic
therapists has been the British 'Independent' group. The origins of the
Independents can be traced back to the beginnings of psychoanalysis in Britain.
The British Psycho-Analytical Society was formed in 1919, under the leadership
of Ernest Jones. In 1926, Melanie Klein, who had been trained in Berlin, moved
to London and became a member of the British Society. From the beginning
Klein was critical of conventional psychoanalysis. She pioneered child analysis,
insisted on the primary importance of destructive urges and the death instinct,
and paid more attention to early development than to Oedipal issues. The contrast between the views of Klein and her followers, and those of more orthodox
Freudians, came to a climax with the emigration of Freud and his daughter Anna
Freud, along with several other analysts from Vienna, to London in 1938. Anna
Freud represented the mainstream of Freudian theory, and in the years immediately following the death of Freud in 1939, the relationship between her group
and the Kleinians became tense. In the 1940s there were a series of what came
to be known as 'controversial discussions' in the Society. The drama of this
period in psychoanalysis is well captured by Rayner (1990: 18–19):

> by 1941 the atmosphere in scientific meetings was becoming electric . . .
> It is puzzling that there should be such passion on matters of theory in the
> midst of a world war. The situation was that London was being bombed
> nearly every night, and many did not know whether they would survive,
> let alone what would happen to analysis – to which they had given their
> lives. They felt they were the protectors of precious ideas which were

threatened not only by bombs but from within their colleagues and themselves. Also, it was hardly possible to go on practising analysis, which is vital to keep coherent analytic ideas alive. Ideological venom and character assassination were released under these circumstances. Where many people found a new communality under the threats of war, the opposite happened to psychoanalysts in London.

In what can be seen as a reflection of the British capacity for compromise, the Society decided by 1946 to divide, for purposes of training, into three loose groups: the Kleinians, the Anna Freud group, and the 'middle' group, who later became known as the 'Independents'. The rule was introduced that analysts in training must be exposed to the ideas and methods of more than one group. This principle has resulted in a tradition of openness to new ideas within the British psychodynamic community. The influence of the 'independent mind' in psychoanalysis has been documented by Kohon (1986) and Rayner (1990).

Although the independents have inevitably generated new ideas across the whole span of psychodynamic theory (Rayner, 1990), the group is particularly known for its reappraisal of the concept of counter-transference. It is not without significance that a group of therapists who had gone through the kind of personal and professional trauma described by Rayner (1990) should become particularly sensitive to the role of the personality and self of the therapist in the therapeutic relationship. The contribution of the independents has been to draw attention to the value of the feelings of the counsellor in the relationship with the client. Previously, counter-transference had been regarded with some suspicion by analysts, as evidence of neurotic conflicts in the analyst. Heimann (1950) argued, by contrast, that counter-transference was 'one of the most important tools' in analysis. Her position was that

the analyst's unconscious understands that of the patient. This rapport on a deep level comes to the surface in the form of feelings which the analyst notes in response to [the] patient.

Another member of the independent group, Symington (1983), suggested that 'at one level the analyst and patient together make a single system'. Both analyst and patient can become locked into shared illusions or fantasies, which Symington (1983) argues can only be dissolved through an 'act of freedom' by the analyst. In other words, the analyst needs to achieve insight into the part he or she is playing in maintaining the system. The approach to counter-transference initiated by the independents involved a warmer, more personal contact between client and therapist (Casement, 1985, 1990), and anticipated many of the developments associated with time-limited psychodynamic counselling.

Psychodynamic counselling within a time-limited framework

In the early years of psychoanalysis, it was not assumed by Freud or his colleagues that patients need necessarily be in treatment for long periods of time.

For example, in 1908 Freud is reported to have carried out successful therapy of a sexual problem in the composer Gustave Mahler in the course of four sessions (Jones, 1955). However, as psychoanalysts became more aware of the problem of resistance in patients, and more convinced of the intractable nature of the emotional problems they brought to therapy, they began to take for granted the idea that psychoanalysis in most cases would be a lengthy business, with patients attending therapy several times a week, perhaps for years.

Among the first psychoanalysts, however, there were some critics of this trend, who argued for a more active role for the therapist, and definite time limits for the length of therapy. The two most prominent advocates of this view were Sandor Ferenczi and Otto Rank. There was strong opposition to their ideas from Freud and the inner circle of analysts, and eventually both men were forced to leave. The next important event in the progress of this debate about psychoanalytic technique came with the publication in 1946 of a book by Alexander and French which advocated that psychoanalysts take a flexible approach to treatment. Over a period of seven years at the Chicago Institute for Psychoanalysis, they had experimented with a range of variations of standard psychoanalytic technique, for example trying out different numbers of sessions each week, the use of the couch or chair, and the degree of attention paid to the transference relationship. The Alexander and French book was highly influential and, in the spirit of openness to new ideas that followed the death of Freud in 1939, it stimulated many other analysts to tackle the issues of technique involved in offering psychodynamic therapy or counselling on a time-limited basis. The main figures in the subsequent development of what is often known as 'brief therapy' are Mann (1973), Malan (1976, 1979), Sifneos (1979) and Davanloo (1980).

It is essential to recognize that the emergence of brief psychodynamic therapy and counselling arose as much from the pressures of social need and client demand as from the deliberations of therapists themselves. In the 1940s in the USA, for example, counsellors and psychotherapists were being expected to help large numbers of members of the armed forces returning from war with emotional problems. In the 1960s there was substantial political pressure in the USA to move mental health facilities into the community, and to make them more readily available for large numbers of clients. Even clients seeing therapists in private practice did not want 'interminable' therapy. For example, Garfield (1986), in a review of studies of the length of treatment in a variety of therapy settings, found that the largest group of clients were those who came for five or six sessions, with the majority seeing their counsellor or therapist on fewer than twenty occasions. These factors led counsellors and therapists from all orientations to examine closely the problem of time-limited interventions, and the literature on brief psychodynamic work is paralleled by writings on brief cognitive, client-centred and other modes of work.

Writers on brief psychodynamic therapy have different ideas about what they mean by 'brief', which can refer to anything between three and forty sessions. Most are agreed that brief treatment is that involving fewer than twenty-five sessions. More fundamental, however, is the idea that the number of sessions is rationed, and that a contract is made at the start of counselling that there will only be a certain number of sessions. Although there are many styles of brief psychodynamic work that have been evolved by teams of therapists in different clinics (see Gustafson (1986) for a review of some of the main currents of thought within this movement), there is general agreement that brief work is focused on three discrete stages: beginning, the active phase and termination (Rosen, 1987).

If the time to be spent with a client is limited, then the maximum use must be made of each and every client–counsellor interaction. The beginning phase is therefore a site for a variety of different kinds of counsellor activity, encompassing assessment, preparing the client, establishing a therapeutic alliance, starting therapeutic work and finding out about the life history and background of the client. The first meeting with the client, and indeed the first words uttered by the client, can be of great significance. This point is well made by Alexander and French (1946: 109):

> The analyst during this period may be compared to a traveller standing on top of a hill overlooking the country through which he is about to journey. At this time it may be possible for him to see his whole anticipated journey in perspective. When once he has descended into the valley, this perspective must be retained in the memory or it is gone. From this time on, he will be able to examine small parts of this landscape in much greater detail than was possible when he was viewing them from a distance, but the broad relations will no longer be so clear.

It is generally assumed that time-limited counselling is appropriate only for particular kinds of clients. For example, clients who are psychotic or 'borderline' are usually seen as unlikely to benefit from time-limited work (although some practitioners, such as Budman and Gurman (1988), would dispute this, and would view all clients as potentially appropriate for time-limited interventions). In brief counselling or therapy it is therefore necessary to carry out an assessment interview. The objectives of the assessment session might cover exploration of such issues as:

- the attitude of the client towards a time-limited treatment contract;
- motivation for change and 'psychological-mindedness';
- the existence of a previous capacity to sustain close relationships;
- the ability to relate with the therapist during the assessment interview;
- the existence of a clearly identifiable, discrete problem to work on in therapy.

Positive indications in all, or most, of these areas are taken to suggest a good prognosis for brief work. Techniques for increasing the effectiveness of the assessment interview include asking the client to complete a life history questionnaire before the interview, recording the interview on video and discussing the assessment with colleagues, and engaging in 'trial therapy' during the interview. The last refers to the practice of the interviewer offering some limited interpretation of the material offered by the client during the interview (Malan, 1976), or devoting a segment of the assessment time to a very short therapy session (Gustafson, 1986).

It is of course important that care is taken with clients who are assessed as unsuitable for brief work, and that alternative referrals and forms of treatment are available. Special training is usually considered necessary for those carrying out assessment interviews. The beginning stage of brief work also encompasses negotiation with the client over the aims and duration of the counselling or therapy contract, and preparation of the client for what is to follow by explaining to the client the nature of his or her therapeutic responsibilities and tasks.

One of the principal tasks of the brief therapist is to find a focus for the overall therapy, and for each particular session. The therapist is active in seeking out a focus for the work, and in this respect differs from the traditional psycho-analyst, who would wait for themes to emerge through free association. In find-ing a focus, the counsellor brings to the session some assumptions about the type of material with which he or she is seeking to work. These assumptions are derived from psychoanalytic and object relations theory, and guide the counsellor in the choice of which threads of the client's story to follow up. For example, Budman and Gurman (1988) describe an 'IDE' formula which they use in deciding on a focus for a session. They view people as inevitably grappling with developmental (D) issues arising from their stage of psycho-social develop-ment, involved in interpersonal (I) issues arising from relationships, and faced with existential (E) issues such as aloneness, choice and awareness of death. Gustafson (1986) emphasizes the central importance of finding a focus when he writes that 'I will not go a step until I have the "loose end" of the patient's preoccupation for today's meeting.'

It is often valuable, in finding the focus for client work, to consider the ques-tion 'Why now?' In brief psychodynamic work it is assumed that the problem the client brings to therapy is triggered off by something currently happening in his or her life. The client is seen as a person who is having difficulties coping with a specific situation, rather than as a fundamentally 'sick' individual. The question 'Why now?' helps to begin the process of exploring the roots of the troublesome feelings which are evoked by current life events. Sometimes the precipitating event can be something that happened many years ago, which is being remembered and re-lived because of an anniversary of some kind. For example, a woman who requested counselling because of a general lack of satisfaction with her relationship with her husband reported that what seemed to be happening now somehow seemed to be associated with her daughter, who was 16 and starting to go out to parties and have boyfriends. The client found herself remembering that, when she had been 16, she had become pregnant and quickly found herself with all the responsibilities of a wife and mother. Her daughter was now at that same stage in life, and bringing home to the client her buried feelings about the stage of development in her life she had missed out on. This case illustrates how the question 'Why now?' can open up developmental issues.

Another set of central issues which are often the focus for brief work arise from experiences of *loss*. The case just mentioned in fact included a component of grieving for the loss of youth and adolescence. One of the major contributors to the understanding of loss from a psychodynamic perspective has been the British psychoanalyst John Bowlby (1969, 1973, 1980, 1988). In his research and writing, Bowlby argued that human beings, like other animals, have a basic need to form attachments with others throughout life, and will not function well unless such attachments are available. The capacity for attachment is, according to Bowlby, innate, but is shaped by early experience with significant others. For example, if the child's mother is absent, or does not form a secure and reliable bond, then the child will grow up with a lack of trust and a general inability to form stable, close relationships. If, on the other hand, the mother or other family members have provided the child with what Bowlby calls a 'secure base' in childhood, then later close relationships will be possible.

Similarly, according to Bowlby, early experiences of loss can set an emotional pattern that persists into adulthood. Bowlby and Robertson observed that children separated from their parents, for example through hospitalization, initially respond through protest and anger, then with depression and sadness, and finally by behaving apparently normally. This normality, however, masks a reserve and unwillingness to share affection with new people. If the parents return, there will be reactions of rejection and avoidance before they are accepted again. For the young child, who is unable to understand at a cognitive level what is happening, this kind of experience of loss may instil a fear of abandonment that makes him or her cling on to relationships in later life. For the older child, the way he or she is helped (or not) to deal with feelings of grief and loss will likewise set up patterns that will persist. For example, when parents divorce it is quite common for a child to end up believing that he or she caused the split and subsequent loss, and would have a destructive impact on any relationship.

The events which stimulate people to seek counselling help encompass many different types of loss. The death of someone in the family, being made redundant, leaving home or the surgical removal of a body part are all powerful loss experiences. Usually, loss themes in counselling encompass both interpersonal and existential dimensions. Most experiences of loss involve some kind of change in relationships as well as change in the way the person experiences self. The experience of loss particularly challenges the illusion of self as invulnerable and immortal (Yalom, 1980). The other existential facet of loss is that it can throw the person into a state of questioning the meaningfulness of what has happened: 'nothing makes sense any more'. Finally, current experiences of loss will reawaken dormant feelings about earlier losses, and may thereby trigger off strong feelings related to early childhood events.

The aims of the counsellor or therapist working with loss from within a brief psychodynamic approach will include *uncovering* and *working through*. The uncovering part of the counselling will involve the client exploring and expressing feelings, and generally opening up this whole area of inner experience for exploration. Techniques for assisting uncovering may include retelling the story of the loss, perhaps using photographs or visits to evoke memories and feelings. The working through phase involves becoming aware of the implications of what the loss event has meant, and how the person has coped with it personally and interpersonally. In the latter phase, the counsellor may give the client information about the 'normal' course of reactions to loss.

It can be seen that, although the active phase of brief psychodynamic therapy involves the use of interpretation of current feelings in terms of past events, it also includes encouragement from the therapist or counsellor to express feelings in the here-and-now setting of the counselling room. The aim is to allow the client to undergo what Alexander and French (1946) called a 'corrective emotional experience'. They saw one of the principal aims of therapy as being 'to reexpose the patient, under more favorable circumstances, to emotional situations which he/she could not handle in the past' (Alexander and French, 1946: 66). So, for example, a client who had always been afraid to express his anger at the loss of his job, in case his wife could not handle it, can allow this feeling to be shown in the presence of the counsellor, and then, it is hoped, become more able to have this type of emotional experience with his wife or other people outside the counselling room. Part of the active stance of the brief therapist is therefore to assist the communication of feelings which are 'under the surface' by using questions such as 'What do you feel right now?' and 'How do you feel inside?' (Davanloo, 1980).

In any kind of time-limited counselling, the existence of a definite date after which therapy will no longer be available raises a whole range of potential issues for clients. The ending of counselling may awaken feelings associated with other kinds of endings, and lead the client to act out in the relationship with counsellor the ways he or she has defended against previous feelings of loss. The end of counselling may similarly have a resonance for the client of the separation-individuation stage of development (Mahler, 1968), the stage of leaving the protective shell of the parental relationship and becoming a more autonomous individual. There may also be a sense of ambivalence about the end of a counselling relationship, with feelings of satisfaction at what has been achieved and frustration at what there still is to learn. The fact of a time limit may bring into focus the client's habitual ways of living in time, for example by existing only in a future-orientation (in this case, being obsessed with how much time there is left) and being unwilling to be in the present or with the past. The intention of the brief therapist is to exploit the time-limited format by predicting that some of these issues will emerge for the client, and actively challenging the client to confront and learn from them when they do.

The ending of a counselling relationship can also raise issues for the counsellor, such as feelings of loss, grandiosity at how important the therapy has been for the client, or self-doubt over how little use the therapy has been. Dealing with termination is therefore a topic that receives much attention in the counsellor's work with his or her supervisor.

It should already be clear that the role of the counsellor in brief psychodynamic work is subtly different from that in traditional psychoanalysis. In the latter, the therapist takes a passive role, acting as a 'blank screen' on to which may be projected the transference reactions of the client. In brief work, by contrast, the therapist is active and purposeful, engaging the client in a therapeutic alliance in which they can work together. The use that is made of the transference relationship is therefore of necessity quite different.

In long-term analysis, the therapist encourages the development of a strong transference reaction, sometimes called a 'transference neurosis', in order to allow evidence of childhood relationship patterns to emerge. In brief work, strategies are used to avoid such deep levels of transference, for example by identifying and interpreting transferences as soon as they arise, even in the very first session, and by reducing client dependency by explaining what is happening and maintaining a clear focus for the work. In brief therapy, the here-and-now feeling response of the client towards, the therapist or counsellor, the transference, is used instead as the basis for making links between present behaviour with the therapist and past behaviour with parents (Malan, 1976).

Some useful principles for the interpretation of transference behaviour have been established by Malan (1979) and Davanloo (1980). The *triangle of insight* (Davanloo, 1980) refers to the links between the behaviour of the client with the therapist (T), with other current relationship figures (C) and with past figures such as parents (P). Clients can be helped to achieve insight by becoming aware of important T–C–P links in their lives. For example, a woman who treats her counsellor with great deference, depending on him to solve her problems, may make the connection that her mother was someone who had a strong need to take care of her. The next step might be to unravel the ways in which she is deferential and dependent with her husband and work colleagues. The triangle of insight would allow this client to understand where her behaviour pattern came from, how it operates (through careful, detailed exploration of how she is in relationship to her counsellor) and what effects the pattern has in her current life.

It can be seen here that the basic techniques of psychoanalysis – transference, resistance and interpretation – are used in brief psychodynamic work, but with important modifications. Just as in any kind of psychoanalytic work, the effectiveness of these techniques will depend on the skill of the therapist.

An appraisal of the psychodynamic approach to counselling

Psychoanalysis has provided a set of concepts and methods which have found application in a wide variety of contexts. Psychodynamic ideas have proved invaluable not only in individual therapy and counselling, but also in groupwork, couples counselling and the analysis of organizations. The ideas of Freud have been robust and resilient enough to withstand critique and reformulation from a number of sources. Psychodynamic perspectives have made a significant contribution to research into the process of counselling and therapy. Throughout this book there are many examples of the ways psychodynamic ideas have been used in different contexts and settings. All counsellors and therapists, even those who espouse different theoretical models, have been influenced by psychodynamic thinking and have had to make up their minds whether to accept or reject the Freudian image of the person.

There are clearly innumerable similarities and differences between psychodynamic and other approaches. The most essential difference, however, lies in the density of psychodynamic theory, particularly in the area of the understanding of development in childhood. Cognitive–behavioural theory is largely silent on child development, and the person-centred approach, in its use of the concept of 'conditions of worth', is little more than silent. Psychodynamic counsellors, by contrast, have at their disposal a highly sophisticated conceptual net. At issue is the question of how this theoretical apparatus affects the counselling process. From a psychodynamic perspective, it represents the net that catches the prey. From other counselling perspectives, it is a net that can entangle both counsellor and client, and prevent movement and change.

Topics for reflection and discussion

1 Coltart (1986: 187) has written of

> the need to develop the ability to tolerate not knowing, the capacity to sit it out with a patient, often for long periods, without any real precision as to where we are, relying on our regular tools and our faith in the process, to carry us through the obfuscating darkness of resistance, complex defences, and the sheer *unconsciousness* of the unconscious.

Discuss this statement in the light of the themes introduced in this chapter.
2 To what extent does time-limited counselling dilute the distinctive aims and meaning of psychodynamic work?
3 What are the main similarities and differences between psychodynamic counselling and the other principal approaches reviewed in the following chapters?

THREE

THE ORIGINS AND DEVELOPMENT OF THE COGNITIVE–BEHAVIOURAL APPROACH

The cognitive–behavioural tradition represents an important approach to counselling, with its own distinctive methods and concepts. This approach has evolved out of behavioural psychology and has three key features: a problem-solving, change-focused approach to working with clients, a respect for scientific values, and close attention to the cognitive processes through which people monitor and control their behaviour.

The origins of the cognitive–behavioural approach

To understand the nature of cognitive–behavioural counselling, it is necessary to examine its historical emergence from within the discipline of academic psychology. The cognitive–behavioural approach represents the most overtly 'scientific' of all the major therapy orientations. The behavioural dimension of the cognitive–behavioural approach has its origins in behavioural psychology, which is widely seen as having been created by J. B. Watson, particularly through the publication in 1919 of *Psychology From the Standpoint of a Behaviorist*.

Watson was a psychology professor at the University of Chicago at a time when psychology as an academic discipline was in its infancy. It had only been in 1879 that Wilhelm Wundt, at the University of Leipzig, had first established psychology as a field of study separate from philosophy and physiology. The method of research into psychological topics, such as memory, learning, problem-solving and perception, that Wundt and others such as Titchener had used was the technique known as 'introspection', which involved research subjects reporting on their own internal thought processes as they engaged in remembering, learning or any other psychological activity. This technique tended to yield contradictory data, since different subjects in different laboratories reported quite dissimilar internal events when carrying out the same mental tasks. The weakness of introspection as a scientific method, argued Watson, was that it was not open to objective scrutiny. Only the actual subject could 'see' what was happening, and this would inevitably result in bias and subjective distortion. Watson made the case that, if psychology was to become a truly scientific discipline, it would need to concern itself only with *observable* events and phenomena. He suggested that psychology should define itself as the scientific study of actual, overt behaviour rather than invisible thoughts and images, because these behaviours could be controlled and measured in laboratory settings.

Watson's 'behavioural' manifesto convinced many of his colleagues, particularly in the USA, and for the next thirty years mainstream academic psychology was dominated by the ideas of the behavioural school. The main task that behaviourists like Guthrie, Spence and Skinner set themselves was to discover the 'laws of learning'. They took the position that all the habits and beliefs which people exhibit must be learned, and so the most important task for psychology is to find out how people learn. Moreover, they suggested that the basic principles of learning, or acquisition of new behaviour, would be the same in any organism. Since there were clearly many ethical and practical advantages in carrying out laboratory research on animals rather than human beings, the behaviourists set about an ambitious programme of research into learning in animal subjects, mainly rats and pigeons.

All this may seem strange from a contemporary perspective. The assumption that the psychology of people can be explained through studies of the behaviour of animals is one that few people would now see as sensible. In fact there have been many attempts to make sense of the behaviourist era in psychology. Many writers have suggested that these psychologists were merely following a model of science, known as 'logical positivism', which was dominant in academic circles at that time. Other observers have suggested that behavioural psychology became popular in the USA because it was consistent with the growth of the advertising industry, with its need for techniques for controlling and manipulating the behaviour of consumers. It is perhaps significant that J. B. Watson himself left academic life to become an advertising executive.

In his analysis of the social origins of behaviourism, Bakan (1976) points out that many of the behaviourists, like Skinner, had grown up around animals and machines, and were therefore inevitably attracted by the idea of carrying out laboratory experiments on small animals. There were also powerful pressures in academic life to pursue 'pure' science (Bakan, 1976), and the experimental approach adopted by the behaviourists enabled them to conform to this academic norm. Another factor in the development of behaviourism was the parallel growth at this time in the influence of psychoanalysis, which was viewed by behavioural psychologists as dangerously unscientific and quite misguided. To some extent the threat of becoming like psychoanalysis served to keep the attention of behaviourists firmly on the objective and observable rather than subjective and unconscious aspects of human experience.

Although the behaviourist movement, in the form in which it existed in the 1930s and 1940s, may appear to many people involved in counselling and psychotherapy to represent an impoverished and inadequate vision or image of the human person, it is essential to acknowledge the immense influence it had over psychologists in the USA. Anyone from this era who entered counselling or psychotherapy with a psychology background (for example, Carl Rogers) brought at least some residue of behavioural thinking and behaviourist attitudes.

Within behaviourism itself, however, there came to be a recognition that a stimulus–response model was insufficient even to account for the behaviour of laboratory animals. Tolman (1948), in a series of experiments, had demonstrated that rats who had originally learned to swim through a flooded laboratory maze could later find their way through it successfully on foot. He pointed out that the behaviour they had acquired in the first part of the experiment – a series of swimming movements – was in fact irrelevant to the second task of running round the maze. What they must have learned, he argued, was a 'mental map' of the maze. In this manner, the study of inner mental events, or cognitions, was introduced to the subject matter of behavioural psychology. The new interest in cognition within behaviourism was matched by the work in Switzerland of Piaget, who initiated the study of the development of thinking in children, and at Cambridge by Bartlett, who examined the ways in which people 'reconstruct' the events they recall from long-term memory. These pioneering studies in the 1930s, by Tolman, Bartlett, Piaget and a few others, eventually resulted in what has been labelled the 'cognitive revolution' in psychology. By the 1970s, academic psychologists as a whole had in effect reversed the tide of behaviourism, and were no longer locked into a stimulus–response analysis of all human action. The preoccupation of the introspectionists with inner, cognitive events had returned to dominate psychology once more, but allied now to more sophisticated research methods than naive introspection.

Throughout its history, behavioural psychologists looked for ways to apply their ideas to the explanation of psychological and emotional problems. Probably the first theorist to look at emotional problems from a behavioural perspective was Pavlov, a Russian physiologist and psychologist working at the end of the nineteenth century, who noted that when he set his experimental dogs a perceptual discrimination task that was too difficult (for example, they would be rewarded with food for responding to a circle, but not when the stimulus was an ellipse) the animals would become distressed, squeal and 'break down'. Later, Liddell, carrying out conditioning experiments at Cornell University, coined the phrase 'experimental neurosis' – a pattern of behaviour characterized by swings from somnolence and passivity to hyperactivity – to describe the behaviour of his experimental animals exposed to monotonous environments. Watson himself carried out the well-known 'Little Albert' experiment, where a conditioned fear of animals was induced in a young boy by frightening him with a loud noise at the moment he had been given a furry animal to hold. Masserman, in a series of studies with cats, found that 'neurotic' behaviour could be brought about by creating an approach–avoidance conflict in the animal, for example by setting up a situation where the animal had been rewarded (given food) and punished (given an electric shock) at the same area in the laboratory.

Skinner (1953) found that when animals were rewarded or reinforced at random, with there being no link between their actual behaviour and its outcome in terms of food, they began to acquire 'ritualistic' or obsessional behaviour.

More recently, Seligman (1975) has conducted studies of the phenomenon of 'learned helplessness'. In Seligman's studies, animals restrained in cages and unable to escape or in any other way control the situation are given electric shocks. After a time, even when they are shocked in a situation where they are able to escape, they sit there and accept it. They have learned to behave in a helpless or depressed manner. Seligman views this work as giving some clues to the origins of depression. Further documentation of the origins of behaviour therapy in experimental studies can be found in Kazdin (1978).

To behaviourists, these studies provided convincing evidence that psychological and psychiatric problems could be explained, and ultimately treated, using behavioural principles. However, the strong identification of the behavioural school with the values of 'pure' science meant that they restricted themselves largely to laboratory studies. It was not until the years immediately after the Second World War, when there was a general expansion of psychiatric services in the USA, that the first attempts were made to turn behaviourism into a form of therapy. The earliest applications of behavioural ideas in therapy drew explicitly upon Skinner's operant conditioning model of learning, which found practical expression in the behaviour modification programmes of Ayllon and Azrin (1968), and on Pavlov's classical conditioning model, which provided the rationale for the systematic desensitization technique devised by Wolpe.

Behaviour modification is an approach which takes as its starting point the Skinnerian notion that in any situation, or in response to any stimulus, the person has available a repertoire of possible responses, and emits the behaviour that is reinforced or rewarded. This principle is known as *operant conditioning*. For example, on being asked a question by someone, there are many possible ways of responding. The person can answer the question, he or she can ignore the question, he or she can run away. Skinner (1953) argued that the response which is emitted is the one which has been most frequently reinforced in the past. So, in this case, most people will answer a question, because in the past this behaviour has resulted in reinforcements such as attention or praise from the questioner, or material rewards. If, on the other hand, the person has been brought up in a family in which answering questions leads to physical abuse and running away leads to safety, his or her behaviour will reflect this previous reinforcement history. He or she will run off. Applied to individuals with behavioural problems, these ideas suggest that it is helpful to reward or reinforce desired or appropriate behaviour, and ignore inappropriate behaviour. If a behaviour or response is not rewarded it will, according to Skinner, undergo a process of extinction, and fade out of the repertoire.

Ayllon and Azrin (1965, 1968) applied these principles in psychiatric hospital wards, with severely disturbed patients, using a technique known as 'token economy'. With these patients specific target behaviours, such as using cutlery to eat a meal or talking to another person, were systematically rewarded by the ward staff, usually by giving them tokens which could be exchanged for rewards such as cigarettes or visits, or sometimes by directly rewarding them at the time with chocolate, cigarettes or praise. At the beginning of the programme, in line with Skinner's research on reinforcement schedules, the patient would be rewarded for very simple behaviour, and the reward would be available for every performance of the target behaviour. As the programme progressed, the patient would only be rewarded for longer, more complex sequences of behaviour, and would be rewarded on a more intermittent basis. Eventually, the aim would be to maintain the desired behaviour through normal social reinforcement.

The effectiveness of behaviour modification and token economy programmes is highly dependent on the existence of a controlled social environment, in which the behaviour of the learner can be consistently reinforced in the intended direction. As a result, most behaviour modification has been carried out within 'total institutions', such as psychiatric and mental handicap hospitals, prisons and secure units. The technique can also be applied, however, in more ordinary situations like schools and families if key participants such as teachers and parents are taught how to apply the technique. It is essential, however, that whoever is supplying the behaviour modification is skilled and motivated so that the client is not exposed to contradictory reinforcement schedules. Furthermore, because behaviour modification relies on the fact that the person supplying the reinforcement has real power to give or withhold commodities which are highly valued by the client, there is the possibility of corruption and abuse. It is not unusual for people with only limited training in behavioural principles to assume that punishment is a necessary component of a behaviour modification regime. Skinner, by contrast, was explicit in stating that punishment would only temporarily suppress undesirable behaviour, and that in the long term behaviour change relies on the acquisition of new behaviour, which goes hand-in-hand with the extinction of the old, inappropriate behaviour.

Another way in which behaviour modification can be abusive in practice is by too much emphasis on the technique known as 'time out'. In residential settings, problematic behaviour patterns, such as aggressive and violent behaviour, can be interrupted by placing the person in a room to 'cool off'. The intention is that their violence is not rewarded by attention from staff or other residents, but that resumption of rationality is rewarded, by the person being allowed out of the room. In principle this can be a valuable intervention strategy, which can help some people to change behaviour that can lead them into severe trouble. The danger is that staff may use time out in a punitive manner, to keep a resident quiet to discharge their own anger at him or her. This technique may result in an abuse of the rights and civil liberties of the client.

Behaviour modification does not sit easily within a counselling relationship, which is normally a collaborative, one-to-one relationship in which the client can talk about his or her problems. Nevertheless, the principles of behaviour modification can be adapted for use in counselling settings, by explaining behavioural ideas to the client and working with him to apply these ideas to bring about change in his own life. This approach is often described as 'behavioural self-control', and involves functional analysis of patterns of behaviour, with the aim not so much of 'knowing thyself' as that of 'knowing thy controlling variables' (Thoresen and Mahoney, 1974). The assumption behind this way of working is that, following Skinner, any behaviour exhibited by a person has been elicited by a stimulus, and is reinforced by its consequences. The client can then be encouraged to implement suitable change at any, or all, of the steps in a sequence of behaviour.

A simple example of what is known as *functional analysis* (Cullen, 1988) of problem behaviour might involve a client who wishes to stop smoking. A behaviourally oriented counsellor would begin by carrying out a detailed assessment of where and when the person smokes (the stimulus), what he does when he smokes (the behaviour), and the rewards or pleasures he experiences from smoking (the consequences). This assessment will typically identify much detailed information about the complex pattern of behaviours that constitutes 'smoking' for the client, including, for example, the fact that he always has lunch with a group of heavy smokers, that he offers round his cigarettes and that smoking helps him to feel relaxed. This client might work with the counsellor to intervene in this pattern of smoking behaviour by choosing to sit with other, non-smoking colleagues after lunch, never carrying more than two cigarettes so he cannot offer them to others, and carrying out an 'experiment' where he smokes one cigarette after the other in a small room with other members of a smoking-cessation clinic, until he reaches a point of being physically sick, thus learning to associate smoking with a new consequence: sickness rather than relaxation.

The other technique that represented the beginning of a behavioural approach to counselling and therapy was the systematic desensitization method pioneered by Wolpe. This approach relies on Pavlov's classical conditioning model of learning. Pavlov had demonstrated, in a series of experiments with dogs, that the behaviour of an animal or organism includes many reflex responses. These are unlearned, automatic reactions to particular situations or stimuli (which he called 'unconditioned stimuli'). In his own research he looked at the salivation response. Dogs will automatically salivate when presented with food. Pavlov discovered, however, that if some other stimulus is also presented at the same time as the 'unconditioned' stimulus, the new stimulus comes to act as a 'signal' for the original stimulus, and may eventually evoke the same reflex response even when the original, unconditioned stimulus is not present. So Pavlov rang a bell just as food was brought in to his dogs, and after a time they would salivate to the sound of the bell even when there was no food around. Furthermore, they would begin to salivate to the sound of other bells (generalization) and would gradually lessen their salivation if they heard the bell on a number of occasions in the absence of any association with food.

Wolpe saw a parallel between classical conditioning and the acquisition of anxiety or fear responses in human beings. For a vivid example, imagine a person who has been in a car crash. Like one of Pavlov's dogs, the crash victim can only passively respond to a situation. Similarly, he experiences an automatic reflex response to the stimulus or situation, in this case a reflex response of fear. Finally, the fear response may generalize to other stimuli associated with the crash, for instance travelling in a car or even going out of doors. The crash victim who has become anxious or phobic about travelling, therefore, can be understood as suffering from a conditioned emotional response. The solution is, again following Pavlov, to re-expose the person to the 'conditioned' stimuli in the absence of the original fear-inducing elements. This is achieved through a process of *systematic desensitization*. First of all, the client learns how to relax. The counsellor either carries out relaxation exercises during counselling sessions, or gives the client relaxation instructions and tapes to practise at home. Once the client has mastered relaxation, the client and counsellor work together to identify a hierarchy of fear-eliciting stimuli or situations, ranging from highly fearful (for example, going for a trip in a car past the accident spot) to minimally fearful (for example, looking at pictures of a cars in a magazine). Beginning with the least fear-inducing, the client is exposed to each stimulus in turn, all the while practising his relaxation skills. This procedure may take some time, and in many cases the counsellor will accompany the client into and through fear-inducing situations, such as taking a car journey together. By the end of the procedure, the relaxation response rather than the fear response should be elicited by all the stimuli included in the hierarchy.

Although systematic desensitization takes its rationale from classical conditioning, most behavioural theorists would argue that a full account of the development of maladaptive fears and phobias requires the use of ideas from operant, or Skinnerian, as well as classical conditioning. They would point out that, while the initial conditioned fear response may have been originally acquired through classical conditioning, in many cases it would have been extinguished in the natural course of events as the client allowed himself to re-experience cars, travel and the outside world. What may happen is that the person actively avoids these situations, because they bring about feelings of anxiety. As a result, the person is being reinforced for avoidance behaviour – he is rewarded or reinforced by feeling more relaxed in the home rather than outside, or walking rather than going in a car. This 'two-factor' model of neurosis views the anxiety of the client as a conditioned emotional response which acts as an avoidance drive. Through systematic desensitization, the counsellor can help the client to overcome his avoidance.

The techniques of behavioural self-control and systematic desensitization are explicitly derived from the behavioural 'laws of learning' of operant and classical conditioning. However, in a process which reflected the general movement within psychology towards a more cognitivist approach, critics such as Breger and McGaugh (1965) and Locke (1971) began to question whether the therapeutic processes involved in these techniques could actually be fully understood using behaviourist ideas. In the words of Locke (1971), the issue was: 'Is behaviour therapy "behaviouristic"?' Behavioural therapists and counsellors typically asked their clients to report on and monitor their inner emotional experiences, encouraged self-assertion and self-understanding, and aimed to help them to develop new plans or strategies for dealing with life. These activities encompass a wide variety of cognitive processes, including imagery, decision-making, remembering and problem-solving. The thrust of this critique is that behavioural approaches may have generated many useful techniques, but these techniques draw heavily upon the capacity of clients to make sense of things, to process information cognitively, and that a more cognitive theory is needed in order to understand what is going on. There arose an increasing acceptance among behaviourally oriented counsellors and therapists of the need for an explicit cognitive dimension to their work. The social learning theory approach of Bandura (1971, 1977) made an important contribution to these developments. This interest in cognitive aspects of therapy coincided with the emergence of the cognitive therapies, such as *rational emotive therapy* (RET) (Ellis, 1962) and Beck's (1976) *cognitive therapy*.

The cognitive strand

The development of the 'cognitive' strand of cognitive–behavioural counselling is well described in Ellis (1989). One of the earliest attempts to work in a cognitive mode with clients took place, Ellis (1989) points out, within the field of sex therapy. The pioneers of sex therapy found that, of necessity, they needed to give their clients information about sexuality and the varieties of sexual behaviour. In other words, they needed to challenge the inappropriate fantasies and beliefs which their clients held about sex. The aim of helping clients to change the way they think about things remained the central focus of all cognitive approaches.

Both Ellis, the founder of rational emotive therapy, and Beck, the founder of cognitive therapy, began their therapeutic careers as psychoanalysts. Both became dissatisfied with psychoanalytic methods, and found themselves becoming more aware of the importance of the ways in which their clients thought about themselves. The story of his conversion to a cognitive therapeutic perspective is recounted by Beck (1976) in his book *Cognitive Therapy and the Emotional Disorders*. He notes that he had 'been practising psychoanalysis and psychoanalytic psychotherapy for many years before I was struck by the fact that a patient's cognitions had an enormous impact on his feelings and behavior' (p. 29). He reports on a patient who had been engaging in free association, and had become angry, openly criticizing Beck. When asked what he was feeling, the patient replied that he felt very guilty. Beck accepted this statement, on the grounds that, within psychoanalytic theory, anger causes guilt. But then the patient went on to explain that while he had been expressing his criticism of Beck, he had 'also had continual thoughts of a self-critical nature', which included statements such as 'I'm wrong to criticize him . . . I'm bad . . . He won't like me . . . I have no excuse for being so mean' (pp. 30–1). Beck (1976: 31) concluded that 'the patient felt guilty *because* he had been criticizing himself for his expressions of anger to me' (emphasis added).

Beck (1976) described these self-critical cognitions as 'automatic thoughts', and began to see them as one of the keys to successful therapy. The emotional and behavioural difficulties which people experience in their lives are not caused directly by events but by the way they interpret and make sense of these events. When clients can be helped to pay attention to the 'internal dialogue', the stream of automatic thoughts which accompany and guide their actions, they can make choices about the appropriateness of these self-statements, and if necessary introduce new thoughts and ideas, which lead to a happier or more satisfied life. Although Beck had been a psychoanalyst, he found that his growing interest in cognition was leading him away from psychoanalysis and in the direction of behaviour therapy. He cites some of the commonalities between cognitive and behavioural approaches: both employ a structured, problem-solving or symptom reduction approach, with a highly active therapist style, and both stress the 'here-and-now' rather than making 'speculative reconstructions of the patient's childhood relationships and early family relationships' (Beck 1976: 321).

Albert Ellis had, a decade earlier, followed much the same path. Also trained in psychoanalysis, he evolved a much more active therapeutic style characterized by high levels of challenge and confrontation designed to enable the client to examine his or her 'irrational beliefs'. Ellis argued that emotional problems are caused by 'crooked thinking' arising from viewing life in terms of 'shoulds' and 'musts'. When a person experiences a relationship, for example, in an absolutistic, exaggerated manner, he or she may be acting upon an internalized, irrational belief, such as 'I *must* have love or approval from all the significant people in my life.' For Ellis, this is an *irrational* belief because it is exaggerated and overstated. A rational belief system might include statements such as 'I enjoy being loved by others' or 'I feel most secure when the majority of the people in my life care about me.' The irrational belief leads to 'catastrophizing', and feelings of anxiety or depression, if anything goes even slightly wrong in a relationship. The more rational belief statements allow the person to cope with relationship difficulties in a more constructive and balanced fashion.

Following the lead provided by Ellis (1962) and Beck (1976; Beck *et al.*, 1979; Beck and Weishaar, 1989), many other clinicians and writers within the cognitive–behavioural tradition have contributed to the further elaboration and construction of this approach to counselling. The cognitive–behavioural approach is historically the most recent of the major therapy orientations, and is perhaps in its most creative phase, with new ideas and techniques being added to it every year (Dryden and Golden, 1986; Dryden and Trower, 1988; Dobson, 1988; Freeman *et al.*, 1989). In this brief review of the most important developments within the cognitive behavioural domain it will be necessary to divide the field into three main areas of work: cognitive processes, maladaptive beliefs and strategies for cognitive intervention.

Cognitive processes

In directing her attention to cognitive aspects of the client's way of dealing with problems in living, the cognitive–behavioural counsellor recognizes that there are two distinct types of cognitive phenomenon that are of interest. First, people differ in the way in which they process information about the world. Second, people differ in the beliefs they hold about the world, in their cognitive content. Cognitive–behavioural counsellors have devised intervention strategies for addressing issues in both of these domains.

The best-known model of cognitive processing used by cognitive–behavioural counsellors is that of Beck (1976), which is known as the *cognitive distortion* model.

In this framework, it is assumed that the experience of threat results in a loss of ability to process information effectively:

> Individuals experience psychological distress when they perceive a situation as threatening to their vital interests. At such times, there is a functional impairment in normal cognitive processing. Perceptions and interpretations of events become highly selective, egocentric and rigid. The person has a decreased ability to 'turn off' distorted thinking, to concentrate, recall or reason. Corrective functions, which allow reality testing and refinements of global conceptualizations, are weakened.
>
> (Beck and Weishaar, 1989)

Beck (1976) has identified a number of different kinds of cognitive distortion which can be addressed in the counselling situation. These include *overgeneralization*, which involves drawing general or all-encompassing conclusions from very limited evidence. For example, if a person fails her driving test at the first attempt she may overgeneralize by concluding that it is not worth bothering to take it again because it is obvious that she will never pass. Another example of cognitive distortion is *dichotomous thinking*, which refers to the tendency to see situations in terms of polar opposites. A common example of dichotomous thinking is to see oneself as 'the best' at some activity, and then to feel a complete failure if presented with any evidence of less than total competence. Another example is to see other people as either completely good or completely bad. A third type of cognitive distortion is *personalization*, which occurs when a person has a tendency to imagine that events are always attributable to his actions (usually to his shortcomings), even when no logical connection need be made. For example, in couple relationships it is not unusual to find that one of the partners believes that the mood of the other partner is always caused by his or her conduct, despite ample proof that, for instance, the irritation of the partner is caused by work pressures or other such external sources.

These cognitive distortions are similar in practice to the 'absolutistic' and 'catastrophizing' thinking described by Ellis (1962). The ideas behind these cognitive–behavioural concepts are familiar ones within the broader field of cognitive psychology. For example, it has been demonstrated in many studies of problem-solving that people frequently make a 'rush to judgement', or overgeneralize on the basis of too little evidence, or stick rigidly to one interpretation of the facts to the point of avoiding or denying contradictory evidence. The concept of 'personalization' is similar to the Piagetian notion of egocentricity, which refers to the tendency of children younger than about four years of age to see everything that happens only from their own perspective – they are unable to 'decentre' or see things from the point of view of another person. It is to some degree reassuring that the phenomena observed by cognitive–behavioural therapists in clinical settings should also have been observed by psychological researchers in other settings. On the other hand, these researchers, particularly in the studies of problem-solving, were studying ordinary adult people who were not under emotional threat or suffering from psychological problems. If cognitive distortions are part and parcel of the way that people cope in everyday life, it is difficult to make a case that they should necessarily be regarded as factors which cause emotional problems, and therefore as elements to be eliminated from the cognitive repertoire of the client.

The cognitive distortion model of cognitive processing is similar in many respects to the Freudian idea of 'primary process' thinking. Freud regarded human beings as capable of engaging in rational, logical thought ('secondary process' thinking), but also as highly prone to reverting to the developmentally less mature 'primary process' thinking, in which thought is dominated by emotional needs. The crucial difference between the primary process and cognitive distortion models is that in the former emotion controls thought, whereas in the latter thought controls emotion.

The other main approach to understanding cognitive process within cognitive-behavioural counselling and therapy is concerned with the operation of *metacognition*. This refers to the ability of people to reflect on their own cognitive processes, to be aware of how they are going about thinking about something, or trying to solve a problem. A simple example to illustrate metacognition is to reflect on your experience of completing a jigsaw puzzle. You will find that you do not just 'do' a jigsaw in an automatic fashion (unless it is a very simple one) but that you will be aware of a set of strategies from which you can choose as needed, such as 'finding the corners', 'finding the edges' or 'collecting the sky'. An awareness of, and ability to communicate, metacognitive strategies is very important in teaching children how to do jigsaws, rather than just doing it for them. Meta-cognition is a topic widely researched within developmental psychology in recent years.

Although the name of Meichenbaum (1977, 1985, 1986) is most closely associated with the issue of metacognition in counselling and therapy, the principle of metacognitive processing is in fact central to the work of Ellis, Beck and other cognitive–behavioural practitioners. For example, Ellis (1962) has devised an A–B–C theory of personality functioning. In this case, A refers to the activating event, which may be some action or attitude of an individual, or an actual physical event. C is the emotional or behavioural consequence of the event, the feelings or conduct of the person experiencing the event. However, for Ellis A does not cause C. Between A and C comes B, the person's beliefs about the event. Ellis contends that events are always mediated by beliefs, and that the emotional consequences of events are determined by the belief about the event rather than the event itself. For example, one person may lose her job and, believing that this event is 'an opportunity to do something else', feel happy. Another person may lose her job and, believing that 'this is the end of my usefulness as a person', feel deeply depressed.

The significance of the A–B–C formula in relation to metacognition is that the RET counsellor will teach the client how to use it as a way of monitoring cognitive reactions to events. The client is then able to engage in metacognitive processing of his or her thoughts in reaction to any event, and is, ideally, more able to make choices about how he or she intends to think about that event.

Cognitive content

Cognitive–behavioural counsellors and therapists have been active in catalogu-
ing a wide variety of cognitive contents, referred to by different writers as irrational beliefs (Ellis, 1962), dysfunctional or automatic thoughts (Beck, 1976),
self-talk or internal dialogue (Meichenbaum, 1986) or 'hot cognitions' (Zajonc,
1980). One of the central aims of much cognitive–behavioural work is to replace
beliefs that contribute to self-defeating behaviour with beliefs that are associated
with self-acceptance and constructive problem-solving. The following set of 'irrational beliefs', as identified by Ellis, provides the counsellor with a starting point
for exploring the cognitive content of the client.

> I *must* do well at all times.
> I am a *bad* or *worthless* person when I act in a weak or stupid manner.
> I *must* be approved or accepted by people I find important.
> I am a *bad, unlovable* person if I get rejected.
> People *must* treat me fairly and give me what I *need*.
> People who act immorally are undeserving, *rotten* people.
> People *must* live up to my expectations or it is *terrible*.
> My life *must* have few major hassles or troubles.
> I *can't stand* really bad things or difficult people.
> It is *awful* or *horrible* when important things don't turn out the way I want them
> to.
> I *can't stand* it when life is really unfair.
> I *need* to be loved by someone who matters to me a lot.
> I *need* immediate gratification and *always* feel *awful* when I don't get it.

The belief statements used in RET reflect the operation of a number of distorted
cognitive processes. For example, overgeneralization is present if the client
believes he or she needs to be loved *at all times*. Cognitive therapists would
dispute the rationality of this statement, inviting the client perhaps to reframe
it as 'I enjoy the feeling of being loved and accepted by another person, and if
this is not available to me I can sometimes feel unhappy.' Other cognitive distortions, such as dichotomous thinking ('if people don't love me they must hate
me'), arbitrary inference ('I failed that exam today so I must be totally stupid'),
personalization ('the gas man was late because they all hate me at that office')
are also evident in irrational beliefs.

Within RET approaches to working with cognitions, the counsellor is looking
out for examples of deeply held general statements which sum up the assumptions the client holds about the world. Another approach, used by Meichenbaum
and other cognitive–behavioural counsellors, is to uncover the statements that
accompany actual behaviour. For example, a client who has problems dealing
with job interviews may be carrying on an 'internal dialogue' during the interview, which might include messages such as 'I will fail,' 'Here we go again, its
just like the last time' or 'I know that was the wrong thing to say.' These beliefs
or self-statements are very likely to undermine the performance of the interview
candidate, by initiating and reinforcing feelings of anxiety, and by devoting

attention to internal states rather than listening to the questions being asked by the interviewer.

One of the difficulties in this area of cognitive–behavioural counselling lies in gaining access to the beliefs or self-statements of the client. Some of the main techniques used in the assessment of cognitions (Hollon and Kendall, 1981; Kendall and Hollon, 1981) are:

- unobtrusive tape-recording of spontaneous speech;
- recording speech following specific instructions (e.g. 'imagine you are taking an exam');
- 'thinking out loud' when doing a task;
- questionnaires (e.g. *assertiveness self-statements test*);
- thought listing;
- dysfunctional thoughts record (worksheet on which client records activating event, belief and behavioural consequences).

It is important to be aware of the fact that the process of eliciting beliefs may in itself have an impact. For example, there is evidence that depressed people report more negative thoughts if asked to report on what they were thinking in the past, but will produce more positive cognitions if reporting what they are thinking in the here-and-now (Hollon and Kendall, 1981). Verbal communication would also appear to be more productive than writing thoughts down (Blackwell *et al.*, 1985).

The principal strategy for facilitating change in beliefs, once they have been brought out into the open, is to encourage the client to experiment with alternative beliefs or self-statements in particular situations, to discover for himself or herself the effects of acting according to a different set of guiding assumptions. This strategy demonstrates the behavioural as well as cognitive nature of cognitive–behavioural counselling. The client is not merely engaged in 'thought exercises', but is given opportunities to learn about the behavioural consequences of the cognitions, and to extend the available repertoire of behaviours in problem situations.

It is apparent that maladaptive cognitive processes and maladaptive cognitive contents are linked. It may be useful to see both as aspects of the operation of an overall cognitive structure (Meichenbaum, 1986) or model of the world. The task of the cognitive–behavioural counsellor can be viewed as assisting the client to act as a scientist in discovering the validity of this personal map or model, and in making choices about which elements to keep and which to change.

The techniques and methods of cognitive–behavioural counselling

Unlike the psychodynamic and person-centred approaches to counselling, which place a great deal of emphasis on exploration and understanding, the cognitive-behavioural approach is less concerned with insight and more oriented towards client action to produce change. Although different practitioners may have different styles, the tendency in cognitive–behavioural work is to operate within a structured stage-by-stage programme, such as (Kuehnel and Liberman, 1986; Freeman and Simon, 1989):

1 Establishing rapport and creating a working alliance between counsellor and client. Explaining the rationale for treatment.
2 Assessing the problem. Identifying and quantifying the frequency, intensity and appropriateness of problem behaviours and cognitions.
3 Setting goals or targets for change. These should be selected by the client, and be clear, specific and attainable.
4 Application of cognitive and behavioural techniques.
5 Monitoring progress, using ongoing assessment of target behaviours.
6 Termination and planned follow-up to reinforce generalization of gains.

The cognitive–behavioural counsellor will usually employ a range of intervention techniques to achieve the behavioural objectives agreed with the client (Haaga and Davison, 1986; Meichenbaum, 1986). Techniques which are frequently used include:

1 Challenging irrational beliefs.
2 Reframing the issues; for example, perceiving internal emotional states as excitement rather than fear.
3 Rehearsing the use of different self-statements in role plays with the counsellor.
4 Experimenting with the use of different self-statements in real situations.
5 Scaling feelings; for example, placing present feelings of anxiety or panic on a scale of 0–100.
6 Thought stopping. Rather than allowing anxious or obsessional thoughts to 'take over', the client learns to do something to interrupt them, such as snapping a rubber band on his or her wrist.
7 Systematic desensitization. The replacement of anxiety or fear responses by a learned relaxation response. The counsellor takes the client through a graded hierarchy of fear-eliciting situations.
8 Assertiveness or social skills training.
9 Homework assignments. Practising new behaviours and cognitive strategies between therapy sessions.
10 *In vivo* exposure. Being accompanied by the counsellor into highly fearful situations; for example, visiting shops with an agoraphobic client. The role of the counsellor is to encourage the client to use cognitive–behavioural techniques to cope with the situation.

Further examples of cognitive–behavioural methods can be found in Kanfer and Goldstein (1986), Kuehnel and Liberman (1986) and Freeman et al. (1989).

Another set of ideas and techniques that have come to be widely used by cognitive–behavioural counsellors is associated with the concept of *relapse prevention*. Marlatt and Gordon (1985) observed that while many clients who are helped, through therapy, to change their behaviour may initially make good progress, they may at some point encounter some kind of crisis, which triggers a resumption of the original problem behaviour. This pattern is particularly common in clients with addictions to food, alcohol, drugs or smoking, but can be found in any behaviour-change scenario. Marlatt and Gordon (1985) concluded that it is necessary in cognitive–behavioural work to prepare for this eventuality, and to provide the client with skills and strategies for dealing with relapse events. The standard approaches to relapse prevention involve the application of cognitive–behavioural techniques. For example, the 'awful catastrophe' of 'relapse' can be redefined as a 'lapse'. The client can learn to identify the situations which are likely to evoke a lapse, and acquire social skills in order to deal with them. Marlatt and Gordon (1985) characterize three types of experience as being associated with high rates of relapse: 'downers' (feeling depressed), 'rows' (interpersonal conflict) and 'joining the club' (pressure from others to resume drinking, smoking, etc.). Clients may be given written instructions on what action to take if there is a threat of a lapse, or a phone number to call. Wanigaratne et al. (1990) describe many other ways in which the relapse prevention concept can be applied in counselling.

These examples of techniques and strategies illustrate the fundamental importance of scientific methods in cognitive–behavioural counselling. There is a strong emphasis on measurement, assessment and experimentation. This philosophy has been called the 'scientist-practitioner' model (Barlow et al., 1984), because it stresses that therapists should also be scientists and integrate the ideas of science into their practice. At the time this perspective on counselling and therapy was also known as the 'Boulder model', since it emerged from a conference held at Boulder, Colorado, in 1949 to decide the future shape of training in clinical psychology in the USA.

An appraisal of the cognitive–behavioural approach to counselling

Cognitive–behavioural concepts and methods have made an enormous contribution to the field of counselling. Evidence of the energy and creativity of researchers and practitioners in this area can be gained by inspection of the ever-increasing literature on the topic. Cognitive–behavioural approaches appeal to many counsellors and clients because they are straightforward and practical, and emphasize action. The wide array of techniques provide counsellors with a sense of competence and potency. The effectiveness of cognitive–behavioural therapy for a wide range of conditions is amply confirmed in the research literature.

There are, however, two significant theoretical areas in which the cognitive–behavioural approach is particularly open to criticism. The first of these concerns the notion of the therapeutic relationship. Cognitive–behavioural therapists take very seriously the necessity of establishing a good working alliance with the client. This relationship is often characterized as educational rather than medical: teacher–student as opposed to doctor–patient. Unfortunately, this practical awareness of the relationship factor is not extended to the realms of theory and training. For example, there is no cognitive–behavioural concept equivalent to 'counter-transference' in psychodynamic theory or 'congruence' in person-centred theory. Nor is there, usually, any requirement for cognitive–behavioural counsellors to undergo personal therapy as part of their training, with the aim of facilitating the development of appropriate self-awareness in the counselling relationship. The absence of a real appreciation of the impact of the self or person of the counsellor is all the more regrettable when it is realized that the approach gives counsellors permission to challenge and confront clients. At these moments, can the cognitive–behavioural counsellor be sure of for whose benefit the challenge or confrontation is being made? From a psychodynamic perspective, for example, the achievement of a rational, equal relationship between counsellor and client would be seen as the end-point of very successful work, rather than as something which could be readily set up before the real work begins. Many clients come to counselling because of relationship difficulties, and these difficulties can often be acted out in the counselling room itself.

A second issue that presents theoretical dilemmas for cognitive–behavioural counsellors concerns the way cognition is understood and conceptualized. A basic tenet of the approach is that change in thinking can result in change in behaviour and feelings. The research evidence to support this position is, however, not without problems. For example, in a study of cognitive processes in people who were depressed, Alloy and Abramson (1982) found that these individuals exhibited thinking which was pessimistic and negative, but which was in fact less distorted than the cognitive processing of 'normal' people. They argued that depressed people see the world accurately, while non-depressed people view things through 'rose-tinted lenses'. In their experiment, depressed people remembered both good and bad information about self, while non-depressed people remembered only the positive information. In another study, Lewinsohn et al. (1981) followed up a group of people over a one-year period. Some of these people developed symptoms of depression during that time, but there was no correlation between irrational beliefs and cognitive processes measured at the beginning and the subsequent development of depression. Lewinsohn et al. (1981) interpreted these findings to mean that distorted cognitions were not a cause of depression, as Beck et al. (1979) would assume, but were by-products of it. Beidel and Turner (1986) draw the conclusion from these studies that cognitive processes are secondary to behavioural processes in the development of emotional problems, and that the 'cognitivist' revolution is misguided. This point of view is supported by Cullen (1991) and by Wolpe (1978: 444), who has reasserted the radical behaviourist, determinist position in stating that 'our thinking is behaviour and is as unfree as any other behaviour . . . all learning takes place automatically . . . we always do what we must do.' Beidel and Turner (1986) also suggest that the cognitive strand of cognitive–behavioural counselling and therapy could be strengthened by paying more attention to new developments in cognitive psychology.

Both the issue of the nature of the counsellor–client relationship in cognitive-behavioural therapy, and the question of the validity of the theoretical assumptions employed in the approach, can be understood as deriving from the same ultimate source. Compared to most other mainstream approaches to counselling and therapy, the cognitive–behavioural orientation is more of a technology than a framework for understanding life. Recurring themes in cognitive–behavioural writings are management, control and monitoring. It is a highly effective way of fixing people quickly. In being the most recently emergent of the major schools of therapy, it is also the approach best fitted to a 'post-modern' world suspicious of grand theory and ideology.

Topics for reflection and discussion

1 Does it make sense to understand cognition as a type of behaviour? What are the implications for counselling practice of taking this idea seriously?
2 Ellis (1973: 56) has suggested that 'there are virtually no legitimate reasons for people to make themselves terribly upset, hysterical or emotionally disturbed, no matter what kind of psychological or verbal stimuli are impinging on them.' Do you agree? What is the 'image of the person' implicit in this statement?
3 What are the advantages and disadvantages of the explicitly scientific emphasis of the cognitive–behavioural approach?

FOUR

THEORY AND PRACTICE OF THE PERSON-CENTRED APPROACH

The brief account in Chapter 1 of the social and cultural background which shaped the work of Carl Rogers gives some indication of the extent to which his approach to counselling was rooted in the values of American society. The approach associated with Rogers, called at various times 'non-directive', 'client-centred', 'person-centred' or 'Rogerian', has not only been one of the most widely used orientations to counselling and therapy over the past fifty years, but has also supplied ideas and methods which have been integrated into other approaches (Thorne, 1992). The emergence of client-centred therapy in the 1950s was part of a movement in American psychology to create an alternative to the two theories which at that time dominated the field: psychoanalysis and behaviourism. This movement became known as the 'third force' (in contrast to the other main forces represented by the ideas of Freud and Skinner), and as 'humanistic' psychology. Apart from Rogers, the central figures in early humanistic psychology included Abraham Maslow, Charlotte Buhler and Sydney Jourard. These writers shared a vision of a psychology that would have a place for the human capacity for creativity, growth and choice, and were influenced by the European tradition of existential and phenomenological philosophy. The image of the person in humanistic psychology is of a self striving to find meaning and fulfilment in the world.

Humanistic psychology has always consisted of a broad set of theories and models connected by shared values and philosophical assumptions, rather than constituting a single, coherent, theoretical formulation. Within counselling and psychotherapy, the most widely used humanistic approaches are person-centred and Gestalt, although psychosynthesis, Transactional Analysis and other models also contain strong humanistic elements. The common ingredient in all humanistic approaches is an emphasis on *experiential* processes. Rather than focusing on the origins of client problems in childhood events (psychodynamic) or the achievement of new patterns of behaviour in the future (behavioural), humanistic therapies concentrate on the 'here-and-now' experiencing of the client. It can be a source of confusion that the label 'experiential' has been used as a general term to describe all such approaches, but has also been employed as a label for one particular approach (Gendlin, 1973).

The evolution of the person-centred approach

The birth of the person-centred approach is usually attributed to a talk given by Rogers in 1940 on 'new concepts in psychotherapy' to an audience at the University of Minnesota (Barrett-Lennard, 1979). In this talk, which was subsequently published as a chapter in *Counseling and Psychotherapy* (Rogers, 1942), it was suggested that the therapist could be of most help to clients by allowing them to find their own solutions to their problems. The emphasis on the client as expert and the counsellor as source of reflection and encouragement was captured in the designation of the approach as 'non-directive' counselling. In the research carried out at that time by Rogers and his students at the University of Ohio, the aim was to study the effect on the client of 'directive' and 'non-directive' behaviour on the part of the counsellor. These studies were the first pieces of psychotherapy research to involve the use of direct recording and transcription of actual therapy sessions.

In 1945 Rogers was invited to join the University of Chicago, as Professor of Psychology and Head of the Counseling Center. At this time, the ending of the war and the return from the front line of large numbers of armed services personnel, many of them traumatized by their experiences, meant that there was a demand for an accessible, practical means of helping these people cope with the transition back to civilian life. At that time, the dominant form of psychotherapy in the USA was psychoanalysis, which would have been too expensive to provide for large numbers of soldiers, even if there had been enough trained analysts to make it possible. Behavioural approaches had not yet emerged. The 'non-directive' approach of Rogers represented an ideal solution, and a whole new generation of American counsellors were trained at Chicago, or by colleagues of Rogers at other colleges. It was in this way that the Rogerian approach became quickly established as the main non-medical form of counselling in the USA. Rogers was also successful in attracting substantial funding to enable a continuing programme of research.

These developments were associated with a significant evolution in the nature of the approach itself. The notion of 'non-directiveness' had from the beginning implied a contradiction. How could any person in a close relationship fail to influence the other, at least slightly, in one direction or another? Studies by Truax (1966) and others suggested that supposedly non-directive counsellors in fact subtly reinforced certain statements made by clients, and did not offer their interest, encouragement or approval when other types of statement were made. There were, therefore, substantial problems inherent in the concept of non-directiveness. At the same time, the focus of research in this approach was moving away from a concern with the behaviour of the counsellor, to a deeper consideration of the process that occurred in the client, particularly in relation to changes in the self-concept of the client. This change of emphasis was marked by a renaming of the approach as 'client-centred'. The key publications from this period are *Client-centered Therapy* by Rogers (1951) and the Rogers and Dymond (1954) collection of research papers.

The third phase in the development of client-centred counselling came during the latter years at Chicago (1954–7), and can be seen as representing an attempt to consolidate the theory by integrating the earlier ideas about the contribution of the counsellor with the later thinking about the process in the client, to arrive at a model of the therapeutic relationship. Rogers's 1957 paper on the 'necessary and sufficient' conditions of empathy, congruence and acceptance, later to become known as the 'core conditions' model, was an important landmark in this phase, as was his formulation of a 'process conception' of therapy. The book that remains the single most widely read of all of Rogers's writings, *On Becoming a Person* (Rogers, 1961), is a compilation of talks and papers produced during this phase.

In 1957 Rogers and several colleagues from Chicago were given an opportunity to conduct a major research study based at the University of Wisconsin, investigating the process and outcome of client-centred therapy with hospitalized schizophrenic patients. One of the primary aims of the study was to test the validity of the 'core conditions' and 'process' models. This project triggered a crisis in the formerly close-knit team around Rogers (see Kirschenbaum (1979) for a lively account of this episode). Barrett-Lennard (1979: 187), in his review of the historical development of the person-centred approach, notes that 'the research team suffered internal vicissitudes'. The results of the study showed that the client-centred approach was not particularly effective with this type of client. There were also tensions between some of the principal members of the research group, and, although the project itself came to an end in 1963, the final report on the research was not published until 1967 (Rogers *et al.*, 1967).

Several significant contributions emerged from the schizophrenia study. New instruments for assessing concepts such as empathy, congruence, acceptance (Barrett-Lennard, 1962; Truax and Carkhuff, 1967) and depth of experiencing (Klein *et al.*, 1986) were developed. Gendlin began to construct a model of the process of experiencing which was to have a lasting impact. The opportunity to work with highly disturbed clients, and the difficulties in forming therapeutic relationships with these clients, led many of the team to re-examine their own practice, and in particular to arrive at an enhanced appreciation of the role of congruence in the therapy process. Client-centred therapists such as Shlien discovered that the largely empathic, reflective mode of operating, which had been effective with anxious college students and other clients at Chicago, was not effective with clients locked into their own private worlds. To make contact with these clients, the counsellor had to be willing to take risks in being open, honest and self-disclosing. The increase in emphasis given to congruence was also stimulated by the phase of the project where the eight therapists involved made transcripts of sessions available to other leading practitioners, and engaged in a dialogue. In the section of the Rogers *et al.* (1967) report that gives an account of this dialogue, it can be seen that these outside commentators were often highly critical of the passive, 'wooden' style of some of the client-centred team. The fruits of these more experiential sources of learning from the schizophrenia study are included in Rogers and Stevens (1968).

The Wisconsin project has more recently been criticized by Masson (1988), who argues that the acceptance and genuineness of the client-centred therapists could never hope to overcome the appalling institutionalization and oppression suffered by these patients:

> [The] patients lived in a state of oppression. In spite of his reputation for empathy and kindness, Carl Rogers could not perceive this. How could he have come to terms so easily with the coercion and violence that dominated their everyday existence? Nothing [written by Rogers] indicates any genuinely human response to the suffering he encountered in this large state hospital.
>
> (Masson, 1988: 245)

In defence, it can be pointed out that Rogers *et al.* (1967) discuss in great detail the issues arising from working in a 'total institution', and were clearly attempting to deal with the problem that Masson (1988) describes. Rogers *et al.* (1967: 93) commented that

> one of the unspoken themes of the research, largely evident through omission, is that it was quite unnecessary to develop different research procedures or different theories because of the fact that our clients were schizophrenic. We found them far more similar to, than different from, other clients with whom we have worked.

This passage would indicate that at least one of the elements in the power imbalance, the existence of labelling and rejection, was not an important factor.

The end of the Wisconsin experiment also marked the end of what Barrett-Lennard (1979) has called the 'school' era in client-centred therapy. Up to this point, there had always been a definable nucleus of people around Rogers, and an institutional base, which could be identified as a discrete, coherent school of thought. After the Wisconsin years, the client-centred approach fragmented, as the people who had been involved with Rogers moved to different locations, and pursued their own ideas largely in isolation from each other.

Rogers himself went to California, initially to the Western Behavioral Sciences Institute, and then, in 1968, to the Center for Studies of the Person at La Jolla. He became active in encounter groups, organizational change and community-building and, towards the end of his life, in working for political change in East–West relations and in South Africa (Rogers, 1978, 1980). He did not engage in any further developments of any significance regarding his approach to one-to-one therapy. The extension of client-centred ideas to encompass groups, organizations and society in general meant that it was no longer appropriate to view the approach as being about *clients* as such, and the term 'person-centred' came increasingly into currency as a way of describing an approach to working with larger groups as well as with individual clients (Mearns and Thorne, 1988).

Of the other central figures at that time, Gendlin and Shlien went back to

Chicago, the former to continue exploring the implications of his experiential approach, the latter to carry out research in the effectiveness of time-limited client-centred therapy. Barrett-Lennard eventually returned to Australia, and remained active in theory and research. Truax and Carkhuff were key figures in creating new approaches for training people in the use of counselling skills. In Toronto, Rice was the leader of a group which explored the relationship between client-centred ideas and the information-processing model of cognitive psychology. Various individuals, such as Gendlin, Gordon, Goodman and Carkhuff, were instrumental in setting up programmes with the aim of enabling ordinary, non-professional people to use counselling skills to help others (see Larson, 1984).

The post-Wisconsin developments in client-centred theory and practice are summarized by Lietaer (1990), who notes that while there have been many useful new directions, the approach as a whole has lacked coherence and direction in the absence of the powerful, authoritative voice provided by Rogers. So, although the periodic reviews of client-centred and person-centred theory, research and practice compiled by Hart and Tomlinson (1970), Wexler and Rice (1974), Levant and Shlien (1984) and Lietaer et al. (1990) contain much useful material, there is also a sense of a gradual drifting apart and splitting, and consequent reduction in impact. The client-centred or person-centred approach has been becoming less influential in the USA, partly because its central ideas have been assimilated into other approaches, although it remains a major independent force in Britain, Belgium, Germany and Holland (Lietaer, 1990).

The evolution of the person-centred approach over a fifty-year period illustrates many important social and cultural factors. Client-centred therapy was created from a synthesis of European 'insight' therapy and American values (Sollod, 1978). The emphasis in the model on self-acceptance and its theoretical simplicity made it wholly appropriate as a therapy for soldiers returning from war, and allowed it to gain a peak of influence at that time. In the post-war years in the USA, the increasing competitiveness of the 'mental health industry' resulted in the gradual erosion of this influence, as other therapies which could claim specific techniques, special ingredients and rapid cures became available. Moreover, the insistence of insurance companies in the USA that clients receive a diagnosis before payments for therapy could be authorized went against the grain of the client-centred approach. Finally, the failure to maintain a solid institutional base, either in the academic world or in an independent professional association, contributed further to its decline. In other countries, and for example in Europe, counsellors and therapists working in state-funded educational establishments and in voluntary agencies were largely protected from these pressures, enabling the person-centred approach to thrive. In these other countries there have also been Rogerian institutes and training courses.

The image of the person in person-centred theory

The main concern of Rogers and other person-centred theorists was to develop an approach which was effective, rather than to engage in speculation on theoretical matters. Compared to the massive edifice of psychodynamic theory, the conceptual apparatus of the person-centred approach is an insubstantial scaffolding. It is important to recognize that this apparent absence of theoretical content necessarily accompanies any attempt to pursue a phenomenological approach to knowledge. Phenomenology is a method of philosophical inquiry evolved by Husserl, and widely employed in existential philosophy, which takes the view that valid knowledge and understanding can be gained by exploring and describing the way things are experienced by people. The aim of phenomenology is to depict the nature and quality of personal experience. Phenomenology has been applied to many areas of study other than therapy, for example the experience of the social world. The technique of phenomenology involves 'bracketing off' the assumptions one holds about the phenomenon being investigated, and striving to describe it in as comprehensive and sensitive a manner as possible. The act of 'bracketing off' or 'suspending' assumptions implies that the phenomenological researcher (or therapist) does not impose his or her theoretical assumptions on experience. As a result, theory in phenomenological approaches to counselling, such as the person-centred approach, acts more as a general pointer towards potentially significant areas of experience, rather than making any assumptions about the actual content of that experience.

The person, in the person-centred approach, is viewed as acting to fulfil two primary needs. The first is the need for self-actualization. The second is the need to be loved and valued by others. Both these needs are, following Maslow, seen as being independent of biological survival needs. However, the person is very much seen as an embodied being, through the concept of 'organismic valuing'.

The idea of the 'self-concept' has a central place in person-centred theory. The self-concept of the person is understood as those attributes or areas of experiencing about which the person can say 'I am . . .' So, for example, a client in counselling may define himself or herself in terms such as, 'I am strong, I can be angry, I sometimes feel vulnerable.' For this person, strength, anger and vulnerability are parts of a self-concept, and when he or she feels vulnerable, or angry, there will usually be a *congruence* between feelings and resulting words and actions. But if this person does not define himself or herself as 'nurturing', and is in a situation where a feeling of care or nurturance is evoked, he or she will not be able to put that inner sense or feeling accurately into words, and will express the feeling or impulse in a distorted or inappropriate way. Someone who is not supposed to be nurturing may, for instance, become very busy 'doing things' for someone who needs no more than companionship, comforting or a human touch. Where there is a disjunction between feelings and the capacity for accurate awareness and symbolization of these feelings, a state of *incongruence* is said to exist. Incongruence is the very broad term used to describe the whole range of problems which clients bring to counselling.

Why does incongruence happen? Rogers argued that, in childhood, there is a strong need to be loved or valued, particularly by parents and significant others. However, the love or approval that parents offer can be conditional or unconditional. In areas of unconditional approval, the child is free to express his or her potential and accept inner feelings. Where the love or acceptance is conditional on behaving only in a certain way, and is withdrawn when other behaviour or tendencies are exhibited, the child learns to define himself or herself in accordance with parental values. Rogers used the phrase 'conditions of worth' to describe the way in which the self-concept of the child is shaped by parental influence. In the example above, the person would have been praised or accepted for being 'useful', but rejected or scorned for being 'affectionate' or 'soft'. Incongruence, therefore, results from gaps and distortions in the self-concept caused by exposure to conditions of worth.

Another idea that is linked to the understanding of how the self-concept operates is the notion of 'locus of evaluation'. Rogers observed that, in the process of making judgements or evaluations about issues, people could be guided by externally defined sets of beliefs and attitudes, or could make use of their own internal feelings on the matter, their 'organismic valuing process'. An over-reliance on external evaluations is equivalent to continued exposure to conditions of worth, and person-centred counselling encourages people to accept and act on their own personal, internal evaluations. Rogers had a positive and optimistic view of humanity, and believed that an authentic, self-aware person would make decisions based on an internal locus of evaluation that would be valid not only for himself or herself, but for others too. Although it is perhaps not explicitly articulated in his writings, his underlying assumption was that each person carried a universal morality, and would have a bodily sense of what was right or wrong in any situation.

It is perhaps worth noting that the simple phrase 'conditions of worth' encompasses the entirety of the person-centred model of child development. The person-centred counsellor does not possess a model of developmental stages into which to fit the experience of the client. The simple idea of conditions of worth merely points the counsellor in the direction of anticipating that some unresolved childhood process may be around for the client. The task is not to go looking for these childhood episodes, but to allow the client to pursue an understanding of them if he or she chooses to do so. Also of interest is the fact that childhood experiences are seen as leaving an enduring influence in the form of internalized values and self-concepts. This is clearly different from the psychodynamic idea that people grow up with internalized images of the actual people who were formative in childhood, usually the mother and father (see Chapter 2).

The person-centred theory of the self-concept suggests that the person possesses not only a concept or definition of self 'as I am now', but also a sense of self 'as I would ideally like to be'. The 'ideal self' represents another aspect of the consistent theme in Rogers's work concerning the human capacity to strive for fulfilment and greater integration. One of the aims of person-centred therapy is to enable the person to move in the direction of his or her self-defined ideals.

One of the distinctive features of the person-centred image of the person is its attempt to describe the 'fully functioning' person. The idea of the 'actualized' or fully-functioning individual represents an important strand in the attempt by humanistic psychologists to construct an alternative to psychoanalysis. Freud, reflecting his background in medicine and psychiatry, created a theory which was oriented towards understanding and explaining pathology or 'illness'. Rogers, Maslow and the 'third force' regarded creativity, joyfulness and spirituality as intrinsic human qualities, and sought to include these characteristics within the ambit of their theorizing. The main features of the fully functioning person were described by Rogers (1963: 22) in the following terms:

> he is able to experience all of his feelings, and is afraid of none of his feelings. He is his own sifter of evidence, but is open to evidence from all sources; he is completely engaged in the process of being and becoming himself, and thus discovers that he is soundly and realistically social; he lives completely in this moment, but learns that this is the soundest living for all time. He is a fully functioning organism, and because of the awareness of himself which flows freely in and through his experiences, he is a fully functioning person.

The person envisioned here is someone who is congruent, and is able to accept and use feelings to guide action. The person is also autonomous rather than dependent on others: 'the values of being and becoming himself'.

One of the difficulties involved in grasping the person-centred image of the person is that textbook versions of what is meant are inevitably incomplete. This is an area of counselling theory where the gap between the lived, oral tradition and the written account is particularly apparent (see Chapter 5). For Rogers, the actualizing tendency or formative tendency is central, the person is always in process, always becoming, ever-changing. The task for psychological theory was not to explain change, but to understand what was happening to arrest change and development. The idea of 'becoming a person' captures this notion. From a person-centred perspective, any conceptualization of the person which portrays a static, fixed entity is inadequate. The aim is always to construct a process conceptualization. In this respect, it could well be argued that some of the earlier elements in the theory, such as the idea of the self-concept, place too much emphasis on static structures. It would be more consistent to talk about a 'self-process'. The image of the fully functioning person can similarly give an impression that this is an enduring structure that can be permanently attained, rather than part of a process that can include phases of incongruence and despair. The process orientation of the model is also expressed through the absence of any ideas about personality traits or types, and the strong opposition in person-centred practitioners to any attempts to label or diagnose clients.

The significance of the image of the person employed by this approach is underlined by the fact that this orientation attaches relatively little importance to the technical expertise of the counsellor, and concentrates primarily on the attitude or philosophy of the counsellor and the quality of the therapeutic relationship (Combs, 1989).

The therapeutic relationship

At its heart, person-centred counselling is a relationship therapy. People with emotional 'problems in living' have been involved in relationships in which their experiencing was denied, defined or discounted by others. What is healing is to be in a relationship in which the self is fully accepted and valued. The characteristics of a relationship which would have this effect were summarized by Rogers (1957: 95) in his formulation of the 'necessary and sufficient conditions of therapeutic personality change'. For constructive personality change to occur, it is necessary that these conditions exist and continue over a period of time:

1 Two persons are in psychological contact.
2 The first, whom we shall term the client, is in a state of incongruence, being vulnerable and anxious.
3 The second person, whom we shall term the therapist, is congruent or integrated in the relationship.
4 The therapist experiences unconditional positive regard for the client.
5 The therapist experiences an empathic understanding of the client's internal frame of reference, and endeavours to communicate this to the client.
6 The communication to the client of the therapist's empathic understanding and unconditional positive regard is to a minimal extent achieved.

No other conditions are necessary. If these six conditions exist, and continue over a period of time, this is sufficient. The process of constructive personality change will follow.

This formulation of the therapeutic relationship has subsequently become known as the 'core conditions' model. It specifies the characteristics of an interpersonal environment that will facilitate actualization and growth.

The three ingredients of the therapeutic relationship that have tended to receive most attention in person-centred training and research are the counsellor qualities of acceptance, empathy and genuineness. In the list above the term 'unconditional positive regard' is used, rather than the everyday idea of 'acceptance'.

The core conditions model represented an attempt by Rogers to capture the essence of his approach to clients. It also represented a bold challenge to other therapists and schools of thought, in claiming that these conditions were not just important or useful, but sufficient in themselves. The view that no other therapeutic ingredients were necessary invited a head-on confrontation with psychoanalysts, for example, who would regard interpretation as necessary, or behaviourists, who would see techniques for inducing behaviour change as central. The model stimulated a substantial amount of research, which has broadly supported the position taken by Rogers (Patterson, 1984). However, many contemporary counsellors and therapists would regard the 'core conditions' as components of what has become known as the 'therapeutic alliance' (Bordin, 1979) between counsellor and client.

In the person-centred approach there is considerable debate over the accuracy and comprehensiveness of the necessary and sufficient conditions model. For example, Rogers (1961: Chapter 3) himself described a much longer list of characteristics of a helping relationship:

Can I *be* in some way which will be perceived by the other person as trustworthy, as dependable or consistent in some deep sense?
Can I be expressive enough as a person that what I am will be communicated unambiguously?
Can I let myself experience positive attitudes towards this other person – attitudes of warmth, caring, liking, interest, respect?
Can I be strong enough as a person to be separate from the other?
Am I secure enough within myself to permit his or her separateness?
Can I let myself enter fully into the world of his or her feelings and personal meanings and see these as he or she does?
Can I accept each facet of this other person when he or she presents it to me?
Can I act with sufficient sensitivity in the relationship that my behaviour will not be perceived as a threat?
Can I free the other from the threat of external evaluation?
Can I meet this other individual as a person who is in the process of *becoming*, or will I be bound by his past and by my past?

This list includes the qualities of empathy, congruence and acceptance, but also mentions other important helper characteristics, such as consistency, boundary awareness, interpersonal sensitivity and present-centredness. Later, Rogers was also to suggest that therapist 'presence' was an essential factor (Rogers, 1980). Thorne (1991) has argued that 'tenderness' should be considered a core condition. These modifications of the model may be seen as attempts to articulate more clearly what is meant, or to find fresh ways of articulating the notion of a uniquely 'personal' relationship (Van Balen, 1990), but do not change the basic framework, which has remained the cornerstone of person-centred practice (Mearns and Thorne, 1988).

Re-visioning the concept of empathy

The importance attributed to empathic responding has been one of the distinguishing features of the person-centred approach to counselling. It is considered that, for the client, the experience of being 'heard' or understood leads to a greater capacity to explore and accept previously denied aspects of self. However, there were a number of difficulties apparent in the conception of empathy contained within the 'core conditions' model. When researchers attempted to measure the levels of empathic responding exhibited by counsellors, they found that ratings carried out from different points of view produced different patterns of results. A specific counsellor statement to a client would be rated differently by the client, the counsellor and an external observer (Kurtz and Grummon, 1972). It was difficult to get raters to differentiate accurately between empathy, congruence and acceptance: these three qualities all appeared to be of a piece in the eyes of research assistants rating therapy tapes. Finally, there were philosophical difficulties arising from alternative intepretations of the concept. Rogers characterized empathy as a 'state of being'. Truax and Carkhuff defined empathy as a communication skill, which could be modelled and learned in a structured training programme.

Many of these issues associated with the concept of empathy are addressed in the 'empathy cycle' model proposed by Barrett-Lennard (1981):

> Step 1: *empathic set by counsellor*. Client is actively expressing some aspect of his or her experiencing. Counsellor is actively attending and receptive.
>
> Step 2: *empathic resonation*. The counsellor resonates to the directly or indirectly expressed aspects of the client's experiencing.
>
> Step 3: *expressed empathy*. The counsellor expresses or communicates his or her felt awareness of the client's experiencing.
>
> Step 4: *received empathy*. The client is attending to the counsellor sufficiently to form a sense or perception of the counsellor's immediate personal understanding.
>
> Step 5: *the empathy cycle continues*. The client then continues or resumes self-expression in a way that provides feedback to the counsellor concerning the accuracy of the empathic response and the quality of the therapeutic relationship.

In this model, empathy is viewed as a process that involves intentional, purposeful activity on the part of the counsellor. It can be seen that the perceptions of different observers reflect their tendency to be aware of what is happening at particular steps in the process rather than others. The counsellor will consider himself or herself to be in good empathic contact with the client if he or she is 'set' and 'resonating' in response to what the client has expressed (steps 1 and 2). An external observer will be most aware of the actual behaviour of the counsellor (expressed empathy – step 3). The client, on the other hand, will be most influenced by the experience of 'received' empathy (step 4). The Barrett-Lennard (1981) model also makes sense of the definition of empathy as communication skill or way of being. In so far as the counsellor needs to be able to receive and resonate to the expressed feelings of the client, empathy is like a state of being. But in so far as this understanding must be offered back to the client, it is also a communication skill.

The empathy cycle raises the question of the interconnectedness of the core conditions. The Barrett-Lennard model describes a process that includes non-judgemental openness to and acceptance of whatever the client has to offer. It also describes a process in the counsellor of being congruently aware of his or her inner feelings, and using these in the counselling relationship. In the flow of the work with the client the effective person-centred counsellor is not making use of separate skills, but is instead offering the client a wholly personal involvement in the relationship between them. There is a sense of mutuality, or the 'I–thou' relationship described by Buber (Van Balen, 1990). Bozarth (1984) has written that, at these points in counselling, an empathic response to a client may bear little resemblance to the wooden 'reflection of meaning' statements much favoured in the early years of client-centred therapy. For Bozarth (1984), the ideal is to respond empathically in a manner that is 'idiosyncratic' and spontaneous.

This notion of the unity of the 'core conditions' is to some extent a return to the very earliest formulation of the principles of client-centred therapy. Before Rogers and his colleagues began to use terms like empathy, congruence and unconditional regard, they described the approach as an attitude or philosophy of 'deep respect for the significance and worth of each person' (Rogers, 1951: 21).

The therapeutic process

From a person-centred perspective, the process of therapeutic change in the client is described in terms of a process of greater openness to experience. Rogers (1951) characterized the direction of therapeutic growth as including increasing awareness of denied experience, movement from perceiving the world in generalizations to being able to see things in a more differentiated manner, and greater reliance on personal experience as a source of values and standards. Eventually, these developments lead to changes in behaviour, but the 'reorganization of the self' (Rogers, 1951) is seen as a necessary precursor to any new behaviour.

Rogers (1961) conceptualized the process of counselling as a series of stages, and his model formed the basis for subsequent work by Gendlin (1974) and Klein et al. (1986) and on the concept of 'depth of experiencing'. In successful counselling the client will become able to process information about self and experiencing at greater levels of depth and intensity. The seven stages of increasing client involvement in his or her inner world (Rogers, 1961; Klein et al., 1986) are summarized as follows:

1 Communication is about external events. Feelings and personal meanings are not 'owned'. Close relationships are construed as dangerous. Rigidity in thinking. Impersonal, detached. Does not use first-person pronouns.
2 Expression begins to flow more freely in respect of non-self topics. Feelings may be described but not owned. Intellectualization. Describes behaviour rather than inner feelings. May show more interest and participation in therapy.
3 Describes personal reactions to external events. Limited amount of self-description. Communication about past feelings. Beginning to recognize contradictions in experience.
4 Descriptions of feelings and personal experiences. Beginning to experience current feelings, but fear and distrust of this when it happens. The 'inner life' is presented and listed or described, but not purposefully explored.

5 Present feelings are expressed. Increasing ownership of feelings. More exact-
ness in the differentiation of feelings and meanings. Intentional exploration of
problems in a personal way, based in processing of feelings rather than
reasoning.
6 Sense of an 'inner referent', or flow of feeling which has a life of its own.
'Physiological loosening', such as moistness in the eyes, tears, sighs or
muscular relaxation, accompanies the open expression of feelings. Speaks in
present tense or offers vivid representation of past.
7 A series of felt senses connecting the different aspects of an issue. Basic trust
in own inner processes. Feelings experienced with immediacy and richness of
detail. Speaks fluently in present tense.

Research using this seven-stage model has shown that clients who begin therapy
at level 1 are less likely to be able to benefit from the process. Mearns and
Thorne (1988) have commented on the importance of the 'readiness' of the client
to embark on this type of self-exploration. Rogers (1961) also comments that the
changes associated with stage 6 appear to be irreversible, so the client may be
able to move into stage 7 without the help of the counsellor.

The process in the client is facilitated by the empathy, congruence and acceptance of the counsellor. For example, sensitive empathic listening on the part of
the counsellor enables him or her to reflect back to the client personal feelings
and meanings implicit in stage 1 statements. The acceptance and genuineness
of the counsellor encourages the growth of trust in the client, and increased risk-
taking regarding the expression of thoughts and feelings which would previously
have been censored or suppressed. Then, as this more frightening material is
exposed, the fact that the counsellor is able to accept emotions which had been
long buried and denied helps the client to accept them in turn. The willingness
of the counsellor to accept the existence of contradictions in the way the client
experiences the world gives the client permission to accept himself or herself as
both hostile and warm, or needy and powerful, and thus to move towards a more
differentiated, complex sense of self.

This process model offers an account of some of the changes which can be
observed over fairly long periods of time, perhaps over several months of
therapy. Other person-centred writers have presented models of much briefer
process episodes. An example of one attempt to capture the momentary
experiencing and communication of empathy, the Barrett-Lennard (1981)
'empathy cycle' model, was discussed earlier. Rice (1984) has suggested that the
therapeutic process can be understood in terms of a series of tasks to be performed by client and counsellor. In her research, tapes and transcripts of therapy
sessions are intensively analysed in order to identify the precise sequence of
steps taken by both therapist and client to resolve a particular type of problem
or issue.

Rice (1974, 1984) has described a series of stages in the resolution of 'problematic incidents'. These are incidents in the client's life when he or she felt
as though his or her reaction to what happened was puzzling or inappropriate.

Rice (1984) has found that effective counselling in these situations tends to follow four discrete stages. First, the client sets the scene for exploration, by labelling an incident as problematic, confirming what it was that made the reaction to the incident unacceptable, and then reconstructing the scene in general terms. The second stage involves the client and counsellor working on two parallel tasks. One task is to tease out different facets of the feelings experienced during the incident; the other is to search for the aspects of the event which held the most intense meaning or significance. This second stage is centred on the task of discovering the meanings of the event for the client. In the third phase, the client begins to attempt to understand the implications for his or her 'self-schema' or self-concept of what has merged earlier. The final phase involves the exploration of possible new options. Rice (1984: 201) describes this whole process as being one of 'evocative unfolding', in which 'the cognitive–affective reprocessing of a single troubling episode can lead into a widening series of self-discoveries.'

Another framework widely employed in the person-centred approach as a means of understanding process is the model of experiential focusing, which represents perhaps the single most influential development in person-centred theory and practice in the post-Wisconsin era (Lietaer, 1990). The technique of focusing and the underlying theory of experiencing are supported by thorough philosophical analysis (Gendlin, 1962, 1984a) and considerable psychological research (Gendlin, 1969, 1984c).

The focusing process is built on an assumption that the fundamental meanings which events and relationships have for people are contained in the 'felt sense' experienced by the person. The felt sense is an internal, physical sense of the situation. In this inner sense the person knows there is more to the situation than he or she is currently able to say. According to Gendlin (1962), this 'inner referent' or felt sense holds a highly differentiated set of implicit meanings. For these meanings to be made explicit, the person must express the felt sense in a symbol, such as a word, phrase, statement, image or even bodily movement. The act of symbolizing an area of meaning in the felt sense allows other areas to come to attention. Accurate symbolization therefore brings about a 'shift' in the inner felt sense of a situation or problem.

Gendlin takes the view that the experiential process described here is at the heart of not only person-centred counselling but of all other therapies too. He regards the therapeutic movement or shifts brought about by interpretation, behavioural methods, Gestalt interventions and so on to be reducible to episodes of effective experiential focusing. This experiential process is also a common feature of everyday life. The problems which bring people to counselling are caused by an interruption of the process, an unwillingness or inability of the person to achieve a complete and accurate picture of the felt sense of the problem. The basic tasks of the counsellor are therefore to help the client to stay with the inner referent rather than avoiding it, and to facilitate the generation of accurate symbols to allow expression of implicit meanings.

The process of 'focusing on a problem' can be broken into a number of stages or steps:

1 Clearing a space. Taking an inventory of what is going on inside the body.
2 Locating the inner felt sense of the problem. Letting the felt sense come. Allowing the body to 'talk back'.
3 Finding a 'handle' (word or image) which matches the felt sense.
4 Resonating handle and felt sense. Checking symbol against feeling. Asking 'does this really fit?'
5 A felt shift in the problem, experiencing either a subtle movement or 'flood of physical relief'.
6 Receiving or accepting what has emerged.
7 Stop, or go through process again.

These steps can occur, or be helped to occur, in the dialogue or interaction between counsellor or client, or the counsellor can intentionally instruct and guide the client through the process. The technique has been taught to clients and used in peer self-help groups.

An appraisal of the person-centred approach

The early phase of the development of the person-centred approach, the 'school' years (Barrett-Lennard, 1979) represents a unique achievement in the history of counselling and psychotherapy. Between 1940 and 1963, Rogers and others evolved a consistent, coherent body of theory and practice which was informed and shaped by ongoing research. Despite the later fragmentation of the approach, it remains a powerful strand of thought in the contemporary counselling world. However, recent developments resulted in the appearance of some fundamental tensions between alternative conceptualizations of the legacy of Rogers.

One of these issues concerns the identity of the person-centred approach as a distinctive mode of counselling. Many counsellors and therapists regard themselves as 'client-centred' or 'person-centred' because their intention is to focus on the experience or needs of the client, rather than to impose their own definitions or structures, and because they find the ideas encompassed in the 'core conditions' model a useful framework for understanding the nature of the therapeutic alliance. However, these values are often combined with a view that, while the core conditions might be necessary, they are in themselves insufficient to bring about change (Bohart, 1990; Tausch, 1990). These counsellors use the core conditions as a basis for the employment of therapeutic techniques derived from other approaches. For example, Boy and Pine (1982) describe two phases of counselling. In the first phase, the counsellor employs reflective listening, genuineness and acceptance to form a good working relationship with a client. Then, in the second phase:

> the counselor adopts any pattern of responses that serve to meet the unique needs of the individual client . . . [drawing upon] the attitudes, techniques

and approaches inherent in, and available from, *all other* existing theories of counseling.

(Boy and Pine, 1982: 18–19)

This approach is characteristic of that of many counsellors who use the person-centred perspective as a basis for integration (see Chapter 5). The end product is a way of working which is *a* person-centred approach rather than *the* person-centred approach. There is support for this kind of endeavour in Rogers's writings. He suggested in relation to the core conditions that empathy, congruence and unconditional positive regard could be communicated to the client in many different ways, for example through psychoanalytic interpretation (Rogers, 1957). On the other hand, there is the danger that counsellors working in this fashion may merely use person-centred ideas as a gloss beneath which they are operating in a quite different fashion. For example, a rigorous interpretation of person-centred principles involves a reliance on the actualizing tendency of the client, and continual use of self in the relationship. These are characteristics that can easily become lost when ideas from other approaches are introduced.

Another central issue arising in contemporary person-centred practice concerns the role of skill and technique. Truax and Carkhuff, and others, developed structured programmes for training people in the use of empathy, acceptance and other person-centred qualities. These programmes (reviewed in Chapter 10) engage in a reduction of the person-centred approach to a set of behavioural skills. From a different direction, Gendlin and his colleagues have developed training in 'focusing' as a means of enabling people to make use of the experiential processes found in person-centred (and other) forms of therapy. These skills programmes are thoroughly consistent with the egalitarian philosophy of the person-centred approach, in that they serve to demystify the role of therapist and allow many more people to participate in and benefit from counselling. The concept of empowerment is central to these programmes: giving people the power to change their own lives.

On the other hand, however, the theoretical framework of the person-centred approach places great emphasis on the quality of the relationship between counsellor and client, for example in terms of a gradual growth in trust and safety. It also states that this mode of working relies on the presence of a set of attitudes and beliefs in the counsellor. Clearly, brief skills training and self-help programmes can do little to address relationship and attitude issues in any serious or systematic manner. There are times when this split between technique and underlying philosophy produces uncomfortable results, for example when managers are taught empathic listening skills in the context of organization-centred or profit-centred rather than person-centred relationships with employees.

A debate has emerged in person-centred counselling over the role of spiritual or transcendent dimensions of experience. Although Rogers himself had originally intended to join the ministry, for most of his career his psychological theorizing was conducted within a strictly secular humanistic framework. It was only towards the end of his life that Rogers (1980) wrote of his experience of 'transcendent unity' and 'inner spirit'. These ideas have been both welcomed (Thorne, 1992) and criticized (Van Belle, 1990) within the person-centred movement.

In 1968, Carl Rogers was asked to speak at a symposium entitled 'USA 2000', sponsored by the Esalen Institute, the spiritual home of the humanistic psychology movement. He chose to talk about his vision of the kinds of directions in which he thought relationships between people were moving in the modern world, and about the ways in which therapy and groups could contribute to this process. His paper expresses very clearly his fundamental assumptions about the nature and role of person-centred counselling and therapy. Rogers (1968: 266) states that 'the greatest problem which man faces in the years to come . . . is the question of how much change the human being can accept, absorb and assimilate, and the rate at which he can take it.' In this statement can be seen the central problematic for Rogers: coming to terms with change in the modern world. Rogers himself was a person who lived through huge social change, in his own life and in the world around him. His own life transitions included leaving a small rural town to go to college in New York, moving from the world of clinical practice to that of academic teaching and research, and then finally leaving that to enter a new world in California. His approach to counselling proved itself most effective with clients undergoing life transitions, such as the transition to adulthood marked by entry to university and the transition from soldier back to civilian status. The theory and method of the person-centred approach have been finely tuned to the needs of people in a changing world. Internal, personal values are to be preferred in the absence of secure external structures of meaning. Relationships must be flexible, whether in therapy or elsewhere:

> I believe there will be possibilities for the *rapid* development of closeness between and among persons, a closeness which is not artificial, but is real and deep, and which will be well suited to our increasing mobility of living. Temporary relationships will be able to achieve the richness and meaning which heretofore have been associated only with lifelong attachments.
>
> (Rogers, 1968: 268)

This statement sums up the immense appeal that the writing of Rogers have had to people in a world where so many factors operate to deny the possibility of lifelong attachments. The promise of rich, meaningful temporary relationships fulfils a deep longing in many people who find themselves isolated by the collapse of their familiar social ecology.

At the same time, the person-centred approach can be set alongside other counselling approaches that have resonance with other dimensions of social life. The psychodynamic and object relations approaches, for example, present an image of a person invaded by other objects and troubled not by 'conditions of worth' but by internalized representations of sometimes abusive parents. The cognitive–behavioural approach yields a portrait of a person struggling to 'manage' his or her life and be a successful, rational problem-solver. These themes can also be pursued through a person-centred perspective but are less immediately salient.

Topics for reflection and discussion

1 How valid do you find the 'necessary and sufficient conditions' model? What other conditions would you add?
2 What are the strengths and weaknesses of the person-centred approach, in comparison with the psychodynamic and cognitive–behavioural approaches described in previous chapters?

FIVE

UNDERSTANDING THEORETICAL DIVERSITY: BRAND NAMES AND SPECIAL INGREDIENTS

In previous chapters, the three-core theoretical models in contemporary counselling – psychodynamic, cognitive–behavioural and person-centred – were introduced. However, these are merely the most popular of a wide range of theoretical orientations presently in use. The current situation in counselling and psychotherapy is one of great theoretical diversity and creativity. Just as quickly as new theories are spawned, new attempts are enjoined to unify, combine or integrate them. The aim of this chapter is to place theoretical diversity in context, to begin to make sense of how and why there are so many systems and models on offer. This issue will be tackled by first establishing the underlying similarities between all counselling approaches, then examining the social factors which encourage either fragmentation or integration, and finally exploring the ways in which individual counsellors actually use theory in their practice.

The underlying unity of approaches to counselling: 'non-specific' factors

From the very beginnings of the emergence of counselling and psychotherapy as mainstream human service professions, there have been people who have pointed out that the similarities between approaches were much greater than the differences. For example, in 1940 the psychologist Goodwin Watson organized a symposium at which well-known figures such as Saul Rosenzweig, Carl Rogers and Frederick Allen agreed that factors such as support, a good client–therapist relationship, insight and behaviour change were common features of all successful therapy (Watson, 1940). An early piece of research by Fiedler (1950) found that therapists of different orientations held very similar views regarding their conception of an ideal therapeutic relationship.

Perhaps the most influential writer in this area has been Jerome Frank (1973, 1974), who argued that the effectiveness of therapy is not primarily due to the employment of the specific thereputic strategies advocated by approaches (e.g. free association, interpretation, systematic desensitization, disowning irrational beliefs, reflection of feeling), but is attributable instead to the operation of a number of general or 'non-specific' factors. Frank (1974) identified the principal non-specific factors as being the creation of a supportive relationship, the provision of a rationale by which the client can makes sense of his or her problems, and the participation by both client and therapist in healing rituals. Frank (1974: 272) writes that although these factors are delivered in different ways by different counselling approaches, they all operate to 'heighten the patient's sense of mastery over the inner and outer forces assailing him by labeling them and fitting them into a conceptal scheme, as well as by supplying success experiences.'

The 'non-specific' hypothesis has stimulated extensive debate within the field (Parloff, 1986; Strupp, 1986; Hill, 1989), since it directly challenges the beliefs of most counsellors and therapists that their own specific techniques and intervention strategies do have a positive effect on clients. Some of the research into this issue is reviewed in Chapter 11 and in the discussion of non-professional therapists in Chapter 9. One of the outcomes of this scholarly activity has been the generation of a large number of suggestions regarding a whole range of non-specific factors not mentioned by Frank (1974). The literature on non-specific or 'common' factors has been reviewed by Grencavage and Norcross (1990), who compiled a list of all the factors mentioned by at least 10 per cent of the fifty articles and books included in their review (Table 2). Grencavage and Norcross (1990) identified four broad categories of non-specific factors, reflecting client characteristics, therapist qualities, change processes and treatment methods. They found that the highest levels of consensus in this review of professional opinion were concerning the therapeutic alliance (with 56 per cent of authors citing this factor), the opportunity for catharsis (38 per cent), acquisition and practising of new behaviours (32 per cent), the client having positive expectations (26 per cent), the qualities of the therapist (24 per cent) and the provision of a rationale (24 per cent).

There are three important sources of evidence which lend support to the non-specific hypothesis. The first arises from research which demonstrates that different theoretical orientations, using different specific strategies, report similar success rates (Luborsky et al., 1975). The second is that non-professional counsellors, who have not received enough training to be able to claim mastery of specific techniques, appear to be as effective as highly trained professional therapists (Hattie et al., 1984). The third piece of evidence arises from studies of the experiences of clients in counselling. When clients are asked what they find most helpful (e.g. Llewelyn and Hume, 1979), they tend to rate non-specific elements more highly than specific techniques.

In the context of this chapter, the importance of the work on non-specific factors is that it points to a huge area of shared common ground between different therapies. It is a misunderstanding of the non-specific hypothesis to conclude that effective counselling consists only of these common factors. There are all sorts of complex interactions between common factors, specific techniques and theoretical models. But it makes sense to acknowledge that at the heart of any

Table 2   Non-specific or common factors that facilitate therapeutic change

Client characteristics
Positive expectations, hope or faith
Distressed or incongruent client
Client actively seeking help

Therapist qualities
The personal qualities of the therapist
Cultivates hope and positive expectations
Warmth and positive regard
Empathic understanding
Being a socially sanctioned healer
Non-judgemental and accepting

Change processes
Opportunity for catharsis or ventilation of emotions
Acquisition and practice of new behaviours
Provision of a rationale/model for understanding
Foster insight/awareness
Emotional and interpersonal learning
Suggestion
Success and mastery experiences
Persuasion
Placebo effects
Identification with the therapist
Behavioural self-control
Tension reduction
Desensitization
Providing information/education

Treatment methods
Use of rituals/techniques
Focus on 'inner world'
Adherence to a theory
Creating a healing setting
Interaction between two people
Communication
Explanation of client and therapist roles

Source: Grencavage and Norcross (1990)

counselling relationship there are a set of generic, common processes. The diversity of theories and approaches can therefore be viewed as different versions of one common activity, rather than as fundamentally different activities.

Brand names and special ingredients

One way of interpreting theoretical diversity in counselling is in commercial terms. All counsellors and therapists are offering clients the same basic product.

The exigencies of the marketplace, however, mean that there are many pressures leading in the direction of product diversification. It is obvious to anyone socialized into the ways of the market economy that in most circumstances it is not a good idea merely to make and sell 'cars' or 'washing powder'. Who would buy an unbranded car or box of detergent? Products which are on sale usually have 'brand names', which are meant to inform the customer about the quality and reliability of the commodity being sold. To stimulate customer enthusiasm and thereby encourage sales, many products also boast 'special ingredients' or 'unique selling features', which are claimed to make the product superior to its rivals.

This analogy is applicable to counselling and therapy. The evidence on the non-specific hypothesis implies that counsellors and therapists are, like car manufacturers, all engaged in selling broadly similar products. But for reasons of professional identity, intellectual coherence and external legitimacy there have emerged a number of 'brand name' therapies. The best known of these brand name therapies have been reviewed in earlier chapters. Psychodynamic, person-centred and cognitive–behavioural approaches are widely used, generally accepted and universally recognized. They are equivalent to the Mercedes, Ford and Toyota of the therapy world. Other, smaller, 'firms' have sought to establish their own brand names. Some of these brands have established themselves in a niche in the marketplace.

The main point of this metaphor is to suggest the influence of the marketplace, the 'trade in lunacy', on the evolution of counselling theory. The huge expansion in therapies was associated with the post-war expansion of modern capitalist economies. This economic growth has slowed and stopped, as the costs of health and welfare systems, struggling to meet the needs of an ageing population and an increasing demand for more costly and sophisticated treatments, have had to be kept within limits. At this time, when counselling and therapy services are under pressure to prove their cost-effectiveness, there are strong pressures in the direction of consolidating around the powerful brand names, and finding ways to combine resources through merger or integration.

The three main brand-name approaches have been discussed in earlier chapters. It can be seen that each of these major approaches contains within it sub-groupings of practitioners who have developed their own versions of the approaches. Hovering above and between these mainstream approaches are a range of integrationist frameworks that will be discussed in the next chapter. However, there are also a substantial number of approaches which contain distinctive ideas that cannot readily be assimilated into one of the major approaches, but that have not been as influential as the 'big three'. These alternative approaches are briefly summarized below.

It was suggested in Chapter 1 that philosophical ideas have permeated the theory and practice of counselling and therapy. One of the counselling orientations that most vividly illustrates this trend is the *existential* approach, which draws upon the ideas of existential philosophers such as Heidegger, Kiekegaard and Sartre (see Macquarrie, 1972). The aim of existential philosophy is to understand or illuminate the experience of 'being-in-the-world'. The focus is therefore on the way of being of the person, the qualitative texture of his or her relationship with self (*Eigenwelt*), others (*Mitwelt*) and the physical world (*Umwelt*). There have been three main strands of existential therapy. The first has evolved from the work of European therapists such as Boss (1957) and Binswanger (1963). The second strand consists of American therapists such as May (1950), Bugental (1976) and Yalom (1980). Finally, in Britain the writings of R. D. Laing (1960, 1961) comprise an important contribution to existential psychology.

One of the distinguishing features of the existential approach is its complete lack of concern for technique. The task of the existential counsellor or therapist is to explore the meaning for the client of problematic areas of experience. In line with some of the findings of existential philosophy, this exploration of meaning may focus on the significance for the person of broad categories of experience, such as choice, identity, isolation, love, time, death and freedom. The basic assumption being offered to the client is that human beings create and construct their worlds, and are therefore responsible for their lives.

The core text in existential therapy remains May *et al.* (1958). This book is, however, a difficult read, and more accessible introductions to the principles and practice of existential counselling are to be found in Bugental (1976), Yalom (1980) and van Deurzen-Smith (1988). Yalom (1989) has also produced a collection of case studies from his own work with clients.

The *Jungian* approach, also known as *analytic psychology*, was created by C. G. Jung (1875–1961). Jung was a Swiss psychiatrist who was one of the earliest members of the circle around Freud, the 'favourite son' who was predicted to take over from Freud as leader of the psychoanalytic movement. Jung split with Freud in 1912 through disagreement over theoretical differences. In particular, Jung diverged from the Freudian position on the predominance of sexual motives in the unconscious. Jung developed a concept of the 'collective unconscious', which he saw as structured through 'archetypes', symbolic representations of universal facets of human experience, such as the mother, the trickster, the hero. Perhaps the best known of the Jungian archetypes is the 'shadow', or animus (in women) or anima (in men), which represents those aspects of the self that are denied to conscious awareness. Another difference between Freud and Jung was highlighted in their views on development. Freudian thinking on development is restricted largely to events in childhood, particularly the oral, anal and Oedipal stages. Jung, on the other hand, saw human development as a lifelong quest for fulfilment, which he called 'individuation'. Jung also evolved a system for understanding personality differences, in which people can be categorized as 'types' made up of sensation/intuition, extraversion/introversion and thinking/feeling.

There is substantial common ground between psychodynamic approaches to counselling and the 'analytic' approach of Jung, in the shared assumptions regarding the importance of unconsious processes and the value of working with dreams and fantasy. There are, however, also significant areas of contrast, centred on the understanding of the unconscious and ideas of development and personality. Jung was also highly influenced by religious and spiritual teachings, whereas Freud was commited to a more secular, scientific approach.

In recent years there has been a strong interest in Jungian approaches within the counselling and psychotherapy community. There has been a proliferation of new texts elaborating Jungian concepts and methods. The application of a Jungian perspective to gender issues has been a particularly successful area of enquiry. Although the process of Jungian analysis is lengthy, and more appropriate for the practice of psychotherapy than for counselling (at least as counselling is defined in most agencies), many counsellors have read Jung or interpreters of his work (such as Kopp, 1972, 1974) and have integrated ideas such as the 'shadow' into their own way of making sense of therapy. The Jungian model of personality type has also influenced many counsellors through the use in personal development work of the Myers–Biggs Type Indicator (MBTI), a questionnaire devised to assess personality type in individuals.

The most accessible of Jung's writings are his autobiography, *Memories, Dreams, Reflections* (Jung, 1963), and *Man and His Symbols* (Jung, 1964). Other valuable introductory texts are Fordham (1986), Kaufmann (1989) and Carvalho (1990).

The spiritual theme in Jungian analysis has been further developed in a number of psychotherapeutic approaches, which can be described as *transpersonal* in nature. The best established of these approaches is *psychosynthesis*, founded by the Italian psychiatrist R. Assagioli (1888–1974). The transpersonal perspective seeks to include in the therapy process dimensions of experience beyond the personal or interpersonal. Sutich (1986) defines transpersonal therapy as being directed towards enabling the person to achieve the 'realization of an ultimate state', through finding his or her own spiritual path. The broad field of transpersonal counselling and therapy encompasses elements from psychosynthesis and the Jungian approach, as well as drawing upon ideas and techniques from meditation, Chakras, dreamwork, imagery, healing, Sufism, Buddhism, astrology and after-death experiences (Boorstein, 1986). Further information about psychosynthesis and transpersonal therapy can be found in Hardy (1987), Hardy and Whitmore (1988) and Gordon-Brown and Somers (1988).

Transactional Analysis (TA) is another of the approaches to counselling and therapy which has clear origins in psychoanalysis. The founder of TA, Eric Berne (1910–70), was a Canadian psychoanalyst who became critical of classical Freudian ideas and in reaction constructed his own theoretical model. The central innovation in TA has been the replacement of the Freudian superego–ego–id structure with a model consisting of three 'ego states': parent, adult and child. The use of everyday language here, as in other parts of TA theory, serves to demystify psychodynamic ideas and make them more accessible and relevant to ordinary people. The concept of ego states also implies a great deal more conscious awareness of these structures and how they operate than is assumed in traditional psychoanalysis. The other powerful innovation in TA was the construction of a model which explicitly addressed aspects of interpersonal as well as intrapersonal functioning. Berne proposed structural analysis (the use of the ego-state model) as a tool for understanding internal processes in individuals. He also evolved models for Transactional Analysis (processes occurring between two people), games analysis (sequences of behaviour between two or, more usually, more participants) and finally script analysis (the relationship between the individual and society as a whole over a lifetime).

TA is probably the most comprehensive theoretical framework currently available in the field of counselling and psychotherapy. Some critics would argue that the conceptual richness of TA can in some instances be a weakness. Counsellors and clients using TA can allow themselves to get wrapped up in talking about problems rather than in resolving them, but this is a pitfall that can be anticipated and avoided by experienced practitioners and supervisors. TA has not been associated with any major innovations in therapeutic technique, and many counsellors using TA may implement it through interventions and exercises drawn from other approaches, for example from Gestalt therapy (James and Jongeward, 1971). A significant contribution of TA has been the development of theoretical models for understanding problems associated with alcoholism (Steiner, 1971) and schizophrenia (Schiff et al., 1975).

Although the number of counsellors and therapists trained in TA remains relatively small, the model has had a significant impact on the field as a whole, in supplying practitioners with an accessible and highly creative therapeutic language. Readers interested in learning more about TA are recommended to begin with Steiner (1971), Berne (1975), Dusay and Dusay (1989) and Clarkson and Gilbert (1990).

Gestalt therapy was created by Fritz and Laura Perls in the 1950s and is yet another approach founded by a psychiatrist (Fritz Perls) originally trained in psychoanalysis. The distinctive feature of this orientation to counselling is that it draws heavily on the 'Gestalt' school of psychology, which was an influential force in the field of the psychology of perception and cognition in the period 1930–50 (Kohler, 1929; Koffka, 1935). 'Gestalt' is a German word which means 'pattern', and the key idea in this psychological model is the capacity of people to experience the world in terms of wholes, or overall patterns, and, more specifically, to have a tendency to complete unfinished patterns. The actual Gestalt psychologists were primarily interested in studying human perception and thought, and were responsible for familiar ideas, such as 'mental set' (viewing later phenomena as if they were similar to the first configuration the viewer had originally encountered) and the 'Zeigarnik effect' (having a better recollection of tasks that had not been completed than of tasks that had been fully finished).

Fritz Perls saw the relevance of these ideas for psychotherapy, and Gestalt therapy was established with the publication of *Ego, Hunger and Aggression* (Perls, 1947) and *Gestalt Therapy* (Perls et al., 1951). The later writings of Perls (1969, 1973) mainly articulated the approach through examples of his work with clients, rather than through a formal theoretical presentation, although Perls also demonstrated his work extensively in training workshops. An essential feature of Gestalt therapy as practised by Fritz Perls was an extreme hostility to over-intellectualization, or what he called 'bullshit'. His approach, therefore, focused rigorously on the here-and-now experiencing or awareness of the client, with the aim of removing the blocks to authentic contact with the environment caused by old patterns ('unfinished business').

The emphasis on working with immediate experience and the rejection of theorizing has meant that Gestalt therapy is generally thought of as a source of practical techniques for exploring current awareness, and enabling clients to express buried feelings, rather than as a distinctive theoretical model. There is some validity to this view, since Gestalt has been responsible for a wide range of techniques and exercises, such as two-chair work, first-person language and ways of working with art materials, dreams and guided fantasies. Writers on Gestalt Therapy appear to have been reluctant to engage in theoretical discourse. Nevertheless, this approach includes a theoretical framework that contains many important ideas.

The writings of Fritz Perls do not present a particularly balanced view of the Gestalt approach. He has been described as a 'brilliant, dramatic, controversial and charismatic teacher' (Parlett and Page, 1990) who modelled a style of working with clients that was significantly more confrontational and anti-intellectual than that adopted by subsequent Gestalt practitioners (see Shepard, 1975; Masson, 1992). Useful introductions to the current theory and practice of Gestalt can be found in Passons (1975), Van de Riet *et al.* (1980), Yontef and Simkin (1989), Clarkson (1989) and Parlett and Page (1990).

Psychodrama was one of the earliest approaches to psychotherapy, developed by the Viennese psychiatrist J. L. Moreno (1889–1974) in the 1930s. Moreno emigrated to the USA in 1925. His wife Zerka Moreno later became a key figure in the evolution of the approach, and continues to be involved in training. Although Moreno did meet Freud, his mode of therapy represents a radical departure from the assumptions and methods of any of the psychodynamic therapies. The emphasis in psychodrama is on spontaneity, creativity and action. Moreno believed that people co-act with each other, and this sense of mutuality or reciprocation is known within psychodrama as *tele*. The aim of therapy is to enable the release of these qualities in individuals and relationships through the use of ideas and techniques borrowed from drama. Participants in psychodrama groups act out problem situations in their lives, using fellow group members to enact the roles of significant others. The primary client, or protagonist, is encouraged to act out his or her conflicts in the here-and-now, rather than emotionally distancing himself or herself from them by talking about them in the past tense. The intensity of the drama can be enhanced by the use of role reversal (for example, the protagonist may switch into playing the role of his or her mother) or doubling (where another member of the group may speak for the protagonist to express feelings that are blocked from awareness). This process of dramatic enactment produces insight, catharsis and finally reflection and consolidation of learning.

As with many of the other approaches discussed in this section, the number of counsellors or therapists who practise psychodrama in its pure form is relatively small. However, much larger numbers of therapists have been influenced by the ideas and techniques pioneered by the Morenos. In particular, psychodrama liberates therapists from the physical passivity of the seated conversation, and introduces the possibility for self-expression through action, movement, posture and the use of objects. Psychodrama also brings into the world of therapy concepts and methods from drama and the arts, which provide a valuable counterpoint to the predominantly scientific assumptions of psychology and psychiatry. Like Gestalt, psychosynthesis and many of the other humanistic therapies, psychodrama needs to be experienced rather than read about. However, useful introductions to theory and practice can be found in Greenberg (1974), Badaines (1988), Marineau (1989) and Brazier (1991). Another counselling approach that has its origins in the arts and humanities is *art therapy* (Dalley, 1984; Dalley and Case, 1992), in which clients express themselves through painting and clay modelling. Anderson (1977) provides a valuable discussion of the interface between therapy and the arts in general.

One of the basic building blocks of psychodynamic theory is the concept of defence. Freud himself, and his daughter Anna Freud, made major contributions to the understanding of the human capacity to block off unwelcome thoughts, feelings and impulses, through defence mechanisms such as projection, repression and denial (see Chapter 2). Wilhelm Reich, who worked with Freud, took a special interest in the functioning of defence mechanisms, and came to the conclusion that these processes could usefully be regarded as actually physically located in bodily, anatomical structures. Reich argued that the build-up of repressed libidinal or sexual energy brought about by defences led to the formation of a 'body armour'. The most effective way of helping clients, therefore, was to work directly with the physical embodiment of the defence, rather than merely talking about it. The approach known as *bioenergetics* is based on these ideas of Reich, and on the later work of Alexander Lowen, who was a client and student of Reich. The bioenergetic approach has not been institutionalized into a rigid framework or school, and there are therapists influenced by Reich and Lowen who would label themselves Reichian or practitioners of biosynthesis (Boadella, 1988) or biodynamic therapy (Southwell, 1988).

The aim of bioenergetic counselling and therapy is to enable a free flow of energy through the body of the person, resulting in vitality, energy and pleasure. In practice, the therapist will insist that the client is 'grounded', and will encourage him or her to be in physical contact with the ground, for example by standing. Another important practical principle is attention to breathing, as people who are anxious or afraid will often attempt to muffle their feelings by breathing slowly or superficially, or holding their breath. A third technique is awareness of the flow of energy, by observing muscle tone, skin temperature and colour. Using these principles, the bioenergetic therapist will work with the client to bring about release and discharge of bodily energy blocks.

The 'special ingredient' in bioenergetic work is its systematic attention to the body. Unlike many other approaches, which treat clients as if they were disembodied intellectual entities, bioenergetics operates primarily on a non-verbal, intuitive level. The popularity of this mode of therapy has undoubtedly been badly affected by the unfortunate image presented by the later career of Reich himself. Reich went to the USA in 1954, where his ideas were wildly at odds with the highly conservative psychiatric establishment of the time. In response to their rejection, he became more extreme in his views, advocating radical sexual freedom and experimenting with the use of the 'orgone accumulator'. He was imprisoned for some time, and died in obscurity. It is fair to say that current practitioners of Reichian therapy make use of the more sensible of his ideas. More detailed information about this approach is available in Whitfield (1988).

A very different approach to counselling and therapy has emerged from the field of family therapy. This approach is fundamentally *systemic* in nature. In other words, the therapist is not intervening at the level of the individual person, but at the level of the family system. The attention of the therapist shifts from the 'disturbed' individual to the dysfunctional system. The relationship between family members is seen as forming an interlocking network of patterns of inter-action. It is impossible to understand what is happening in any one part of the system without grasping what is going on in the system as a whole. It is assumed that the system (as opposed to the individual people in the system) has no memory, so the aim is to work with here-and-now current interactions. For example, a family may come to the attention of a helping agency because one of the children is mentally ill and behaving in a disturbed manner. On explora-tion of what is happening in the family system as a whole, it may become apparent that the disturbance of the 'sick' child is allowing the mother and father to avoid communicating with each other over financial difficulties, and at the same time giving the grandmother an opportunity to spend more time with the other children. The behaviour of the sick child cannot change until some way is found to alter these other elements in the system. The role of the therapist (or team of therapists) is not to enter into a close relationship or alliance with individuals in the family, but to act as a catalyst for change in the system as a whole. As a result, the skills and assumptions made by systemic counsellors and therapists are often radically different from those employed by those using more traditional relationship-oriented methods. Nevertheless, systemic ideas have influenced many counsellors in the direction of taking into consideration the family dynamics which lie behind the problems of their individual clients. Systemic ideas have also been widely applied in couples counselling.

It is impossible to give an adequate account of the breadth and scope of systemic approaches here. Families can clearly be highly complex in their com-position and functioning, and the nature of systemic theory reflects this complex-ity. The reader wishing to learn more about this topic is recommended to consult Street and Dryden (1988) and Barker (1992).

The roots of theoretical diversity

These brief descriptions of some of the main brand-name approaches are intended to give some idea of the range of current thinking in counselling and psychotherapy. Many other approaches could (and perhaps should) have been included. The supporters of Adlerian therapy, reality therapy, neuro-linguistic programming and many others could make a strong case for the importance of their own preferred orientation to therapy. Outlines of the feminist and transcultural approaches are presented in Chapter 7. However, given the almost endless scope for theoretical choice, it is necessary to draw a line somewhere. But why are there so many approaches? How can we make sense of this extreme degree of theoretical diversity?

There would appear to be several factors that have contributed to the fragmentation of the field and the proliferation of different schools of thought. Broadly speaking, these factors can be classified in three categories: the choice of ideas and concepts included in the theory (the unique mix of 'special ingredients'), the issues and phenomena explained by the theory, and the context in which the theory is created.

The pool of ideas and concepts

One very fundamental source of theoretical complexity is that any psychological theory, or approach to counselling, ultimately relies on a root 'image of the person', a set of basic assumptions about the very nature of what it is to be human.

Shotter (1975) has suggested that two of the dominant images of the person used in psychology have been the image of the machine ('the best way to understand people is to view them as mechanical objects') and the image of the organism ('the best way to understand people is to view them as animal, biological entities'). These two images can certainly be found running through different counselling approaches, from the mechanistic thinking of traditional behaviourism to the many references to bodily functioning in classical psychoanalysis. The ideas of existential philosophy have, more recently, introduced the image of the person not as an organism or mechanism but as a social being. The influence of Eastern philosophies has introduced the image of the person as spiritual being. It has been difficult to reconcile these underlying images at a philosophical level, and so at least some of the differences between counselling theories can be attributed to the different images of the person which underpin them. The situation is even further complicated by the fact that the same theory can encompass more than one root image. For example, psychoanalysis contains mechanistic ideas (e.g. defence mechanisms) and organismic/biological ideas (e.g. libido, oral fixation). Person-centred theory contains organismic images (e.g. the organismic valuing process, the self-actualization motive) as well as existential ones (e.g. congruence, empathy).

The special ingredients upon which brand-name therapies base their claims to distinctiveness are usually derived from these root images or metaphors. Bioenergetics draws upon a strong image of the embodied, sexual person. Jungian and transpersonal approaches draw upon an image of the person as spiritual being. For systemic approaches, the person is primarily a social being.

What is a theory trying to explain?

A key factor behind the multiplication of theories has been the scope for theoretical profusion caused by the complexity of the phenomena which any theory needs to address. Table 3 illustrates some of the ways in which each approach to counselling has tended to focus on some phenomena and devote less

Table 3   Examples of 'specialization' in counselling theories

Phenomenon to be explained	Theories which emphasize this phenomenon	Theories which largely ignore this phenomenon
Links between childhood experience and adult problems	Psychodynamic, TA	Cognitive-behavioural, Gestalt
The client–counsellor relationship	Psychodynamic, person-centred	Cognitive-behavioural, Gestalt
Expression of conflicts through body posture, tension, etc.	Gestalt Bioenergetics	Person-centred, Jungian, Cognitive-behavioural
Helping the client to implement change in behaviour	Cognitive-behavioural, TA	Psychodynamic, person-centred, Transpersonal
Focusing on relationships between the client and family members	Systemic, psychodrama, TA	Person-centred, Gestalt
The experience of death	Existential, transpersonal	Person-centred, cognitive–behavioural

attention to others. The list in Table 3 is not intended to be comprehensive, but merely to show how the aims and areas of emphasis of different theories vary.

The context of theory construction

Another set of factors contributing to theoretical diversity has arisen from the social context in which theorists have operated. A particularly powerful force for diversity has been the economic pressure exerted by the 'mental health industry', particularly in the USA. If approaches to counselling and psychotherapy are considered as competing products in a marketplace, it is inevitable that each therapist or group of therapists will strive to identify the unique features that make their brand of therapy more attractive than all the others on display. Significant material and status rewards accrue, therefore, to practitioners who create new approaches and thereby attract clients, students and book sales. The relative weakness of the academic and research base for counselling and psychotherapy has also contributed to this situation, since the development of systematic critiques of new therapies has not been forthcoming.

The construction and refinement of theory is a process which takes time and necessarily involves numbers of people. Working through the meaning and validity of new ideas, testing them against experience and research evidence, is a collective, collaborative activity. The philosopher Kuhn (1962) introduced the notion of the 'scientific community' to describe the international networks of scientists who are linked by a shared scientific culture consisting of books, journals and conferences. Very few counsellors and psychotherapists are researchers or scholars able to participate in this kind of exchange of ideas and theory-building.

Moving beyond the immediate social milieu of therapists and counsellors, it can be recognized that the modern industrial societies that have given birth to counselling and psychotherapy have themselves been fragmented and complex. Ideas from different political ideologies, such as capitalism, socialism, liberalism and feminism, have exerted an influence on therapy theorists, as have ideas from science and religion. It would be unrealistic, therefore, to expect therapy in a 'post-modern' world to comprise a monolithic universal theory.

The use of theory in practice

The existence of theoretical diversity in counselling can be partially understood in terms of the range of social factors discussed above. This analysis does not, however, examine the ways in which theories are used in practice, the manner in which counsellors actually employ theories in their work with clients. The importance of looking at theory in practice is that it is limiting and misleading to conceive of counselling theory as only, or even mainly, a set of ideas and concepts existing in books and journal articles. Theorizing is an active, subtle, personal and interpersonal process. Rycroft (1966) has suggested that there are profound differences between theories of therapy and scientific theories in fields such as physics and chemistry. The latter can yield cause-and-effect statements which can be used to predict future events. The former are used by people largely to attribute meaning to events which have already taken place.

Theorizing is embedded in social life, and the written word inevitably abstracts ideas and concepts from their actual usage. A great deal of the learning that informs the work of counsellors comes from talking with colleagues, supervisors and tutors rather than reading books and journals (Morrow-Bradley and Elliott, 1986). It is possible to view counsellors and therapists who adhere to a particular approach, such as person-centred counselling, as members of a language community. Within this language community, much of what is said and done may be written down, particularly by key figures such as Rogers, but the oral tradition from which the writing emerges always contains a richer, more comprehensive, more open-textured version of what is known and believed. Books and articles convey a version of the approach, rather than the approach in its entirety. The basis for much critical debate is the discrepancy between the linear, logical, systematized version of theory that appears in books, and the theory as used in practice.

The philosopher Polanyi (1958) introduced the term 'implicit knowledge' to refer to the kind of knowing used by people who belong in a community of scientists. Implicit or 'tacit' knowledge is picked up informally and unconsciously rather than being explicitly written down. This idea is equally applicable to the world of therapy, perhaps even more applicable given the highly interpersonal nature of the work. For example, counsellors are seldom comfortable about employing a technique or exercise with a client on the basis of only having read about it in a book. There is usually a need to see it demonstrated, or even be the recipient of it, before the counsellor can have a 'feel' for how it will be in practice. The gap between the written description of the technique and the 'feel' is what Polanyi (1958) means by implicit knowledge.

The relationship between theoretical concepts and feelings is further explored by Gendlin (1962). His model of experiencing, developed within the client-centred or person-centred approach, proposes that meaning arises from the symbolization of a 'felt sense'. The 'felt sense' is a bodily, multifaceted area of feeling which the person experiences in response to events. This felt sense contains all the diverse meanings that the event might have for the person, but these meanings can only be accessed through symbolization, usually in words, but potentially also through images. When a symbol, for example a word or phrase, captures the meaning contained within a feeling, there is a sense of fit, and then a sense of movement or change as this clarification of meaning allows other meanings to emerge. This approach to understanding experiencing has been highly influential within person-centred counselling (see Chapter 4). However, Gendlin (1966) has also pointed out that it provides a framework for validating the use of theory, through the process of 'experiential explication'. He suggests that the test of whether a concept or idea is helpful in therapy depends on whether its use brings about a shift in the felt sense of a problem. Gendlin is proposing that theories and concepts have a subjective truth value as well as an objective, scientifically verified validity. His framework also draws attention to the importance of using language in a creative and sensitive manner. The technical language of much counselling theory does not mean a great deal to clients, and it is essential for counsellors to communicate their ideas through a mutually constructed 'feeling language' (Hobson, 1985) that makes sense to the client.

The use in practice of theoretical ideas and constructs is also dependent on the structure of the theory. Rapaport and Gill (1959) have argued that there are three levels to any theoretical model used in counselling and therapy. First, there are statements about observational data. Second, there are theoretical propositions which make connections between different observations. Third, there are statements of philosophical assumptions, or 'metapsychology'. Rapaport and Gill (1959) looked at the theoretical structure of psychoanalysis, and came to the conclusion that statements about, for example, defence mechanisms such as projection or denial were fundamentally simple observations of behavioural events. Psychoanalytic concepts such as 'anal personality', on the other hand, went 'beyond the information given', and made inferences about the connectedness of events separated by time and space. The idea of anal personality implies a link between childhood events and adult behaviour, and this association is inferred rather than directly observed. However, in principle, given good enough research, the truth of the inference could be tested through observation. Finally, concepts such as the 'unconscious' and 'libido' referred to philosophical abstractions that could not be directly observed but were used as general explanatory ideas.

Rapaport and Gill's (1959) discussion of these issues has a number of implications for the application of theory in practice. The use of lower-level, observational constructs can be seen to carry little in the way of theoretical 'baggage'. For example, describing a client as 'always in his child ego state' might be an effective shorthand means of giving information to a supervisor. However, it would be a straightforward matter to use everyday ordinary language to communicate the same information. Different counselling theories tend to include their own uniquely phrased observational labels, and counsellors often find it helpful to use these labels. In doing so, they are not necessarily using the theoretical model from which the label is taken, but are merely borrowing a useful turn of phrase.

Higher-level constructs and concepts, by contrast, cannot be so easily taken out of the context of their parent theoretical model. A term such as 'libido' or 'self-actualization' cannot be used without making a substantial number of philosophical assumptions about what it means to be a person. As a result, any attempt to combine 'libido' and 'self-actualization' in the same conversation, case study or research project is likely to lead to confusion.

This exploration of how theory is used in practice provides another perspective on theoretical diversity. It is clear that, first of all, it is highly unlikely that any single counselling theory is adequate to provide a comprehensive set of observables, propositions and metatheoretical assumptions appropriate to all circumstances: the theories we have are just not well enough worked out to deliver this kind of coverage. Second, the formal theoretical concepts which we use always exist in relation to a felt sense, an unsymbolized feeling, of what is happening, or to an informal oral tradition. Third, the theory we use depends on whom we use it with. In circumstances where the only colleagues a counsellor would talk with come from the same language community, a high degree of theoretical purity can be maintained. For many counsellors and therapists, however, the realities of their work bring them into contact with colleagues from other backgrounds, and they are forced to assimilate concepts and terminology from other approaches in order to establish a basis for communication. Ryle (1978, 1987), in response to this situation, has argued that therapists should deliberately work together to create a 'common language'.

Conclusion: the place of theory in counselling

The aim of this chapter has been to make some sense of the bewildering array of theories presently employed by counsellors and psychotherapists. It is hoped that it is possible to find a way through this swirling fog of theories and concepts by holding on to some firm points of reference. The apparent differences between theories and approaches can be viewed more as differences in emphasis rather than differences in substance. As Frank (1973, 1974) and others have argued, behind the alternative theories and models there are a set of common factors used by all therapists. The differences in emphasis can be explained by taking into consideration the particular interests of the person who created the theory. Jung was interested in religion, Reich was interested in the body, Moreno was interested in action and spontaneity. These differences have been reinforced and maintained by commercial pressures to market a 'brand-name' product, and by the gravitation of therapists and clients towards approaches whose 'special ingredients' appealed to them. At the same time, the reality of using a theory in practice introduces another level of complexity. The struggle to make sense of a client, or the experience of working with certain colleagues, may lead a counsellor towards new areas of theory.

Theory is important in counselling. The counsellor is called upon to participate in lives which may be breaking down. The client may be very confused, overwhelmed by feeling, lost in despair. Being able to use a theoretical model to make sense of what is happening in these circumstances is highly desirable. In the words of Kurt Lewin, 'there is nothing as practical as a good theory'. Counsellors can enhance the practical value of their theory by ensuring that it is consistent, coherent and comprehensive. In doing so, they inevitably need to address the question of how best to combine or integrate ideas from different models. This issue is discussed in depth in the next chapter.

Topics for reflection and discussion

1 Make a list of the theoretical terms and concepts you routinely use in talking about counselling. Identify which you employ as 'observational' labels and which refer to more abstract theoretical assumptions. What does this tell you about the theoretical model(s) you use in practice?
2 How important are non-specific or common factors? Do you believe that they are more influential than the actual techniques used by therapists? What are the implications of this perspective for the ways that counsellors work with clients? What are the implications for counsellor training?

SIX

COMBINING APPROACHES: ISSUES IN INTEGRATION AND ECLECTICISM

Historically, as a profession psychotherapy has been largely structured around distinct, separate sets of ideas or theoretical models, each backed up by its own training institute or professional association. Most counselling textbooks are organized around chapters on individual theorists, such as Freud, Rogers, Perls and Ellis, or are specifically devoted to single schools of thought. The impression given by these characteristics is that counsellors would in general be members of one or another of these sub-groups, and adhere to one specific approach. Increasingly, however, counsellors and therapists are looking beyond the confines of theoretical purity. A series of studies in the 1960s and 1970s showed that more and more practitioners were describing themselves as 'eclectic' or 'integrationist' in approach, rather than being followers of any one single model.

Garfield and Kurtz (1974), for example, carried out a survey of 855 clinical psychologists in the USA, and found that 55 per cent defined themselves as eclectic, 16 per cent as psychoanalytic/psychodynamic, 10 per cent as behavioural and 7 per cent as Rogerian, humanistic and existential (the remaining 12 per cent were divided between a wide range of other orientations). Garfield and Kurt (1977) followed up the eclectic clinical psychologists from their 1974 study and found that 49 per cent had at some time in the past adhered to a single theory and 45 per cent had always seen themselves as eclectic. Of those who had once been single approach oriented, the main shift was from psychoanalysis and Rogerian to eclecticism. Prochaska and Norcross (1983), in a survey of 410 psychotherapists in the USA, reported figures of eclectic 30 per cent, psychodynamic 18 per cent, psychoanalytic 9 per cent, cognitive 8 per cent, behavioural 6 per cent, existential 4 per cent, Gestalt 3 per cent, humanistic 4 per cent, Rogerian 2 per cent and other approaches 15 per cent. O'Sullivan and Dryden (1990) found that 32 per cent of clinical psychologists in one region in Britain designated themselves as eclectic in orientation. The trend across all these surveys has been that eclecticism has emerged as the single most popular approach.

The roots of the trend towards eclecticism and integrationism can be found in some of the earliest writings in the field. For example, as behaviourism began to be influential in the 1930s and 1940s, a number of writers, such as Dollard, Miller and Rosenzweig, were beginning to explore ways in which parallels and connections could be made between behavioural and psychoanalytic ideas and methods (see Marmor and Woods, 1980). As humanistic thinking achieved prominence in the 1950s the commonalities and divergences between it and existing approaches were widely debated. It could well be argued that there is no such thing as a 'pure' theory. All theorists are influenced by what has gone before. Freudian ideas can be seen as representing a creative integration of concepts from philosophy, medicine, biology and literature. The client-centred model encompasses ideas from psychoanalysis, existential and phenomenological philosophy, and social psychology. The cognitive–behavioural approach is an example of an overt synthesis of two strands of psychological theory: behaviourism and cognitive psychology.

The emergence of the idea that all therapies might largely function through the operation of common or 'non-specific' factors, discussed in the previous chapter, further reinforced the movement towards eclecticism and integration. The argument put forward by Frank (1973) that therapy, alongside other forms of behaviour change, achieved its effectiveness through very general processes, such as the provision of a rationale for understanding life problems, the instillation of hope and the opportunity for emotional release, made it easier to see the common ground between therapies and to begin to consider ways in which they might fit together.

Nevertheless, even though there has been an integrationist 'underground' within the field of counselling, up until the 1960s, it is probably reasonable to suggest that the dominant view was that different models and approaches provided perfectly viable alternative ways of working with clients, and that, on the whole, theoretical 'purity' was to be preferred. The situation today is more complex and fragmented. Many practitioners, influenced not only by their own experience with clients but also by research which has shown different approaches to be equivalent in their effectiveness (Smith *et al.*, 1980), have been convinced that no one model was adequate in itself. These practitioners looked beyond their initial training in a single approach and sought to acquire skills and ideas from other approaches. As a result, increasing numbers now describe themselves as eclectic in orientation. This trend is matched by the parallel development of the institutionalization of eclecticism and integrationism, through the formation of the Society for the Exploration of Psychotherapy Integration (SEPI) in 1983, the inauguration in 1982 of the *International Journal of Eclectic Psychotherapy* (later renamed the *Journal of Integrative and Eclectic Psychotherapy*), the establishment of systematic training in integrative therapy (Clarkson, 1992) and the publication of a number of important books on the topic (Norcross, 1986; Dryden, 1992).

In opposition to this movement, a significant number of practitioners remained convinced that eclecticism or integrationism was associated with muddle and confusion, and that it was necessary to stick to one, consistent approach. Voices speaking out against the integrationist trend include Eysenck (1970: 145), who vividly asserts that to follow in the direction of theoretical integration would lead us to nothing but a mishmash of theories, a huggermugger of procedures, a gallimaufry of therapies, and a charivaria of activities having no proper rationale, and incapable of being tested or evaluated. What is needed in science and in medicine are *clear-cut* theories leading to *specific* procedures applicable to *specific* types of patients.

Eysenck (1970) argues that, in his view, only behaviour therapy can provide the kind of logically consistent and scientifically evaluated approach he seeks. Another critic of integrationism, but this time from a psychoanalytic perspective, is Szasz (1974: 41):

> The psychotherapist who claims to practice in a flexible manner, tailoring his therapy to the needs of his patients, does so by assuming a variety of roles. With one patient, he is a magician who hypnotizes; with another, a sympathetic friend who reassures; with a third, a physician who dispenses tranquilizers; with a fourth, a classical analyst who interprets; and so on . . . The eclectic psychotherapist is, more often than not, a role player; he wears a variety of psychotherapeutic mantles, but owns none and is usually truly comfortable in none. Instead of being skilled in a multiplicity of therapeutic techniques, he suffers from what we may consider, after Erikson, 'a diffusion of professional identity'. In sum, the therapist who tries to be all things to all people may be nothing to himself; he is not 'at one' with any particular method of psychotherapy. If he engages in intensive psychotherapy, his patient is likely to discover this.

Theoretical purists argue that there are conflicting philosophical assumptions underlying different approaches, and that any attempt to combine them is likely to lead to confusion (Eysenck) or inauthenticity (Szasz). For example, within psychoanalysis the actions of a person are regarded as ultimately determined by unconscious motives arising from repressed childhood experiences. By contrast, humanistic theories view people as capable of choice and free will. It could be argued that these are irreconcilably opposing ways of making sense of human nature, and can only breed contradiction if combined into one approach to counselling (Patterson, 1989). Another type of confusion can be created by taking ideas or techniques out of context. For example, systematic desensitization is a therapeutic technique that has been developed within a behavioural perspective in which anxiety is understood in terms of a conditioned fear response to a stimulus. A humanistic counsellor who understood anxiety in terms of threat to the self-concept might invite the client to engage in a process which could superficially resemble systematic desensitization, but the meaning of the procedure would be radically different. A final source of confusion which can result from an eclectic approach reflects the difficulties involved in mastering concepts and methods from different theories. It is hard enough, according to this line of argument, to be a competent counsellor within one approach, without attempting to achieve a depth of understanding and experience in them all.

If the main objection to eclecticism is that it can result in confusion and misunderstanding, a secondary objection is that it may undermine effective training, supervision and support. If a theoretical model provides a language through which to discuss and reflect on the complex reality of work with clients, it is surely helpful to work with trainers, supervisors and colleagues who share the same language. Similarly, research or scholarship in a field of study are facilitated when everyone involved can agree on the meaning of terminology. This is a strong argument in favour of at least a strong degree of theoretical purity. The language of psychoanalysis and the psychodynamic approach, for example, is over 100 years old, and constitutes a rich and extensive literature on just about every aspect of human psychological and cultural functioning that can be imagined. Only specialists within a psychodynamic approach, it is argued, can really make effective use of these resources. Integrationist practitioners with a more superficial grasp of psychodynamic language would be much less able to find their way through this material.

The field of counselling and psychotherapy is therefore currently involved in an important debate over the relative merits of theoretical purity as against integration or eclecticism. Behind this debate is a much larger question, of whether it is even in principle possible to create a universally acceptable framework for understanding human behaviour. It would seem plausible to many people trained within Western science and philosophy that advances in human understanding arise from attempts to assess the validity of competing theories, or to refute the predictions of a dominant theory. For observers with these values and beliefs, the absence of debate over fundamental assumptions about human nature and society is associated with totalitarian and authoritarian states. From another point of view, however, the Western tendency to divide reality into competing dualisms can be seen as equally dangerous.

The several strands of the purism versus eclecticism or integrationism debate are summarized in Table 4. The issue is further complicated, however, by the fact that there are important differences between eclecticism and integrationism, and also several different types of integrationism.

Eclecticism and integrationism

An eclectic approach to counselling is one in which the counsellor chooses the best or most appropriate ideas and techniques from a range of theories or models, in order to meet the needs of the client. Integration, on the other hand, refers to a somewhat more ambitious enterprise in which the counsellor brings together elements from different theories and models into a new theory or model. To be an eclectic it is merely necessary to be able to recognize or identify what you like in the approaches on offer. To be an integrationist it is necessary not only to identify what is useful, but also to weld these pieces into a whole. Some of the differences in meaning between the two terms are presented in Table 5. The term 'eclectic' was more fashionable in the 1960s, but subsequently has perhaps dropped out of favour. 'Integrative' and 'integrationist' imply to many people a greater degree of intellectual rigour. However, there have recently been attempts to rehabilitate the concept of eclecticism. In practice, both concepts

Table 4   A force-field analysis of the integrationism–separatism debate

Factors leading towards integrationism or eclecticism	Factors leading towards theoretical purity
Perceived limitations of existing theories	Commitment to theoretical consistency
The experience of working with colleagues from different orientations	Marketability of distinctive 'product'
Personal desire to learn	Assumption that science is advanced through testing competing theories against each other
Belief in the unity of psychotherapies, e.g. the historical search for convergence	Existence of extensive literature and experience within well-established approaches
Belief in common or non-specific factors	Institute-based education and training – membership of approach-based associations and societies
Research evidence which suggests all approaches are equally effective	
The gap between theory and practice – counsellors do not adhere to their approach in practice	
Resistance to the further proliferation of approaches	
University-based counsellor and therapist education and training – membership of discipline-based associations and societies	

Table 5   A comparison of the meanings of eclecticism and integrationism

Eclecticism	Integrationism
Technical	Theoretical
Divergent (differences)	Convergent (commonalities)
Choosing from many	Combining many
Applying what is	Creating something new
Collection	Blend
Selection	Synthesis
Applying the parts	Unifying the parts
Atheoretical but empirical	More theoretical than empirical
Sum of parts	More than sum of parts
Realistic	Idealistic

Source: Norcross and Grencavage (1989)

depend on an act of combining, and signify that the counsellor involved is not satisfied with a single-theory approach to his or her work.

Varieties of integration

So far, the general principle of combining or unifying counselling approaches has been discussed, but not the practicalities. How can different theories and techniques be combined? Within the counselling and psychotherapy literature, the urge to create a broader, more all-encompassing approach has taken a number of contrasting forms. The options for integration have been described by a number of writers. For example, Mahrer (1989) argues that there have been six distinctively different strategies for achieving integration:

1 The development of a substantive new theory. This strategy involves the ambitious and complex endeavour of creating a genuinely new way of looking at human beings, one that will encompass and satisfactorily replace all existing theories. This approach to integration is the equivalent of a scientific revolution, such as the replacement of Newtonian with Einsteinian ideas about time, space and gravity, and is obviously extremely difficult to achieve. However, the identification of 'transtheoretical' constructs or frameworks goes some way towards this goal.
2 The development of one of the current theories to the point where it would be capable of assimilating all other competing or alternative theories. This strategy is fundamentally mistaken, according to Mahrer (1989), because each of the current theories is based upon a radically different image of the person.
3 To concentrate on the vocabularies, the sets of words, phrases and concepts used in different approaches, and work at the development of a common language for counselling and therapy (e.g. Ryle, 1978, 1987). This strategy is valuable in enabling counsellors from different orientations to communicate effectively with each other.
4 To focus on areas of agreement or commonality between different approaches, in order to produce integrative concepts and techniques within specific domains or components of therapy, rather than at the level of the theory or approach as a whole. Areas of commonality which have been explored in this manner include the therapeutic alliance (Bordin, 1979) and the formulation of stages of change (Prochaska and DiClemente, 1982).
5 More extensive sharing between practitioners of specific techniques or 'operating procedures'. In this strategy, counsellors and therapists would observe each other at work (for example, on tape) and acquire new ways of working with clients, but at a practical not theoretical level.
6 Using research findings to enable practitioners to identify those intervention techniques which are most effective with specific client problems and issues. Mahrer (1989) describes this strategy for integration as 'diagnose-the-problem-and-prescribe-the-treatment'. Dryden (1984) describes it as *technical eclecticism*.

The framework offered by Mahrer (1989) reflects the complexity of the current debate over eclecticism and integrationism. These six strategies for combining approaches can be placed on a continuum, which at one end involves close attention to concepts and theory-building, and at the other end represents a primarily atheoretical, pragmatic and empirical approach. In the middle of the continuum are counsellors and therapists who are neither solely technicians nor grand theorists, but are grappling with problems of translating one approach or theory into another. These are counsellors who are trying to learn from each other, by asking questions such as 'What does that concept mean to me?' or 'How does that way of working with a client fit into my scheme of things?'

This chapter has examined in some detail the debate over integrationism and theoretical purity, focusing on the many aspects of this complex issue. It would seem reasonable to ask, at this point, whether integrationist counsellors and therapists do anything different from practitioners who operate within a single model. The answer must be that, to a large extent, they do not do anything significantly different. They are, after all, drawing upon the same pool of therapeutic resources. There would appear to be two distinctive features of integrative work as it is currently practised. The first is a concern with client assessment, which is a central feature of technical eclecticism. The second is the use of 'transtheoretical' concepts.

The use of client assessment in integrative approaches

The basic rationale for client assessment within integrative approaches derives from the fact that the integrationist or eclectic practitioner has at his or her disposal a range of intervention tools and techniques. The form of intervention that is chosen will depend on the particular needs and personality of the client. By contrast, the single-theory practitioner, it could be suggested, can only work with each client in the same way. One of the most explicit examples of this kind of assessment can be found in multimodal therapy (Lazarus, 1989a,b; Eskapa, 1992). Within the multimodal approach clients are viewed as presenting problems that can be located within seven distinctive areas: behaviour, affect, sensation, imagery, cognition, interpersonal relationships, drugs/biology. Lazarus (1989a,b), the founder of the approach, uses the term 'BASIC-ID' as a mnemonic for these areas. The task of the counsellor is to identify the main focus for client work, using an assessment interview and the multimodal life history questionnaire, and then choose the relevant intervention techniques, based on research findings.

The multimodal approach is a good example of what can be called 'technical eclecticism' (Dryden, 1984). In other words, it is a framework for selecting therapeutic techniques. One major advantage that this perspective on integration can claim is that it is atheoretical and thus avoids pointless debate over the compatibility (or otherwise) of theoretical constructs. A major disadvantage, on the other hand, is that, strictly speaking, it relies on the existence of sound research evidence concerning the effectiveness of particular techniques with particular categories of client. Such evidence is frequently not available, forcing the clinician to rely on his or her personal experience, which will have been at least partly shaped by theoretical assumptions and suppositions. Many other eclectic or integrationist therapists use rigorous client assessment procedures without specifically following the multimodal model (see, for example, the work of Norcross described in Dryden, 1991).

The use of 'transtheoretical' concepts in integrative approaches

In practice, the main strategy for achieving integration has been to find a central theoretical concept or framework within which some or all existing approaches can be subsumed. Barkham (1992) has suggested that integrationist counsellors and therapists attempt to identify *higher-order constructs* which can account for change mechanisms beyond the level of any single model. The aim is to produce a cognitive 'map' that will enable the links and connections between ideas and techniques to be understood. There are several examples of approaches to counselling and therapy which employ such higher-order or *transtheoretical* constructs.

One example of a transtheoretical approach to integration, which is widely used within counselling, is the 'skilled helper' model constructed by Egan (1990). The key integrating concept chosen by Egan is that of *problem management*. Egan suggests that clients who seek assistance from counsellors and other helpers are experiencing difficulties in coping with difficulties in their lives, and that the primary task of the helper is to enable the person to find and act on appropriate solutions to these problems. The emphasis is therefore on a problem-solving process, which involves three stages. First, the client is helped to describe and explore the 'present scenario', the problem situation which he or she is faced with at present. The second stage is to articulate a 'preferred scenario', which includes future goals and objectives. The third stage is to develop and implement action strategies for moving from the current to the preferred scenario. Egan (1990) describes sub-stages within each stage, and identifies the client tasks and helper skills necessary to facilitate this problem-solving process.

The Egan model can usefully be viewed as a 'map' through which the usefulness of relevant elements of other approaches can be located and evaluated. For example, the concept of empathy is taken from client-centred theory and regarded as a communication skill essential to the helping process, and the idea of congruence is included under 'immediacy'. From a psychodynamic perspective, the aim of insight is included in Egan's goal of identifying and challenging 'blind spots' in the client. Many counsellors and therapists have used the Egan model as a framework through which they can employ techniques and methods from a wide range of approaches, for example Gestalt exercises as a way of challenging blind spots or assertiveness training a way of developing action strategies. The brief case study in Inskipp and Johns (1984) illustrates some of the ways in which various ideas can be included within the skilled helper model.

The main strengths of the skilled helper model are that it offers an intensely practical and pragmatic approach to working with people, and that it is applicable to a wide variety of situations, ranging from individual counselling to organizational consultation. As an integrationist approach, its limitation is that it is primarily based in a cognitive–behavioural perspective. Although the model clearly encompasses some elements of humanistic and person-centred thinking, through such concepts as respect, immediacy and empathy, it includes very little from the psychodynamic approaches. Key concepts from psychodynamic approaches, such as the importance of childhood object relations, the idea of defence mechanisms and unconscious processing, or the notion of transference, are all absent.

Another integrative approach which employs a central unifying concept as a device for combining different approaches is the *self-confirmation* model developed by Andrews (1991). The core idea in this model is that the individual acts in the world to reaffirm his or her self-concept. The process of self-confirmation involves a feedback loop consisting of a number of stages. The self-concept of the person represents the way he or she perceives his or her attitudes, feeling states, ways of acting in situations and all other dimensions of 'what is me'. This sense of self generates characteristic needs and expectations. For example, a person who views herself as 'dominant' may experience a need or drive to be powerful and controlling in relationships, and will expect other people to follow her directives. Patterns of behaviour and action will ensue that are consistent with the underlying needs and expectations and even more fundamental self-concept. This behaviour is, in turn, perceived and reacted to by others, some of whom are people with whom the person is actually in relationship (e.g. friends, colleagues) but some also being 'internalized others' (e.g. mental images of parents or other significant others). The person then perceives the response of these others, and not only cognitively interprets that response but also has a feeling or emotional reaction to it. These inner experiences are assimilated into the self-concept, and the process resumes.

At the heart of the self-confirmation model is that at all these stages the person acts in order to prevent outcomes which are dissonant or in conflict with his or her self-concept. Problems in living occur when the person engages in distortion at one or more of the stages in the feedback loop, in order to protect the self-concept from contradictory information from the environment. The objective of counselling or psychotherapy is, therefore, to enable the client to understand how self-confirmation operates in his or her life, and to change what is happening at those stages of the loop where the most serious distortion is occurring. The model enables an integration of a wide variety of therapeutic concepts and strategies, by providing a model which combines all of the issues (self-concept, motivation, behaviour, object relations and so forth) from all other models.

A third transtheoretical approach is *cognitive–analytic therapy* (CAT) (Ryle and Cowmeadow, 1992), originally developed by Ryle (1990). This model is based on some recent ideas from cognitive psychology, concerning the ways that people engage in intentional activity through sequences of mental and behavioural acts. In pursuing their life goals, people run into trouble when they encounter *traps*, *dilemmas* and *snags*. The psychoanalytic dimension of this model includes the

Freudian idea of defence mechanisms as examples of cognitive 'editing', and takes account of the origins of traps, dilemmas and snags in early parent–child interactions. In practice, CAT is implemented through brief (sixteen-session) therapy, which begins with an exploration of the life-history and current functioning of the client. This leads on to a *reformulation* of the difficulties being experienced by the client, in which the counsellor or therapist identifies targets for change.

By considering together these three integrative approaches, the Egan skilled helper model, the Andrews self-confirmation model and Ryle's CAT, some of the fundamental difficulties involved in integration can be examined. Although all three models successfully integrate previously existing sets of ideas, they all arrive at a different result regarding a suitable overarching concept or principle. In effect, Egan, Andrews and Ryle have arrived at new theories of therapy. In doing so, they have inevitably fragmented the counselling and therapy world even further. It is noticeable, for example, that little or no research has been conducted into the Egan model, even though it has been in use for some time, and there exists a wealth of research studies into cognitive–behavioural therapy, which it resembles in important respects. The other notable feature of these integrative approaches is that they bring together some ideas but clearly reject others; they are partial integrations of previous theory.

The missing dimension: counsellor development

The search for ways to combine or synthesize the massive array of ideas and techniques in counselling and therapy is probably an inevitable consequence of the explosion of writing on therapy in the past thirty years. It seems reasonable to assume that these writers have not in reality all uncovered insights that are fresh and unique. There must be a broad area of common ground between many competing approaches. However, it may be inappropriate to assume that the integrationist urge must necessarily take the form of creating new theories, such as those presented by Egan, Andrews and Ryle. A more fertile approach to understanding integrationism may be to view it as a personal process undertaken by individual counsellors and therapists.

Several writers have commented that one of the central tasks for any counsellor is to develop his or her own *personal* approach. Smail (1978) and Lomas (1981) have been particularly insistent that theory and techniques must be assimilated into the person of the therapist. Lomas (1981: 3) writes that the essence of counselling or therapy is 'the manifestation of creative human qualities' rather than the operation of technical procedures. In Chapter 12, the idea of the *counsellor's journey* is introduced as a way of understanding the development in counsellors of a professional identity. On this journey, there may be times when particular areas of theory and technique may resonate with developments in the personal life of the counsellor, and lead to the cultivation of particular knowledge and skills, or the adoption of a specific approach. The autobiographical essays included in Dryden and Spurling (1989) illustrate some of the ways in which professional interests interact with personal needs to create a unique professional identity.

It would appear to be necessary, therefore, to regard eclecticism and integration not as abstract theoretical exercises, but as choices intimately connected with the process of counsellor development. Significantly, the literature on therapeutic convergence is dominated by the writings of mature 'master' therapists who have had the benefit of extensive training and are able to employ a sophisticated and highly differentiated conceptual map in making sense of the similarities and differences between alternative theories and techniques. Such individuals are not in the majority in the world of counselling. Often, counsellors working in an eclectic mode may be relatively inexperienced and have limited training in the techniques they are employing. A great many counsellors have been trained within a generic skills model, of the kind described by Culley (1992). This kind of training package usually consists of a combination of ideas from person-centred and cognitive–behavioural approaches, but focused on practical skills at the expense of theoretical understanding. Although research evidence is lacking, it is not uncommon for counsellors initially trained in a generic model to choose later in their career to specialize in a pure, brand-name approach, as a means of consolidating their professional identity and sense of competence.

Conclusion: the future of integrationism

It should be clear that there is no one 'eclectic' or 'integrated' approach to counselling. There is, rather, a powerful trend towards finding ways of combining the valuable ideas and techniques developed within separate schools and approaches. At the same time, however, there are also strong forces within the counselling and psychotherapy world acting in the direction of maintaining the purity of single-approach training institutes, professional associations and publications networks. The only prediction that would appear warranted would be that this tension between integration and purity is unlikely to disappear, and that it is to be welcomed as a sign of how creative and lively this field of study is at this time.

Beyond the current debates over eclecticism and integrationism is a broader historical perspective. The intellectual history of counselling and psychotherapy is not extensive. Psychoanalysis is about 100 years old, humanistic approaches have been established for forty years, cognitive models came on the scene less than thirty years ago. If the founders of an approach, and their first generation of students, usually fight to establish the distinctiveness and uniqueness of their creation, and subsequent generations of adherents become secure enough to feel less threatened about making links with other approaches, then we are only just entering a period when such collaborations are even possible. This trend has, of course, been complicated and slowed down by the tendency towards splitting and factionalism in the therapy world. But it may well be that we are beginning to see the beginnings of an emergent consensus over the aims, concepts and methods of counselling and psychotherapy. Yet, as the study of group dynamics demonstrates, true consensus is only possible when differences are acknowledged and respected.

Finally, the trend towards integrationism and eclecticism has important practical implications in the area of counsellor training. Is it possible to train counsellors to an adequate level of competence in a range of different techniques? Are beginning counsellors in a position to appreciate the theoretical issues involved in integrating different theoretical models? Can supervisors or tutors appropriately assess the work of trainees who use their own idiosyncratic integration of ideas? These issues will be addressed in Chapter 13.

Questions for reflection and discussion

1 Where do you stand on the question of eclecticism and integration? In terms of your own current counselling work is it more useful to keep to one approach, or to combine different approaches? Might this change in the future?
2 John Norcross (in Dryden, 1991: 13) has stated that 'a single unifying theory for all psychotherapies is neither viable nor desirable in my opinion'. Do you agree?

SEVEN

DISCRIMINATION, DISADVANTAGE AND DIFFERENCE IN COUNSELLING

In Chapter 1 a brief sketch was offered of the historical development of counselling and psychotherapy within Western industrial society. In this chapter, to that earlier account of some of the social, economic and political factors which have shaped counselling will be added a consideration of the influence of race, gender, sexual orientation and other social categories. The importance for counsellors and counselling of an understanding of social factors cannot be underestimated. Both the clients who come for counselling and the counsellors themselves are participants in social life and bearers of the attitudes, values and behaviours espoused by the particular social groups to which they belong. The power of any social system to shape or determine the lives of its members is immense.

On the whole, the theory and practice of counselling and psychotherapy have served the dominant groups in society and largely ignored the problems of people who are disadvantaged or discriminated against. A theme throughout this chapter will be the lack of research articles, or even general articles in professional journals, devoted to this area. In this chapter counselling issues arising from work with clients from a range of different categories of social disadvantage will be discussed. Following this, various options for increasing the relevance and accessibility of counselling for such clients will be explored.

Social class

Research is the USA, reviewed by Bromley (1983) and Garfield (1986), has found that counselling and psychotherapy services are most widely used by people in middle and upper income and social class groups, either because others do not seek therapy or because when they do seek therapy they are more likely to be refused or offered drug treatment. Lower-class clients are also more likely to drop out of counselling prematurely. Why does this happen?

From surveys carried out in both the USA and Britain, there is ample evidence that there is a strong association between social class and mental health, with people of lower social class being more likely to be hospitalized for a psychiatric problem and reporting higher levels of symptoms in community studies (Cochrane, 1983). Sociologists interested in social class and mental health have proposed two alternative models for explaining these differences. The first is known as the 'social causation' hypothesis, and views the high levels of psychological disturbance in working-class people as caused by poverty, poor housing and other environmental factors. Although the social causation seems highly plausible on common-sense grounds, there is significant evidence which would appear to contradict it. Several pieces of research, for example Goldberg and Morrison (1963), have found that although the social class distribution of psychiatric patients is weighted towards a high representation of lower-class individuals, the social class distribution of the parents of these patients resembles the class distribution in the general population. This type of result has led to the development of what is known as the 'social selection' or 'drift' hypothesis, which suggests that the high numbers of disturbed people in lower-class groups is caused by the inability of these people, because of their illness, to maintain the social class and income levels of their family of origin. In this model, the downward 'drift' is understood to be at least partly caused by genetic factors.

Substantial efforts have been expended in attempts to test these competing hypotheses but have failed to reach an unequivocal answer (see Cochrane (1983) and Lorion and Felner (1986) for reviews and further discussion). The significance of these studies for counselling is that they have a direct bearing on the aims of counselling and the attitudes of counsellors towards lower-class clients. From a social selection point of view, counselling or psychotherapy is likely to be of very limited utility for lower-class clients, because of the lack of personal resources and history of failure experienced by the client. From a social causation perspective, by contrast, counselling may have a lot to offer in empowering clients to cope with their current situation and fulfil their potential.

The debate over social class and mental illness illustrates well the political ideologies underlying this area of research and practice. Most counsellors and psychotherapists are middle class, and have undergone several years of professional education and training. Their world-view, personal values and way of using language are quite different from those of working-class clients. Where counselling and psychotherapy agencies use client assessment and diagnosis to screen applicants for therapy, there is evidence that working-class people are more likely to be referred elsewhere or allocated to drug treatment rather than individual therapy (Bromley, 1983).

Perhaps the most obvious explanation for the different patterns of diagnosis and treatment in different social classes is the *gatekeeper* theory. The professional providers of counselling and psychotherapy are themselves middle class and therefore find it more congenial to work with clients or patients from similar backgrounds. Middle-class and educated clients are possibly more articulate and assertive in seeking out counselling, or may be better informed about its benefits. Finally, the costs of regular visits, which could include time off work, travel and childcare costs (even when the counselling itself might be free), to a counsellor or therapist may be beyond the means of people on low incomes.

These are all factors that prevent working-class clients from entering counselling.

The attitudes and expectations of working-class clients regarding the counselling process have also received some attention. It is often said that psychoanalysis, for example, is more acceptable to highly educated intellectual and artistic clients, whereas people from lower-class or less educated groups prefer counselling that is more directive, structured and advice-giving in nature. There is, however, very little evidence to support this proposition (Bromley, 1983).

Probably the most important aspect of social class in relation to counselling is that working-class clients will almost always find themselves with middle-class counsellors. As an occupational group, counsellors are almost entirely middle class. Even counsellors from families of working-class origin will usually have entered counselling through higher education or primary training in a profession such as nursing, the Church, teaching or social work. This may make it difficult for the counsellor to empathize with the needs and aspirations of the working-class client (e.g. for financial security rather than personal fulfilment).

There have been few attempts to develop a theoretical understanding of the issues involved in counselling people from lower-class groups, a situation that Pilgrim (1992) attributes to the general avoidance of political issues by counsellors and psychotherapists. However, Arsenian and Arsenian (1948) suggested that it is necessary for therapists to grasp the difference between 'tough' and 'easy' cultures. In a 'tough' social environment, people have fewer options open for satisfying their needs, those options which are available do not reliably lead to desired outcomes, and the link between action and goal achievement can be difficult to identify. Living in such a culture results in feelings of frustration and low self-esteem. The lack of positive expectations for the future and belief in the efficacy of personal action resulting from socialization in a tough culture would make counselling more difficult. Meltzer (1978) has argued that social class differences in psychotherapy are due to linguistic factors. Research carried out by Bernstein (1972) found that communication in working-class cultures took place through a 'restricted' code, which is largely limited to describing concrete, here-and-now events rather than engaging in reflexive, abstract thought. The implication for counselling of this linguistic theory is that working-class language does not lend itself to 'insight' or exploratory therapies, and that clients from this group would be better served by behaviour therapy or family therapy (Bromley, 1983).

It is necessary to treat these analyses of working-class personality and communication style with considerable caution. The characteristics that are interpreted as deficits of working-class culture can equally well be seen as assets. For example, middle-class people who grow up in an 'easy' culture can become narcissistic and self-absorbed. Similarly, the capacity of middle-class people to engage in abstract intellectualization, rather than describing their concrete experience, is viewed by many counsellors as a barrier to effective work. It may be more correct to regard these ideas as indicative of potential areas of mismatch between counsellors and clients. In this respect, it is relevant to note that, in her study *Therapy in the Ghetto*, Lener (1972) found a strong relationship between client improvement and 'democratic attitudes' in their therapists. The effective therapists in this study were those who were able to reach out across the class divide and accept their clients.

The report by Holland (1979) of a counselling centre that operated in a deprived area of London draws a number of relevant conclusions concerning the adaptation of counselling methods in such a setting. Holland noted that many clients preferred to see a counsellor once or twice, and then to return some time later for additional help, rather than entering into continuing long-term work. Some clients would not commit themselves to a formal counselling contract, although they would talk at length to staff about themselves and their problems if given informal opportunities to do so. The common factor in both these observations would appear to be the importance for the client of remaining in control of the counselling relationship. Working-class clients may have been on the receiving end of many welfare agencies and government departments that will have treated them as 'cases' and taken decisions on their behalf.

Counselling women

In contrast to the field of social class and counselling, the significance of gender in counselling has been the source of a great deal of theory and research over the past twenty years. This work has explored two main areas of interest: the development of a feminist approach to counselling and psychotherapy, and the impact on process and outcome of the gender match (or mismatch) of counsellor and client.

At a theoretical level, the feminist re-examination of psychoanalysis carried out by Mitchell (1974) has been followed by a steady stream of publications devoted to integrating feminist principles with psychotherapeutic (usually psychodynamic) practice. These theoretical studies have involved carrying out a systematic critique of male-dominated approaches, as well as constructing an explicitly feminist alternative. The feminist critique of psychoanalysis has, for example, drawn attention to the intensely sexist basis of Freud's concept of 'penis envy', and to the fact that the memories of child sexual abuse reported by many women (and some men) clients are not, as Freud supposed, based in fantasy but are real memories of actual events. The feminist critique of conventional sex therapy has drawn attention to the 'phallocentric' assumptions made by most sex therapists (Tiefer, 1988; Stock, 1988). Another element in the development of an approach to counselling which acknowledges that there can be fundamental differences between male and female experience in society has been the giving of emphasis in theory and research to issues which particularly affect women. For example, in recent years there has been a major growth in theory and practice relating to 'women's' issues, such as working with rape and sexual abuse survivors, depression, women's drinking and assertiveness (Howell and Bayes, 1981; Rosewater and Walker, 1985).

Virtually all of the key historical figures in counselling and psychotherapy have been men, and they have written, whether consciously or not, from a male perspective. There have been extensive efforts by women writers and practitioners to envision theories and approaches in counselling and psychotherapy that are more consistent with the experiences and needs of women. Many of these efforts were inspired by the consolidation of feminism in the 1960s as a central force for social change. The work of feminist authors such as Simone de Beauvoir, Germaine Greer, Kate Millett and others encouraged female psychologists and therapists to look again at established ideas in these disciplines. It would be mistaken to assume, however, that women had no voice at all in counselling and psychotherapy before that time. Within the psychoanalytic movement, Melanie Klein and Karen Horney had played a crucial role in emphasizing the part of the mother in child development. Other women therapists, such as Laura Perls, Zerka Moreno and Virginia Axline, had been important contributors to the founding of Gestalt therapy, psychodrama, and client-centred therapy respectively, but had received much less attention than the men alongside whom they had worked.

The guiding force behind most contemporary work on women and counselling has, nevertheless, been feminism. The basic assumption of feminism is that, in the great majority of cultures, women are systematically oppressed and exploited. Howell (1981) describes this state of affairs as 'the cultural devaluation of women'; other people would label it as 'sexism'. Feminists have approached the problem of sexism from several directions. The ways in which a male-dominated social order is created and maintained have been subjected to critical analysis. A language for describing and understanding the experience of women has been created. Finally, new forms of social action and social institutions have been invented with the aim of empowering women. All these aspects of the feminist agenda have been pursued within counselling and psychotherapy.

The field of mental health affords multiple examples of the oppression and exploitation of women. There is ample evidence of experimentation on and sexual abuse of women clients and patients (Masson, 1984; Showalter, 1985). Studies of perceptions of mental health in women have shown that mental health workers view women in general as more neurotic and less well-adjusted than men (Broverman et al., 1970). The psychiatric and mental health professions, which provide the intellectual and institutional context for counselling and psychotherapy, can be seen to be no less sexist than any other sector of society.

Moving more specifically to counselling and psychotherapy, there has been a powerful re-examination of theoretical assumptions, particularly those of psychoanalysis, from a feminist point of view. Two of the fundamental ideas in psychoanalysis have received special attention: the concept of penis envy, and the formulation of childhood sexuality. The notion of penis envy was used by Freud to explain the development of femininity in girls. Freud supposed that when a little girl first saw a penis, she would be 'overcome by envy' (Freud, 1905). As a result of this sense of inferiority, the girl would recognize that

> this is a point on which she cannot compete with boys, and that it would be therefore best for her to give up the idea of doing so. Thus the little girl's recognition of the anatomical distinction between the sexes forces her away from masculinity and masculine masturbation on to new lines which lead to the development of femininity.
>
> (Freud, 1924: 340)

These 'new lines' included a motivation to look attractive to compensate for the missing penis, and a tendency to a less mature type of moral sensitivity due to the absence of the castration anxiety, which Freud saw as such an important element in male moral development.

From a contemporary perspective the penis envy hypothesis seems incredible, ludicrous and objectionable. However, such was the domination of Freud that this doctrine remained in force within the psychoanalytic movement for many years after his death (Howell, 1981). It was only in the writings of Mitchell (1974) that a thorough critique of this aspect of Freudian theory was carried out.

It is possible to regard the penis envy hypothesis as an example of a lack of understanding of women in Freudian theory, an ill-conceived idea which can be reviewed and corrected without threat to the theory as a whole. The other main feminist objection to psychoanalysis is, however, much more fundamental. In the early years of psychoanalysis, Freud had worked with a number of women patients who had reported distressing memories of sexual attacks on them which had taken place in their childhood. Freud was uncertain how to interpret these memories, but in the end came to the conclusion that the childhood events which these women were reporting could not have taken place. Freud, at heart, could not believe that middle-class, socially respectable men could engage in this kind of behaviour. Freud therefore interpreted these reports as 'screen memories', or fantasies constructed to conceal the true nature of what had taken place, which was the acting out by the child of her own sexual motives. From a modern perspective, when so much more is known about the prevalence of child sexual abuse and the barriers of secrecy, collusion and adult disbelief which confront child victims, the classical Freudian approach to this issue can be seen to be deeply mistaken. Masson (1984), one of the leading critics of this aspect of Freudian theory, was driven to label this set of ideas an 'assault on truth'.

Through time, many women therapists came to agree with Taylor, M. (1991: 96) that 'a careful reading of Freud's writings reveals that he thoroughly rejected women as full human-beings.' The next step, the construction of an alternative feminist approach to counselling and psychotherapy, was based on the work of key figures such as Miller (1976), Gilligan (1982) and Chodorow (1978). Feminist counselling and therapy has been described by Llewelyn and Osborn (1983) as being built on four basic assumptions about the social experience of women:

1 Women are consistently in a position of deference to men. For example, women tend to have less power or status in work situations. Miller (1987) has observed that women who seek to be powerful rather than passive are viewed as selfish, destructive and unfeminine.
2 Women are expected to be aware of the feelings of others, and to supply emotional nurturing to others, especially men.
3 Women are expected to be 'connected' to men, so that the achievement of autonomy is difficult.
4 The issue of sexuality is enormously problematic for women. This factor arises from a social context in which images of idealized women's bodies are used

to sell commodities, assertive female sexuality is threatening to many men, and sexual violence against women is widespread.

The theoretical framework developed by feminists to articulate the psychological dimensions of these social inequalities has largely been constructed around a core concept of 'relatedness' or 'self-in-relation' (Miller, 1976). In her study of gender differences in moral reasoning, for example, Gilligan (1982) found that, in general, men make moral judgements based on criteria of fairness and rights, while women assess moral dilemmas according to a sense of responsibility in relationships. The male way of looking at things, in Gilligan's (1982) words, 'protects separateness', and the female way 'sustains connections'. Gilligan goes on from this finding to suggest that men and women use different styles of constructing social reality: men fear intimacy, women fear isolation.

Miller (1976) and colleagues from the Stone Centre at Wellesley College in Massachussetts (e.g. Kaplan, 1987) have explored the implications of this 'relational' perspective in understanding patterns of development in childhood. They conclude that there is a basic difference between social development in boys and girls. For a girl, the relationship with the primary caretaker, the mother, is one of mutuality. Both are the same sex, both are engaged in, or preparing to be engaged in (Chodorow, 1978), the tasks of mothering and nurturing. For boys the situation is one of achieving development and maturity only through increasing separation and autonomy from the mother. Men, as a result, are socialized into a separate, isolated way of being, and in counselling need help to understand and maintain relationships. Women, by contrast, spend their formative years in a world of relationships and connectedness, and in counselling need help to achieve autonomy.

This is a necessarily oversimplified account of a complex and powerful theoretical model. Nevertheless, taken together with an awareness of social factors as discussed by Llewelyn and Osborn (1983) and Taylor (1990, 1991), it can be seen that it points the way towards a distinctive approach to feminist counselling. Although it is probably misleading to imagine that there is one agreed, 'textbook', feminist mode of counselling, many women practitioners would agree with the following guidelines (Worell, 1981):

• An egalitarian relationship with shared responsibility between counsellor and client. For example, being cautious about the imposition of interpretations on the client's experience.
• Using a consciousness-raising approach. For example, differentiating between personal problems and political or social issues.
• Helping women to explore and express their personal power.
• Helping women to get in touch with unexpressed anger.
• Assisting women to define themselves apart from their role relationships to men, home and children.
• Encouraging women to nurture themselves as well as others.
• Promoting skills development in areas such as assertiveness and employment.

Another, more controversial corollary of feminist therapy theory is the argument that, if women are specialists in being in relationship, and if counselling is in essence a relational process, then it follows that women should be, on the whole, more effective counsellors than men (Collier, 1987).

It could well be argued that feminist perspectives have represented the most significant area of advance in counselling theory and practice over the past ten or fifteen years. Apart from the theoretical ideas contributed by Miller (1976) and others, feminist practitioners have been responsible for opening up counselling to new groups of clients, including women undergoing surgical procedures such as mastectomy or hysterectomy, survivors of sexual abuse and rape, and women from ethnic minority groups (see Howell and Bayes, 1981; Braude, 1987).

Sexual orientation

The social world in which counselling has developed over the past century is a world marked by a high degree of homophobia. Many industrial societies still enforce laws that restrict or criminalize homosexual behaviour, and there is widespread stigmatization of gay and lesbian relationships, despite the fact that around 10 per cent of the population is homosexual. Although gay and lesbian clients in counselling will seek help for the same wide range of general relationship, self-esteem and stress problems felt by heterosexual people, there are some distinctive issues which may be presented by clients from this group. These include dilemmas and anxieties about the process of 'coming out' and accepting a gay or lesbian identity. There may be additional problems for the heterosexual counsellor of being aware of his or her own possible homophobia, and achieving an understanding of the language and norms of gay and lesbian sub-cultures.

Many lesbian and gay counselling agencies have been set up to offer telephone or face-to-face counselling and self-help support networks. This trend has been motivated in part by the hostility to homosexuals shown by the mental health profession. It was only in 1974 that homosexuality ceased being classified as a psychiatric disorder by the American Psychiatric Association (Bayer, 1987). The considerable opposition to this change included psychoanalysts and psychotherapists as well as 'medical model' psychiatrists. The founder of rational emotive therapy, Albert Ellis, was also in the 1950s a proponent of the view that exclusive homosexuality was a neurotic disorder that could be resolved through effective psychotherapy (Bayer, 1987). Mainstream counselling research, training and practice largely ignore the existence or needs of non-heterosexual clients. For example, in a survey of articles published between 1978 and 1989 in the six most widely read and prestigious counselling psychology journals, Buhrke et al. (1992) found that out of a total of 6661 articles and reports, only 43 (0.65 per cent) focused on lesbian and gay issues in any way. The majority of these articles were theoretical discussions or reviews of the literature, rather than empirical studies of counselling process or outcome. Over one-third of the articles over this twelve-year period had appeared in one special issue of the *Journal of Counseling and Development* (Dworkin and Gutierrez, 1989).

Counsellors working with gay and lesbian clients have evolved an 'affirmative' (Hall and Fradkin, 1992) stance towards the problems presented by clients. A key element in the approach is to reinforce the validity and acceptability of homosexual behaviour and relationships. To accomplish this, it is often necessary to challenge the homophobic attitudes which the client has internalized through socialization. The provision of accurate information about homosexuality can often be a part of this process, as is sensitive rehearsal with the counsellor of how the client will tell others about his or her decision to come out. Many counsellors working with gay and lesbian clients adopt a developmental approach, viewing the experience of 'coming out' as a set of developmental tasks. The model of coming out constructed by Coleman (1982) has been widely utilized in counselling. Coleman (1982) postulates five developmental stages in the coming-out process: pre-coming out, coming out, exploration, first relationships and integration. Other issues that are often present in counselling gay and lesbian clients include family conflicts, sexual problems, attitudes to ageing and coping with AIDS/HIV (Coleman, 1988; Harrison, 1987).

Ethnicity

Racism is part of the value system and fabric of contemporary society, and represents a factor of enormous significance for counselling. Counselling remains a predominantly 'white' occupation, with relatively few black counsellors or black clients. Racial and ethnic minority research is significantly under-represented in the professional literature (Ponterotto, 1988). On the other hand, there has in recent years been an increasing awareness in counselling of the importance of cultural differences between counsellors and clients. The work in this area has been variously described as concerned with 'cross-cultural' (Pedersen, 1985), 'intercultural' (Kareem and Littlewood, 1992) or 'transcultural' (d'Ardenne and Mahtani, 1989) counselling, or focused on 'cultural difference' (Sue, 1981) or 'ethnic minorities' (Ramirez, 1991). Each of these labels has its own unique meaning, but all these approaches are essentially exploring the same set of issues regarding the impact of race, culture and ethnic identity on the counselling process.

Some of the dilemmas that emerge in cross-cultural counsellor–client interactions are described by d'Ardenne and Mahtani (1989). These include: using appropriate names and forms of address, deciding on whether to use an interpreter, dealing with different assumptions about the helping process, and negotiating differences in non-verbal communication and time boundaries. Behind these tangible and practical issues, which can stand in the way of establishing an effective therapeutic alliance, there lie less concrete factors associated with the attitudes and knowledge of the counsellor. If counsellors are to respond in ethnically sensitive ways, it is useful for them to possess accurate information about the cultural background of clients. However, counsellors also need to be aware of their own stereotypes, attitudes and feelings in relation to people from other ethnic groups. Given the racist and nationalist nature of

Western industrial society, it is likely that these attitudes will contain at least some elements of rejection.

The client, too, may have difficulties in accepting and trusting the counsellor. As d'Ardenne and Mehtani (1989: 78) write:

> clients who have had a lifetime of cultural and racial prejudice will bring the scars of these experiences to the [therapeutic] relationship. For the most part, counsellors are from the majority culture, and will be identified with white racist society. Thus, counsellors are seen by their clients as both part of the problem and part of the solution.

This ambivalence toward the counsellor may well be exhibited in resistance, or transference reactions. There is some evidence from research studies to suggest that black clients seeking help from 'majority culture' agencies will drop out of treatment more quickly than white clients (Sattler, 1977; Abramowitz and Murray, 1983). There is also evidence that in these situations black clients receive more severe diagnostic labels and are more likely than white clients to be offered drug treatment rather than therapy, or to be referred to a non-professional counsellor rather than a professional (Atkinson, 1985). Research studies have also shown that clients tend to prefer counsellors from the same ethnic group (Harrison, 1975). In one study, Sue *et al.* (1991) checked the client files of 600,000 users of therapy services from the Los Angeles County Department of Mental Health between 1973 and 1988. Ethnic match between client and therapist was strongly associated with length of stay in treatment (i.e. fewer early drop-outs). For those clients whose primary language was not English, ethnic match was also associated with better therapy outcomes.

While acknowledging that clients from ethnic minority groups represent a wide variety of diverse cultural communities, Ramirez (1991) argues that the common theme running through all cross-cultural counselling is the challenge of living in a multicultural society. He proposes that a central aim in working with clients from all ethnic groups should be the development of 'cultural flexibility'. Ramirez (1991) points out that even members of a dominant, majority culture report the experience of 'feeling different', of a sense of mismatch between who we are and what other people expect from us. Within the field of cross-cultural counselling, Ramirez (1991) uses the distinction between *traditional* and *modern* cultures as a way of defining the nature of cultural flexibility. Both types of culture embody distinctive, contrasting sets of values and beliefs, styles of cognition and communication, and family structures. Some of the differences Ramirez has observed between behaviour in the counselling of 'traditional' and 'modern' clients are listed in Table 6.

The counselling approach taken by Ramirez (1991) involves the counsellor matching the cultural and cognitive style of the client in initial settings, then moving on to inform the client about the cultural flexibility model, and to encourage experimentation with different forms of cultural behaviour. This approach obviously requires a high degree of self-awareness and cultural flexibility on the part of the therapist.

A distinctive feature of the cross-cultural approach to counselling is its

Table 6 Behaviour in counselling of clients from traditional and modern cultural backgrounds

Traditional	Modern
Behaves deferentially towards the therapist	Seeks to establish equal status with the therapist
Expects the therapist to do most of the talking	Does most of the talking
Appears shy and self-controlling	Appears assertive and self-confident
Is observant of social environment	Seems to ignore social environment
Focuses on important others in relating reason(s) for seeking therapy	Focuses on self in relating reason(s) for seeking therapy

Source: Ramirez (1991)

recognition of the value of indigenous modes of helping. Every ethnic and cultural group contains its own approach to understanding and supporting people with emotional and psychological problems, and counsellors can draw upon these resources, such as traditional healers, religious groups and social networks, when working with clients (d'Ardenne and Mahtani, 1989). It is also possible to integrate indigenous and Western counselling approaches, to create a mode of help that is tailored to meet the needs of a specific client group.

The field of cross-cultural counselling has received relatively little attention in the research literature. In addition, many counselling agencies and individual counsellors in private practice have so many clients applying from their majority cultural group that there is little incentive for them to develop expertise in cross-cultural work. The multicultural nature of contemporary society, and the existence of large groups of dispossessed exiles and refugees experiencing profound hopelessness and loss, make this an increasingly important area for future investment in theory, research and practice.

Religious orientation

Religion may often represent a core element in the distinctive social identity of an ethnic group. Alternatively, some ethnic groups are fragmented into many competing religious sub-groups or sects, and there are world religions that unite many diverse races and ethnic groups. On the whole, counselling and counsellors have been reluctant to be explicit in addressing religious concerns. It has already been suggested in Chapter 1 that many of the values and practices of counselling have been derived from the Judaeo-Christian religious tradition. These influences have been disguised by the generally scientific, humanistic and secular framework provided by counselling theory. Although surveys of religious affiliation and activity in counsellors and psychotherapists carried out in the 1960s and 1970s found lower levels of religious affiliation than in the general population (Henry *et al.*, 1971; Bergin, 1980), more recent surveys have found an increasing interest in and commitment to religious and spiritual values and beliefs, with counsellors and psychotherapists now demonstrating equivalent levels to the population at large (Bergin and Jensen, 1990; Shafranske and Malony, 1990).

Several writers and practitioners have addressed the question of how existing counselling techniques or approaches can be adapted to meet the needs of clients from particular religious groups, for example Mormons (Koltko, 1990) and Christian fundamentalists (Young, 1988; Moyers, 1990). These approaches have concentrated on acquiring a comprehensive understanding of the beliefs and way of life of clients from such backgrounds, to facilitate the understanding of client symptoms.

Other writers have explored the possibilities for modifying established counselling principles in work with clients with specific religious value systems and behaviours (Stern, 1985). Another strategy has been to attempt to integrate ideas from both religion and counselling, with the intention of developing a new and more effective approach. One example of this type of direction is the Christian counselling movement. Johnson and Ridley (1992) have identified four sources of benefit to clients that can result from integrating Christian beliefs with counselling practice.

1 The accommodation of Christian beliefs and values within established counselling techniques and approaches. An example of this strategy can be found in a study by Propst *et al.* (1992), in which religious cognitive–behavioural therapy was offered to depressed clients, all of whom labelled themselves as actively Christian. This therapeutic intervention consisted of standard techniques derived from cognitive therapy (Beck *et al.*, 1979) and RET (Ellis, 1962), but with religious arguments supplied to counter irrational thoughts and religious images suggested to facilitate positive change. Clients in a comparison group received the same cognitive–behavioural treatment, but without religious imagery or rationales. Although clients in both groups reported significant benefit from the therapy, those who had received religious therapy showed slightly higher rates of improvement. One additional point of interest from the Probst *et al.* (1992) study was that even the non-religious therapists achieved good results when using a religious approach. Another example of an accommodation strategy can be found in a psychodynamic approach to pastoral counselling, in which the stories or narratives told by clients are interpreted in the light of religious stories and teachings (Foskett and Lyall, 1988; Foskett and Jacobs, 1989).

2 Mobilizing hope. Yalom (1980, 1986) has argued that hope can enable the client to enter and stay in counselling, and increases compliance with therapeutic interventions. Christian beliefs and practices, such as prayer, can be a powerful source of hope for the future.

3 The use of scriptural truth. Christian counsellors and clients believe that the Bible can provide guidelines for action and explanations for problems.

4 Intervention by a divine agent. Some Christian counselling approaches seek to facilitate inner healing through the acceptance of a divine agent, such as God, Jesus or the Holy Spirit.

The integration of an explicitly Christian approach to counselling can be seen to offer 'resources for mental health or well-being that are not available to the non-believer' (Jeske, 1984). If the efficacy of non-religious counselling can be viewed as depending on the resources of the counsellor and client, then religious counselling introduces a third type of resource: an external, transcendent power. From a theoretical perspective, this idea is difficult to assimilate into mainstream counselling approaches. It is just not included in the 'image of the person' implicit in psychodynamic, person-centred or cognitive–behavioural theory. This discrepancy can be overcome by reinterpreting familiar counselling concepts from a Christian standpoint. For example, Malony (1983: 275) has written that 'to the degree that empathic understanding, therapeutic congruence, acceptance, permissiveness and unconditional positive regard exist in the therapeutic hour, there God is present.' It is also possible to interpret religious statements from a psychological standpoint. The 'twelve step' programme for change employed by Alcoholics Anonymous, for example, includes the suggestion that the alcoholic's behaviour is controlled by a higher power. The effects of this piece of 'cognitive reframing', according to Mack (1981), are to give the person who has difficulty controlling his or her drinking a means of 'governing the self' that is not dependent on personal will power or social sanctions.

So far this discussion has concentrated on Christian approaches to counselling. It is worth noting that there do not appear to have been any systematic published attempts to look at counselling from an Islamic, Hindu or Sikh perspective. Surprisingly, given the over-representation, compared to the general population, of practitioners from Jewish backgrounds in surveys of counsellors and therapists (Henry et al., 1971; Bergin and Jensen 1990; Shafranske and Malony, 1990), there have been few publications on Jewish counselling. There has, however, been substantial interest in the relationship between Buddhism and Western psychotherapy and counselling (Suzuki et al., 1970), but this has consisted for the most part of incorporating ideas and techniques from Buddhism into therapy offered to non-Buddhist clients, rather than attempting to develop services for clients from that religious persuasion itself.

Another dimension of the relationship between religion and counselling has been the insistence of a number of practitioners and theorists that counselling itself is incomplete if it does not give serious consideration to the spiritual aspects of human existence. Bergin (1980) has made a useful distinction between spirituality and religiosity, with the former being concerned with a personal quest for transcendent meaning, while the latter refers to participation in organized religious institutions. An acknowledgement of the spiritual dimension of existence has become a highly significant theme in contemporary counselling and therapy (see Chapter 5).

Other sources of social disadvantage and difference

There are many other social groups that could be discussed in this chapter. For example, the counselling needs of older people represent an important area of work (Knight, 1986; Hanley and Gilhooley, 1986). Counselling and therapy around explicitly male issues is also beginning to receive some attention (Scher *et al.*, 1987; Fine, 1988). The issues arising from counselling with people with learning difficulties and physical handicaps would also repay further consideration if space was available.

Approaches to anti-discriminatory practice in counselling

One of the themes that emerges from this examination of counselling with people from different social groups is that traditional approaches to counselling can be seen to discriminate against those in society who are disadvantaged or marginalized. There are many reasons for this. The historical origins of psychiatry and psychotherapy, reviewed in Chapter 1, suggest that mental health services have often been used to confine, or hide from view, people who do not conform to the requirements or standards of capitalist, industrial society. The founders of psychotherapy and counselling, key figures like Freud, Rogers and Ellis, were limited by their own socialization and world-view. Ultimately, therapy reflects the prejudices and discrimination of the society within which it exists.

There have, however, been many attempts to introduce anti-discriminatory practice and procedures into the field of counselling. Most of these endeavours have been specific to particular areas, such as work with women and working-class or ethnic minority clients. Nevertheless, although the areas of application have differed, a number of general strategies can be identified. There are five distinctive forms which anti-discriminatory programmes have taken: constructing a critique of mainstream or 'majority' theory and practice; awareness training for counsellors; development of new counselling techniques; the adaptation of existing services and agencies to meet the needs of previously excluded client groups; and the creation of new, specialist agencies and services.

Critiques of mainstream, 'majority' theory and practice

Often the first steps in initiating change involve not direct action but creating a framework for understanding what is happening, and how things might be different. Counsellors and therapists committed to opening up access to counselling for members of disadvantaged groups have engaged in a number of activities designed to change the prevailing climate of opinion in their professional organizations. These activities have included publishing critical reinterpretations of theory, carrying out research into the needs and problems of the particular client group, arranging debates at conferences and in professional journals, and pressurizing committees to accept changes to discriminatory regulations and procedures. Examples of this type of enterprise can be seen in the fight to de-pathologize homosexuality (Bayer, 1987), the publication of the classic text on cross-cultural counselling by Sue (1981), and the feminist attack on Freudian theory (Howell, 1981).

This phase of change can hold dangers for those people engaged in it, who may be risking their reputations and careers by espousing unpopular causes. There is also the possibility that little may be achieved beyond recognition that there is a problem. The critique must be followed up by appropriate action if it is to have an effect on the lives of clients. However, the existence of a plausible rationale for introducing new methods and services is of inestimable value to those who are in the position of having to justify and even defend their proposals in the field.

Awareness training for practitioners

In all these fields of anti-discriminatory practice, one of the first approaches to making practical change happen has been to set up training courses and workshops to enable counsellors to become more aware of their own prejudices and better informed on the needs of 'minority' clients. This is basically an individualistic solution to a social issue, but it is one that has great appeal to counsellors and therapists whose previous training has already prepared them to adopt an individualistic or psychologistic approach. The case for systematic racism awareness training for counsellors is made by Lago and Thompson (1989), who point out that such courses can be painful for participants, perhaps resulting in conflict with colleagues or family members and re-examination of core beliefs and assumptions.

LaFramboise and Foster (1992) describe four models for providing training in cultural awareness. The first is the 'separate course' model, where trainees take one specific module or workshop in cross-cultural issues. The second is the 'area of concentration' model, where trainees undertake a placement working with a particular ethnic minority group. The third is the 'interdisciplinary' model, in which trainees go outside the course and take a module or workshop run by an external college department or agency. Finally, there is the 'integration' model, which describes a situation where cross-cultural awareness is addressed in all parts of the course rather than being categorized as an option, or as outside the core curriculum. LaFramboise and Foster (1992) observe that, while integration represents an ideal, resource constraints and lack of suitably trained staff mean that the other models are more widely employed.

Harway (1979) and Frazier and Cohen (1992), writing from a feminist perspective, have suggested a set of revisions to existing counsellor training courses to make them more responsive to the counselling needs of women. Their model is just as appropriate as a way of promoting awareness of the needs of other 'minority' or disadvantaged client groups. They propose that training courses should:

- employ a significant proportion of 'minority' staff;
- enrol a significant proportion of 'minority' students;
- provide courses and placement experiences of the type outlined by LaFramboise and Foster (1992);
- encourage research on topics relevant to counselling with disadvantaged groups;

- provide library resources in these areas;
- require experiential sessions for both staff and students to facilitate examination of attitudes and stereotypes;
- encourage staff to use culturally aware language and teaching materials.

It is difficult to assess the effectiveness of cultural awareness training programmes. Few courses have been run, and there is an absence of research evidence regarding their impact on counselling practice. However, in one recent study, Wade and Bernstein (1991) provided brief (four-hour) training in cultural awareness to four women counsellors, two of whom were black and two white. Another four women counsellors, who did not receive the training, acted as a comparison group. The effectiveness of these counsellors was assessed through evaluating their work with eighty black women clients, who had presented at a counselling agency with personal and vocational problems. Results showed large differences in favour of the culturally trained counsellors, who were seen by clients as significantly more expert, attractive, trustworthy, empathic and accepting. The clients of the culturally aware counsellors reported themselves as being more satisfied with the counselling they had received, and were less likely to drop out of counselling prematurely. For this group of black women clients, the impact of training was more significant than the effect of racial similarity; the black counsellors who had received the training had higher success rates than those who had not. The Wade and Bernstein (1991) study illustrates that even very limited cultural awareness training can have measurable effects on counselling competence. Other studies are needed to assess the generalizability of this finding to other training packages and client groups.

The development of new counselling techniques

In many respects, the actual counselling process with a member of one of the disadvantage groups discussed earlier will be much the same as with any other client. However, one special feature is the tendency for the counsellor or therapist to encourage the client to be clear about the difference between personal problems and political/social realities. Holland (1990: 262) describes this as a distinction between *loss* and *expropriation*:

> In my work . . . we return over and over again to the same history of being separated from mothers, rejoining mothers that they did not know, leaving grandmothers they loved, finding themselves in a totally different relationship, being sexually abused, being put into care, and so on: all the kinds of circumstances with which clinicians working in this field are familiar. That is loss, but expropriation is what imperialism and neo-colonialism does – it steals one's history; it steals all kinds of things from black people, from people who don't belong to a white supremacist race.

Holland is here writing about her work with working-class black women in Britain. But the experience of having things stolen by powerful others is a common theme in the lives of those who are gay, lesbian or religiously differ-ent. Loss can be addressed and healed through therapy, but expropriation can only be remedied through social action. The theme of empowerment, within an individual life, through self-help groups or by political involvement, is therefore a distinctive and essential ingredient of this sphere of counselling.

Adapting existing services and agencies to meet the needs of previously excluded client groups

Counsellor awareness training is of fundamental importance, given that ethnocentric counsellor attitudes are sure to impede the formation of a good working relationship with clients from other cultures or social groups. There are, however, limits to what can be achieved through this strategy. No counsellor can acquire an adequate working knowledge of the social worlds of all the clients he or she might encounter. In any case, many clients prefer to have a counsellor who is similar to them in sexual orientation, social class or gender, or they may not believe that they will find in an agency someone who will understand their background or language. In response to these considerations, some counsellors have followed the strategy of aiming for organizational as well as individual change. To meet the needs of disadvantaged clients, they have attempted to adapt the structure and operation of their agencies.

Rogler *et al.* (1987) and Gutierrez (1992) describe a range of organizational strategies that have been adopted by counselling and therapy agencies to meet the needs of ethnic minority clients, and that are also applicable in other situations. One approach they describe focuses on the question of access. There can be many factors (financial, geographical, attitudinal) which prevent people from seeking help. Agencies can overcome these barriers through publicizing their services differently, employing outreach workers, hiring bilingual or bicultural staff, opening offices at more accessible sites and providing crèche facilities. A second level of organizational adaptation involves tailoring the counselling to the target client group. Services are modified to reflect the issues and problems experienced by a particular set of clients. One way of doing this is to offer courses or groups which are open to these people only, for example a bereavement group for older women, an assertiveness class for carers or a counselling programme for women with drink problems. Rogler *et al.* (1987) describe the invention of *cuento*, or folklore therapy, as a therapeutic intervention specifically designed to be of relevance to a disadvantaged group, in this case disturbed Hispanic children. This approach is based on cognitive–behavioural ideas about modelling appropriate behaviour, but the modelling is carried out through the telling of Puerto Rican folktales, followed up by discussion and role play.

A further stage in the adaptation of a counselling agency to the needs of minority clients occurs when the actual structure, philosophy or aims of the organization are changed in reaction to the inclusion within it of more and more members of formerly excluded groups. When this happens, initiatives of the type described above can no longer be marginal to the functioning of the organizations, but come to be seen as core activities. Gutierrez (1992: 330) suggests that without this kind of organizational development, 'efforts toward change can be mostly symbolic and marginal'.

Creating new specialist agencies

Within the world of counselling and therapy, existing agencies have generally had great difficulty in responding to the demands of minority clients. The direction that many socially aware counsellors have taken has been to set up specialist agencies which appeal to specific disadvantaged groups. There is a wide array of agencies that have grown up to provide counselling to women, people from different ethnic and religious communities, gay and lesbian people, and so on. These services are based on the recognition that many people will choose to see a counsellor who is similar to them. One of the difficulties these agencies face is that, usually, they are small and suffer recurring funding crises. They may also find it difficult to afford training and supervision.

Conclusions

The expansion of counselling and psychotherapy from the 1950s to the present has been largely achieved by responding to the needs of the better off members of dominant social groups in Western industrial nations. Counselling is now at a point where the huge gaps in provision and access for people who are disadvantaged or socially different can no longer be ignored. The task of revisioning counselling so that it is no longer 'monocultural' (Holdstock, 1990) is a massive undertaking, requiring a thoroughgoing critical re-examination of theory, research and practice.

Topics for reflection and discussion

1 Critics of counselling and psychotherapy have argued that these forms of response to personal problems ignore the social origins and conditions which ultimately produce these problems (Smail, 1991; Pilgrim, 1992). How successful, in your view, have the counsellors discussed in this chapter been in addressing this critique? How adequately have they demonstrated the relevance and value of counselling for their client groups?

2 Why is it important for people from minority or oppressed groups to receive counselling from someone from their own cultural background?

3 Discuss the strengths and weaknesses of different theoretical orientations in counselling with clients from disadvantaged groups. Is there a theoretical perspective which you find most (or least) applicable in this context?

4 Briefly list the categories of people to whom you feel you can readily offer a facilitative counselling relationship, and those with whom you would have greater difficulty in being congruent, empathic and accepting. Would you be willing to act as counsellor for members of these latter groups? What kinds of training or learning experiences would be necessary for you to change your perception of them?

EIGHT

THE ORGANIZATIONAL CONTEXT OF COUNSELLING

The theoretical models that were explored in earlier chapters tended to view counselling purely as a process which takes place in the immediate encounter between helper and client. The focus of these models is on what happens in the counselling room itself. They do not consider, at least in any systematic fashion, the context in which counselling takes place. When a counsellor and client meet, it is not merely two individuals, but in fact two social worlds which engage with each other. Two sets of expectations, assumptions, values, norms, manners and ways of talking must accommodate each to the other. More than this, usually it is the client who is required to enter the social world of the counsellor, by visiting his or her consulting room or office. The physical and emotional environment in which counselling takes place forms the backdrop for the counselling process, and the quality of this environment is largely determined by organizational factors.

Counselling organizations can exert a strong influence on both their clients and their staff. The type of agency or setting, and the way it is organized and managed, may have an impact on many aspects of counselling, including the:

- number, length and frequency of sessions that are offered to clients;
- approach to counselling that is employed;
- adequacy of supervision and training provided for counsellors;
- morale and motivation of counsellors;
- sex, age and ethnicity of counsellors;
- furnishing in the interview room;
- perceptions clients have of the counsellor;
- security of confidential information;
- financial cost of counselling to client.

Types of counselling organization

Much of the counselling and psychotherapy literature, influenced by the American experience, is written as though the most common type of counselling or psychotherapy organization is the private practice, which might be characterized as the simplest or most minimal form of organization, with an absence of hierarchies, committees or other structures. In private practice the client makes contact directly with a named therapist, and personally reimburses that therapist for each session or course of sessions. Some practices consist of a number of practitioners, who may set themselves up as a partnership or a limited company. The private practice as a counselling organization most clearly exemplifies the image of the counsellor as autonomous professional. The financial structure of private practice is that it provides a service to people who can afford it, and therefore depends on fees.

Although private practice may represent an ideal for many counsellors, in that it maximizes the freedom of the therapist, it accounts for a relatively small proportion of all counselling and therapy which is offered. Most counselling is provided through larger organizations, or 'agencies'. An important type of counselling agency has traditionally been the voluntary agency, which uses unpaid or minimally paid volunteers and which, originally at least, would have a central social mission to fulfil. One of the voluntary counselling agencies in Britain that has had a significant impact on the field is Relate (formerly the National Marriage Guidance Council), which was formed in 1947 in response to what was perceived as a crisis in married life (Tyndall, 1985). Similarly, Childline was formed as a telephone counselling agency in 1986 in reponse to general concern about the rising prevalence of child sexual abuse. Relate and Childline are both large voluntary agencies, with substantial budgets and hierarchical organizational structures which encompass central management, decision-making and fund-raising functions as well as local branches. Many other voluntary counselling agencies are much smaller. For example, in many cities there are locally based gay and lesbian counselling networks, women's therapy centres, rape crisis centres and bereavement counselling agencies. Some of these smaller voluntary agencies may be run by less than a dozen volunteers.

The difference in size between the large national voluntary agencies and the small local ones can have implications in terms of organizational structure and functioning. For example, large organizations inevitably need to develop bureaucratic procedures, whereas smaller agencies can rely on decision-making in face-to-face meetings of everyone involved. On the other hand, the larger agencies are often better placed to afford and provide good quality selection, training and supervision. There are also common organizational issues found in all voluntary agencies, regardless of size. These include: integrating the efforts of a small group of core professional staff with those of a large workforce of volunteers; maintaining standards with minimally trained volunteers; dealing with the demands of volunteers to be able to enter paid, professional positions; raising money from clients without jeopardizing access; and expending effort and energy on collecting charitable donations from the public. These pressures and dilemmas have become more acute over the past decade, as the government has cut the resources for statutory services in fields such as social work and mental health, and has come to expect more of the burden of care to be met by the voluntary sector. Lewis *et al.* (1992) have documented the operation of these organizational processes and pressures during the evolution of Relate/ Marriage Guidance.

A significant amount of counselling is also provided by people employed by statutory agencies, such as the Probation Service, Social Services and the National Health Service. Within this statutory sector there are many different forms of organization, ranging from the lone probation officer or social worker who sees part of his or her role as counselling, to the established psychotherapy units which have been set up by some health authorities (Aveline, 1990). An area of great expansion in recent years within taxpayer-funded counselling has been the use of counsellors in general practice, working as members of primary health care teams.

There are a whole range of general organizational issues encountered by counsellors working in statutory settings. One of the very basic issues is that the ethos or philosophy of the organization may be in tension with the values of a counselling approach. For example, in some NHS settings the dominance of the medical/biological model may make it difficult for counsellors to find acceptance for work with relationships and feelings. Or in some social services settings there may be an emphasis on mobilizing resources for the client, rather than working with the client. In some instances, the legal requirements for probation officers, social workers and nurses to act as agents of the court may make it impossible to offer clients the kind of voluntary, confidential relationship which is usually considered essential in counselling. There may also be rivalry or jealousy from colleagues in these agencies, who regard counselling as part of their role. Many of these issues arise from the challenge of inter-professional work, when counsellors need to work alongside people from other professional groups who have their own roles, norms and organizational 'territories'. Some of the problems and dilemmas that can emerge when counselling is offered within a primarily non-counselling organizational setting, such as a hospital, social services department or school, are:

- being pressured to produce results desired by the agency rather than the client;
- maintaining confidentiality boundaries;
- justifying the cost of the service;
- dealing with isolation;
- educating colleagues about the purpose and value of counselling;
- justifying the cost of supervision;
- avoiding being overwhelmed by numbers of clients, or becoming the 'conscience' of the organization;
- avoiding the threat to reputation caused by 'failure' cases;
- coping with the envy of colleagues who are not able to take an hour for each client interview;
- creating an appropriate office space and reception system.

A final type of counselling setting occurs when counselling is made available to employees of large organizations. For example, many police forces, insurance companies, and other commercial and service organizations have recognized that counselling is a valuable means of taking care of their 'human resources', their employees. One of the distinctive aspects of employee counselling schemes, often known as 'employee assistance programmes' (EAPs), is that counselling is set in an organizational context which is not primarily focused on caring or helping people. The tension between the values and philosophy of the organization and those of the counsellor can be even more acute than in statutory health and social services agencies, and many of the issues highlighted in the list above may apply. Employee counselling can be provided 'in-house', by counsellors employed by the organization, or can be delivered 'out-house', through an external counselling agency under contract to the organization to supply counselling for its employees. In either case, the counselling is being paid for by the employer, rather than the client himself or herself, which can lead, for example, to client suspicion over confidentiality and pressure on the counsellor to produce results consistent with the needs of the organization rather than those of the client. Counselling in educational settings, such as schools, colleges and universities, shares many of the organizational features of employee counselling.

From this brief discussion of some of the organizational issues which can arise in different types of counselling organizations, it is evident that there are many aspects of organizational life of potential relevance to counsellors. The field of organizational studies or organizational behaviour is a well-established area of research, scholarship and teaching. Further, more detailed overviews of current thinking about organizations can be found in Handy (1990), Robbins (1991), Hosking and Morley (1991) and many other texts. Some of the specific issues in organizational theory which are relevant to counselling are explored in the remainder of this chapter.

The nature of counselling organizations

One of the most valuable concepts to have emerged from the field of organizational studies has been the idea of the 'open system' (Katz and Kahn, 1978). From this perspective, organizations are seen as consisting of sets of overlapping and interconnecting parts, which combine to form an organizational system. Change in any element or part of the system will affect what happens elsewhere in the system. Furthermore, the system exists in an environment, and is open to influence from external factors. The purpose of the organizational system is to produce 'throughput': there is an input of 'raw materials', which are processed and then leave the system as 'output'. A typical counselling agency, therefore, could be viewed as a system made up of clients, counsellors, supervisors, managers and administrators, receptionists and fund-raisers. The throughput of the agency is represented by the number of clients seen, and the external environment may include funding agencies, professional bodies and members of the general public. A systems perspective is particularly useful in providing a framework for beginning to understand the ways in which other parts in the system may have an impact on the client–counsellor relationship. For example, successful publicity and outreach work may increase the number of clients applying for counselling. The long waiting lists which may then result can lead to pressure to place a limit on the number of sessions offered to clients. Some of the counsellors may find this policy unacceptable, and leave. This very brief, simplified (but not fictional) example gives a sense of how an organizational system might operate. Other examples will be explored later in the chapter.

In his analysis of the organization of human services providers, Hasenfeld (1992) makes two observations that are highly relevant to counselling agencies. He suggests that an appreciation of the nature of these organizations must take into account that they are engaged in 'moral' work and in 'gendered' work. Counselling organizations ultimately exist because of an assumption that certain groups of people deserve help and resources. A person who is depressed, or who is abusing drugs, is entitled to the time of a therapist. The fact that a counselling agency has been set up to provide counselling for such clients implies a value position. Other people, however, may not share this value position, and may argue on moral grounds that these problems do not deserve a share of public resources. Counselling agencies may, as a result, need to work to establish their legitimacy in the eyes of external groups, such as funding bodies and the public at large.

Historically, the task of caring for people has been work for women. In counselling and other human service organizations, women predominate in frontline service delivery roles, although men are proportionally more heavily represented in management roles. This pattern is even more apparent in voluntary counselling agencies, where male counsellors can be thin on the ground. In general, female occupations enjoy lower status and rates of pay than male occupations, and this tendency can be seen in the field of counselling. Another issue arising from the gendered nature of counselling is the influence of feminist values on counselling organizations. Taylor (1983: 445) has suggested that organizations dominated by women are more likely to espouse values such as 'egalitarianism rather than hierarchy, cooperation rather than competition, nurturance rather than rugged individualism, peace rather than conflict'. This set of values is congruent with the values of counselling as a whole, and can lead to misunderstanding, tension or difficulty when counselling agencies attempt to develop hierarchical structures, or operate in host organizations which embody different beliefs.

Another set of issues that must be faced by counselling organizations concerns the position to be taken regarding professionalism and voluntarism. There is a long and respectable tradition of counselling as voluntary work. People trained and practised as counsellors on a part-time basis because of the intrinsic satisfaction of the work, and also for the altruistic motive of giving to others who were less fortunate. There is also a tradition of counselling as a profession, carried out by paid experts. Difficulties arise in situations where these traditions confront each other, for example in voluntary agencies where some training and supervisory staff are paid, but counsellors are not, or in agencies seeking to make the transition from voluntary to professional status.

Organizational culture

Just as different nations have different cultures, so do organizations and work groups. The experience of walking through the centre of Paris is quite distinct from the experience of walking through London. There are a different language, different rules regarding physical space and contact, driving on the other side of the road, different values and ways of feeling implied by the architecture and use of leisure, and so on. These are two different cultures. The social anthropologist Clifford Geertz (1973) has suggested an essential quality of any culture: it is 'thick'. By this, Geertz means that there are always many layers and levels to a culture, and that describing or understanding it is never a simple matter. The method used by social anthropologists to study cultures, known as 'ethnography', reflects their recognition of the complexity of cultures. Ethnographic studies involve immersion in the life of a group, using participant observation and interviewing, for long periods of time.

Studies of organizational cultures have looked at such aspects as the kinds of roles and relationships which exist in the organization, the language, imagery and humour of the organization, social norms and rules, and the underlying values and philosophy that underpin behaviour and decision-making. All these factors interact with each other in complex ways, to create an organizational system. In counselling agencies, the concept of organizational culture can be employed to make sense of the tension that can often exist between bureaucracy, which is associated with formal procedures and impersonal rules, and the informality and personal relationships which can be cultivated by counsellors being in supervision or being trained together. The rational decision-making inherent in bureaucracy can also be at odds with the use of feelings as a guide to action, as advocated by some approaches to counselling.

Expectations about what is supposed to happen here are also communicated by the culture of an agency. Crandall and Allen (1981), for example, found in one study that different drug abuse therapy agencies embodied quite different levels of demand regarding client change. In some agencies there was a strong expectation that client's behaviour would change in basic ways. In other agencies there were low therapeutic demands on clients. The promotion of a 'culture of excellence' will be expressed through various aspects of organizational culture, such as allocation of rewards and praise, availability of training, and provision of support and resources (Hackman and Walton, 1986).

The culture of an organization is reflected in the use of language within the organization. People in formal, hierarchical organizations, for example, address each other by title or surname; people in informal, 'flat hierarchy' organizations are more likely to be on first name terms. There may be shared images of the agency or unit which express a sense of the organizational culture: the agency may be a 'family', a 'team', a 'sinking ship'. People are usually consciously aware of the meanings of these uses of language. Some writers on organizations have suggested, however, that a group or organizational culture operates largely at an unconscious level. These theorists have borrowed from Freud the idea that the most powerful motives in people are deeply hidden and emerge only indirectly, in patterns of behaviour and in fantasies and dreams. Members of organizations may hold powerful fantasies about other people, or groups in the organization, or about their clients. According to this theory, the most funda-mental elements of the culture of an organization are unconscious and are revealed only through fantasies, jokes and other non-conscious processes.

Institutional defence mechanisms

One of the most influential analyses of organizational life in terms of unconscious processes has been the study of hospital nurses carried out by Menzies (1959). The very nature of the nursing task involves nurses in intimate contact with patients, through being exposed to physical and sexual bodily functions which are usually private, and to pain, anxiety and death. Menzies argued that this kind of contact can be emotionally threatening to nurses, and as a consequence they have evolved, on a collective or group basis, organizational defence mechanisms with which to cope with their emotional reactions to the job. These collective defences include 'objectifying' the patient, denying his or her humanity (e.g. 'the appendix in bed fourteen'), and projecting their vulnerabilities on to other colleagues. Menzies found that more senior nurses, for example, tended to view student nurses as irresponsible and unreliable, thereby projecting their unconscious fears over their own ability to cope on to this group.

These two processes, objectifying patients and blaming colleagues rather than acknowledging personal feelings of vulnerability, are of general relevance and can be found in many counselling agencies. The fundamental value placed in counselling on acceptance, respect and empathy for clients has evolved in response to the powerful tendency for busy caring professionals to lose their sense of the client as a unique individual person rather than as a representative of a category of problem. The process of blaming colleagues can also be found in counselling agencies, particularly where there is inter-professional working.

Parallel process

The key idea in Menzies's (1959) approach is that a group of staff can collectively develop a set of defences for coping with the emotional challenge of dealing with clients. This basic idea has been expanded and specifically applied to counselling and psychotherapy agencies through the concept of 'parallel process'. Crandall and Allen (1981) suggest that there can often be significant parallels between counselling issues and organizational issues. In other words, what happens between counsellor and client is influenced by what happens between counsellor and agency, and vice versa. For example, in a marriage counselling agency that works a lot with couples, counsellors often come across the combination of one rational, unfeeling spouse with a partner who is the emotionally sensitive, feeling, but illogical one. This splitting of logic and feeling can become inherent in the agency itself, perhaps through managers and administrators being perceived by counsellors as unfeeling insensitive bureaucrats, and the counsellors being perceived by administrators as disorganized and unwilling to make decisions.

The parallel process can also take place in the other direction, from agency to client. For example, in an agency with an authoritarian and directive management style, where counsellors are told what to do, counsellors may find themselves becoming more structured and directive in their work with clients. Even the choice of furniture for counselling rooms in an agency can influence the counselling process. A counselling room with floor cushions gives a different message about expressing feelings than would a room with upright tubular chairs (see Rowan, 1992b).

The developmental history of the agency

Another important perspective on organizational functioning is linked to the age of the organization, and its stage of development. Chester (1985) has suggested that many counselling agencies begin existence with a strong sense of mission and commitment. The agency is set up because its founders believe passionately that there is a powerful social need for something to be done about a particular problem. Chester (1985) calls this the 'social movement' stage in the development of an agency. As time goes by, however, the original excitement and sense of mission becomes diluted by the requirement to provide a service to clients. The agency then begins to move into a professional, 'service agency' stage, where expertise and professional competence is valued over commitment and passion. The work of the agency becomes consolidated and routinized. This transition can be painful and difficult, with agencies becoming 'stalemated' (Hirschhorn, 1978) as opposing groups of staff adopt positions on one side or another of a movement–professionalism split.

A version of this kind of organizational crisis can be observed when an agency is set up in the first place by a charismatic, inspirational leader. Such people are more effective in the mission stage of the life of an agency than in the later consolidation phase, and may leave once the initial task is complete. But, because their influence over other staff is so strong, their departure may threaten the very existence of the service. This pattern has been observed in therapeutic communities (Manning, 1989), and has led to caution about the usefulness of founders who adopt the role of 'hero-innovator'.

Counselling has not been established long enough for agencies to develop beyond the consolidation/professionalization stage. In the domain of religious life, however, there have been religious communities and organizations that have been in existence for hundreds of years. Research into the lifespan of religious orders indicates a similar early process to that observed in counselling agencies, with high levels of mission and commitment followed by consolidation and maintenance. After this stage, though, there is a further stage of decline, in which the membership of the order diminishes, and the organization may cease to function unless a new leader emerges to inspire new directions. Fitz and Cada (1975) suggest that the life cycle of a religious congregation follows five discrete stages: foundation, expansion, stabilization, breakdown and transition. This whole process can take centuries to complete.

Role conflict

The idea of 'role' refers to the behaviour expected from a person who holds a particular position in a social group. Role conflict occurs when other people hold contradictory expectations in relation to that person. One of the guiding principles of counselling is to avoid allowing role conflicts to occur in relation to a client. For example, it is generally considered bad practice for a counsellor or therapist to be a friend, colleague or relative of a client, since the expectations and behaviours elicited through these other relationships will get in the way of the counselling relationship. This is one reason, incidentally, for the difficulty in establishing counselling agencies in rural settings where everyone knows everyone else and the kind of anonymity required for role 'purity' can be impossible to guarantee. The avoidance of role conflict is also one of the reasons why many counsellors idealize private practice. Only in private practice can the counsellor be responsible solely to the client. A counsellor who works for an agency is responsible to the agency, and can be seen as representing the agency. The counsellor who is paid by a third party, such as the employer of the client, inevitably has a role in relation to that other person or institution as well as to the client. The issue of role conflict emerges in supervision if the supervisor is also a manager or tutor of the counsellor.

Why is role conflict considered in such a negative light by counsellors? After all, it could be argued that it could in some circumstances be a valuable learning experience for the client to work out the implications of different role expectations he or she held in relation to the counsellor. A key factor involves the capacity of the counsellor to be there solely for the client. Any role other than counsellor carries with it the danger that the counsellor is using the relationship at least partially to gratify his or her needs. Counsellors working within a psycho-dynamic approach place particular importance on the maintenance of strict counsellor–client boundaries, since the introduction of other types of relationship into the equation makes transference more difficult to understand. Counsellors working within a humanistic or person-centred approach can be more flexible in the roles they are willing to develop in relation to a client (see, for example, Thorne, 1985, 1987).

The issue of role conflict arises frequently in counselling agencies. It is impossible to work in a counselling organization of any complexity without fulfilling a range of roles: counsellor, colleague, fundraiser, peer supervision group member, friend. Sometimes the training requirements of agencies and institutes (see Chapter 13) require counsellors to be in personal therapy with another member of the same organization. It is essential, therefore, for agencies to have some means of monitoring and dealing with these issues when they arise, usually through the employment of outside consultants. Role conflict can also raise a number of ethical issues, which are discussed in Chapter 10 under the heading of 'dual relationships'.

The role of the paraprofessional or voluntary counsellor

The use of unpaid volunteer counsellors raises a number of issues in counselling organizations. Whereas paid professional employees receive a salary to reward their efforts, and may be motivated by hopes of promotion and career development, voluntary workers seek personal satisfaction and rewards intrinsic to the job itself. The perceptions and attitudes of paid and unpaid counselling staff may therefore be quite different, leading to difficulties when they work side-by-side in the same agency. Feild and Gatewood (1976) have identified a number of problems of mutual adjustment which can occur when professional and volunteer staff work together:

1 Volunteer counsellors may be given little encouragement or opportunity for career development. They may be allocated simple tasks which do not allow them to express their skills adequately, or may not be allowed to attend courses that would allow them to develop new skills.
2 Because they are only involved for a few hours each week, volunteers or paraprofessionals may have little power or influence within the agency, and may become frustrated at their inability to influence policy and practice.
3 Professionals may fear that the introduction of volunteer workers will threaten their livelihoods.
4 Volunteers may have little previous experience of working in an organization, and may find it difficult to comply with administrative procedures and expectations.
5 When a counselling agency uses volunteers selected on the basis of their similarity to the client population (e.g. sex, age, ethnicity, specific life experience), there may be a tendency for these workers to over-identify with clients, or to experience conflict between allegiance to clients and adherence to agency policies.

Feild and Gatewood (1976) suggest that counselling agencies using volunteers can overcome many of these difficulties through appropriate supervision and training.

Organizational stress and burnout

As with all organizations, working in a counselling agency can affect the health and well-being of staff. Studies of many different types of organizations have demonstrated that stress and emotional and physical ill-health can be caused by overwork, unplanned change and a poor working environment. In human service organizations, a specific type of stress has been identified, which has been labelled 'burnout' (Freudenberger, 1974; Farber, 1983b; Maslach and Jackson, 1984). The phenomenon of burnout occurs when workers enter a human service profession (such as social work, nursing, the police or counselling) with high and unrealistic aspirations regarding the degree to which they will be able to help other people. In many instances the amount of help that can be offered, or the effectiveness of an intervention, is limited. There are also, usually, too many clients for them all to be dealt with in an ideal manner. The result is that the helper becomes caught between his or her own high standards and the impossibility of fulfilling these standards, and after a while is unable to maintain the effort and energy required in functioning at such a high level. This is the state of burnout.

Maslach and Jackson (1984) have identified three main dimensions of the burnout syndrome. People experiencing burnout report emotional exhaustion, a persistent fatigue and a state of low motivation. They also exhibit depersonalization, gradually coming to see their clients not as unique people with individual problems but as 'cases' or representatives of diagnostic categories. Finally, burnout is associated with feelings of lack of personal accomplishment, or powerlessness. Prevention of burnout has been shown, in a number of studies of different groups of human services personnel, to be correlated with the presence of support from colleagues, realistic workloads, clarity about job roles and demands, variety and creativity in the job specification, and recognition and positive feedback from clients and management (Maslach and Jackson, 1984).

A number of studies of burnout with counsellors and therapists have been carried out. Farber and Heifitz (1982) interviewed sixty psychotherapists about their experiences of job-related stress. The primary source of stress reported by these therapists was 'lack of therapeutic success'. Other burnout factors included overwork, work with clients raising personal issues, and isolation. Most of the interviewees stated that they could only see four to six clients a day before becoming depleted, although male therapists claimed they could see greater numbers before being affected. The therapists in this study also felt they were particularly prone to burnout when under stress at home. Hellman and Morrison (1987) administered a 350-item stress questionnaire to psychologists engaged in therapy, and found that those working with more disturbed clients were likely to experience more professional doubt and personal depletion. Therapists working in institutions reported more stress from organizational factors, while those in private practice found it more stressful to deal with difficult clients. Jupp and Shaul (1991) surveyed the stress experiences of eighty-three college counsellors in Australia, and found that more experienced counsellors reported more burnout symptoms than their less experienced colleagues. In all of these studies, the existence of effective social support networks was associated with lower levels of stress and burnout.

The potential for burnout in counselling work is considerable. Counsellors are routinely exposed to clients who are in great distress and whose problems do not readily resolve themselves in the face of therapeutic interventions. There are many references in the therapy literature to therapists who have been driven to the very depths of their personal resources through working with particular clients (e.g. Hobson, 1985). The high suicide rate of psychiatrists, who are more likely to be involved with highly disturbed clients, has been noted in a number of studies (Farber, 1983a). Many counselling agencies have long waiting lists and are under external pressure regarding continued funding. Feedback concerning the effectiveness of the work can sometimes be meagre.

The implementation of organizational procedures to forestall burnout is therefore of immense importance. There are a range of organizational strategies designed to prevent stress and burnout. Regular, effective supervision is essential. Opportunities for counsellor career development, through expanding interests in training, supervision, writing and research, are also helpful. Peer support, either within an agency (Scully, 1983) or through training workshops and conferences, also contributes to burnout prevention. Cherniss and Krantz (1983) have argued that burnout results from the loss of commitment and moral purpose in the work. This absence of meaningfulness can be counteracted by the establishment of 'ideological communities' comprised of groups of colleagues sharing a set of beliefs and values. Boy and Pine (1980) similarly advocate the benefits of associating with committed, concerned colleagues.

It is difficult to estimate the overall prevalence of burnout in counsellors and therapists. An unknown number of trained counsellors either leave the profession or gravitate towards teaching and administration rather than frontline therapy (Warnath and Shelton, 1976). Although Farber and Heifitz (1981) have argued that the majority of practitioners see therapeutic work as offering a unique opportunity for personal affirmation and fulfilment, the issue of counsellor burnout clearly requires further research attention, all the more so at a time when cut-backs in the funding of health and social service agencies have increased workloads and job insecurity.

Stability of funding

The type and quality of funding that a counselling agency receives can have a profound impact on its approach to clients. In private practice, the pressure to maintain income from client fees can lead indirectly to longer-term rather than time-limited approaches, and to an unconscious reluctance to complete the therapy of lucrative clients (Kottler, 1988). The counsellor in private practice may need to develop knowledge and skills in such areas as marketing and business planning (Woody, 1989). In voluntary or non-profit organizations a number of different issues may emerge.

Gronbjerg (1992) observes that most voluntary organizations rely on three sources of income: client fees, donations from individuals, trusts and companies, and contracts with government agencies. The task of maintaining stable funding is complex, with administrators or managers being required to meet the criteria and demands of three different groups. The agency may have little control over these sources of funding, and may therefore find itself periodically in crisis when a donor or government agency reduces or fails to renew its commitment to it. In addition, grants or contracts from government or local authority departments usually carry strict deadlines, formalized reporting procedures and other forms of external control. These features all result in a great deal of administrative work, and possibly the need to appoint staff who are skilled in this particular area.

In a study of six voluntary agencies in Chicago, Gronbjerg (1992) identified three contrasting strategies for dealing with funding issues. The first was to adopt a 'client-driven' approach, in which services were developed in response to client demand. This strategy was only possible for agencies whose main sources of finance were client fees and reliable private donations. The second approach was to aim for maximum flexibility and cushioning against funding jolts by continually seeking increases in grants (to counteract the possibility of cuts), finding ways of commercially marketing some services, and looking for different sources of finance for the same projects. In emergencies, cash-flow problems would be dealt with by borrowing, delaying the payment of bills and delaying salary payments. The third financial strategy for voluntary agencies could be described as 'expansionist'. This approach involves engaging in political activity, attempting to establish relationships with staff in charitable trusts, and forming networks and joint initiatives with other non-profit organizations. Gronbjerg (1992) suggests that although this final strategy may be effective in securing finance and resources, it does so at the risk of losing touch with client needs. On the other hand, the pure 'client-driven' approach is highly vulnerable to the vicissitudes of funding sources.

Conclusions

Theory and research in counselling have concentrated mainly on the immediate process occurring between client and counsellor. This chapter has explored some of the ways in which the 'macro' environment of the counselling agency or setting can influence the 'micro' process of the counselling interview. Many of the issues that have been discussed would be equally relevant in relation to other human service agencies, such as social services departments, hospitals, residential homes, and police, fire and rescue services. However, unlike these other forms of helping, counselling claims to offer people a special kind of relationship, characterized by high levels of empathy, honesty and acceptance. The concept of 'parallel process' implies that the relationship offered to clients will reflect the relationships between people in the organization. It would seem, therefore, that counsellors have a particular responsibility for ensuring that the life of the organization models the assumptions, values and roles to which it intends that clients will aspire. Sensitivity to and awareness of organizational factors is also important because of the relatively recent expansion of counselling into many new areas of work. Many counselling agencies now in existence have only been set up very recently, and many counsellors find that they are the first people to have held their particular post. The continued health of these agencies and counsellors will depend on the establishment of appropriate organizational norms and practices.

The history of counselling includes many examples of counsellors breaking away from organizations and entering private practice. In many respects the people who become counsellors are not good followers of bureaucratic procedures. Nevertheless, the needs of socially disadvantaged groups (see Chapter 7) will never be met through private practice. If counselling is to respond to these needs, it will require further research and experimentation to find the most appropriate ways of creating organizational structures that respect the ethos of counselling but can survive in the current harsh political and economic climate.

Topics for reflection and discussion

1 Consider either the counselling setting where you currently work, or another counselling setting with which you are familiar. In what ways does the way counselling is organized limit the effectiveness of the help offered to clients? What organizational changes could be introduced to overcome these problems?
2 Is there an optimum size for a counselling agency? Discuss the advantages and disadvantages of both very large and very small agencies.
3 In what ways could the underlying theoretical orientation of a counselling organization (e.g. psychodynamic, person-centred, cognitive–behavioural, integrative/eclectic) have an effect on the way it is administered and managed?

NINE

ALTERNATIVE MODES OF DELIVERY

The somewhat clumsy phrase 'modes of delivery' refers to the differing shapes and forms that counselling can take. The chapters on core theoretical models such as psychodynamic, person-centred and cognitive–behavioural, and the discussion of integrative approaches, were largely based on the practice of one-to-one counselling, where the counsellor and client are the only people involved. This type of counselling can be seen as representing a 'pure' form of the genre, one in which principles and processes are readily identifiable and well-documented. There are, however, several other formats within which counselling can occur. In this chapter some of these alternative modes of delivery will be discussed, including variants of one-to-one counselling, group counselling, telephone counselling, working with couples and bibliotherapy. These approaches provide a range of fascinating challenges for counsellors primarily trained in face-to-face individual work, as well as enabling the benefits of counselling to achieve a wider impact in society.

Variants on one-to-one counselling

Normally, counselling is regarded as taking place between a trained, professional counsellor and a client over a number of meetings. The main variants on this pattern have been to limit the number of sessions and to use minimally trained volunteers rather than professional practitioners.

A considerable amount of research evidence has demonstrated that most counselling and therapy takes place within a fairly limited number of sessions, and that clients seem to benefit more from earlier than from later sessions (the literature on this topic is reviewed by Howard *et al.*, 1986). These findings, as well as other theoretical and pragmatic considerations, have led to a growth in interest in developing forms of 'brief therapy', in which the client is offered a limited number of sessions. Psychodynamic brief therapy is discussed in Chapter 2, but the principle of time limits has also been applied in counselling

Table 7 A comparison of the values underlying long-term and short-term counselling

The long-term therapist	The short-term therapist
Seeks change in basic character	Pragmatic, does not believe in concept of 'cure'
Sees presenting problems as indicative of underlying pathology	Emphasizes client's strengths and resources
Wants to be there as client makes significant change	Accepts that many changes will occur after termination of therapy, and will not be observable by therapist
Is patient and willing to wait for change	Does not accept the 'timelessness' of some approaches
Unconsciously recognizes the fiscal convenience of maintaining long-term clients	Fiscal issues often muted by the nature of the organization for which therapist works
Views therapy as almost always benign and useful	Views therapy as sometimes useful and sometimes harmful
Being in therapy is the most important part of the client's life	Being in the world is more important than therapy

Source: Budman and Gurman (1988)

delivered from a cognitive–behavioural or person-centred orientation (Dryden and Feltham, 1992). The decision to adopt a time-limited rather than open-ended approach to working with clients has been viewed by Budman and Gurman (1988) as reflecting a shift in underlying counsellor or therapist values (see Table 7).

Recently, some researchers and practitioners have addressed the question of how few sessions are necessary to enable effective counselling to take place. The attraction of very brief counselling is that its implementation can avoid the necessity for long waiting lists. In addition, clients may also be encouraged and given hope by the assumption that they can make progress quickly. Major research into very brief therapy is being carried out by the Psychotherapy Research Project at the University of Sheffield, who are examining the efficacy of a '2 + 1' model. In this approach, clients are offered two sessions one week apart, then a follow-up meeting around three months later (Barkham and Shapiro, 1989, 1990a, b; Dryden and Barkham, 1990). One of the aims of the study is to identify the types of client most likely to benefit from this approach. Initial results, based on counselling offered to white-collar workers referred for job-related stress and relationship difficulties, suggest that at six-month follow-up, around 60 per cent of clients exhibited significant benefits (Barkham and Shapiro, 1990a).

The practice of structuring counselling around time limits makes special demands on counsellors, and requires careful training and supervision. Counsellors and counselling agencies employing time-limited approaches also need to organize themselves to enable effective and sensitive selection of clients, and appropriate referral of clients who turn out to require longer-term work. From the wide array of theory and research into brief therapy, some central principles for time-limited counselling are clearly emerging. These include initial assessment of clients, an active approach by the counsellor, structuring the therapeutic process in terms of stages or phases, engaging the active involvement and cooperation of the client, and providing the client with new perspectives and experiences (Steenberger, 1992; Dryden and Feltham, 1992).

The use of non-professional, paraprofessional or lay counsellors in one-to-one work has attracted a great deal of controversy in recent years, following the publication by Karlsruher (1974) and Durlak (1979) of reviews of studies assessing the therapeutic effectiveness of non-professional helpers. Durlak (1979), in a review of forty-two studies, reported that research evidence indicated that lay or non-professional counsellors tended to be *more* effective than highly trained expert practitioners. This conclusion, not unexpectedly, provoked a strong reaction within the profession (Nietzel and Fisher, 1981; Durlak, 1981). The accumulation of further evidence has, however, supported the original position taken by Durlak (1979). In two more recent reviews of the research literature, Hattie *et al.* (1984) concluded that paraprofessionals were more effective than trained therapists, and Berman and Norton (1985), using more rigorous criteria for accepting studies as methodologically adequate, concluded that there were no overall differences in effectiveness between professional and non-professional therapists.

Although the general trend in these studies does not confirm the prediction that most people would make, that years of professional training should lead to positive advantages, it is necessary to be cautious in interpreting the results. The studies cover a wide range of client groups, including psychiatric patients, schizophrenic people in the community, people in crisis, students with study problems and children with behavioural difficulties. The non-professional helpers have included adult volunteers, parents of children and college students. Modes of treatment have encompassed one-to-one and group counselling, behavioural methods and telephone counselling. So although the general effectiveness of non-professionals has been demonstrated, there are insufficient studies in specific areas to allow the claim that the efficacy of using volunteers for that specific client group has been established. Moreover, when the factors that are associated with effective non-professional counselling are considered, some interesting results emerge. Non-professionals who are more experienced and have received more training achieve better results (Hattie *et al.*, 1984). Non-professionals did better with longer-term counselling (over twelve weeks), while professionals were comparatively more effective with short-term work (one to four weeks) (Berman and Norton, 1985).

Why do non-professionals, such as volunteer counsellors, achieve such good results? The discussion of this issue has generated a number of suggestions for contributory factors:

- perceived by clients to be more genuine;
- less likely to apply professional labels to clients;
- restrict themselves to straightforward, safe interventions;
- clients will attribute success and progress to self rather than to expertise of therapist;
- able to refer difficult cases to professionals;
- limited case-load;
- highly motivated to help;
- may be more likely to come from similar cultural background to client;
- able to give more time to clients.

This list, derived from the writings of Durlak (1979) and Wills (1982), indicates that there are advantages in non-professional status and relative lack of experience which balance the advantages conferred by professional authority, experience and advanced training. There are also disadvantages associated with expertise, such as the danger of burnout due to overwork, and the development of professional distancing or detachment from clients. One possible explanation for the effectiveness of non-professional counsellors may be that they are selected from a pool of naturally talented, untrained listeners in the community. In a unique piece of research, Towbin (1978) placed an advertisement in the personal column of his local paper to seek out non-professional 'confidants'. The entry began, 'Do people confide in you?' Towbin interviewed seventeen of those who replied. These people were self-confident and open, and had felt deeply loved as children. With regard to the relationships with those who confided in them, they saw themselves as trustworthy and able to be fully present in the situation.

Perhaps the most detailed piece of research comparing professional and non-professional counsellors is the study at Vanderbilt University carried out by Strupp and Hadley (1979). In this study, male college students seeking counselling were assessed using a standardized personality questionnaire. Those who exhibited a profile characterized by depression, isolation and social anxiety were randomly allocated either to experienced therapists or to college professors without training in counselling who were 'selected on the basis of their reputation for warmth, trustworthiness, and interest in students' (Strupp and Hadley, 1979: 1126). A comparison group was formed from prospective clients who were required to wait for treatment. The effectiveness of the counselling (twice weekly, up to twenty-five hours) was evaluated using standard questionnaires and ratings administered at intake, termination and a one-year follow-up. In addition, sessions were either video- or audio-taped.

Both treatment groups showed more improvement than the control group, but there was no difference in outcome between those clients seen by experienced therapists and those counselled by untrained college professors. The non-professional counsellors proved to be just as helpful as their professional colleagues. However, there were marked differences in the counselling style of the two sets of helpers. The non-professionals were more likely to give advice, discuss issues other than feelings and conflicts, and run out of relevant material to explore (Gomes-Schwartz and Schwartz, 1978).

In a detailed examination of counselling carried out by one of the college professors in the study, Strupp (1980a, b, c, d) presents a picture of a professor of statistics who was genuinely interested in his clients, offered high levels of encouragement and acceptance, and communicated a sincere belief in their capacity to change for the better. With a client who was ready to try out new behaviours, he proved to be a highly effective therapist. With one of his more difficult clients, a young man who turned out to have deep-rooted difficulties arising from his relationship with his father, therapy broke down because of the counsellor's inability to understand or challenge high levels of client resistance and negative transference. The overall conclusion that can be drawn from this study is that volunteer, non-professional counsellors can achieve a great deal through 'the healing effects of a benign human relationship' (Strupp and Hadley, 1979: 1135), but are less well equipped to cope with some of the dilemmas and difficulties that can occur in particular cases.

An important area requiring further research is the relationship between professional and volunteer counsellors. For example, in Strupp and Hadley's (1979) study, the college professors acting as counsellors were all carefully selected by professional therapists, and had the option of passing clients on to the university counselling service. Clearly, professionals are heavily involved in volunteer counselling schemes, through delivering training and supervision, and in taking referrals for clients whose difficulties are beyond the competence of volunteer counsellors to handle. Unfortunately little is known about the distinct training and supervision needs or the development of skills and awareness in volunteer counsellors. Another useful area of enquiry concerns the theoretical basis for volunteer counselling. Non-professionals with limited time to attend courses or explore the literature often lack a consistent theoretical orientation, even though they may possess good counselling skills. It is significant that theoretical models employed in training courses for volunteers, such as the Egan (1990) skilled helper model, are broadly integrative and action-oriented rather than exploratory in nature (Culley, 1992).

Telephone counselling

In terms of numbers of client contacts made each year, telephone counselling agencies such as Samaritans, Childline, Nightline and Gay Switchboard do much more counselling than any other type of counselling agency. For example, Childline alone answers over 1000 calls each day. Despite the overwhelming importance of telephone counselling as a means of meeting public needs for emotional support, there has been relatively little effort devoted to theory and research in this area. The task of supplying counselling help over a telephone raises several fundamental questions. In what ways do counselling techniques and approaches need to be modified? Do telephone counsellors have different training and support needs? How much, and in what ways, do users benefit from telephone counselling? Which problems are amenable to telephone counselling and which require ongoing face-to-face contact with a counsellor?

The circumstances of telephone counselling make it difficult to evaluate the benefits that callers may experience. In studies that have asked callers, either at the end of the conversation or at subsequent follow-up, to assess their satisfaction with the service, it has been found that consistently two-thirds or more of clients have reported high levels of satisfaction (Stein and Lambert, 1984). The types of counsellor behaviour which are perceived by callers to be helpful include understanding, caring, listening, offering feedback, exhibiting a positive attitude, acceptance, keeping a focus on the problem, and giving suggestions (Slaikeu and Willis, 1978; Young, 1989). These counsellor behaviours are similar to effective counsellor interventions in face-to-face counselling.

There does, however, appear to be one important process dimension along which telephone counselling differs from face-to-face work. Lester (1974) has suggested that telephone counselling is a situation which increases the positive transference felt by the caller. The faceless helper is readily perceived as an 'ideal', and can be imagined to be anything or anyone the caller needs or wants. Grumet (1979) points out the elements of the telephone interview which contribute to increased intimacy: visual privacy, the speaker's lips being, in a sense, only inches from the listener's ear, and a high level of control over the situation. Rosenbaum (1974) has written that: 'the ringing of the phone symbolically represents the cry of the infant and there was an immediate response, namely my voice itself being equivalent to the immediate response of the mother.'

One consequence of the positive transference found in telephone counselling would appear to be to make the caller tolerant of counsellor errors. Delfin (1978) recorded the way clients responded to different types of statements made by telephone counsellors. It was found that clients appeared to react positively to counsellor responses that were viewed by trained observers as clichéd or inaccurate.

Most telephone counselling agencies are staffed by part-time volunteer workers who receive only very limited training and supervision. It would appear, from the research evidence already reviewed, that the personal qualities and presence of the counsellor are more important in telephone work than are technical skills. Most clients will have one contact with any individual counsellor, so some of the complexities of other forms of counselling, such as action planning, overcoming resistance to change and building a therapeutic alliance, are not present to the same extent. On the other hand, telephone counsellors need to work quickly, to be flexible and intuitive, and to be able to cope with silence. Hoax calls and sex calls draw on skills which are less frequently used in face-to-face counselling. Telephone counsellors are required to enter into the personal worlds of people actually in the middle of crisis, and are thereby exposed to strong emotions. They may become remote participants in suicide. Not only are telephone counsellors involved in a potentially raw and harrowing type of work, they are also less liable to receive feedback on the results of their efforts. Indeed, they may never know whether a caller did commit suicide, or did escape from an abusive family environment. The rate of turnover and burnout in telephone counselling agencies, and provision of adequate support and supervision, are therefore topics of some concern, which require further study and research.

From the point of view of the caller or client, telephone counselling has two major advantages over face-to-face therapy: access and control. It is easier to pick up a phone and speak directly to a counsellor than it is to make an appointment to visit a counselling agency at some time next week. Telephone counselling therefore has an important preventative function, in offering a service to people who would not submit themselves to the process of applying for other forms of help, or whose difficulties have not reached an advanced stage. Moreover, most people are ambivalent about seeking help for psychological problems. The telephone puts the client in a position of power and control, able to make contact and then terminate as he or she wishes.

Reading and writing as therapy

The concept of 'bibliotherapy' refers to the therapeutic effect of reading books. In general, there are two categories of book which are used in bibliotherapy. The first category consists of explicit self-help manuals, which are designed to enable people to understand and resolve a particular area of difficulty in their lives. Self-help books will usually contain exercises and suggestions for action, and are therefore often thought of as behavioural in orientation. Other books often employed in bibliotherapy are texts, usually on a psychological topic, that essentially discuss ideas and experiences rather than being explicitly oriented towards behaviour change. These may be originally written for a professional audience, but become taken up by the general public or achieve cult status. Examples of this second type of bibliotherapy text are *The Road Less Travelled* by Scott Peck (1978) and Alice Miller's (1987) *The Drama of Being a Child*.

The use of self-help manuals and books raises a number of theoretical issues (Craighead *et al.*, 1984). Much theory and research in counselling emphasizes the importance of the therapeutic relationship, yet in bibliotherapy there is no direct relationship. Self-help manuals also assume that the same techniques will be effective for all people who experience a particular problem, rather than individualizing the intervention for separate clients. Finally, the suggestions made in self-help books must have a relatively low risk of side-effects.

Starker (1988) carried out a questionnaire survey of psychologists in the USA, asking them about their prescription of self-help books in therapy. Some 69 per cent of these therapists reported that some of their clients had been 'really helped' by such books. More than half of the practitioners at least occasionally recommended self-help books to supplement treatment. Psychodynamic therapists were less likely to use bibliotherapy than were therapists from other orientations. The most popular bibliotherapy texts were in the areas of parenting, assertiveness, personal growth, relationships, sexuality and stress. Other studies have looked at the effectiveness of bibliotherapy. In one study, Ogles *et al.* (1991) supplied self-help books for coping with loss to sixty-four people who had recently experienced divorce or the break-up of a relationship. Levels of depression and psychiatric symptoms were assessed before and after reading the book.

Clinically significant benefits were reported. It was also found that those readers who initially had high positive expectations that the book would help subsequently showed greater gains, which might imply that a book or self-help manual received on the recommendation of a therapist might be particularly valuable. Some projects have combined the prescription of self-help manuals with telephone counselling, either using a telephone hotline that clients can phone, or calling clients at regular intervals to encourage them to use the manual (Orleans *et al.*, 1991; Ossip-Klein *et al.*, 1991). Although most self-help manuals are written from a cognitive–behavioural perspective, the remarkable *Barefoot Psychoanalyst* book (Southgate and Randall, 1978) demonstrates that it is possible to employ even Kleinian and Reichian ideas in a self-help mode.

In a review of evaluative studies of self-help manuals, Craighead *et al.* (1984) came to the conclusion that, although totally self-administered manuals may be effective for some people, most clients want or need some additional personal contact with a helper. They also noted that particularly positive results had been obtained with self-help manuals for problem drinking, anxiety control, vocational guidance and study skills problems. The effectiveness of bibliotherapy in other areas, such as obesity, smoking cessation, sexual problems and assertiveness, was difficult to assess because of methodological weaknesses in the studies which had been carried out. Scogin *et al.* (1990), in a more recent review of the literature, largely confirmed these conclusions, and suggested that bibliotherapy appeared to be more effective with older, more highly educated clients.

The results of research would seem to confirm that bibliotherapy can be an effective way of facilitating insight and change in clients, particularly in combination with face-to-face counselling or telephone contact. The exploration of feelings and experiences through writing can also be helpful. Some therapists encourage clients to write on particular topics (e.g. Maultsby, 1971; McKinney, 1976). Others suggest the use of ongoing diaries or journals, perhaps using structures and techniques developed by Progoff (1975) or Rainer (1985). Additional writing-based modes of counselling intervention include correspondence, poetry writing and autobiography (Greening, 1977).

Group counselling and therapy

Group counselling and therapy represents a major area of theory, research and practice in its own right, and interested readers are recommended to learn more about the topic by consulting some of the major texts in the field (Whitaker, 1985; Corey, 1990; Forsyth, 1990). The aim of the present discussion is to identify some of the possibilities and issues arising from this mode of delivery of counselling help, rather than attempting a comprehensive review of this area of specialization.

There are several parallel historical sources of the origins of group therapy. Early forms of groupwork were pioneered by Moreno, with psychodrama, by Lewin, through the invention of 'T-groups', and by Bion, in his psychoanalytic groups. These various initiatives came together in the late 1940s and early 1950s to form what has become a strong tradition in the various branches of the helping professions. Group-based approaches are used in counselling, psychotherapy, social work and organizational development. The three main theoretical orientations in counselling – psychodynamic, humanistic and cognitive–behavioural – are all represented in distinctive approaches to the theory and practice of working with groups.

The first systematic psychodynamic group theory was formulated by Bion, Foulkes and Jacques, initially during the Second World War through work with psychologically disturbed and traumatized soldiers at the Northfield Hospital in Birmingham, and later at the Tavistock Institute in London. The key idea in psychodynamic groupwork is its focus on the 'group-as-a-whole'. Bion (1961) argued that, just as individual patients in psychoanalysis exhibit defences against reality, so do groups. He coined the phrase 'basic assumptions' to describe these collective patterns of defence and avoidance in groups. At the heart of a 'basic assumption' is a shared, unconscious belief that the group is acting 'as if' some imaginary state of affairs were true. For example, a group can act 'as if' the leader was all-knowing and all-powerful (dependency), 'as if' the only option in a group was to engage in conflict with others (fight–flight), or 'as if' the main purpose of the group was the formation of two-person friendships or sexual liaisons (pairing). The role of the group leader was similar to that of the analyst in individual psychoanalyst, in saying little and thereby acting as a blank screen on to which members could project their fantasies.

The benefits to be gained from therapy in this kind of group lie in gaining personal insight from participating in a group that was learning to understand issues concerning authority, boundaries, sexuality and aggression, which emerged in the culture of the group-as-a-whole. Whitman and Stock (1958) introduced the notion of the 'group focal conflict' as a way of making sense of the link between group process and individual learning. If the group becomes emotionally engaged in, for instance, the question of whether it is acceptable for members to meet outside of sessions, this issue will resonate in each individual member of the group in so far as it resembles similar issues in their own lives. One member may bring strong feelings about betrayal, another anger about having been controlled by his parents, and so on.

The process of a psychodynamic group takes time, and it may be possible to see phases or stages in the life of the group. Bennis and Shepard (1956) have constructed a model which envisages two general stages in the life of a group. The first stage is concerned with issues of control and authority, the second with issues of intimacy and interdependence. During the first stage, group members behave in the group in line with previously learned ways of coping with authority: some may be conformist, others rebellious. In the process of the group as an entity sorting out how it can reconcile these tensions, there is opportunity for individual insight and therapeutic change. The practical implications, in terms of running counselling groups, of these ideas about group dynamics are fully explored in Agazarian and Peters (1981) and Whitaker (1985), and current issues in the theory and application of this approach are discussed in Pines (1983) and Roberts and Pines (1991).

The humanistic approach to group counselling devotes particular attention to ideas of growth and encounter. The main aim of this approach is the personal development or self-actualization of group members, and traditionally there have been two contrasting methodologies employed by practitioners. Some group facilitators utilize a high degree of structure in their groups, providing the group with exercises and tasks to promote exploration and growth. This tradition has its origins in psychodrama and the T-group, or sensitivity training group, movement. The other tradition is to offer very little structure, and for the facilitator to strive to create a group environment characterized by respect, empathy and congruence. This latter tradition is associated with the work of Rogers and the person-centred approach. A central aim in much groupwork informed by humanistic thinking is the creation of a 'cultural island' where people can experiment with different behaviour, share experiences and receive feedback from others in a setting that is outside everyday life and thereby allows greater freedom.

The third of the approaches to group counselling has evolved from the cognitive–behavioural tradition, and is primarily concerned with using the group to foster behavioural change in clients. Examples of this type of groupwork are social skills groups (Trower et al., 1978), assertiveness training and short-term groups focused on a specific problem behaviour, such as alcohol abuse, eating or offending. Social skills training groups exhibit many of the key features of the approach. There is a didactic component, with the group leaders supplying teaching and modelling appropriate skills. Group members practise skills through exercises, simulations and role play, and will usually be given homework assignments to encourage generalization of the skill to ordinary life situations. The emphasis is on action and behaviour change rather than reflection and encounter.

These three approaches to working with groups have different aims, along a continuum with insight and personal development at one end and behaviour change at the other. The form of group that is set up will also reflect the needs of clients and the agency or organization within which it takes place. Agazarian and Peters (1981) propose a categorization of helping groups into three levels of challenge, depending on clients' needs. However, organizational factors can also have a bearing on group practice. Psychodynamic, Tavistock-oriented groups and Rogerian encounter groups, for example, will usually need to meet over many hours, to allow the dynamics of the group to develop. If the agency can only afford to allocate ten or twenty hours of staff time to running a group, then a more behaviourally oriented experience will probably be selected.

Most counsellors are initially trained to work with individual clients, and the contrast between one-to-one and group facilitation can present a significant challenge. The interactions which take place in a group are more complex than those occurring between a single client and counsellor. The group facilitator must monitor the relationships between himself or herself and the group members, but also those occurring between group members. The facilitator also needs to have a sense of what is happening to the group as a whole system. The emotional demands, or transference, that the facilitator absorbs from the group may at times be much more intense than in individual counselling. Bennis and Shepard (1956) for example, identify the 'barometric event' in the life of a group as the moment when all group members combine together to reject the authority of the leader. There are case management issues unique to groupwork, for example designing and forming the group, selecting members, combining group and individual counselling, introducing new members once the group is underway, and dealing with the process of people leaving the group (Whitaker, 1981). There are distinctive ethical issues arising in groups, mainly concerning the conformity pressure that can be exerted on individuals and the difficulty of maintaining confidentiality (Lakin, 1988). Finally, it is common practice to work with a co-leader or co-facilitator when running a group, as a way of dealing with some of the complexities of the task. There is, therefore, a distinctive knowledge base and set of requirements for effective group leadership. It is unfortunate that very few formal training courses exist to prepare people to be group facilitators. Most practitioners working with groups have acquired their groupwork competence through being members of groups and acting in a co-facilitator role as an assistant or apprentice.

Groups offer a number of ways of helping clients which are not readily available in individual counselling. The group provides an arena in which the client can exhibit a much broader range of interpersonal behaviour than could ever be directly observed in a one-to-one relationship with a counsellor. In individual counselling, a client may tell a male counsellor about how he has problems in communication with women. In a group these problems can be expressed in his relationships with the women in the group. Oatley (1980, 1984) has described this process as the acting out of 'role-themes'. Group counselling, therefore, presents the counsellor with a different quality of information about the client, and different opportunities for immediacy and working with the here-and-now. In groups, moreover, there are chances for clients to help each other through clarification, challenge and support. This is useful not only in that there is more help available, but also in that the client who is able to be helpful to another will benefit in terms of enhanced self-esteem. The group setting can be viewed as akin to a drama, where the interaction between group members is a means of acting out personal and collective issues (McLeod, 1984). In this drama, not all participants are on centre stage at the same time. Some will be in the role of audience, but this ability to be able to observe how other people deal with things can in itself be a powerful source of learning.

One of the most fertile lines of research into group counselling and therapy in recent years has developed out of the work of Yalom (1975) in identifying and defining the 'curative' or 'therapeutic' factors in groups. Struck by the complexity of what went on in his groups, Yalom set about reviewing the literature with the aim of bringing together ideas about the factors or processes in groups that help people. He arrived at a set of twelve factors:

Group cohesiveness
Instillation of hope
Universality
Catharsis

Altruism
Guidance
Self-disclosure
Feedback
Self-understanding
Identification
Family re-enactment
Existential awareness.

The presence of these factors in a group can be assessed through questionnaire or Q-sort (a kind of structured interview) techniques devised by Yalom and others. Bloch *et al.* (1981) have developed a similar approach based on asking group members at the end of each group session to write briefly about what they found helpful. The 'curative factors' research is of particular interest to many group facilitators because it is grounded in the perceptions of clients regarding what is helpful or otherwise, and because it provides valuable pointers to how the group might be run.

While the work of Yalom (1975) and Bloch *et al.* (1981) focuses on what is helpful in groups, it is also valid to take account of group processes that may be harmful or damaging. In a large scale, comprehensive study of twenty encounter groups run for students at Stanford University, Lieberman *et al.* (1973) found that around 10 per cent of the people who had participated in the groups could be classified at the end as 'casualties'. Being in the group had caused more harm than good to these people. This piece of evidence stimulated a lively debate in the literature, with some critics claiming that there were aspects of the Stanford study which would exaggerate the casualty estimate. Nevertheless, it is fair to say that the Lieberman *et al.* (1973) research does draw attention to some of the potentially worrying aspects of group approaches. Situations can arise in groups where individual members are put under pressure to self-disclose or take part in an exercise despite their resistance or defences against doing so. The reactions of other members of the group may be destructive rather than constructive, for example when a group member shares his fears over 'coming out' as gay and is met by a homophobic response from others. The ensuing distress may be hidden or difficult to detect. These are some of the factors which lead group facilitators to be careful about selecting people for groups, setting up arrangements for providing support outside the group session and ensuring that the facilitators receive adequate supervision.

Self-help groups

A great deal of group counselling takes place in self-help groups, which consist of people with similar problems who meet together without the assistance of a professional leader. The appeal of the self-help movement can be seen to rest on two main factors. The first is that self-help groups can be created in the absence of professional resources, and can thereby transcend the budgetary limitations of health and welfare agencies. The second is that people who participate in self-help groups appreciate the experience of talking to others who 'know what it feels like' to have a drink problem, to have lost a child in a road accident or to be a carer of an infirm elderly parent.

The effectiveness of self-help groups for a variety of client groups has been well documented. In the field of alcohol dependence, there is even evidence that Alcoholics Anonymous is on the whole more effective than individual or group counselling offered by professional experts (Emrick, 1981).

One of the issues can lead to difficulties in self-help groups is the establishment of an unhelpful or inappropriate group culture. For example, the group may come to be dominated by one or two people who have covert needs *not* to change, and who create groups where people collude with each other to remain agoraphobic, overweight or problem drinkers. Another difficulty may be that the group does not evolve clear enough boundaries and norms, so that being in the group is experienced as risky rather than as a safe place to share feelings. Antze (1976) has suggested that the most effective self-help groups are those which develop and apply an explicit set of ground rules or an 'ideology'. Women's consciousness-raising groups, for example, can draw upon an extensive literature which details the philosophy and practice of feminist approaches to helping. Alcoholics Anonymous uses a clearly defined 'twelve-step' rulebook.

Professional counsellors may be involved in enabling self-help groups to get started, either through taking a proactive role within their organization, or because people in the group seek guidance about where to meet and how to proceed. For example, student counsellors may encourage the formation of self-help groups among mature students, or overseas students. Counsellors in hospitals may work with self-help groups of nursing staff suffering from work stress, or of patients with cancer. The relationship between the 'expert' and the group requires sensitive handling, with the counsellor being willing to act as external consultant rather than coming in and taking charge (Robinson, 1980).

Couples counselling

A substantial number of people seek counselling as a couple, because they recognize that their problems are rooted in their relationship rather than being attributable to individual issues. Counselling agencies specifically devoted to working with couples, or with individuals on relationship issues, have been established in many countries. Many of these agencies, like the British National Marriage Guidance Council (Relate) began life as a result of fears about the sanctity of married life, and were in their early years mainly 'marriage saving' organizations. In recent years, however, the realities of changing patterns of marriage and family life have influenced these agencies in the direction of defining their work as being more broadly based in relationship counselling in general.

The field of couples counselling is dominated by two major approaches: psychodynamic and behavioural. Useful comparisons between these styles of working with couples can be found in Paolino and McCrady (1978) and Scarf

(1987). The psychodynamic approach aims to help couples gain insight into the unconscious roots of their marital choice, and into the operation of projection and denial in their current relationship. One of the fundamental assumptions of psychodynamic couples counselling is that each partner brings to the relationship a powerful set of ideas about being a spouse and being a parent, which originate in his or her family of origin. Each partner also brings to the relationship a set of interpersonal needs shaped by experience in early childhood. For example, the person whose mother died at a critical age in childhood may have a need for acceptance but a fear of allowing himself to trust. A person who was sexually abused in childhood may express needs for intimacy through sexualized relationships. The job of the counsellor is, just as in individual work, to help the couple to achieve insight into the unconscious roots of their behaviour, and to learn to give expression to feelings which had been repressed.

The psychodynamic counsellor in marital or couples work also brings to the task a set of ideas about relationships. The dynamics of the Oedipal situation, with its triangular configuration of child, same-sex parent and opposite-sex parent, can serve as a template for understanding difficulties currently experienced by the couple, such as husband, wife and wife's mother, or husband, wife and first child. Another triangular pattern in couples work is that consisting of husband, wife and the person with whom one of them is having an affair. Many counsellors find object relations theory (Chapter 2) valuable in disentangling the processes of jealousy, attachment, loss and rivalry that can occur in couples work.

The concepts of marital 'choice' and marital 'fit' help in making sense of the basis for the emotional bond between a couple. According to psychodynamic theory, a couple will choose each other because, at least partially, the unconscious needs of each will be met by the other. So, for example, a man who gets angry may find a partner who is even-tempered. However, this marital fit may become less and less comfortable as one or both of the partners develops in such a way as to claim back the unconscious territory ceded to the other. Some couples are able to re-negotiate the basis of their relationship as and when such changes occur. Others are not able to do so, and after some time there is an explosion as the pressure becomes too great and the original pattern of relationship is torn apart in a crisis of violence, splitting up or conducting an affair. It is often in such crisis that the couple will come for help.

A psychodynamic perspective brings to couples counselling a sophisticated model of personality development. Behind the conflict and dissent projected by many couples who arrive for counselling are fundamental developmental issues. A woman who married at sixteen finds herself experimenting with new partners and nightclubs when her daughter reaches the same age. A man in his mid-twenties is terrified by the transition to parenthood; his wife is ready to have a child now. The *Educating Rita* scenario, where a woman who has missed out on her opportunity to fulfil her potential in the world of study or work, is not uncommon as a source of marital conflict.

The technique of psychodynamic couples work involves the same careful listening and exploration as in individual counselling. Some couples counsellors recommend that the counselling is provided by a pair of counsellors, a man and a woman, to facilitate different types of transference, but this is an option that is only feasible in well-resourced, counselling centres. On the whole, it is necessary for counsellors working in this way to be more active and interventionist than they might be with individual clients, to keep the focus of the couple on the therapeutic work rather than on acting out arguments in the counselling room. Further information about the theory and practice of psychodynamic work with couples is available in Skynner and Cleese (1983) and Clulow and Mattinson (1989).

The cognitive–behavioural approach to couples counselling is quite different. There is very little theoretical baggage, little exploration of the past and a predominant emphasis on finding pathways to changed behaviour. The central assumption in this approach is that people in an intimate relationship act as a source of positive reinforcement for each other. At the time of first meeting each other, and through courtship, there is usually a high level of positive reinforcement or reward associated with the relationship. Later on, as the couple perhaps live together, work together or bring up children, the opportunities for rewarding contact diminish and the costs of the relationship, the compromise and stress, increase. As a result, the 'reward–cost ratio' reduces, and there is a loss of satisfaction. At the same time, the couple may encounter difficulties in such areas as communication, problem-solving and sexuality.

The remedy for these problems, in a cognitive–behavioural mode, is to apply behavioural principles to initiate change, such as the use of contracts between spouses. Cognitive–behavioural methods have been particularly successful in couples work in the area of sex therapy. Other theoretical perspectives have had only a limited impact on couples work. Some couples counsellors find it valuable to think about couples in terms of family systems models. Greenberg and Johnson (1988) have developed *emotionally focused* couples therapy, which takes an experiential approach.

One of the central issues and debates in couples counselling concerns the decision to work with partners individually, or to see them together as a couple. There are many occasions when this decision is made by the clients, when only one member of the couple is willing to see the counsellor. Even in these circumstances, however, there is an issue about how much to involve the absent partner or spouse (Bennun, 1985).

This discussion of couples counselling can do no more than introduce some of the central themes running through theory and practice in this field. The reader interested in finding out more about this type of counselling is recommended to consult Dryden (1985a), Scarf (1987), Freeman (1990) and Hooper and Dryden (1991).

Conclusions

This review of alternative modes of providing counselling help for people in need indicates that there is a wide range of formats which can be used. There is scope for counsellors and counselling agencies to be creative in their use of resources.

It would appear that the approaches described in this chapter have the potential to reach people who might be reluctant to seek out conventional one-to-one counselling or therapy. Each of these approaches, however, requires training and awareness based in an acknowledgement that they demand different skills and methods from counsellors.

Topics for reflection and discussion

1 Take any one face-to-face counselling agency. How could the service offered by that agency be enhanced by introducing some of the other modes of delivery of counselling discussed in this chapter?

2 Do different modes of counselling help (e.g. groups, bibliotherapy, telephone counselling, individual face-to-face work) produce different outcomes in clients? Is the learning process for clients the same whatever type of intervention is used, or are there change elements unique to each format?

3 Discuss the extent to which alternatives to traditional individual counselling represent attempts to deal with power issues in the helper–helpee relationship. How successful are these alternative approaches empowering clients?

4 You have been asked to run a training course intended to enable counsellors who work with individual clients in face-to-face settings to undertake either telephone counselling, groupwork, or couples counselling. What would you include in the course?

5 Reflect on the experience of reading a self-help book, preferably one which you consulted some time ago. Why did you decide to use the book? Did you discuss it with anyone else, or merely work through it on your own? What impact, either in the short-term or of a more lasting nature, has the book made on you? What was it about the book that you felt was most and least helpful?

TEN

MORALS, VALUES AND ETHICS IN COUNSELLING PRACTICE

The practice of counselling includes a strong moral and ethical dimension. It is clear that one of the central characteristics of the social groups in which counselling and psychotherapy have become established is the experience of living in a world in which it is difficult to know what is the 'right' way to live. In an increasingly secular society where there may be much questioning or rejection of tradition and authority, and where different moral or religious codes coexist, individuals are required to make choices about moral issues to an extent unknown in previous generations. In Chapter 1 it was argued that much of the need for psychotherapy is due to the fact that in modern society moral controls are for the most part internalized rather than externalized. Because we do not live in communities dominated by single, comprehensive moral codes, individuals must possess within them the means of deciding what is right and wrong, and also the means of punishment, for example feeling guilty, if they transgress these rules.

Many, perhaps even most, people who seek counselling are struggling with moral decisions. Should I finish my course or quit college? Should I stay in a marriage that is making me unhappy? Should I have this baby or arrange for an abortion? Should I come out and acknowledge that I am gay? Shall I take my own life? These, and many other counselling issues, are problematic for people because they involve very basic moral decisions about what is right and what is wrong.

One of the fundamental principles of most approaches to counselling is that the counsellor is required to adopt an accepting or non-judgemental stance or attitude in relation to the client. In general, most counsellors would agree that the aim of counselling is to help people to arrive at what is right for them, rather than attempting to impose a solution from outside. Nevertheless, at the same time counselling is a process of influence. In the end, the client who benefits from counselling will look back and see that the counselling process made a difference, and influenced the course of his or her life. The dilemma for the counsellor is to allow herself to be powerful and influential without imposing her own moral values and choices. Good counsellors, therefore, need to possess an informed awareness of the different ways in which moral and ethical issues may arise in their work.

In most societies, the principal source of moral and ethical thinking has been organized religion. Historically, there have been strong links between therapy and religion (discussed in Chapter 1). However, although Christian ideas about morality have been influential in the counselling world, it is also apparent that at least some of the people who have come into counselling from a previous religious background have done so because they have rejected elements of traditional religious thinking, or have been seeking something beyond these traditions. There has also been a steady influence on counselling and psychotherapy of non-religious moral philosophy, particularly existentialism, and of political and social movements, such as feminism. Finally, there has been a growing interest in non-Western religious thinking, particularly Buddhism.

Counsellors need to be aware of the moral dilemmas faced by their clients, and of the moral or ethical assumptions they themselves bring to their practice. However, as professionals accredited by society to deal with clients who may be vulnerable, needy and ill-informed, counsellors also have a responsibility to act towards their clients in an ethical manner. There are, therefore, two broad areas in which ethical and moral considerations are particularly relevant to counselling. The first is rooted in the actual counselling process. Clients may need help to resolve the moral issues involved in the life crises or problems that have brought them to counselling. The counsellor must also be sensitively aware of her own moral stance, and its interaction with the value system of the client. The second area is in behaving towards the client in an ethical and responsible manner.

Values in counselling

A *value* can be defined as an enduring belief that a specific end-state or mode of conduct is preferable. Rokeach (1973) differentiates between 'instrumental' and 'terminal' values. The latter refer to desirable end-states, such as wisdom, comfort, peace or freedom. Instrumental values correspond to the means by which these goals are to be achieved, for example through competence, honesty or ambition. Rokeach (1973) argues that most people will be in favour of a value such as 'equality', and that the best way to uncover the personal value system that guides the behaviour of an individual is to inquire about his or her value preferences. For example, one person might value equality higher than freedom, whereas another might place these two values in the other order. The study of values is, therefore, a complex matter. However, several studies have shown that the values of the counsellor influence the values held by clients. The trend shown in most studies has been for the values of the client to converge with those of the counsellor (Kelly, 1989). This finding raises questions for the practice of counselling. Are counsellors imposing their values on clients? Should counselling be seen as a form of socialization into a particular set of values?

Table 8 Comparison of religious and therapeutic value systems

Religious/theistic	Clinical-humanistic
God is supreme; humility and obedience to the will of God are virtues	Humans are supreme; autonomy and the rejection of authority are virtues
Relationship with God defines self-worth	Relationships with others define self-worth
Strict morality; universal ethics	Flexible morality; situational ethics
Service and self-sacrifice central to personal growth	Self-satisfaction central to personal growth
Forgiveness of others who cause distress completes the restoration of self	Acceptance and expression of accusatory feelings are sufficient
Meaning and purpose derived from spiritual insight	Meaning and purpose derived from reason and intellect

Source: Bergin (1980)

In Chapter 1, the cultural origins of counselling and psychotherapy in religious forms of helping and meaning-making were discussed. Bergin (1980) claims that the espousal by psychology of scientific beliefs and attitudes was associated with a rejection of religious values. His view is that, since many people in the general population hold strong religious views, there is a danger that therapy will be seen as irrelevant or even damaging. Bergin (1980) has carried out a systematic analysis of the differences between what he calls 'theistic' and 'clinical-humanistic' value systems (Table 8). The contrasts made by Bergin highlight divergences rather than acknowledging possible points of similarity and convergence, and his formulation has been criticized by Walls (1980), Ellis (1980) and Brammer *et al.* (1989). Nevertheless, his work makes it possible to see that there can be radically different views of what is 'right' or 'good'. Counsellors, trained in institutions which may embody clinical-humanistic values, may perhaps lose touch with the values of their clients. The power imbalance of the counselling situation may make it impossible for the client to assert his or her values except by deciding not to turn up. The issue of value differences is particularly relevant in cross-cultural counselling, or when the client is gay or lesbian (see Chapter 7). It is significant that many clients from these groups deliberately seek out counsellors whom they know to have a similar background and values.

Ethics and moral reasoning

In responding to moral and ethical questions which arise in their work, counsellors can make reference to a variety of levels of moral wisdom or knowledge. Kitchener (1984) has identified four discrete levels of moral reasoning which are drawn upon by counsellors: personal intuition; ethical guidelines established by professional organizations; ethical principles; and, finally, general theories of moral action.

Personal intuition

People generally have a sense of what feels right in any situation. This personal moral or ethical response is best understood as intuitive, since it is implicit rather than explicit, taken for granted rather than systematically formulated. Most of the time, and particularly during an actual counselling session, counsellors rely on their intuitive moral judgement of 'what feels right' rather than on any more explicit guidelines. There are, however, a number of limitations or dangers involved in relying only on this way of responding to moral choices. The first difficulty is that this kind of intuitive response is accumulated at least partially through experience and beginning counsellors may need to have some other way of dealing with moral issues, for example by reference to supervision or professional codes of ethics. Even for experienced counsellors, there may always be a sense in which their personal intuition is incomplete, especially in unusual or unforeseen situations. Other difficulties arise when the personal moral belief or choice of the client is outside the personal experience of the counsellor; for example, the Christian counsellor working with an Islamic client. Finally, it must be recognized that personal intuition can lead to unethical or immoral action as well as to more desirable behaviour. A counsellor in private practice, for instance, may persuade herself that a client who pays well would benefit from another ten sessions of therapy.

Despite the limitations of personal, intuitive moral reasoning, its presence is nevertheless absolutely essential in counsellors. Trainers or tutors assessing candidates for counsellor training are concerned that the people they select are trustworthy, have developed a firm moral position for themselves, and are capable of respecting boundaries. Counselling is an occupation in which external monitoring of ethical behaviour is extremely difficult, and therefore much depends on personal moral qualities.

Ethical guidelines developed by professional organizations

Counselling in Britain and other countries has become increasingly regulated by professional bodies. One of the functions of professional organizations such as the British Association for Counselling or the British Psychological Society is to ensure ethical standards of practice, and to achieve this objective both have produced ethical guidelines for practitioners, accompanied by procedures for dealing with complaints about unethical behaviour. In the USA, ethical guidelines have been published by the American Psychiatric Association, the American Psychological Association, the American Association for Marital and Family Therapy, and the American Association for Counseling and Development. In addition, some State legislatures in the USA have constructed ethical codes, as have numerous other professional groupings and agencies. All trained and competent counsellors currently in practice should be able to indicate to their clients the specific ethical guidelines within which they are operating.

The British Association for Counselling (BAC) Code of Ethics and Practice for Counsellors covers the nature of counselling, responsibility, competence, management of the work, confidentiality and advertising, and consists of a total of twenty-eight paragraphs. BAC has also published ethical guidelines for trainers and supervisors of counsellors. The AACD Ethical Standards statement, which also covers training and supervision, runs to ninety-nine paragraphs.

Although these guidelines are undoubtedly helpful in placing on record a consensus view on many of the ethical dilemmas in counselling, they are by no means unambiguous. For example, Table 9 presents the key statements on confidentiality drawn from the BAC and AACD ethical codes.

Finally, it is important to note that these ethical codes have been developed not only to protect clients against abuse or malpractice by counsellors, but also to protect the counselling profession against state interference and to reinforce its claims to control over a particular area of professional expertise. Ethics committees and codes of practice serve a useful function in demonstrating to the outside world that the counselling house is in order, that counsellors can be relied upon to give a professional service.

Ethical principles

On occasions when neither personal intuition nor ethical codes can provide a solution to a moral or ethical issue, counsellors need to make reference to more general philosophical or ethical principles. These are the ideas or more general moral injunctions which underpin and inform both personal and professional codes. Kitchener (1984) has identified five moral principles that run through most thinking about ethical issues: autonomy, non-maleficence, beneficence, justice and fidelity.

One of the fundamental moral principles in our culture is that of the *autonomy* of individuals. People are understood as having the right to freedom of action and freedom of choice, in so far as the pursuit of these freedoms does not interfere with the freedoms of others. The concept of the autonomous person is an ideal which has clearly not been achieved in many societies, in which coercion and control are routine. Nevertheless, in the societies where counselling and psychotherapy have become established, individual freedom and rights are usually enshrined in law. This concept of autonomy has been so central to counselling that many counsellors would assert that counselling cannot take place unless the client has made a free choice to participate. Another implication for counselling of the concept of autonomy lies in the notion of informed consent, that it is unethical to begin counselling, or initiate a particular counselling intervention, unless the client is aware of what is involved and has given permission to proceed.

Although it may be morally desirable to act as though clients are autonomous people capable of freedom of thought and action, there are many counselling situations in which the concept of autonomy is problematic. From a theoretical perspective, counsellors working from a psychoanalytic or radical behaviourist

Table 9   Confidentiality guidelines from two codes of ethics

British Association for Counselling (1984)
1 Counsellors treat with confidence personal information about clients, whether obtained directly or indirectly by inference. Such information includes name, address, biographical details, and other descriptions of the client's life and circumstances which might result in identification of the client.
2 'Treating with confidence' means not revealing any of the information noted above to any other person or through any public medium, except to those to whom counsellors owe accountability for counselling work (in the case of those working within an agency or organizational setting) or on whom counsellors rely for support and supervision.
3 Notwithstanding the above sections, if counsellors believe that a client could cause danger to others, they will advise the client that they may break confidentiality and take appropriate action to warn individuals or the authorities.
4 Information about specific clients is only used for publication in appropriate journals or meetings with the client's permission and with anonymity preserved when the client specifies.
5 Counsellors' discussion of the clients with professional colleagues should be purposeful and not trivializing.

American Association for Counseling and Development (1988)
1 Members make provisions for maintaining confidentiality in the storage and disposal of records and follow an established record retention and disposal policy. The counseling relationship and information resulting therefrom must be kept confidential, consistent with the obligations of the member as a professional person. In a group counseling situation, the counselor must set a norm of confidentiality regarding all group participants' disclosures.
2 If an individual is already in a counseling relationship with another professional person, the member does not enter into a counseling relationship without first contacting and receiving the approval of that other professional. If the member discovers that the client is in another counseling relationship after the counseling relationship begins, the member must gain the consent of the other professional or terminate the relationship, unless the client elects to terminate the other relationship.
3 When the client's condition indicates that there is clear and imminent danger to the client or others, the member must take reasonable personal action or inform responsible authorities. Consultation with other professionals must be used where possible. The assumption of responsibility for the client's behavior must be taken only after careful deliberation. The client must be involved in the resumption of responsibility as quickly as possible.
4 Records of the counseling relationship, including interview notes, test data, correspondence, tape recordings, electronic data storage, and other documents are to be considered professional information for use in counseling, and they should not be considered a part of the records of the institution or agency in which the counselor is employed unless specified by state statute or regulation. Revelation to others of counseling material must occur only upon the expressed consent of the client.
5 In view of the extensive data storage and processing capacities of the computer, the member must ensure that data maintained on a computer is: (a) limited to information that is appropriate and necessary for the services being provided; (b) destroyed after it is determined that the information is no longer of any value in providing services; and (c) restricted in terms of access to appropriate staff members involved in the provision of services by using the best computer security methods available.
6 Use of data derived from a counseling relationship for purposes of counselor training or research shall be confined to content that can be disguised to ensure the full protection of the identity of the subject client.

position would question the very possibility of individual autonomy, arguing that most of the time the behaviour of individual people is controlled by powerful external or internal forces. Counsellors influenced by feminist or family therapy perspectives would argue that in many instances autonomy may not be an ideal, and that very often clients need to move in the direction of greater relatedness or interdependence.

The freedom of choice and action of clients is also limited by a variety of practical circumstances. For example, few people would suppose that young children are capable of informed consent regarding the offer of counselling help, but it is difficult to decide at just what age a young person is able to give consent. Even with adult clients, it may be hard to explain just what is involved in counselling, which is an activity that is centred on first-hand experiential learning. Furthermore, the limits of client autonomy may be reached, at least for some counsellors, when the client becomes 'mentally ill', suicidal or a danger to others. In these situations, the counsellor may choose to make decisions on behalf of the client.

To summarize, the principle of freedom of choice and action is a theme which lies at the heart of much counselling practice. However, it is also evident that the concept of personal autonomy is not a simple one, and certainly not sufficient as a guide to action and good practice in all circumstances.

Non-maleficence refers to the instruction to all helpers or healers that they must 'above all do no harm'. *Beneficence* refers to the injunction to promote human welfare. Both these ideas emerge in the emphasis in codes of practice that counsellors should ensure that they are trained to an appropriate level of competence, that they must monitor and maintain their competence through supervision, consultation and training, and that they must work only within the limits of their competence.

One of the areas in which the principle of non-maleficence arises is that of the riskiness or harmfulness of therapeutic techniques. It would normally be considered acceptable for a client to experience deeply uncomfortable feelings of anxiety or abandonment during a counselling session, if such an episode were to lead to beneficial outcomes. But at what point does the discomfort become sufficient to make the intervention unethical? Some approaches to counselling advocate that clients be encouraged to take risks in experimenting with new forms of behaviour. The principle of autonomy might suggest that, if the client has given informed consent for the intervention to take place, then he or she has responsibility for the consequences. However, in practice it can be difficult explicitly to agree on every step in the therapy process. The counsellor or therapist may well not know about the potential riskiness of a technique, given the lack of research on many aspects of practice and the infrequency with which practitioners are influenced by research studies. Research studies also tend to focus on what works rather than on what does not work, and rarely draw attention to procedures which go badly wrong.

Moral dilemmas concerning beneficence are often resolved by recourse to utilitarian ideas. The philosopher John Stuart Mill defined ethical behaviour as that which brought about 'the greatest good for the greatest number'. The question of whether, for example, it was ethical to refer a highly socially anxious client to group counselling might depend on whether it could be predicted that, on balance, the benefits of this type of therapy outweighed the costs and risks. Quite apart from the uncertainty involved in ever knowing whether a therepeutic intervention will be helpful or otherwise in a particular case, the application of utilitarian ideas may conflict with the autonomous right of the client to make such decisions for himself or herself, or might lead to paternalism.

The principle of *justice* is primarily concerned with the fair distribution of resources and services, on the assumption that people are equal unless there is some acceptable rationale for treating them differently. In the field of counselling, the principle of justice has particular relevance to the question of access to services. If a counselling agency has a lengthy waiting list, is it ethical for some clients to be offered long-term counselling while others go without help? If the agency introduces a system of assessment interviews to identify the clients most in need of urgent appointments, can it be sure that its grounds for making decisions are fair rather than discriminatory? Is it just for a counselling agency to organize itself in such a way that it does not attract clients from minority or disadvantaged groups? Kitchener (1984: 50) points to the special significance of justice for counselling in writing that

> psychologists ought to have a commitment to being 'fair' that goes beyond that of the ordinary person. To the extent we agree to promote the worth and dignity of each individual, we are required to be concerned with equal treatment for all individuals.

The point here is that the conditions of trust and respect which are fundamental to the counsellor–client relationship are readily undermined by unjust behaviour.

The principle of *fidelity* relates to the existence of loyalty, reliability, dependability and action in good faith. Lying, deception and exploitation are all examples of primary breaches of fidelity. The rule of confidentiality in counselling also reflects the importance of fidelity. One aspect of counselling that is very much concerned with fidelity is the keeping of contracts. The practitioner who accepts a client for counselling is, either explicitly or implicitly, entering into a contract to stay with that client and give the case his or her best efforts. Situations in which the completion of the contract is not fulfilled, because of illness, job change or other counsellor factors, need to be dealt with sensitively to prevent breaches of fidelity.

This discussion of moral principles of autonomy, non-maleficence, beneficence, justice and fidelity has provided several illustrations of the fact that while these moral ideas are probably always relevant, they may equally well conflict with each other in any particular situation. Beauchamp and Childress (1979) have suggested that, following legal terminology, such principles should be regarded as prima facie binding. In other words, they must be abided by unless they conflict with some other principle, or there are extenuating circumstances. But when they are in conflict, or when such special circumstances do exist, what should be done?

General moral theories

Kitchener (1984) reviews some of the general theories of moral philosophy that can be called upon to resolve complex ethical dilemmas. Utilitarianism, the theoretical perspective which was mentioned in relation to beneficence, can be useful in this respect. The application of a utilitarian approach would be to consider an ethical decision in the light of the costs and benefits for each participant in the event, for example the client, the family of the client, other people who are involved and the counsellor. Another core philosophical approach is derived from the work of Kant, who proposed that ethical decisions should be universalizable. In other words, if it is right to breach confidentiality in this case, it must be right to do so in all similar cases in the future.

A more practical approach to resolving ethical disputes has been put forward by Stadler (1986). She advocates that any ethical decision should be subjected to tests of 'universality', 'publicity' and 'justice'. The decision-maker should reflect on the following questions:

1 Would I recommend this course of action to anyone else in similar circumstances? Would I condone my behaviour in anyone else? (Universality)
2 Would I tell other counsellors what I intend to do? Would I be willing to have the actions and the rationale for them published on the front page of the local newspaper or reported on the evening news? (Publicity)
3 Would I treat another client in the same situation differently? If this person was a well-known political leader, would I treat him or her differently? (Justice)

Throughout this discussion of ethical issues, it has been taken for granted that the counsellor is a person of integrity who is acting according to the highest values, and that ethical dilemmas arise because of the conflicting demands of clients and others. This is far from being the case. There is ample evidence of ethical malpractice among counsellors and psychotherapists. Austin et al. (1990) report that the insurance company contracted by the American Psychological Association to provide professional cover for psychologists paid out $17.2 million in claims in 1985. Table 10 indicates that over half of the cost of these claims was due to cases of unethical behaviour, such as sexual abuse of clients and breach of confidentiality, rather than technical incompetence. The implication of this state of affairs is that it is necessary for counsellors, individually and collectively, to acknowledge their fallibility. Much of the writing on counsellor training and education implies impossibly high standards of individual adjustment (see Chapter 13), which, perhaps, raise barriers to the disclosure of imperfections. The involvement of colleagues in collective maintenance of ethical standards, through supervision, peer support and relevant training, is also essential.

Following this introduction to some of the philosophical principles and ideas in this area, the practical intricacies of moral, legal and personal considerations which can be involved in ethical dilemmas in counselling will be examined through some examples.

Table 10   Causes of malpractice costs in the USA, 1976–1986

Cause of complaint	Percentage of total insurance pay-out
Sexual contact	44.8
Treatment error	13.9
Death of patient/other	10.9
Faulty diagnosis	7.9
Loss from evaluation	3.2
Breach of confidentiality	2.8
Failure to warn or protect	2.7
Bodily injury	2.4
Dispute over fees	2.2
Assault and battery	1.8

Source: Pope (1986)

Whose agent is the counsellor?

In August 1969, Prosenjit Poddar was a voluntary outpatient at the university health service in Berkeley, California, receiving therapy from a psychologist, Dr Lawrence Moore. Poddar had informed his therapist of his intention to kill his girlfriend, Tatiana Tarasoff, when she returned from a trip to Brazil. In consultation with two psychiatrist colleagues, Dr Moore recommended that Poddar be committed to hospital for observation. This decision was overruled by the chief of psychiatry. Poddar moved into an apartment with Tatiana's brother, near to where she stayed with her parents. Dr Moore wrote to the chief of police asking him to confine Poddar, and verbally asked the campus security service to detain him if he was seen. They did so. Poddar assured the campus officers he meant no harm, and they released him. Poddar subsequently murdered Tatiana Tarasoff. No warning had been given to either the victim or her family. The chief of psychiatry asked the police to return the letter written by Dr Moore and directed that the letter and case notes be destroyed. The University of California was sued by the parents of Tatiana Tarasoff, on the grounds that they should have been warned of the danger to their daughter. The defence stated that, after Poddar had been involved with the police, he had broken off all contact with the hospital, and was no longer one of their patients. A lower court rejected the case, but on appeal a higher court found for the parents.

The outcome of this case clearly carries a number of implications for counsellors and psychotherapists. Counsellors need to be willing to breach client-therapist confidentiality when the safety of others is at risk. Counsellors need to do everything possible to 'warn and protect' those in danger from their clients. Many states in the USA have enacted laws which make the failure to protect a criminal offence (Fulero, 1988; Austin *et al.*, 1990). Counsellors should be able to assess accurately and reliably the potential dangerousness of clients.

Finally, counselling agencies must enact specific policies and procedures for dealing with such cases.

The Tarasoff case demonstrates some of the complexities of ethical decision-making in counselling, and how ethical considerations can affect the counselling process itself. The right of the client, Prosenjit Poddar, to respect for his autonomy and for the confidentiality of his disclosures to his therapist was in conflict with the fundamental duty to protect life. The information about his intention to kill his girlfriend was shared with his therapist because they had a strong therapeutic relationship, but this relationship was destroyed by the action taken in an attempt to prevent violence. The therapist himself was faced with contradictory advice and guidance from professional colleagues. The situation necessitated him liaising with the police, a course of action which he had not been trained to undertake effectively.

Many clients express anger and resentment towards others in their counselling sessions. From some theoretical perspectives, such episodes can be interpreted as 'cathartic' and beneficial. On the other hand, as the Tarasoff case and many other such cases (see Austin *et al.* (1990) for details of seventeen similar cases heard in courts in the USA between 1975 and 1986) reveal, there are occasions when such client intentions are turned into action.

The Tarasoff case and the ensuing discussions over the 'duty to protect and warn' are part of a broader ethical issue relating to the problem of agency. Is the counsellor an agent only of the client, or is he or she also accountable to other people with an interest in the case? There are many counselling situations where conflicts of agency can arise. A client who is HIV positive may be engaging in unsafe sex which puts his or her partners or family at risk. An employee counsellor being paid by a company may be under pressure to achieve a particular type of result with a client. A counsellor working with an adolescent may find the parents giving suggestions or seeking information. Agency is very often an issue in relationship or marital counselling. Some practitioners and researchers (e.g. Hurvitz, 1967) would argue that conducting therapy with one spouse is likely to lead to feelings of alienation and rejection in the other spouse, and eventually to separation and divorce. Even in work with both spouses, the interests of the children of the marriage can become a central consideration.

Conflict between fidelity to the client and other demands on the counsellor can also occur in 'third party' counselling settings, such as employee counselling or employee assistance programmes (Wise, 1988). In these situations, the counsellor may be paid or employed by an organization, and may in fact be viewed by the organization as being primarily responsible to it rather than to the client (Bond, 1992). There may be both overt and subtle pressures on the counsellor to disclose information about the client, or to ensure that the counselling arrives at a predetermined outcome (e.g. a troublesome employee being 'counselled' to take early retirement). Sugarman (1992) makes a number of recommendations concerning the maintenance of ethical standards in workplace counselling:

- discover the objectives the organization is attempting to fulfil by providing a counselling service;

- identify any points at which the counselling provision might benefit the organization at the expense of the individual;
- identify any points at which the organization exceeds its right to control aspects of the employee's behaviour;
- negotiate with the organization about what is to be understood by 'confidentiality', and the conditions under which it will or will not be maintained;
- discover whether the resources being allocated to counselling are sufficient to do more good than harm;
- develop a written policy statement concerning the provision of counselling within the organization.

In most counselling theory, there is an implicit assumption that throughout the counselling process the therapist acts solely as an agent of the client. To take this view is to over simplify the situation. An important task for the counsellor is to be aware of these other relationships and systems, and to be willing to explore, and at times defend, the appropriate boundaries.

How far should the client be pushed? The use of persuasion and challenge

One of the fundamental tensions in counselling and psychotherapy arises from the definition and perception of the role of the therapist. In the client-centred/person-centred and psychodynamic traditions, the position is generally taken that the role of the therapist is to be reflective and patient, and on the whole to allow the client to use the time to arrive at his or her own understandings and insights. There is another tradition, represented by Gestalt therapy, the 'body' therapies and cognitive–behavioural approaches, which favours a much more active stance on the part of the therapist through the use of interventions that attempt to accelerate the pace of change or force breakthroughs. It is essential not to exaggerate the dichotomy between these positions: client-centred counsellors challenge clients and Gestalt therapists engage in empathic listening. However, the use of confrontative and manipulative tactics in therapy has been seen by many (Lakin, 1988) as raising a number of ethical issues.

A central ethical issue here is the principle of informed consent. The ethical value of autonomy implies that clients should have a choice regarding treatment. The notion of choice rests on the idea that the person responds to information in a rational manner. The aim of confrontation techniques, by contrast, is to break through the rationalizations and intellectualized defences which the client has erected. To tell the client exactly what will happen would nullify the effectiveness of the intervention. Moreover, some techniques, such as 'paradoxical' methods, require giving the client contradictory information; for example, asking an insomniac client to check the time on an alarm clock every hour through the night.

These techniques also raise questions regarding beneficence. There is little research evidence to support the effectiveness of approaches that are highly confrontative. In fact, in their tightly controlled study of encounter groups, Lieberman *et al.* (1973) found that there were more casualties in the groups run by leaders who were high on challenge and emphasized catharsis. Lakin (1988: 13) considers that confrontation may at times be performed to meet the needs of the therapist rather than those of the client: 'active and aggressive interviewing may be based on egotistical wishes to prove one's effectiveness.'

An extreme example of a brand of highly active therapy which went beyond any acceptable limit to become overtly abusive is given by Masson (1988) in his account of the history of 'direct psychoanalysis' developed by the psychiatrist John Rosen, which included the use of physical violence, verbal assault, deception and imprisonment. Lakin (1988) describes a similar case, relating to the Centre for Feeling Therapy, where therapists again engaged in physical and verbal violence, and also encouraged extra-marital affairs among couples who were in therapy. The leading figures in both these enterprises were sued by patients, and debarred from practice. Although the levels of abuse and cruelty to clients exhibited in these cases may seem outrageous, it is important to note, as Masson (1989) and Lakin (1988) both point out, that the founders of these therapies were highly qualified and trained, had published widely and had been commended by leaders in their profession for their pioneering work.

Dual relationships

Dual relationships in counselling and psychotherapy occur when the therapist is also engaged in another, significantly different, relationship with a client. Examples of dual relationships include: being a counsellor to someone who is a neighbour, friend or business partner; accepting payment from a client in the form of services (e.g. childminding); or being the landlord to a client. Pope (1991) identifies five main ways in which dual relationships conflict with effective therapy.

First, they compromise the professional nature of the relationship. Counselling depends on the creation of an environment of emotional safety created in part by the construction of reliable professional boundaries. The existence of dual relationships makes these boundaries unclear. Second, dual relationships introduce a conflict of interest. No longer is the counsellor there solely for the client. Third, the counsellor is unable to enter into a business or other non-therapy relationship on an equal footing, because of the personal material the client has disclosed and the likelihood of transference reactions, such as dependence. Finally, if it became acceptable for counsellors to engage in dual relationships after counselling had terminated, it would become possible for unscrupulous practitioners to use their professional role to set up relationships engineered to meet their needs. Research on the prevalence of dual relationships (Pope, 1991) has shown that around one-third of therapists have at some time developed non-sexual non-therapy relationships with current or former clients. It would also appear that male therapists engage in this behaviour more often than women.

Dual relationships may be a particularly significant problem in counselling in educational settings. Bond (1992) points out that many counsellors in schools and colleges are also employed as teachers or tutors, and so it is essential to be clear about the boundaries between these roles.

Sexual exploitation of clients

Carolyn Bates was a client in psychotherapy who was sexually abused by her therapist over a period of months. Her story is told in a book, *Sex in the Therapy Hour*, co-written with a psychologist, Barbara Brodsky (Bates and Brodsky, 1989). Their account offers a unique insight into the ways in which therapy can become transformed into a sexually abusive situation which is unethical and destructive.

Carolyn Bates was a shy, overweight teenager whose father had died after a long illness when she was fifteen. She 'staved off' her feelings of grief and loss by immersing herself in a church group. On leaving home to enter college, she met Steve, a Vietnam War veteran, who became her boyfriend and first sexual partner. She became dependent on him 'to ward off the feelings of depression that were nearly always encroaching upon me'. At the same time, she experienced intense guilt about engaging in pre-marital sex in opposition to the teachings of her church. She stopped attending church. The emotional pressure built up, exacerbated by a deteriorating relationship with her mother:

> As the tenuous relationship between Steve and me progressed through the first year, my control over these newly emerging, volatile emotions began to break down. I brimmed over with disillusionment, anger, frustration, and, above all, a pervasive sense of desperation. My reactions to any hints from Steve of ending our relationship were of such inordinate proportions that, in hindsight, I know they were related to my ongoing grief over the separation by death from my father.
>
> (Bates and Brodsky, 1989: 18)

After two years in this situation, with college grades dropping, Carolyn Bates entered therapy with a psychologist, Dr X , who had been recommended by one of her friends.

For the first five months of therapy, Carolyn felt a 'sense of hope and safety', and gradually opened up and explored her feelings about the death of her father and her relationship with Steve. At that point, her relationship with her therapist was close:

> I have no doubt that much of the trust and love I had for my father was directed toward Dr X, for I perceived him as having both wisdom and an unconditional concern for my well-being. I did not recognize at the time that this transference of feelings was occurring, but I did come to perceive him as a parental figure. And so I remained very dependent, working hard in therapy, in my eagerness for his acceptance and approval, believing him to be my sole source of affirmation.
>
> (Bates and Brodsky, 1989: 24)

However, as time went on Dr X began to focus more and more on sexual issues during therapy sessions, encouraging Carolyn to talk about her own sexual behaviour, and explaining his own positive attitude to casual sexual intercourse. He offered an interpretation that perhaps Carolyn was repressing her sexual feelings for him. She described this later as 'the sexualization of the therapeutic relationship'. He began hugging her at the end of sessions, then kissing her goodbye. In one session he suggested that her denial of attraction to him indicated homosexuality.

During the ninth month of therapy, Dr X introduced relaxation exercises which involved Carolyn lying down on the floor of the office. During one of these sessions he raped her. She reports 'terror', 'dissociation' and 'humiliation'. Sexual intercourse continued during eight or ten sessions over the next twelve months, always at the start of a session. During therapy, Dr X began talking more about his own problems. Eventually, some two years after entering therapy, Carolyn Bates was able to overcome her dependency and numbness and leave.

The next few months were a period of 'depression and confusion beyond hope': 'I carried with me a dark secret – I believed myself a failure in therapy . . . and blamed myself for what had occurred' (Bates and Brodsky, 1989: 41). There were nightmares and suicidal thoughts. When Carolyn entered therapy with another counsellor, it became possible to confront what had happened, and to file a complaint against Dr X. Despite the fact that six other women clients of Dr X came forward to testify that they had been the victims of similar sexual exploitation, the case in the civil courts took almost five years before an out-of-court settlement was made. Court appearances involved detailed cross-examination, which was additionally humiliating and distressing. There were other painful experiences arising from appearances before the State Licensing Board, which was considering whether to revoke the professional accreditation of Dr X. The process of achieving some limited redress against this practitioner was also accompanied by media attention. At the end of it all, he reapplied for, and was granted, a licence to practise.

The account given here of this case of therapist sexual abuse presents only some of the main features of what happened. However, by providing a uniquely detailed documentation of the process that occurred, the Bates and Brodsky (1989) study provides an invaluable demonstration of the following more general points:

1 Effective therapy can include phases when the client is highly dependent on the counsellor, and open to such suggestion or manipulation.
2 Within the confidential, secretive environment of the counselling relationship it is possible for counsellors to engage in unethical behaviour with little likelihood of being found out.
3 The focus of counselling on the personality and inner life of the client may readily result in the client blaming himself or herself and his or her own inadequacies for what has happened.
4 Clients who have been sexually abused by professionals encounter great difficulty in achieving redress.

Bates and Brodsky (1989) describe one case. But how general is this form of unethical conduct in counsellors and therapists? A number of surveys of psychologists and psychotherapists in the USA have discovered that sexual contact between therapists and their clients is not uncommon, despite being explicitly prohibited by all the professional associations in that country. Holroyd and Brodsky (1977), in a survey of 1000 psychologists, found that 8.1 per cent of the male and 1.0 per cent of the female therapists had engaged in sex with clients. Some 4 per cent of their sample believed that erotic contact with clients might in some circumstances be of therapeutic benefit to the client. Pope *et al.* (1979) carried out a similar anonymous questionnaire survey of 1000 psychotherapists, and found that 7 per cent reported having had sex with a client. Finally, Pope *et al.* (1986), in another large-scale survey of American practitioners, revealed admission of erotic contact with clients in 9.4 per cent of male and 2.5 per cent of female therapists.

The meaning of these figures is open to interpretation. The estimates made by the surveys cited must be regarded as representing a minimum estimate of the prevalence of client sexual abuse by therapists, because of the many factors which would lead respondents to conceal or under-report their involvement.

The damage that this type of abuse does to clients has been documented in a number of studies. For example, in her research Durre (1980: 242) observed:

> many instances of suicide attempts, severe depressions (some lasting months), mental hospitalizations, shock treatment, and separations or divorces from husbands . . . Women reported being fired from or having to leave their jobs because of pressure and ineffectual working habits caused by their depression, crying spells, anger and anxiety.

One way of making sense of the prevalence of sexual acting out between clients and therapists is to regard it as an inevitable, if unfortunate, consequence of the high levels of intimacy and self-disclosure which occur in therapy. An example of this approach can be found in the work of Edelwich and Brodsky (1991), who regard sex with clients as a professional issue for which therapists should be trained to cope. They take a position of encouraging practitioners to view strong feelings for clients as normal: 'anyone who ministers to the needs of others is bound to have unsettling experiences with emotional currents that run outside the bounds of professional propriety. These crosscurrents arise from normal, universal human feelings' (Edelwich and Brodsky, 1991: xiii). Difficulties arise not because counsellors have these feelings, but because they act on them inappropriately. Edelwich and Brodsky identify a number of guidelines for recognizing seductiveness in themselves and in their clients, and suggest strategies for dealing ethically with feelings of attraction:

- acknowledge your own feelings;
- separate your personal feelings from your dealings with the client;
- avoid overidentifying – the client's problems are not your own;
- don't give your problems to the client;
- talk to someone else about what is happening (e.g. colleagues or supervisor);

- set limits while giving the client a safe space for self-expression;
- don't be rejecting;
- express non-sexual caring;
- avoid giving 'double messages'.

They also point out that most sexual misconduct begins with other 'boundary violations', such as touching the client, seeing him or her socially, or inappropriate counsellor self-disclosure to the client, and recommend that these apparently less significant boundaries be treated with great respect.

An alternative perspective on sexual misconduct can be developed from a Jungian–feminist standpoint. Almost all therapist–client sexual behaviour takes place between male therapists and female clients, and the professional organizations that make it difficult for women to bring perpetrators to justice are dominated by men. In his book *Sex in the Forbidden Zone*, Rutter (1989) agrees with many of the practical guidelines put forward by Edelwich and Brodsky (1991), but profoundly disagrees with their analysis of underlying causes. Rutter argues that sex between professional men (not just therapists and counsellors, but also clergy, teachers, doctors and managers) and women over whom they are in a position of power or authority results from deeply held cultural myths about what it means to be male or female. Many men, according to Rutter, suppress and deny their own emotional pain and vulnerability, but hold on to a fantasy that they can be made whole through fusion with an understanding and accepting woman. The experience of sex with a woman client is, therefore, part of an unconscious search for healing and wholeness. It is, of course only a temporary means of resolving this male dilemma, and soon the sexual intimacy will seem false and the woman will be rejected.

This interpretation of the dynamics of therapist sexual behaviour is consistent with the findings of a study carried out by Holtzman (1984), who interviewed women who had been sexually involved with their therapists. Several of these women spoke of taking care of the therapist, of being aware of gratifying his emotional needs. Searles (1975) has described this process as the client unconsciously acting as therapist to the therapist.

According to Rutter (1989), women bring to this situation a lifetime of assaults to their self-esteem, of being told they are not good enough, particularly by their fathers. The experience of being in a working relationship with a powerful man who appreciates their abilities and qualities, and seeks to help them achieve fulfilment, is, for the woman, a potentially healing encounter. The betrayal of this closeness and hope brought about by sexual exploitation is, therefore, deeply damaging. Chesler (1972) interviewed ten women who had had sexual relationships with their therapists. All were described as being insecure, with low self-regard, and all blamed themselves for what had happened. Pope and Bouhoutsos (1986) suggest that women at particularly high risk of sexual exploitation from therapists are those who have previously survived incest or sexual abuse in earlier life. This point is reinforced by Mann (1989).

Rutter (1989) is perhaps, more simply, making the point that men have a strong tendency to sexualize relationships marked by high degrees of trust and intimacy. He goes further in regarding the public silence of male colleagues in the face of sexual misconduct as evidence of the pervasiveness of the under-lying myth:

> Although the majority of men holding positions of trust behave ethically in the sense that they will never have sexual contact with a woman under their care, they nevertheless hold on to the hope that one day it may actually happen. . . . Men who engage in forbidden-zone sex participate in it vicariously through the exploits of men who do. In a tribal sense, it is as if men who violate the forbidden zone are the designated surrogates for the rest of the men in the tribe.
>
> (Rutter, 1990: 62)

For Rutter, then, the existence of therapist–client sexual contact is not merely a professional issue, to be contained and addressed within the boundary of training programmes, but something which arises from fundamental issues of gender relationships in Western culture. It is, as a result, something from which we can all learn, which casts light on all therapeutic encounters between men and women.

The issue of sexual abuse of clients has been examined at some length, to demonstrate that ethical problems in counselling are not just occasional extreme events, like the Tarasoff murder, which suddenly arise to trap the practitioner in a web of competing moral demands and practical dilemmas. Moral, ethical and value issues are there in each counselling room, in each session. Whatever the counsellor does, or does not do, is an expression of values.

Practitioner malpractice: the response of the professional community

Increasing attention has been devoted by professional organizations in recent years to the question of how to maintain and enforce ethical standards. To some extent, these efforts have been motivated, particularly in the USA but also in other countries, by the recognition that media coverage of cases of misconduct was reducing public confidence and leading government agencies to impose legal penalties, thereby reducing professional autonomy. All professional organiza-tions require their accredited members to abide by a formal code of ethics, and all enforce procedures for disciplining members who violate these codes.

Ethical codes can at best only supply broad guidelines for action. There are always 'grey areas', and situations where different ethical rules might be in conflict. It is therefore necessary for counsellors to acquire an understanding of the broader ethical, moral and value considerations that inform and underpin the statements made in formal codes. Most counselling courses give considerable attention to awareness of ethical issues, drawing on standard texts such as Corey et al. (1988) or Van Hoose and Kottler (1985). This field is also served by an increasing amount of research on ethical issues (Miller and Thelen, 1987; Lakin, 1988).

Finally, some counsellors have contributed to the development of ways of helping clients who have been the victims of malpractice. This work has been mainly concentrated on the needs of clients who have been sexually exploited by therapists, and has included advocacy services, setting up self-help groups and therapy for victims (Pope and Bouhoutsos, 1986). There have been suggestions that the best way to prevent therapist sexual abuse of clients is for all women to be seen by women therapists (Chesler, 1972).

Topics for discussion and reflection

1 Consider the statements on confidentiality extracted from the Ethics Codes of the British Association for Counselling and American Association for the Counseling and Development (page 162). What are the main differences between these statements? What ambiguities can you identify in these guidelines – are there any situations you can imagine where either or both of these Codes would not provide you with a clear-cut recommendation for action? What suggestions do you have for improving these Codes?
2 In the book *Therapists' Dilemmas*, edited by Windy Dryden (1985a), a number of well-known counsellors and therapists are asked to discuss professional dilemmas which they have experienced. The interviews with John Davis, Brian Thorne, Peter Lomas, Paul Brown, Dougal Mackay and Fay Fransella touch on a range of ethical and value issues. Explore one or more of these interviews in the light of the ethical principles introduced in this chapter.
3 What counselling situations can you imagine in which your values would be in conflict with those held by a client? What would you do in such a situation?

ELEVEN

THE ROLE OF RESEARCH IN COUNSELLING AND THERAPY

A great deal of research has been carried out into counselling and psychotherapy, particularly in the past thirty years. The existence of this body of research may seem to imply a paradox: the counselling relationship is private and confidential, while the research process involves external access to information. But it is just this hidden or secret dimension to counselling which has made research so important. Good research should, ultimately, allow the development of a better understanding of events and processes that are experienced by individual counsellors and clients, and therefore enable practitioners to learn from each other. Research can also promote a critical and questioning attitude in practitioners, and help them to improve the quality of service offered to clients. Finally, research is an international activity, and research journals are read by a world audience. Participation in such an international community of scholars helps counsellors to achieve a broader perspective on their work.

The role of research in the field of counselling is complex and multi-faceted. Some of the factors that can motivate people to conduct research in this field are:

- testing the validity of theory;
- evaluating the effectiveness of different approaches or techniques;
- demonstrating to a third-party funding agency (e.g. government department, insurance company, private company) the cost-effectiveness of counselling or psychotherapy;
- enabling an individual practitioner to monitor his or her work;
- allowing individual practitioners to resolve 'burning questions';
- to get a Masters degree or PhD;
- letting colleagues know about particularly interesting cases or innovations;
- establishing the academic credibility of counselling as a subject taught in universities;
- enhancing the professional status of counsellors in relation to other professional groups.

Table 11   The contrast between qualitative and quantitative approaches to research

Qualitative	Quantitative
Description and interpretation of meanings	Measurement and analysis of variables
Quality of relationship between researcher and informants important	Aims for neutral, objective relationship
Necessity for self-awareness and reflexivity in researcher	Aims for value-free researcher
Uses interviews, participant observation, diaries	Uses tests, rating scales, questionnaires
Researcher(s) interpret data	Statistical analysis of data
Strongest in sociology, social anthropology, theology and the arts	Strongest in psychology and psychiatry
Many similar ideas to psychoanalysis and humanistic therapies	Many similar ideas to behavioural and cognitive therapies

It can be seen that there are many different reasons for doing research. Some research studies are inspired by the practical concerns of practitioners. Other studies emerge from the interests of groups of people working together on a set of ideas or theory. Yet other studies are set up to meet external demands. Often, there can be more than one factor motivating a study.

Within the social sciences in general there has been considerable debate over the issue of what constitutes valid research. This debate has generated an enormous literature, which in part can be characterized as an argument between advocates of quantitative approaches and those who would favour qualitative methods of research. Quantitative research involves careful measurement of variables, with the researcher taking a detached, objective role. Qualitative research, by contrast, has as its aim the description and interpretation of what things mean to people, and to achieve this the researcher must develop a relationship with the research informants or co-participants. The differences between the quantitative and qualitative research traditions are displayed in Table 11. Both approaches to research have a lot to offer in the field of counselling and psychotherapy research, and they can be combined effectively (see, for example, Hill, 1989; Stiles *et al.*, 1990; Stiles, 1991). Nevertheless, the split between qualitative and quantitative approaches has been significant for the field as a whole, and remains a source of conflict and tension (Neimeyer and Resnikoff, 1982). The disciplines which have had the strongest professional and institutional influence on counselling have been psychology and psychiatry. These are both disciplines that have been associated with 'hard', quantitative research. On the other hand, the philosophy of the person and values of the qualitative research tradition are very close to those of most counselling and psychotherapy practitioners.

The breadth and scope of research in counselling and psychotherapy is immense. Beutler and Crago (1991), in a recent review, identified forty-one separate research programmes in eight different countries. It would be impossible to attempt meaningful discussion of all aspects of the field in this chapter. Particular attention will therefore be given to three types of research study that have been of central importance: outcome studies, process studies and case studies. Readers interested in pursuing other aspects of research in counselling are recommended to consult Garfield and Bergin (1986), which contains an authoritative review of research findings on a wide range of topics, and Bolger (1989), which looks at counselling research in Britain. Reviews of current research can also be found in the *Annual Review of Psychology* (Gelso and Fassinger, 1990; Goldfried *et al.*, 1990). Readers interested in learning more about research design should consult Parry and Watts (1989), Freeman and Tyrer (1989) or Heppner *et al.* (1992), each of which examines in detail the issues involved in planning and implementing different kinds of research study.

Outcome and evaluation research

Outcome and evaluation studies have the primary aim of finding out how much a particular counselling or therapy intervention has helped or benefited the client. The earliest systematic research into counselling and therapy concentrated entirely on this issue. In the 1930s and 1940s, several studies were carried out into the effects of psychoanalysis. The results of these investigations suggested that, overall, around two-thirds of the psychoanalytic patients followed up improved, with one-third remaining the same or deteriorating after treatment.

These findings appeared highly encouraging for psychoanalysis and, by implication, for other forms of the 'talking cure'. However, in 1952 Eysenck published a devastating critique of this early research. Eysenck pointed out that studies of neurotic people who had not received therapy but had been followed up over a period of time also produced an improvement rate of around 60 per cent. He argued that psychoanalysis could not be considered effective if it produced the same amount of benefit as no therapy at all. Eysenck suggested that there existed a process of 'spontaneous remission', by which psychological problems gradually became less severe over time owing to non-professional sources of help in the community or because the person had learned to deal with a crisis situation which had provoked a breakdown.

The psychotherapy world reacted strongly to Eysenck's critique, but the main effect of his attack was to force researchers to design more adequate studies. In particular, it became accepted that outcome studies should include a control group of clients who do not receive treatment, so that the impact of the counselling or therapy can be compared with the levels of improvement brought about by spontaneous remission. The usual method of creating a comparison group of this kind has been to use a 'waiting list' group of clients who have applied for therapy but who are not offered their first appointment for some time, and are assessed at the beginning and end of that period to detect changes occurring in the absence of professional help.

A good example of outcome research is the Sloane *et al.* (1975) study, which compared the effectiveness of psychodynamic therapy with that of a behavioural approach. The study was carried out in a university psychiatric outpatient clinic, and applicants for therapy were screened to exclude those too disturbed to benefit or who required other forms of help. Ninety-four clients were randomly allocated to behaviour therapy, psychodynamic therapy or a waiting list group. The people on the waiting list were promised therapy in four months, and were regularly contacted by telephone. Clients paid for therapy on a sliding scale, and received an average of fourteen sessions over four months. Before the beginning of therapy, each client was interviewed and administered a battery of tests. In addition, clients identified three target symptoms, and rated the current intensity of each symptom. Ratings of the level of adjustment were also made by the interviewer and a friend or relative of the client. These measures were repeated at the end of the therapy, and at one-year and two-year follow-up. Every fifth session was tape-recorded and rated on process measures of therapist qualities, such as empathy, congruence and acceptance. Speech patterns of therapists and clients were also analysed from these tapes.

The results of the Sloane *et al.* (1975) study indicated that, overall, more than 80 per cent of clients improved or recovered at the end of therapy, with these gains being maintained at follow-up. Both treatment groups improved more than the waiting list group. The quality of the therapist–client relationship was strongly associated with outcome, for both types of therapy. Behaviour therapists were rated on the whole as being more congruent, empathic and accepting than the psychodynamic therapists. There was no evidence for symptom substitution.

Many other studies have been carried out along similar lines to the Sloane *et al.* investigation, and most have arrived at similar conclusions regarding the relative effectiveness of different approaches. With the aim of determining whether the apparent equivalence of approaches was confirmed across the research literature as a whole, several literature reviews have been conducted (Luborsky *et al.*, 1975). The most comprehensive and systematic of these literature reviews was the 'meta-analysis' carried out by Smith *et al.* (1980). Meta-analysis involves calculating the average amount of client change reported for each approach in each separate study, then adding up these change scores to give an overall estimate how much benefit a particular approach (such as psychoanalysis, client-centred therapy or behaviour therapy) yields over a set of studies comprising a large number of clients. In their report, Smith, *et al.* (1980) conclude that they could find no consistent evidence that any one approach to counselling or therapy was any more effective than any other. Although this conclusion has been disputed by some writers (for example, Rachman and Eysenck), who continue to assert the superiority of behavioural methods over all others, there is now general agreement within counselling that different approaches are equally effective, and that counselling or therapy is significantly more beneficial than no treatment.

The story of the development of outcome research might suggest that there is little more to be learned about the effectiveness of counselling and therapy. This is far from being the case. One of the important and significant aspects of studies such as Sloane *et al.* (1975) is that they are difficult to organize and expensive to implement, and as a result have tended to be carried out in 'elite' therapy institutions, such as university psychiatry or counselling clinics. The therapists in these studies are usually experienced and highly trained. There is a need, therefore, for more studies to be carried out into the effectiveness of the work done in agencies that are less well resourced and that may well serve clients who present a wider range of problems or have less counselling sophistication. Relatively few studies of this kind have been carried out, and those that have been completed have not been able to use control groups or to follow up large numbers of clients.

Another gap in the outcome research literature arises from the lack of specificity of many studies. Paul (1967: 111) has made the point that research should be able to identify '*what* treatment, by *whom*, is most effective for *this* individual with *that* specific problem, and under *which* set of circumstances.' At the present time, research evidence is not precise enough to answer these questions.

The outcome and evaluation studies mentioned so far have all comprised the assessment of change in groups of clients receiving counselling or therapy from a number of practitioners. It has already been noted that these studies are complex, expensive and difficult to arrange. Several writers have advocated, by contrast, that it is desirable for individual counsellors to monitor or evaluate their own work in a systematic way. Barlow *et al.* (1984) have called for counsellors and therapists to adopt the role of 'scientist-practitioner' and to use research routinely to help them reflect on their work with clients. They point out that research instruments such as psychological tests or questionnaires may provide clinicians with invaluable information that can be used in therapy. The use of the scientist-practitioner approach normally involves gathering baseline information on the level of problem behaviour in a client, before the commencement of counselling, then continuing to monitor the level of that behaviour throughout counselling and then at follow-up. An essential element of this kind of research is clarity about the goals and objectives of treatment which has made it more popular with the action-oriented behavioural and cognitive-behavioural approaches rather than the more insight-oriented psychodynamic and humanistic approaches.

Examples of some of the many different types of assessment tool that can be used in outcome and evaluation studies are:

- Self-monitoring of problem behaviours (e.g. eating, smoking, occurrence of paranoid or obsessional thoughts) using a notebook or diary.
- Self-ratings of moods or feelings. Examples: rating scales to assess level or intensity of tension, pain, sadness or anxiety.
- Questionnaire measures of general psychological adjustment. Examples: General Health Questionnaire (GHQ), Minnesota Multiphasic Personality Inventory (MMPI).

- Questionnaire measures of specific variables. Examples: Beck Depression Inventory (BDI), Spielberger State-Trait Anxiety Inventory.
- Client-defined variables. Examples: Personal Questionnaire (Phillips, 1986), client ratings of target symptoms (Sloane *et al.*, 1975).
- Client satisfaction questionnaires (Berger, 1983).
- Direct observation of the client. Examples: counting frequency of stuttering or negative self-statements during counselling session, observation of social skills performance during role play, measuring sleep duration of insomniacs.
- Post-therapy ratings of outcome from client, therapist, or friends and family members of the client.

A very wide range of measures and techniques has been employed, reflecting a diversity of aims, client groups and theoretical rationales. Further information on these techniques can be found in Nelson (1981), Lambert *et al.* (1983) and Bowling (1991).

A final type of research that can be carried out in the area of evaluation concerns the assessment of quality of service provided by a counselling agency or organization. In this kind of study, many other factors are investigated in addition to the impact of counselling on individual clients. Maxwell (1984) has suggested six criteria for evaluating service provision: relevance/appropriateness, equity, accessibility, acceptability, effectiveness and efficiency. The question of acceptability introduces the perceptions and judgements of consumers of the service. The issue of efficiency brings in considerations of cost-effectiveness and cost–benefit analysis (McGrath and Lowson, 1986; Mangen, 1988). Parry (1992) has carried out a thorough review of the different methods and approaches that have been employed in service evaluation. She concludes that, in the interests of the many potential clients who might need therapeutic help but are denied it because of inefficient or inaccessible services, 'unmonitored practice is no longer defensible' (Parry, 1992: 14).

Process research

Whereas outcome studies mainly examine the difference in the client before and after counselling, without looking at what actually happens during sessions, process studies take the opposite approach. In a process study, the researcher is attempting to identify or measure the therapeutic elements that are associated with change. Following the conclusions of reviewers such as Luborsky *et al.* (1975) and Smith *et al.* (1980) that counselling and psychotherapy is, on the whole, effective, the energies of many researchers have focused more on questions of process. Having established that therapy 'works', they are seeking to learn *how* it works.

Studies of process from a client-centred perspective

The client-centred approach to counselling and therapy developed by Rogers and his colleagues (Rogers, 1942, 1951, 1961) has been characterized by a consistent emphasis on the process of change in clients, and the process of the client–counsellor relationship. Rogers and his colleagues at the University of Ohio (1940–5) were the first investigators to make recordings of therapy sessions, and the first to study process in a systematic way. The earliest studies within the client-centred framework explored changes in the ways that clients made references to self at different points in their therapy, and the 'directiveness' of counsellor statements, by analysing transcripts of counselling sessions (Snyder, 1945; Seeman, 1949). Other studies from this period focused on the experience of the client in counselling, for example through the exploration of diaries kept by clients (Lipkin, 1948; Rogers, 1951).

In a major piece of research carried out at the University of Chicago, Rogers and Dymond (1954) and their colleagues examined different aspects of change in clients' self-concepts during and after therapy. Self-acceptance, a key concept in Rogerian theory, was assessed using a technique known as the 'Q-sort', in which clients arrange a set of self-statements to describe 'how I see myself now' and 'how I would ideally like to be' (the difference between actual and ideal self being taken as a measure of self-acceptance). Taking a group of twenty-nine clients, they administered the Q-sort, and a range of other tests, at a pre-therapy interview, regularly throughout therapy and at follow-up. Results showed that changes in self-perception were closely associated with good outcomes. One of the main achievements of this phase of research was to demonstrate that research could be undertaken that was phenomenological, respecting the experience of the client, yet at the same time rigorous and quantitative. For the first time, an important aspect of process, change in self-acceptance, had been measured and tracked across a course of therapy. The Rogers and Dymond (1954) report was also noteworthy in containing a systematic analysis of failure attrition cases.

Towards the end of his stay at Chicago, Rogers integrated the fruits of research and practice in client-centred therapy and counselling into two key papers, one on the 'necessary and sufficient' relationship conditions of empathy, congruence and unconditional positive regard (Rogers, 1957), the other on the process of change in therapy (Rogers, 1961: ch. 7). These papers are discussed more fully in Chapter 3. In their next major piece of research, Rogers and his collaborators set out to test these ideas in a study of client-centred therapy with hospitalized schizophrenic patients (Rogers *et al.*, 1967). Rating scales were devised to measure the levels of therapists' unconditional positive regard, congruence, empathy and experiencing level observed in recordings of sessions with clients. Barrett-Lennard developed a questionnaire, the Relationship Inventory, to assess these 'core conditions' as perceived by clients, counsellors or external observers. Although the results of the schizophrenia study were ambiguous, largely due to the difficulty in achieving any degree of substantial change in disturbed clients, the Relationship Inventory and the various rating scales developed during the project have remained standard instruments in process studies (Greenberg and Pinsof, 1986).

The research team around Rogers split up after he moved to California following the Wisconsin study, but the hypothesis of Rogers that the 'core conditions' of adequate levels of acceptance, empathy and congruence, once perceived by the client, represented not only necessary but also sufficient conditions for positive personality change in clients, received a great deal of further study. Reviews of the work on this important theoretical claim (Patterson, 1984; Watson, 1984; Cramer, 1992) suggest that Rogers was largely correct, even though there have been severe practical difficulties in adequately testing his model. Currently the most active research within the client-centred process model has been that concerned with 'depth of experiencing' in clients and counsellors.

The process research carried out by Rogers and his collaborators has made a significant contribution to the field, for a number of reasons. First, it demonstrated that the phenomena and processes of the counselling relationship were not something mysterious and elusive, but could appropriately and effectively be opened up for external scrutiny and research. Second, it represents what is probably still the most successful attempt in counselling and therapy to use research to test theoretical assumptions and evolve new concepts and models. Third, it supplied an example of the fruitful integration of research with practice, since all the people taking part in the research were practitioners as well as researchers. Finally, Rogers and his colleagues showed that it was possible and profitable to give the client a voice, and to explore the experience and perceptions of the client in therapy.

Studies of process from a psychodynamic perspective

Psychodynamic theory contains a wealth of ideas about the process of therapy. For example, the counselling process in psychodynamic work is likely to include instances of free association, interpretation, transference, counter-transference, analysis of dream and fantasy material, and episodes of resistance. Research that could help practitioners to understand more fully the mode of operation of these factors would be of substantial practical utility. However, research that is consistent with the basic philosophical assumptions of psychoanalysis presents a number of distinctive methodological problems. From a psychoanalytic point of view, the meaning of a client statement, or interaction between client and counsellor, can only be understood in context, and can only be interpreted by someone competent in psychodynamic methods. It is insufficient, therefore, to conduct process studies that rely on tape-recordings of segments of an interview, or to use a standardized rating scale administered by research assistants, as in other process research. Psychodynamic process studies are carried out by expert, trained practitioners, and are based on the investigation of whole cases.

One of the best examples of psychodynamic process research is to be found in the use of the core conflictual relationship theme (CCRT) method developed by Luborsky et al. (1986) as a technique for exploring transference. In this technique, a number of expert judges first read a transcript of an entire session. They are then asked to focus on episodes in the transcript where the client makes reference to relationships, and to arrive at a statement of three components of each episode: the wishes or intentions of the client towards the other person, the responses of the other person, and the response of the client himself or herself. Taken together, these components yield a picture of the kind of con-flictual relationships, or transference patterns, experienced by the client in his or her life. The formulations of different judges are checked against each other to arrive at a consensus view.

The CCRT method has been used to investigate a number of hypotheses regarding the transference process in therapy. For example, Luborsky *et al.* (1986) compared the transference themes displayed towards other people and those expressed in relation to the therapist. Results provided strong evidence to confirm the Freudian assumption that the transference relationship with the therapist is a reflection of the way the client characteristically relates to people in everyday life. Crits-Christoph *et al.* (1988), also using the CCRT technique, showed that accuracy of interpretation, assessed by comparing CCRT formula-tions with therapist interpretations of relationship issues, was positively correlated with client benefit in therapy. Similar studies, in which expert readers have been employed to identify psychodynamic themes in session transcripts, have been carried out by Malan (1976), Silberschatz *et al.* (1986) and Kachele (1992).

The 'events paradigm'

Process-oriented research carried out within the client-centred perspective has become less fashionable in recent years, owing to a variety of factors which resulted in diminishing interest in the person-centred approach in the USA. Currently, researchers exploring therapy process are more likely to be working within what has become known as the 'events paradigm' (Rice and Greenberg, 1984a). This approach concentrates on finding change events within therapy sessions, and identifying the therapist's or counsellor's actions or strategies that enabled these events to occur. This is quite different from the client-centred view of process, which focuses not so much on discrete events as on general conditions or the creation of a therapeutic environment.

One of the key figures in events research has been Robert Elliott, based at the University of Toledo in Ohio, who has adapted the interpersonal process recall (IPR) method (see Chapter 13) for use in research (Kagan *et al.*, 1963; Kagan, 1984). In this approach, a video- or audio-tape of a therapy session is played back to either the therapist or the client, with the aim of stimulating their recall of the experience of being in the session, and collecting information about their evaluation or perception of events within it. Early studies using this method looked at process elements, such as client perceptions of what is helpful and dimensions of therapist intentions (Elliott, 1986). However, later research has focused on identifying and analysing actual events, with the aim of describing 'the nature and unfolding of particular types of significant change event' (Elliott, 1986: 507). Another approach to studying significant events has been evolved by Mahrer *et al.* (1987). In these studies, Mahrer and his co-researchers listened to audio-tapes of therapy sessions in order to identify 'good moments' where the client showed movement, progress, process improvement or change. The distri-bution of these moments over the session, and the therapist's behaviour that appeared to facilitate good moments, have been explored. In yet another series of studies of events, Rice and Greenberg have looked at the tasks the therapist must carry out in order to facilitate change in different circumstances.

These studies of key events in the counselling process are all recent or still in progress, and it is too early to tell where they will lead. It is worth noting, however, that unlike the Rogerian studies, which were explicitly informed by theory, the events studies are largely non-theoretical in nature, and so far at least have been devoted to describing change events and processes rather than to developing a theoretical framework for understanding them.

The process as experienced by the client

One of the fundamental issues in research into counselling and psychotherapy concerns the question of who is observing what is happening. Rogers and Dymond (1954) pointed out that different conclusions on process and outcome could be reached depending on whether the perspective of the client, the therapist or an external observer was taken. Most research has relied on either the perspective of the therapist or that of an external observer, since to involve the client could intrude on his or her therapy, or cause distress. Most studies that have involved collecting data from clients have used standardized question-naires or rating scales. In these studies, the experience of the client is filtered through categories and dimensions imposed by the researcher. There have been relatively few studies into the client's experience of the process of counselling as defined by the client (McLeod, 1990).

Maluccio (1979) carried out intensive interviews with clients who had completed counselling. This piece of research illustrates the difficulties inherent in inviting people to talk retrospectively about the *whole* of their counselling experience. The informants interviewed by Maluccio produced large amounts of complex material that was difficult to interpret. Maluccio found that, on the whole, clients experienced their counselling as having passed through discrete stages. Another significant finding from this study was that clients often attributed changes in psychological and emotional well-being not to anything that was happening with their therapist, but to external events such as getting a job or moving house. This finding indicates one of the important differences between the client's and therapist's experience of counselling. The client experiences counselling as one facet of a life that may encompass many other relationships; the counsellor has no first-hand involvement with these other relationships and is limited to his or her experience of the actual sessions. The two types of experience therefore have quite different horizons.

The work of Maluccio (1979), and of other researchers such as Timms and Blampied (1985), has looked at the experience of the client over an extended time, which may span several months of counselling. Clearly, a lot can happen over the course of therapy, and this kind of research will not be able to pick up the fine-grained detail of what the client experiences on a moment-by-moment basis. In a series of studies, Rennie (1990) has focused on the experiences of clients in single sessions. Rennie has used a version of the Interpersonal Process Recall technique (Kagan, 1984) to enable clients to re-live or re-experience what they thought and felt during the session. An audio- or video-tape is made of the session, and as soon as possible after the end of the session the client reviews the tape in the presence of the researcher, stopping the tape whenever he or she remembers what was being experienced at that point. The researcher then sorts through the transcript of the inquiry interview to identify themes and categories of experience.

The client experience studies carried out by Rennie and his associates (Angus and Rennie, 1988, 1989; Rennie, 1990, 1992) have opened up for research an area of the counselling process which is normally inaccessible to counsellors, and have produced some striking results. One of the conclusions Rennie arrives at is that clients are responding to the counsellor on different levels. They may be telling the counsellor about some event in their life, but underneath that narrative may be considering whether or not to take the risk of talking about some previously secret piece of information. They may agree with an interpretation or intervention from the counsellor, while knowing that it is inaccurate or inappropriate.

Exploration of the world of the client, as pioneered by Maluccio (1979) and Rennie (1990), is still at an early stage, and there are undoubtedly significant insights waiting to be discovered. These studies of client experience are rooted in the tradition of qualitative research, and require sensitive, ethically aware contact between researcher and client, as well as much painstaking work categorizing and interpreting themes derived from interview transcripts. The aim of this type of work is to produce 'grounded theory' (Glaser and Strauss, 1967; Glaser, 1978; Rennie et al., 1988), or generalizations and models which are demonstrably rooted in actual experience rather than imposed by the researcher.

Case studies

The final approach to research to be considered is the case study. Traditionally, case studies have been the primary vehicle for research and theory construction in psychodynamic approaches to counselling and psychotherapy. Many of the cases published by Freud, for example, have been widely debated and reinterpreted by other therapists and theorists and represent some of the basic building blocks of psychoanalytic knowledge and training. It would be unusual to find a trained and experienced psychodynamic counsellor or therapist who had not carefully read the cases of Dora (Freud, 1901), the Rat Man (Freud, 1909) or Schreber (Freud, 1910).

From a research point of view, however, there are many methodological issues raised by the manner in which Freud and his colleagues carried out case studies. Freud saw several patients each day, and wrote up notes of his consultations in the evening. Some of these notes were subsequently worked up as papers presented to conferences or published in books and journals. At each stage of this process of producing a case study, there was no possible check on the validity of the conclusions reached by Freud, or on any bias in his recollection or selection of evidence. Critics of Freudian theory such as Eysenck can, as a result, put forward the argument that Freud distorted the evidence to fit his theories. There is little that psychoanalysts can do to counter this charge, given the way the case studies were carried out.

The dilemma that is apparent in this debate over case studies is that, on the one hand, detailed examination of individual cases is invaluable for the development of theory and practice, but, on the other hand, finding a rigorous and unbiased way of observing and analysing individual cases is difficult. The construction of methods for systematic case study research has been a recurrent concern for researchers in the field of personality for many years (Murray, 1938; DeWaele and Harré, 1976; Rabin et al., 1981, 1990). Within the field of counselling and psychotherapy research, there have been three distinctive approaches to systematic case study investigations, reflecting the influence of behavioural, psychoanalytic and integrationist thinking.

Behavioural case studies are sometimes known as '$N = 1$' studies, and are associated with the 'scientist-practitioner' model discussed earlier in this chapter. These case studies concentrate on tracking changes in a limited number of key variables predicted to change as a result of counselling, for example amount of time spent studying or score on a depression inventory. The principal aim of the study is to demonstrate the effectiveness of a particular type of intervention with a particular category of client, and broader process issues are not usually considered. Barlow and Hersen (1986), Barlow et al. (1984) and Morley (1989) provide a useful account of the procedures involved in this type of case study.

Psychoanalytic or psychodynamic systematic case study research is quite different in its aims and methods. The intention in this type of study is to replicate the capacity of the therapist or counsellor to arrive at a formulation of the unconscious dynamics of a case, but using a team of researchers to avoid the bias or distortion which could arise from relying solely on the judgement of the therapist himself or herself. Examples of this kind of study are given in the earlier section on psychodynamically oriented process research.

Case study research from a more integrationist orientation has been conducted by Hill (1989), who carried out a series of eight case studies of brief therapy with depressed women clients, with the aim of identifying the relative contribution to outcome made by non-specific factors and therapist techniques. This study is unique in the exhaustive and comprehensive information that was gathered on each case (see Table 12). A number of other case studies have recently been published in which cases of special interest have been selected from large-scale extensive investigations. For example, Strupp (1980a, b, c, d) presented four comparative pairs (one success and one failure case) of cases drawn from Strupp and Hadley (1979). A similar approach, choosing representative cases for detailed analysis, has been taken by Barkham (1989), Barkham and Shapiro (1990a) and Stiles et al. (1992). The distinguishing features of these integrationist case studies have been the combination of qualitative and quantitative data, the use of group comparisons as well as intensive analysis of individual cases, and the adoption of a trans-theoretical perspective (see Good and Watts, 1989).

Having explored some of the methods and techniques that researchers have

Table 12   The intensive case study method

Pre-therapy, at termination and follow-up
Minnesotta Multiphasic Personality Inventory
Hopkins Symptom Checklist (SCL-90-R)
Tennessee Self-Concept Scale
Target complaints
Hamilton Depression and Anxiety Scales
Interview

After each session
Researchers rated:
   Counsellor verbal response modes
   Counsellor activity level
   Client reactions during session
   Client level of experiencing

Client and therapist completed:
   Post-session questionnaire or interview
   Working Alliance Inventory
   Session Evaluation Questionnaire

Client and therapist separately watched video of session to recall feelings and rate
helpfulness of each counsellor statement

Note: The table shows information gathered on each case by Hill (1989)

used in studying process and outcome in counselling and psychotherapy, we
can now discuss some of the underlying issues and debates in this area.

Ethical dilemmas in counselling research

The purpose of counselling is to help people, or to empower them to help themselves, and the process of counselling can often require disclosure of confidential
information, experience of painful memories and emotions, and the taking of
decisions that affect other people. Counsellors take great care to ensure that this
sometimes risky process does not bring harm to clients. It is easy to see that
research into counselling introduces additional possibilities of harm. Research
may lead to information about clients being disclosed, painful feelings being
re-stimulated, or the relationship of trust with the therapist being damaged.

   Most forms of counselling research contain ethical dangers. For example, in
outcome studies in which there is a control group of 'waiting list' clients, the
decision is taken to offer help immediately to some people, but withhold it from
others. In studies of new types of counselling intervention, clients may be
exposed to therapy that is harmful. If the researcher contacts the client to request
that he or she takes part in the study, the knowledge that this person is a client
is transmitted beyond the counsellor or agency. If the counsellor asks the
client to participate in a study, the client may be unwilling to do so but may

nevertheless comply for fear of antagonizing someone upon whom he or she feels emotionally dependent. In studies where former clients are interviewed about their experience of therapy, the interview itself may awaken a need for further counselling.

For these reasons, counselling and psychotherapy research studies carried out in government agencies, such as hospitals or social services departments, or submitted for funding to charitable trusts will normally need to be assessed by ethical committees, and will need to document in detail their procedures for dealing with ethical issues. However, all research should be designed with ethical considerations in mind, and research training for counsellors and therapists should emphasize awareness of ethical factors.

The problem of reactivity

Connected with ethical issues, but also distinct from them, is the problem of reactivity in counselling research. Reactivity occurs when the research process interferes with or alters what is happening in counselling. In the study by Hill (1989), for example, clients were asked to participate in a great many activities which involved self-exploration and learning (such as watching a video of the therapy session) but were not part of the actual therapy. Hill (1989: 330) acknowledged that 'the research probably influenced the results of all eight cases . . . the [research activities] were probably therapeutic in and of themselves.' In the Sheffield Psychotherapy Research Project (Firth *et al.*, 1986), which compared the effectiveness of brief 'exploratory' or 'prescriptive' therapy, all questionnaires and other data gathering were carried out by a clinic secretary or by interviewers who were independent of the therapists. However, although they knew this, many clients wrote comments on the questionnaires as though they expected their counsellors to read them. Some also admitted sabotaging the research, by completing questionnaires at random, when feeling hostile towards their counsellor.

Another dimension of reactivity is the effect of the research on the counsellor. Many counsellors can be anxious about exposing their work to colleagues, and perhaps risking criticism or censure. In many process studies, transcripts of therapy sessions may be read and rated by a number of judges. Research has shown that there can be wide differences between counsellors and therapists in their levels of effectiveness, so there is a basis in reality for these fears.

In some studies, the research design requires counsellors or therapists to provide standardized treatment, and to conform to the guidelines of a treatment manual, or to offer clients a limited number of sessions. There may be times when these constraints may conflict with the professional judgement of the counsellor regarding how to proceed or how many sessions the client might need.

The relevance of research for practitioners

While there may be a lot of research being carried out, the relevance or utility of that research for practitioners has been extensively questioned. In a study of psychotherapists in the USA, even though 88 per cent of a sample of 279 therapists had PhDs (which meant that they had received extensive training in research, and had carried out research), 24 per cent reported that they never read articles or books about research, and 45 per cent reported that none of the research articles they read had a significant influence on the way they worked with clients (Morrow-Bradley and Elliott, 1986). It would seem highly probable that groups of practitioners in countries with less academically oriented training programmes, or therapists trained in independent institutes rather than in university departments, would report even lower levels of research utilization.

The perceived lack of relevance of much counselling and psychotherapy research has been labelled the 'researcher–practitioner gap', and has been attributed to the differing roles and professional interests and values of researchers and clinicians. Counsellors and therapists typically view research as not giving enough information about the methods of treatment used, looking at groups of clients rather than individuals, and assessing differences between treatment groups on the basis of statistical rather than practical or clinical criteria for significance (Cohen *et al.*, 1986; Morrow-Bradley and Elliott, 1986). In addition, many practitioners may not have access to research libraries or facilities.

Behind the research–practice gap can be detected even more fundamental issues regarding the nature of knowledge about counselling. As mentioned at the beginning of this chapter, counselling and therapy research has been largely dominated by quantitative methods and assumptions borrowed from mainstream psychology and psychiatry, even though many of the ideas and assumptions of qualitative research are probably more congenial to counsellors. This situation will not be resolved until counselling achieves a more explicitly interdisciplinary approach, rather than continuing to define itself as a sub-discipline of psychology. Another fundamental issue concerns the integration of research with theory and practice. For example, during the period spanning 1941 to c. 1965, client-centred counselling and therapy was centred on a group of people headed by Rogers who were all active in seeing clients, teaching students, carrying out research and developing theory. The integration of these activities gave their research a high degree of coherence and impact. In more recent times, there has been a greater fragmentation of professional roles and fewer opportunities to create that kind of research environment.

The relationship between theory and research

One of the distinctive trends apparent in the counselling and psychotherapy research literature over the past twenty years has been the increased reluctance of researchers to engage with theoretical issues. In 1967 and 1968, 69 per cent of therapy research articles published in the *Journal of Consulting and Clinical*

Psychology included a theoretical rationale, but this proportion had fallen to 31 per cent in 1987–8 (Omer and Dar, 1992). This state of affairs can be explained in different ways. It could be that the popularity of integrationist approaches has undermined the relevance of established theoretical models in the eyes of researchers. Alternatively, it could be that the pressure of cutbacks in welfare and health funding in Europe and the USA during this period has temporarily concentrated attention on practical issues of cost-effectiveness at the expense of rather more abstract theoretical speculations.

The image of the person in therapy research

To return to some of the themes and issues introduced in Chapter 1, it can be argued that most research into counselling and therapy draws upon a medical/ biological image of the person. Counselling or therapy is regarded as 'treatment' which is administered to the client, just as a drug is administered to a patient in hospital. The various dimensions of the counselling process, such as empathy or interpretation, can be seen as ingredients of the drug, and process research becomes a search for the best blend of ingredients. Howard *et al.* (1986) have written about the 'dose–effect relationship', meaning the link between the number of sessions (dose) and client improvement. Stiles and Shapiro (1989) have criticized what they call the 'abuse of the drug metaphor' in research. They argue that counselling and therapy involve active, intentional participation on the part of the client rather than passive and automatic responding to ingestion of a drug. The ingredients of therapy, such as empathic reflection, are not fixed and inert, but consist of meanings negotiated between people. These are essential aspects of therapy which do not fit a drug model. Stiles and Shapiro (1989) observe further that even if the drug metaphor is accepted, its use in therapy research is less subtle than in pharmacological research. In studies of real drugs, it is not assumed that 'more is better': some drugs are most effective in small doses, or within certain parameters. Similar effects may well apply in counselling and therapy. For example, a little self-disclosure on the part of the counsellor may be beneficial, but a lot just gets in the way.

The kinds of issues raised by Stiles and Shapiro (1989) have contributed to the need felt by many in the field of counselling and therapy research to construct research informed by alternative metaphors and images of the person.

Topics for reflection and discussion

1 Imagine that a counselling agency (for example, a student counselling service in a college, an employee counselling unit, a Relate branch) had requested you to carry out a study of how much benefit their clients gained from counselling. What would you do? How much would it cost them? How much person time would it require? What ethical issues would need to be considered? How would these ethical issues be dealt with in the design of your study?

2 What research would you like to see carried out? List three research questions that would be of particular interest to you. Consider how you would investigate these questions from both a *qualitative* and a *quantitative* perspective.
3 How relevant is counselling research for you in your work as a counsellor, or how relevant do you think it might be in your future counselling career? In what ways do you see research positively influencing your practice, or in what ways could you see it possibly leading to confusion and poor practice?
4 Read a research article published in one of the research journals. What are the strengths and weaknesses of this particular study? Does the author arrive at conclusions that are fully justified by the evidence, or can you think of other plausible interpretations of the data that the author has not taken into account? How valuable is this piece of research in terms of informing or guiding counselling practice?

TWELVE

THE SKILLS AND QUALITIES OF THE EFFECTIVE COUNSELLOR

In previous chapters, some fundamental questions were asked about the theory and practice of counselling. Ultimately, though, counselling is an activity carried out by people. Theoretical insights or research findings can only be expressed through the behaviour of counsellors. The aim of this chapter is to explore the skills and qualities associated with effective counselling.

Much attention has been given in the counselling and psychotherapy literature to the notion of counselling *skills*. Writers such as Ivey, Carkhuff and Egan (see Larson, 1984) have attempted to identify a set of core skills which are necessary for effective counselling, and which can be acquired through systematic training. Ivey, for example, has broken down the work of the counsellor into a set of *micro-skills* (see Chapter 13). There are, however, serious limitations to the concept of skill, in the context of understanding the activities of counsellors and psychotherapists. The idea of 'skill' was first developed to make sense of fairly simple, short time-scale, observable sequences of behaviour in workers perform-ing simple manual tasks, for example on an assembly line. The aim of an analysis of skilled performance is to break down the actions of a person into simple sequences which can be learned and mastered in isolation from each other. This approach can be seen in the Ivey model.

This way of looking at the task of the counsellor is inappropriate, for three reasons. The first is that many of the essential abilities of the counsellor refer to internal, unobservable processes. For example, a good counsellor is someone who is aware of how she feels in the presence of the client, or who anticipates the future consequences in the family system of an intervention which she plans to initiate with a client. Neither of these counsellor actions is easily understood in terms of observable skills. The second problem of the skills approach lies in the fact that it would appear that one of the differences between truly effective and less able counsellors is that the former are able to see their own actions, and those of the client in the context of the total meaning of the relationship. Therefore, the 'skilfulness' of an intervention can rarely be assessed by dissecting it into smaller and smaller micro-elements. Finally, it can be argued that personal qualities, such as genuineness or presence, are at least as important as skills.

For these reasons it is desirable to find an alternative to the skills approach to understanding counsellor behaviour. A more useful concept would appear to be to adopt the much broader idea of *competence*, which refers to any skill or quality exhibited by a competent performer in a specific occupation. In recent years there has been an increasing amount of research interest devoted to identifying the competencies associated with success in the counselling and psychotherapy. This is an area of research that is very much in progress, and there exist competing models of counsellor competence. For example, Crouch (1992) suggests that there are four main areas of skills development: counsellor awareness, personal work, theoretical understanding and casework skills. Larson *et al.* (1992) have constructed a model which breaks down counsellor competence (which they term 'counsellor self-efficacy') into five areas: micro-skills, process, dealing with difficult client behaviours, cultural competence and awareness of values. Beutler *et al.* (1986), in a review of the literature, identified several categories of 'therapist variables' which had been studied in relation to competence: personality, emotional well-being, attitudes and values, relationship attitudes (e.g. empathy, warmth, congruance), social influence attributes (e.g. expertness, trustworthiness, attraction, credibility and persuasiveness), expectations, professional background, intervention style, and mastery of technical procedures and theoretical rationale. For the purpose of this chapter, subsequent discussion will be structured around consideration of a composite model consisting of six distinct competence areas:

1 *Interpersonal skills.* Competent counsellors are able to demonstrate appropriate: listening, communicating, empathy, presence, awareness of non-verbal communication, sensitivity to voice quality, responsiveness to expressions of emotion, turn-taking, structuring time, use of language.
2 *Personal beliefs and attitudes.* Capacity to accept others, belief in the potential for change, awareness of ethical and moral choices. Sensitivity to values held by client and self.
3 *Conceptual ability.* Ability to understand and assess the client's problems, to anticipate future consequences of actions, to make sense of immediate process in terms of a wider conceptual scheme, to remember information about the client. Cognitive flexibility. Skill in problem-solving.
4 *Personal 'soundness'.* Absence of personal needs or irrational beliefs which are destructive to counselling relationships, self-confidence, capacity to tolerate strong or uncomfortable feelings in relation to clients, secure personal boundaries, ability to be a client. Absence of social prejudice, ethnocentrism and authoritarianism.
5 *Mastery of technique.* Knowledge of when and how to carry out specific interventions, ability to assess effectiveness of interventions, understanding of rationale behind techniques, possession of a sufficiently wide repertoire of interventions.
6 *Ability to understand and work within social systems.* Including awareness of the

family and work relationships of the client, the impact of the agency on the client, the capacity to use support networks and supervision. Sensitivity to the social worlds of clients who may be from a different gender, ethnic, sexual orientation or age group.

Interpersonal skill

Being able to form a productive relationship with a client, to establish rapport or contact, is emphasized by all approaches to counselling. The original analysis of this area of competence in terms of skills led counselling trainers such as Ivey to recommend that counsellors practise listening and reflecting skills. From the broader perspective of a competency analysis, the 'therapeutic alliance' model (Bordin, 1979) emphasizes three of the elements central to the formation of a good working relationship with a client: the creating of an emotional bond between client and counsellor, the achievement of agreement over the goals of counselling, and a shared understanding of the tasks to be performed to fulfil these goals.

The therapeutic alliance model provides a general framework for understanding the interpersonal competencies required in effective counselling. Other theorists have drawn attention to dimensions of interpersonal relating which contribute to the process of forming an alliance. Rogers (1957), for example, has proposed that facilitative therapeutic relationship are those in which the counsellor can provide the 'core conditions' of empathy, congruence and acceptance (see Chapter 4). Hobson (1985) has suggested that the bond between counsellor and client grows from the creation of a shared 'feeling language', a way of talking together that allows expression of the feelings of the client. Rice (1974) has carried out considerable research into the importance of the voice quality of the therapist or counsellor.

Relationships between people are profoundly influenced by general factors, such as social class, age, ethnicity and gender. While it is difficult to generalize about the effect on the counselling relationship of any of these variables, it does seem sensible to conclude that one of the important relationship competencies for a counsellor is that he or she should be aware of the significance of these demographic characteristics, and be able to adjust his or her style or approach accordingly.

Personal beliefs and attitudes

Since the examination by Halmos of the 'faith of the counsellors', there has been a lively interest in the idea that all effective counsellors might possess similar belief systems or ways of making sense of the world. The assumption is that counsellors are able to help people because they see the client's problems in a particular way, and that a helper who took a different perspective might hinder the growth or learning of the client.

The most coherent attempt to identify the beliefs and attitudes associated with effectiveness in counselling has been made by Combs (1986). In a series of fourteen studies, using not only counsellors but also members of other human service professions such as clergy and teachers, Combs and Soper (1963) and Combs (1986) found that more effective helpers in these professions were more likely to view the world from a basically person-centred perspective.

The studies conducted by Combs (1986) have all been firmly based in a client-centred or person-centred orientation, and one of the limitations of his work has been that he restricted himself only to testing the importance of 'person-centred' attitudes. It could be that there is a wider set of beliefs which can be shown to be held by effective counsellors. But the work done by Combs (1986) is especially relevant in contributing to an understanding of the decisions by many people in professions such as nursing, social work and the ministry to change career and enter counselling: the beliefs and attitudes described by Combs may in some circumstances conflict with the practices of these other professions.

Competence in the area of personal beliefs and attitudes consists not only of having certain ways of seeing the world, but also of having accurate self-awareness regarding them. Clients, may well possess quite different sets of beliefs and attitudes, and may even on occasion dispute the legitimacy of what they perceive to be the way the counsellor views things. To be able to handle these situations a counsellor needs to be able to stand back from her own philosophical position in order to let the client know she is capable of accepting his contrasting perspective. Many training courses, therefore, include work on 'values clarification', and this issue is also common in supervision.

Conceptual ability

A great deal of what happens in counselling is about understanding. Clients come to see a counsellor because they have exhausted their own capacity to make sense of what is happening, or to decide what to do about it. Many clients expect their counsellor to tell them what is happening or advise them what to do, and are disappointed when the counsellor suggests that it would be better for the client to arrive at his own understanding and decisions. Nevertheless, counsellors need to be able to work with clients in these areas of difficulty, and therefore require to be competent at thinking about what is happening.

There has been very little research on the conceptual or cognitive abilities of counsellors. In a review of the literature, Beutler et al. (1986) found no relationship between the academic competence of counsellors, as measured by their performance on an undergraduate degree, and their success on a training course. This is not a surprising result, since just through being graduates all of the counsellors would have demonstrated a basic intellectual competence adequate for the role of counsellor. But it does confirm the widely held view that high academic achievement does not correlate with high counselling efficacy. Whiteley et al. (1967) investigated differences in levels of cognitive flexibility in counsellors on a training course, and found a strong association between flexibility and overall counselling competence. Shaw and Dobson (1988) have suggested that 'clinical memory', the capacity to remember information conveyed by the client, constitutes a key cognitive competency. Although the notion of 'clinical memory' makes sense at an intuitive level, there is as yet no research which has looked at the part it plays in counselling. Martin *et al.* (1989) found that more experienced counsellors viewed clients from the basis of a more cognitively complex construct system.

In the absence of research studies into the abilities of effective counsellors, it is instructive to look at the results of studies of effective managers, a field where considerable research has been carried out. Klemp and McClelland (1986) carried out research into the competencies exhibited by effective managers in a number of different organizations, and found that a set of common, or 'generic', competencies tended to be identifiable in all successful managers. One of the main results of this study was clear evidence that more effective managers have a better capacity to conceptualize problems.

Personal 'soundness'

In contrast to the paucity of research into cognitive or conceptual competencies, there is a much more substantial research basis for any discussion of the significance of personality factors and general mental health as variables associated with counselling effectiveness. These studies have concentrated on three main issues: identifying the personality characteristics of effective therapists, and assessing the value of personal therapy for practitioners. Much of the work in this area has been carried out with the aim of giving weight to a critique of skills or technique-oriented approaches. The spirit behind these studies is captured by McConnaughy (1987: 304) in her statement that

> the actual techniques employed by the therapists are of lesser importance than the unique character and personality of the therapists themselves. Therapists select techniques and theories because who they are as persons: the therapy strategies are manifestations of the therapist's personality. The therapist as a person is the instrument of primary influence in the therapy enterprise. A corollary of this principle is that the more a therapist accepts and values himself, or herself, the more effective he or she will be in helping clients come to know and appreciate themselves.

Numerous studies have explored the impact of the personality of the counsellor on counselling outcomes. It can be argued that the whole area of personality research is problematic in that personality traits as measured by questionnaires tend to demonstrate low correlations with actual behaviour in all studies (see Mischel (1968) for a fuller discussion of this debate). Nevertheless, there would seem to be reliable evidence that good counsellors are people who exhibit higher levels of general emotional adjustment and a greater capacity for self-disclosure. It should be noted that personality variables which do *not* appear to be associated with counselling success include introversion–extraversion and dominance–submissiveness. Other studies have explored the possibility that the similarities or differences between counsellor and client personality traits might be associated with outcome. This work has been reviewed by Beutler *et al.* (1986), who found no consistent relationship between client–counsellor similarity and outcome. Many counsellor training courses advocate personal therapy for trainees as a means of ensuring personal growth in the direction of adjustment and openness. There is some evidence that personal therapy enhances the subsequent professional effectiveness of counsellors and psychotherapists by giving a reliable basis for the confident and appropriate 'use of self' (Baldwin, 1987) in relationships with clients.

Personal therapy represents a unique means of learning about the therapeutic process, that it gives insight into the role of client and, finally, that it contributes to a general heightening of self-awareness in the trainee. There are, however, some fundamental difficulties that are raised by the practice of personal therapy for trainees. First, the client is required to attend, rather than depending on voluntary participation. Second, if the trainee becomes deeply caught up in therapeutic work, it may diminish her own emotional availability for her clients. Third, in some training institutes the personal therapist is a member of the training staff, and not only reports on the progress of the trainee in therapy, but, if the trainee completes the programme, will then subsequently become a colleague of the person who was a client. These practices are less prevalent now than they were in the past, but introduce unusual external pressures which may inhibit the benefits to be gained from the therapy. There are, therefore, reasons to expect personal therapy to be associated with greater counsellor competence, but also reasons to expect the reverse. Studies of personal therapy reflect this balance of views. Although, for example, Buckley *et al.* (1981) found that 90 per cent of the therapists in their sample reported that personal therapy had made a positive contribution to their personal and professional development, Norcross *et al.* (1988b) found that 21 per cent felt that, for them, personal therapy had been harmful in some way. Peebles (1980) reported that personal therapy was associated with higher levels of empathy, congruence and acceptance in therapists, while Garfield and Bergin (1971) concluded from a small-scale study that the therapists who had *not* received personal therapy were more effective than those who had.

Surveys in the USA have suggested that around three-quarters of therapists have received at least one course of personal therapy (Norcross *et al.*, 1988a). There is, therefore, a high level of professional commitment to this practice. Evidence is not available concerning the incidence of personal therapy in counsellors. With non-professional counsellors, in particular, the financial and emotional cost of personal therapy might be more difficult to justify in the light of lower caseloads and generally more limited training.

Mastery of technique

There has been a substantial movement over the past few years to identify counsellor competence as primarily a matter of mastery of technique. There is some evidence that practitioners who claim to use different approaches to counselling may work with clients in an identical manner, and that there can be huge differences between practitioners who purport to employ the same model (see, for example, Lieberman *et al.*, 1973). This kind of finding has created difficulties for researchers interested in comparing different approaches. If half the behaviourists in a study are indistinguishable from the psychoanalysts, the study can hardly constitute a comparison of behaviour therapy and psychoanalytic psychotherapy! Increasingly, therefore, researchers have constructed 'manuals' which give detailed instructions to the counsellors or psychotherapists involved in the study regarding just how to implement the particular approach being studied. The competence of the counsellor is assessed, then, in terms of how closely she is able to adhere to the manual.

Valuable though this strategy might be in some research studies, and perhaps also in some training situations, it is of limited use in assessing the competence of most counsellors, who would not claim to be even attempting to follow the dictates of any one approach. Furthermore, one of the characteristics of highly competent or gifted counsellors is that they are adept at creatively modifying techniques or exercises to meet the needs of individual clients. However, it should be noted that in studies which have used manual-instructed counsellors, poor client outcomes are correlated with persistent errors or mistakes in technique. Mastery of technique may be important, therefore, when it is absent rather than when it is present.

It might be supposed that possession of a range of techniques, or what is sometimes called an 'armoury' or 'toolkit' of techniques, would be beneficial. The founder of systematic eclecticism, Lazarus (1989a,b), would certainly recommend that competent counsellors should be familiar with a range of intervention strategies. There is very litle direct research evidence on whether counsellors who employ many techniques are more effective in helping clients than are counsellors with more restricted repertoires. A series of studies by Mahrer (1989; Mahrer *et al.*, 1987) would imply that a large repertoire is not necessarily desirable. Mahrer classified techniques into broad categories and used this set of categories of therapist 'operations' to analyse the behaviour of several well-known 'master therapists', such as Carl Rogers and Irving Polster. He found that each of them regularly uses only a very limited range of strategies. Although further research is clearly required, the results achieved by Mahrer would seem to imply that a thorough grasp of a narrow range of techniques might be more valuable than a more superficial capacity to use a wider range. Mahrer himself would not agree with this conclusion, and sees one of the main objectives of his research programme as being to encourage counsellors and therapists to acquire a broader repertoire of operations.

Ability to understand and work within social systems

It could be argued that one of the weaknesses of most contemporary approaches to counselling is that they take an over-individualistic perspective on the counselling process. They focus on a scenario in which the client is in one chair and the counsellor sits opposite in another chair. In reality, though, there is usually an audience to this performance – encompassing, among others, the family and friends of the client, and the supervisor and colleagues of the counsellor. The counsellor and client always act within a social system, and their actions have consequences for that system. An important competence, therefore, is the capacity to be aware of the operation of social systems. In the earlier discussion of burnout it was suggested that the presence of a support system around the counsellor was a good way of avoiding burnout. In Britain, the BAC and BPS require counsellors to engage in ongoing supervision, an acknowledgement of the necessity for support.

Counsellors who work in or for organizations will be aware of the demands and pressures the organization may make upon them. These pressures, which were discussed more fully in Chapter 8, can include inducements to pass on information confided by clients, expectations to influence the behaviour of clients, and restrictions on the type of work that can be done with clients. Effective counsellors in such settings need to be highly competent in dealing with the social system within which they work.

The counsellor's journey: a developmental model of counsellor competence

The categorization and identification of the skills and qualities associated with effectiveness in counselling have largely focused on competencies exhibited by people who are already practitioners. However, the emphasis in the literature on the importance of personal factors and the value in the area of supervision of models of counsellor identity development (see Chapter 13) suggest that a developmental perspective might also be applied to the question of understanding counsellor competence. Many counsellors find meaning in the metaphor of the 'counsellor's journey' (Goldberg, 1988), an image which allows them to trace the roots of their counselling role back to its earliest origins, and make sense of the different territories and obstacles encountered on the way to becoming a counsellor. The personal and professional pathways followed by counsellors are divisible into five distinct and also overlapping stages:

1 Roles, relationship patterns and emotional needs established in childhood.
2 The decision to become a counsellor.
3 The experience of training.
4 Coping with the hazards of practice.
5 Expressing creativity in the counselling role.

This model draws upon research mainly carried out on psychotherapists in the USA (Henry, 1966, 1977; Burton, 1970), although there is some evidence of similarities in a small-scale study of British therapists (Norcross and Guy, 1989; Spurling and Dryden, 1989). It is important to note that these studies were all carried out on full-time, professional therapists. Research is lacking on the motivational patterns and developmental processes of non-professional or voluntary counsellors.

Studies of the childhood and family life of therapists (Henry, 1966; Burton, 1970; Spurling and Dryden, 1989) have found a number of factors which appear to be related to later career choice. Therapists frequently come from minority groups (for example, the high proportion of Jewish therapists), have lived for some time in another country, or have parents who are exiles or immigrants. As Henry (1977: 49) puts it, in childhood many therapists 'have been exposed to more than one set of cultural influences'. As children, many have experienced illness, loneliness (perhaps through being an only child or living in an isolated location), or bereavement. Conflict in family life is reported fairly often, with the therapist as child taking the role of mediator or subsitute parent. Consistent with this role, therapists often reported that they were the dominant sibling in the family.

These types of childhood experiences can be seen as creating the conditions for embarking on a career as therapist. As Brightman (1984: 295) has written, 'the role of therapist itself may constitute a reenactment of an earlier situation in which a particularly sensitive and empathic child has been pressed into the service of understanding and caring for a parent (usually depressed mother) figure.' The child in this situation grows up with a need to care for others. As the sibling most involved in the family drama, he or she is not able to escape from the responsibility to care. The experience of being a social 'outsider' introduces the additional motivation to learn about and understand relationships and interactions. As Henry (1977) noted, the motive to care on its own is more likely to lead to a career in social work, whereas therapy requires a strong interest in making sense of the inner worlds of clients. The exposure in childhood to periods of loneliness or isolation provides a capacity for exploration of inner life.

Another dimension of the childhood experience of therapists relates to what is known as the 'wounded healer' theory (Guggenbuhl-Craig, 1971; Rippere and Williams, 1985). This idea proposes that the power of the healer (the priest or shaman in primitive societies, the therapist in modern society) derives from his or her inner experience of pain, loss or suffering. The presence of a 'wound' in the healer gives him or her an excellent basis from which to understand and empathize with the wounds of clients. A danger is that the wound of the healer is exacerbated by the demands of those being helped, and the healer is sacrificed for their benefit. The wounded healer concept makes it possible to understand the 'search for wholeness and integration' (Spurling and Dryden, 1989), which characterizes the lives of many counsellors and therapists and which makes it possible to transform the pain of negative life experiences into a resource for helping others.

The pattern of childhood experience is unique for every therapist, but if it contains some of the elements described above it can lead to a motivation to enter counselling as a career. Marston (1984) suggests that the motives for becoming a therapist can include contact, helping others, discovery, social status, power and influence, self-therapy and voyeurism. Clearly, an appropriate balance of motives is necessary. For perhaps the majority of counsellors, the pathway into the occupation unfolds over time. It is common for people to enter professions such as nursing, social work and teaching and then find themselves more and more attracted to and involved in the counselling components of their job. Undergoing personal therapy or counselling as a client can often be a catalyst for the decision to enter counselling training. The experience of meeting therapists or trainers who become influential role models can also be a factor. The decision to become a counsellor can also be facilitated by participation in introductory skills courses. It is important to acknowledge that the decision to become a counsellor is not made lightly by people. It constitutes a significant developmental stage in its own right, and many very talented counsellors do not complete this stage, and enter training, until well into their middle years.

Once the person has decided to become a counsellor, he or she enters the stage of formal training. The training process itself encompasses a developmental process (see Chapter 13) but, viewed from the perspective of the journey as a whole, the main developmental theme of training can be seen to be adequacy to the task. Through training, the counsellor needs to arrive at an answer to the question 'Am I good enough?'

To be 'good enough' to help people who are deeply damaged by life is to make a strong statement about one's own sanity, knowledge and competence. Particularly during the early phase of training, when clients may not return, or present overwhelming problems of staggering complexity and horror, all the evidence points in the direction of inadequacy rather than sufficiency. On the other hand, there is, both in the professional literature and within popular culture, 'the stereotype of the psychotherapist as all-knowing, all-loving, a fusion of the artist and scientist setting forth to battle the dark forces of the human soul' (Brightman, 1984: 295). Counsellors in training may feel vulnerable and incompetent, but they know that they should aspire to the ideal of being a 'potent' role model for their clients (Egan, 1986: 28).

As a means of resolving the tension between expectations of competence and inner fears of inadequacy, some therapists evolve what Brightman (1984) has called a 'grandiose professional self'. Such counsellors and therapists deal with the fears and anxieties arising from their role by identifying with the image of an all-knowing, all-powerful and all-loving therapist. The earliest observation of this phenomenon was made by Ernest Jones, the psychoanalyst who was student and biographer of Freud. Jones (1951) wrote that some analysts kept themselves aloof and mysterious, acted as if they knew everything and never admitted mistakes. He coined the term 'God complex' to describe such therapists. Marmor (1953) described this pattern as a 'feeling of superiority', and commented that it was often reinforced by the tendency of patients to idealize their analysts. Sharaf and Levinson (1964) argue that the enormous responsibility and pressure placed on new therapists result in a desperate quest for all the trappings of a professional role. An account of what it can be like to be on the receiving end of 'grandiose' therapy is given by Allen (1990), who describes her unsuccessful encounter with a therapist who was cold, sat in a chair two inches higher than her chair, and in the end diagnosed her as needing hospital treatment.

The resolution of this phase of grandiosity can be facilitated by appropriate supervision and personal therapy (Brightman, 1984). Often, the transition to a more realistic self-appraisal can be accompanied by depression and a sense of mourning for an idealized state which has been left behind.

The next stage, that of coping with the hazards of practice, brings with it a new set of challenges to competence. The possibility of professional burnout, brought about by high workloads and an increasing discrepancy between the capacity to help and the demands of clients, has been described in Chapter 8. Burnout, and the similar state of 'disillusionment' (Burton, 1970), can be viewed as a consequence of unresolved grandiosity, of the therapist finishing training and taking on a job while still carrying a sense of omnipotence. There are other hazards of practice. Mair (1989: 281) has portrayed counselling and therapy as a trade in secrets:

> Psychotherapists occupy a remarkable position in society. We daily have access to the secrets of our clients, and therefore of the society of which they and we are part. We are secret agents, being told what others try to hide . . . We are ambiguous and liable to be suspect by many in the ordinary world.

Kovacs (1976) has similarly represented the therapist as only participating in life 'from one side', not risking genuine contact but acting as 'observer' or 'witness'.

The main threat to competence during the part of the counsellor's journey that immediately follows training, or may even include the latter phase of training, is that of losing the motivation to help, as a result of burnout, detachment or alienation. Luborsky, in a study which looked at differences in effectiveness between individual counsellors, found motivation to help to be one of the central factors distinguishing effective from ineffective practitioners. McCarley (1975) and Aveline (1986) have both argued for the importance of opportunities for 'self-renewal' being made available to experienced therapists.

The final stage of the counsellor's journey is to achieve a capacity for working creatively with clients. At this stage, the counsellor is no longer merely a technician implementing a specific theoretical approach:

> In the end, each therapist develops his or her own style, and the 'theoretical orientation' falls into the background. What remains salient is a unique personality combining artistry and skill. In this respect, a fine therapist closely resembles a painter, novelist or composer. As is true in all the arts and sciences, few reach the summit.
>
> (Strupp, 1978: 31)

A developmental model of counsellor competence brings into focus a number of issues. Each stage presents the counsellor with a distinctive set of challenges to competence. For the counsellor contemplating a career in counselling, important tasks include checking out the robustness of the adaptation to childhood experiences and being aware of the balance of motives. In selecting people for counsellor training courses, often the most crucial question is whether the person is ready to give help to others, or whether he or she is basically seeking therapy for himself or herself. In training, a principal challenge is to acknowledge vulnerability and accept the 'negative capability' of not knowing everything. As a qualified practitioner, competence depends on periodical renewal and rediscovery of personal meaning in the work, and on establishing sufficient support networks to avoid burning out.

As in any developmental model, the failure to resolve an issue or learning task at one stage will carry implications for the succeeding stages. So, for example, someone who has not gained insight into childhood 'wounds' will find it very difficult to arrive at a sense of being a 'good enough' counsellor. A counsellor who is struggling to meet the everyday demands of clients will lack the time and energy to move to a stage of creative self-expression through his or her work.

Topics for reflection and discussion

1 To what extent, and in what ways, have your early life experiences predisposed you to have an interest in counselling? Have these childhood and adolescent events and experiences influenced your choice of theoretical orientation, or your commitment to work with particular client groups?

2 Does the metaphor of the counsellor's 'journey' apply to your life? Where are you now in terms of that journey? What might be involved in the next stage of the journey? Do any other images or metaphors capture more accurately your sense of your development as a counsellor?

3 Consider the six areas of basic counsellor competence discussed in this chapter: interpersonal skills, personal beliefs and attitudes, conceptual ability, personal 'soundness', mastery of technique and ability to work within social systems. Under each of these headings, list the skills or competencies that you are able to employ well, and those which are more problematic for you. You might invite someone who knows you well to comment on your self-perceptions. What are the implications of this exercise for your training needs as a counsellor?

THIRTEEN

TRAINING AND SUPERVISION IN COUNSELLING

The professionalization of counselling in the past two decades in Britain and Europe has seen increasing attention being devoted to the provision of training and supervision. In North America this process occurred largely during the 1950s. The requirement of professional accountability, and the existence and growing influence of professional associations, have forced colleges, agencies and training institutes to formalize arrangements for training and supervising counsellors. In Britain, for example, the first university-based counsellor training courses began operation only in 1966. In 1986 the British Association for Counselling produced its first criteria and procedures for approving counselling courses, and in 1992 the British Psychological Society published similar guidelines for courses in counselling psychology.

Despite this growth in numbers of courses, relatively little research has been carried out that would assist counselling trainers and tutors in their work. Counsellor training remains, curiously, an underdeveloped area for research and scholarship. Even the knowledge that tutors and trainers have gained through personal and professional experience is seldom written up for publication.

Historical trends in counsellor training

The history of training in psychotherapy, and psychoanalysis in particular, gives some clues to the prevalence of barriers to knowledge about what goes on in training courses. The primary training medium for psychoanalysts has been the training analysis. Trainees in psychoanalytic institutes enter analysis with a senior member of the institute. Through the period of training they may undergo training analyses with two or more analysts in this way. The training analysis was considered to be the only way in which an analyst could learn about what psychoanalysis was really like, although theoretical seminars, case discussions and child observation studies came eventually to be added to the psychoanalytic training programme in many institutes. The assessment of suitability of candidates for qualification as analysts was largely determined by the training analyst. The privacy and secretiveness of these arrangements precluded public discussion of training issues; the suitability of a candidate was assessed solely on the professional judgement, with no appeal possible. The potential oppressiveness of this kind of training has been documented by Masson (1988).

The emergence of client-centred therapy in the 1940s and 1950s brought with it a whole set of new ideas about how to train counsellors. Rogers and his colleagues brought in students to act as co-therapists in sessions with clients. Students practised counselling skills on each other. The 'T-group' or personal growth group was applied to counsellor training, with trainees participating in small experiential groups. Students watched films of sessions and analysed recordings and transcripts. This phase of development of approaches to counsellor training featured a more open and multi-faceted approach to learning technique, and the introduction of other means of facilitating self-awareness (for example, encounter groups) rather a reliance solely on personal therapy. There was also a degree of democratization in the training process, with student self-evaluations being used alongside staff appraisals.

During the 1960s and 1970s the main innovation in counsellor training consisted of the introduction of structured approaches to skills training. These approaches were used not only on counsellor training courses but also in the context of shorter skills courses designed for people in other helping or human service professions, such as teaching, nursing and management. The first of these structured approaches was the human resource development model devised by Carkhuff (1969). Other packages of a similar nature were the micro-skills model (Ivey and Galvin, 1984), the skilled helper model (Egan, 1984), SASHA tapes (Goodman, 1984) and interpersonal process recall (Kagan et al., 1963). Although these models and approaches differed in certain respects, they all contained carefully structured training materials, in the form of handouts, exercises and video or film demonstrations, which would take trainees through a standard programme for learning specific counselling skills.

More recently, significant developments in counsellor training have included increased attention to the role of supervision and personal therapy in training programmes (Bolger, 1985; Thorne and Dryden, 1991).

Key elements in counsellor training courses

The development of different ideas and approaches to the training of counsellors and therapists has resulted in what currently appears to be a broad consensus concerning the elements which need to be included in training courses (Dryden and Thorne, 1991). Different courses may emphasize some of these activities at the expense of others, but all courses will probably include at least some input under each of the headings listed below.

Theoretical frameworks

It is widely accepted that counsellors need to be equipped with a theoretical perspective through which to understand their work with clients. The theory component of courses may include models of counselling, basic psychological theories in areas such as developmental psychology, interpersonal behaviour and group dynamics, an introduction to psychiatric terminology, and some aspects of sociology relating to social class, race and gender. There is potential in counselling courses, therefore, for extensive coverage of theoretical topics, particularly when it is taken into account that specialist areas of counselling, such as marital and couples counselling or bereavement work, have their own well-articulated theoretical models. The challenge of theoretical learning in counselling is further increased by the general recognition that students should not merely know about theory, but should be able to apply it in practice. The aim is to be able to use theory actively to understand clients and the reactions of the counsellor to these clients.

One of the issues that arises in this area of counsellor training is whether it is more appropriate to introduce students to one theoretical orientation in depth, or to expose them to an integration of several theoretical models (Halgin, 1985; Norcross et al., 1986; Beutler et al., 1987). To some extent this issue is linked to the nature of the organization that is offering the training. Independent institutes are often created around proponents of a particular theoretical approach, so that students being trained in these institutes will inevitably be primarily taught that set of ideas. Courses operating in institutions of higher education, such as colleges and universities, are likely to be influenced by academic values concerning the necessity for critical debate between theoretical positions, and will therefore usually teach theory from an integrationist or multiple perspective stance.

Another facet of this debate addresses the question of the order in which theoretical choices should appropriately be made. Is it more helpful to organize initial counsellor training around a broad-based multiple perspective or generic perspective, and encourage counsellors to specialize in a particular approach later on in their careers when they have a solid basis for choice? Or is it more appropriate to begin training with a thorough grounding in a single coherent approach?

Counselling skills

Training in counselling skills has been associated more with person-centred and cognitive–behavioural than with psychodynamic approaches to counselling. The concept of *skill* refers to a sequence of counsellor actions or behaviours carried out in response to client actions or behaviours. Implicit in the idea of skill is an assumption that it makes sense to break down the role of counsellor into discrete actions or behaviours, and this has been an assumption that is difficult to reconcile with psychoanalytic ways of thinking.

As already mentioned, a number of models of counselling skill training have been developed. Even when these models are not adopted in their entirety into training courses, the ideas and procedures contained in them are often put into service. It is therefore worth while to describe the main features of three of the more widely used of these approaches.

The human resource development (HRD) model (Carkhuff, 1971; Cash, 1984) was originally based on the Rogerian 'core conditions' of empathy, unconditional positive regard and congruence. The later evolution of the approach added 'action' skills, such as concreteness, confrontation and immediacy, to the repertoire, and placed these skills within a three-stage model of the helping process. The stages are self-exploration, understanding and action. In an HRD training programme, trainees are exposed to each of the skills in turn. A rationale is presented for the use of the skill in helping relationships, and there is a live or video demonstration of the skill in action. Trainees also take part in a small group experience designed to give them an opportunity of experiencing at first hand the impact of the core conditions.

The micro-counselling or micro-skills training approach (Ivey and Galvin, 1984) also breaks down the task of counselling into a number of discrete skills:

Attending behaviour
Client observation skills
Open and closed questions
Encouraging, paraphrasing and summarizing
Reflecting feelings and meanings
Focusing on problems
Influencing skills
Confrontation
Structuring the interview
Integrating skills.

Trainees are given written descriptions of positive and negative examples of each skill, watch an expert demonstrating the skill on video, then engage in video-taped practice of the skills with other trainees acting as clients. Feedback is provided, and then the trainee attempts the skill once more. This sequence is repeated until the trainee reaches an appropriate level of competence in the skill. One of the primary aims of the micro-skills approach is to enable counsellors to function in an 'intentional' rather than 'intuitive' manner, in other words to be able to select an appropriate response from a wide repertoire rather than being restricted to only one or two modes of communication and intervention. Another area of emphasis has been the identification of skills congruent with particular cultural settings (Ivey et al., 1987).

Interpersonal process recall (Kagan, 1984; Kagan and Kagan, 1990) differs from the HRD and microskills approaches in being based on discovery learning. Trainees initially watch counsellors responding to clients using desirable skills, and briefly practise these skills in response to video-taped 'trigger' vignettes. The next phase, affect simulation, involves trainees responding to vignettes in which actors express intense and distressing emotional statements direct to camera. The final phase involves making a video-tape of a counselling session, then watching it immediately afterwards with the help of an 'enquirer' who urges the trainee to recall any thoughts, feelings or images that he or she experienced during the session. This 'stimulated recall' component is unique to IPR, and is based on an assumption that all helpers, even beginning trainees, are capable of demonstrating a wide repertoire of helpful responses but stop themselves from doing so because of anxiety or social inhibition.

It can be seen that, although there are some differences between these approaches, they nevertheless all embrace many of the same set of learning activities:

- beginning with a generic set of skills, rather than with a theoretical model;
- receiving a description of and rationale for the skill;
- observing an expert modelling the skill;
- learning to discriminate between effective and ineffective examples of the skill;
- practising the skill with a client or colleague;
- the trainee reviewing his or her performance of the skill;
- feedback from other trainees and tutor;
- desensitization of the anxiety level of the helper, particularly in relation to client expression of emotions;
- further practice of skill;
- integration of skills into the counselling role.

Research into the effectiveness of these methods in counsellor training suggests that there is good evidence to support the claims of the micro-skills and HRD approaches, but somewhat less evidence to confirm the value of interpersonal process recall (Baker et al., 1990).

Work on self

The importance of self-knowledge and self-awareness in counsellors is central to many of the mainstream theoretical approaches. Even basically skills-oriented approaches to training, such as the human resource development and interpersonal process recall models described earlier, place considerable emphasis on self-awareness. In psychodynamic work, for example, the counsellor must be able to differentiate between counter-transference reactions that are triggered by client transference, and those that are projections of unresolved personal conflicts. In person-centred work, the congruence of the counsellor, his or her ability to be aware of and act appropriately upon personal feelings, is considered a core condition in creating an effective therapeutic environment. Self-awareness is also necessary in a more general sense, in enabling the counsellor to survive without burning out through the experience of holding and sharing the pain, fear and despair of clients. Most ordinary people to whom clients turn deny the depth of the emotional suffering which is presented to them, or repress their own reactions to it. Effective counsellors cannot afford these defences, but must find ways of staying with clients in their distress. Finally, it is essential for counsellors to be aware of their own motivations and pay-offs for engaging in this kind of work, in order to prevent different types of client exploitation or abuse.

Traditionally, training courses in psychodynamic counselling, or influenced by psychodynamic approaches, have insisted that counsellors in training undergo personal therapy during the period of training. The number of sessions stipulated varies widely, from ten sessions to twice weekly over several years. The rationale for therapy is not only to promote personal development, but to give the student some experience in the role of client, and to enable first-hand observation of a therapist in action. An additional objective, in some training courses, is to enable assessment of the potential of the trainee.

The requirement for personal therapy has been criticized on several grounds. First, this arrangement does not allow the client to choose to enter therapy, which is usually considered essential for productive therapy to take place. This element of choice is particularly relevant when the trainee may have recently completed a course of therapy, before entering training, and has no wish or need to reopen personal issues. Second, if the therapy leads to the uncovering of difficult emotional material, the trainee may not be able to participate effectively in other parts of the course, such as skills training or supervised placements. Third, if the therapy does not go well, for example if there is a mismatch between therapist and client, the trainee may feel that it is necessary to continue, at the risk of emotional damage, for the sake of completing a mandatory part of the course. Fourth, given the scarcity of counselling availability to people in real crisis, it may be difficult to justify using a significant proportion of the time of highly qualified practitioners in supplying personal therapy to trainees. Finally, the financial cost of personal therapy can place counsellor training even further out of the reach of people from socially disadvantaged groups.

None of these arguments against personal therapy is conclusive. For example, if a trainee is thrown into personal crisis as a result of personal therapy, it could be argued that it is better that it happens then rather than as a result of working with one of his or her own clients. It may be extremely valuable for someone to take time out from any kind of training course to reassess personal priorities. A strong argument for the continuation of personal therapy in training is probably that it helps to ensure the centrality of acceptance of the client role: counselling is not a set of techniques applied to others but a learning process in which counsellor as well as client participates. Another reason for including some personal therapy experience in training is that it is necessary for counsellors to know when they themselves need help, and to feel all right about seeking such help, rather than persevering with client work in an impaired state. In some respects, the completion of personal therapy can represent a professional *rite de passage* for trainee counsellors, an entry into a professional role.

Considerable research has been carried out into the impact of personal therapy on the subsequent effectiveness of counsellors and therapists (see Chapter 12). The results of this research have been inconsistent, with no clear benefit being demonstrated. It should be noted, however, that personal therapy is merely one element in a training programme, and it is difficult to identify the unique effects of this component in isolation from everything else that might be happening on a course.

Another approach to work on self that is included in many courses is experiential work in groups. These groups may be called therapy groups, T-groups, or encounter groups, and may be run by external consultants or leaders, course tutors, or even on a self-help or leaderless basis. The aims of such groupwork are similar to those of personal therapy, with the added dimension that the quality of relationships and support developed in the groups will benefit the learning which takes place in other areas of the course as a whole. Work in small groups can also enable counsellors to identify and clarify the values that inform their approach to clients. It is regrettable that there has been no research into the role of groupwork in counsellor training, since there are many issues and dilemmas that would repay systematic study. It would be interesting to know, for instance, whether groups that become highly supportive and cohesive contribute more to counsellor learning than do groups that are fragmented and tense. There are often also serious dilemmas presented by confidentiality boundaries in respect of the acceptability of talking in the rest of the course about topics originating in small groups.

Personal learning diaries and journals are employed in several courses to facilitate personal learning and to record the application of learning in practice (Pates and Knasel, 1989). Guidelines for approaches to writing personal learning diaries can be found in Progoff (1975) and Rainer (1985). The diary or journal is particularly helpful in assisting the transfer of learning and insight beyond the course itself into the rest of the personal and professional life of the trainee. Reading and commenting on diary or journal material can, however, be a time-consuming business for trainers and tutors.

The quality and depth of personal exploration and learning on counsellor training courses can often be facilitated through the creation of suitable physical surroundings. Training groups may use residentials, which are often held in countryside settings away from the usual training premises, to construct a 'cultural island' where relationships are strengthened and new patterns of behaviour tried out. The personal meaning of counsellor training for many trainees is that it is a time of intense self-exploration and change (Battye, 1991), which has implications for partners, family and pre-existing personal roles.

Professional issues

Training courses should include careful consideration of a wide range of professional issues. Principles of ethical practice are usually given substantial attention on courses, mainly through discussion of cases. Other professional issues which are covered are: power and discrimination in counselling, particularly with respect to race, gender, disability and sexual orientation; case management and referral; boundary issues; professional accountability and insurance; inter-professional working; and the organization and administration of counselling agencies.

Supervised practice

At some point in training students will begin work with real clients, rather than practising with course colleagues. It is generally considered essential that participants on training courses should be involved in some supervised practice, to provide them with material to use in other parts of the course, and to give them opportunities to apply skills and concepts. A broader discussion of the nature of supervision is introduced later in this chapter, but at this point it can be mentioned that the delivery of supervision to trainees can be either through regular one-to-one meetings with a supervisor, or through group supervision. The quality and frequency of supervision is of vital importance to people learning to be counsellors. There are, however, aspects of training that make effective supervision difficult to achieve. The first of these arises from the anxieties and dependency which most people experience when first confronted by clients. This stage of counsellor development will be more fully explored in a later section in this chapter. The second issue concerns the relationship between the supervisor and the primary trainers or tutors. It is desirable for supervisors to work with their supervisees in ways that are consistent with the aims and philosophy of a course. It also desirable, on the other hand, for the trainee to know that he or she can be open with the supervisor, with no fear that disclosures will find their way back to those deciding who will pass or fail the course. The role of the supervisor in relation to a training course represents a challenge to achieve an appropriate balance between involvement with the course and autonomy in service of the student.

Research awareness

An exploration of the contribution of research to an understanding of the counselling process is included in many courses. This may take the form of sessions on research awareness, the ability to read research papers and draw appropriate conclusions from them, through training in research methods, and ultimately to designing and implementing a piece of research. The low regard with which most practising counsellors and therapists regard the utility of research findings (reviewed in Chapter 11) would suggest that past efforts on training courses to inculcate an interest in research have not met with any great success.

Issues and dilemmas in counsellor training

Although it might be said that there exists a fair measure of agreement over the broad shape and outline of counsellor training, this apparent consensus should not conceal the fact that there is a wide range of dilemmas and issues to be resolved. In terms of issues arising from the practicalities of operating courses, the two most common dilemmas are balance and time. There are always difficult choices to be made about how much emphasis to give some course elements at the expense of others. No matter how long a course is, the time available could be filled with theory, or could be taken up wholly by experiential work. The other fundamental dilemma is related to time. The process of counsellor development takes a lot of time. People training to be counsellors need to assimilate counselling theory and skills into their own personal way of relating. It probably takes at least four years for most people to become competent as counsellors, and very few courses allow that much time. Other issues that will be addressed include selection of trainees, assessment of competence and course philosophy.

Selection of trainees

There would appear to be very little published research on the selection of applicants for training courses in counselling and psychotherapy. Many courses do little more than interview candidates and take up references. Given the poor evidence concerning the validity of selection interviewing, particularly in situations where job criteria are not clearly defined and the interview itself is not tightly structured, there can be little confidence that this approach to selection is adequate in itself. Best current practice tends to involve taking one or two days to put candidates through an 'assessment centre' procedure, similar to that used in industry, the civil service and the armed forces in the selection of senior managers (see Bray, 1982), in which they are interviewed on different topics by different selectors, observed in group discussion and counselling role play situations, and asked to complete tests that tap relevant aspects of personality, intelligence and counselling aptitude. This procedure gives selectors a range of indicators of counselling potential, with the expectation that such multiple sources of information (which may include peer ratings from the other candidates in the group) will prove to be more reliable and valid than 'one-shot' interviews.

The assessment of counsellor competence

The assessment of competence to practise as a counsellor generates another set of difficult issues. The approach to accreditation or licensing of counsellors as competent to practise that is currently being implemented by professional bodies places a great deal of emphasis on the completion of an acceptable training course. The methods that training courses use to assess competence therefore have important implications for the profession as a whole, and for the quality of service received by clients.

There is a wide range of sources of assessment judgements and techniques for deriving assessment information currently being used on courses. Information about the competence of a counsellor in training can be gathered from tutors or trainers, the supervisor, or an external examiner or consultant. Independent panels of judges can be used to assess samples of the work handed in by the trainee, or to hold an oral assessment of case material (Stevenson and Norcross, 1987). Peer and self-assessment are used on many courses. It is seldom possible to obtain ratings of trainee competence from actual clients, although often fellow students on a course will have been clients for each other, and so a form of client perspective will constitute a component of peer evaluations. All of these diverse assessment sources have a contribution to make, and all also possess limitations. For example, tutors and trainers may be excellent observers of counsellor skills, but trainees may engage in 'impression management' by presenting only their best work to these mentors. Members of the peer group are more likely than tutors to have a rounded view of the weaknesses as well as the achievements of a trainee.

There are a number of different techniques for gathering information on counselling skills and competencies. The most widely used of these techniques are:

Questionnaires and rating scales
Videotapes or audiotapes of work with clients (real or role played)
Learning journals or diaries
Examinations and tests
Computer simulations.

Again, each of these techniques has advantages and disadvantages. The questionnaires and ratings scales that are available (e.g. Linden *et al.*, 1965; Carkhuff, 1969; Myrick and Kelly, 1971) either have been employed mainly for research purposes or lack adequate up-to-date norms. In other words, although these questionnaires would appear to measure relevant counsellor characteristics, such as empathy, there is an absence of valid data on cut-off points, on just how high a score is 'good enough'. In addition, there are aspects of counsellor learning for which questionnaires and rating scales do not exist.

There are several problems associated with the use of tapes in counsellor assessment, including the self-consciousness of the trainee when being taped, the lack of information on internal processes and the question of whether a short tape is representative of the general approach of a counsellor. Learning journals or diaries have often been used as a way of evaluating the development of trainees and the application of learning in practice (Pates and Knasel, 1989). Journals can only present the view of the student, however, and it should also be noted that some students or trainees may lack writing skills and fail to do themselves justice through this medium of communication. Examinations and tests are used on many courses, particularly those located in academic establishments. It is clear that such techniques only assess the cognitive knowledge of students, which may or may not be associated with effectiveness with clients. Finally, computer simulations of patterns of client problems have been used to assess the skill of counsellors in clinical decision-making and case formulation (Berven and Scofield, 1980; Berven, 1987).

Although there is certainly a wealth of ideas about how to assess counsellor competence, the validity and reliability of most of these techniques are unknown (Scofield and Yoxheimer, 1983). In a study by Chevron and Rounsaville (1983), the clinical skills of therapists were assessed through a variety of techniques. The levels of agreement between the techniques was generally low, even though the raters and supervisors used in the study were highly trained and experienced.

Another key issue in the assessment of counsellor competence concerns the sensitivity of the sources and techniques that are used. Davis (1989) has argued that although counsellor errors can be judged more accurately and reliably, it is much harder to differentiate between higher levels of skill, for example between an 'adequate' and an 'excellent' piece of counselling. Sachs (1983) has produced research results which indicate that the absence of counsellor errors is predictive of good client outcomes. It may be, therefore, that there would be advantages in restricting competency assessments merely to arriving at pass–fail distinctions.

As Purton (1991) has observed, the modes of assessment used on training courses reflect the philosophy or theoretical orientation of the course. For example, in his study he found that a person-centred course emphasized student-centred peer assessment, a psychosynthesis course emphasized the use of intuition in assessment, and in a psychodynamic training course close attention was paid in assessment to unconscious personality characteristics that might impede work with clients. The culture of a training course is also significant in determining the way that assessment decisions are made. Tyler and Weaver (1981) consider that policies about access to student records, or the manner in which feedback is given to students, seriously affect the validity of the assessment information that is gathered. The openness of trainers about assessment procedures and criteria is also an important factor. Toukmanian *et al.* (1978) looked at two groups of students participating in equivalent counselling training courses. One group was provided with information about the assessment criteria being used by tutors, while the other group was given no information on this topic. The first group achieved significantly higher grades on the course.

The competency judgements arising from training courses have important implications. The successful completion of a course can often be seen by employers and clients as bestowing a licence to practise. Given the paucity of research in this area, however, it would seem appropriate to take a cautious approach to the use of assessment sources and techniques. It would seem sensible to combine as many sources and techniques as possible, to arrive at a multi-perspective assessment, drawing upon a large sample of relevant behaviour.

Supervision

An important element in counsellor development, not only during training but also throughout the working life of the counsellor, is the use of effective and appropriate supervision. It is a requirement of most professional associations that counsellors accredited by them should receive regular supervision from a qualified person. In this context, it is necessary to emphasize that supervision has a different meaning to that in other work settings. Supervision in counselling is not primarily a management role in which the supervisee is given directions and allocated tasks, but rather is aimed at assisting the counsellor to work as effectively as possible with the client (Carroll, 1988). The supervision role in counselling is similar to that of the tutor or consultant. Hawkins and Shohet (1989) have identified three main functions of supervision in counselling. The first is *educational*, with the aim of giving the counsellor a regular opportunity to receive feedback, develop new understandings and receive information. The second aspect is the *supportive* role of supervision, through which the counsellor can share dilemmas, be validated in his or her work performance and deal with any personal distress or counter-transference evoked by clients. Finally, there is a *management* dimension to supervision, in ensuring quality of work and helping the counsellor to plan work and utilize resources.

There are a number of different formats for providing supervision (Hawkins and Shohet, 1989). Probably the most common arrangement is to make a contract for individual sessions over a period of time with the same person. A variant on this approach is to use separate consultants to explore specific issues, for example going to an expert in family work to discuss a client with family problems, and using a mental health counsellor for consultation on a client who is depressed (Kaslow, 1986). Another possibility is group supervision, where a small group of supervisees meet with a supervisor. The case discussion group is a type of group supervision that gives particular attention to understanding the personality or family dynamics of the client. Peer supervision groups involve a group of counsellors meeting to engage in supervision of each other, without there being a designated leader or consultant. Finally, supervision networks (Houston, 1990) consist of a set of colleagues who are available for mutual or peer supervision, on either a one-to-one or a small group basis.

Each of these modes of supervision has its advantages and disadvantages. Regular individual supervision facilitates the development of a good working relationship between supervisor and supervisee. On the other hand, specific consultants will have a greater depth of experience in particular areas. Group and peer group supervision enable the counsellor to learn from the cases and issues presented by colleagues. In these supervision settings, however, there may be problems in maintaining confidentiality and in dealing with the dynamics of the group. The choice of mode of supervision depends on a wide range of factors, including personal preference, cost, availability, agency policy and organization, and counselling philosophy.

The supervision process is highly dependent on the quality of information which supervisees bring to the supervision setting. Most often, the supervisee will report what he or she has been doing with clients, using notes taken after counselling sessions to augment his or her recollection. Dryden and Thorne (1991) argue that, if the focus of the supervision is to be on the skills employed by the counsellor, the supervisor needs 'actual data' from sessions. These data can be obtained from detailed process notes written immediately after a session, and video- or audio-tapes of sessions. In some situations supervisors may even be able to make live observations of the supervisee working with a client.

One of the principal dilemmas in supervision is deciding on what it would be helpful to discuss. Potentially, the supervisee might need to explore his or her understanding of the client, the feelings he or she holds in reaction to the client, the appropriateness of different intervention or techniques, and many other topics. Hawkins and Shohet (1989) have constructed a model of the supervision process which usefully clarifies some of these issues. They suggest that at any time in supervision there are six levels operating:

1 Reflection on the content of the counselling session. The focus here is on the client, what is being said, how different parts of the life of the client fit together and what the client wants from counselling.
2 Exploration of the techniques and strategies used by the counsellor. This level is concerned with the therapeutic intentions of the counsellor, and the approach he or she is taking to helping the client.
3 Exploration of the therapeutic relationship. The aim at this level is to examine the ways in which the client and counsellor interact, and whether they have established a functioning working alliance.
4 The feelings of the counsellor towards the client. In this area of supervision the intention is to identify and understand the counter-transference reactions of the counsellor, or the personal issues which have been re-stimulated through contact with the client.
5 A focus on what is happening here and now between supervisor and supervisee. The relationship in the supervision session may exhibit similar features to the relationship between the counsellor and his or her client. Paying attention to this 'parallel process' (McNeill and Worthen, 1989) can give valuable insights.
6 Using the counter-transference of the supervisor. The feelings of the supervisor in response to the supervisee may also provide a guide to some of the ways of seeing the cases that are not yet consciously articulated by supervisor or supervisee, as well as contributing to an understanding of the quality of the supervisor–supervisee relationship.

Hawkins and Shohet (1989) argue that good supervision will involve movement between all these levels. Supervisors tend to have a personal style of supervision in which they stick mainly to a particular set of levels, and the model can be used as a framework for both supervisors and supervisees to reflect on their work together and if necessary to negotiate change. The Hawkins and Shohet model has been widely used in training, but has not yet generated research.

The Hawkins and Shohet model examines what takes place within a single supervision setting. There are also processes in supervision that occur over a much longer time-span, which concern the ways in which the stage of development of the counsellor can have an impact on the counselling process. Counsellors of different degrees of experience and maturity have different supervision needs, and numerous models have been devised to portray this developmental track (see Hess (1980) or Stoltenberg and Delworth (1987) for a review of these ideas). One such model is the six-stage model of development of professional identity constructed by Friedman and Kaslow (1986). The stages, which may take several years to pass through, are described as:

1 *Excitement and anticipatory anxiety.* This phase describes the period before the counsellor has seen his or her first client. The task of the supervisor is to provide security and guidance.

2 *Dependency and identification.* The second stage commences as soon as the counsellor begins work with clients. The lack of confidence, skill and knowledge in the counsellor results in a high degree of dependency on the supervisor, who

is perceived as having all the answers. The trainee counsellor at this stage will use the supervisor as a model. However, anxiety about being seen as incompetent may lead the supervisee to conceal information from the supervisor. The personality and dynamics of the client, rather than the therapeutic relationship or counter-transference, is the most common focus of supervision at this stage, reflecting the lack of confidence and awareness of the counsellor in exploring his or her own contribution to the thereputic process.

3 *Activity and continued dependency*. This phase of development is triggered by the realization of the counsellor that he or she is actually making a difference to clients. This recognition enables the counsellor to be more active with clients, and to try out different strategies and techniques. The counsellor is beginning to be more open to his or her own feeling response to clients, and may discuss counselling issues with colleagues and family members as a means of 'spilling affect' (Friedman and Kaslow, 1986: 38). In this burst of enthusiasm for therapy, the counsellor may experiment by applying therapeutic skills and concepts to friends and family members. The primary task of the supervisor at this stage is to be able to accept the needs for dependency as well as active autonomy, and to allow the counsellor to explore different options.

4 *Exuberance and taking charge*. Friedman and Kaslow (1986: 40) write that 'the fourth phase of development is ushered in by the trainee's realization that he or she really *is* a therapist.' Having acquired considerable experience in working with clients, having read widely in the field, and probably having embarked on personal therapy, the counsellor is actively making connections between theory and practice, and beginning to identify with one theoretical perspective rather than trying out diverse ideas and systems. In supervision, there is a willingness to explore counter-transference issues and to discuss theoretical models. The counsellor no longer needs as much support and warmth in supervision, and is ready for a higher degree of challenge. In becoming less dependent on the supervisor, the counsellor comes to view the latter more as a consultant than as a teacher.

5 *Identity and independence*. This is described as the stage of 'professional adolescence'. In beginning to envisage life without the protection and guidance of the supervisor, the counsellor becomes more willing and able to express differences of opinion. Counsellors at this stage of development are often attracted to peer supervision with others at a similar stage. The supervisee has by this time internalized a frame of reference for evaluating client work, and is in a position to accept or reject the advice or suggestions of the supervisor. The counsellor may be aware of areas in which his or her expertise exceeds that of the supervisor. It is necessary for the supervisor at this stage to remain available to the counsellor, and to accept a lack of control.

6 *Calm and collegiality*. By this stage the counsellor has acquired a firm sense of professional identity and belief in his or her competence. The counsellor is able to take a balanced view of the strengths and weaknesses of different approaches to therapy, and is able to use peers and supervisors as consultants, 'from a spirit of genuine respect among colleagues' (Friedman and Kaslow, 1986: 45). At this stage counsellors begin to take an interest in taking on the supervisor role.

The process involved in the formation of a professional identity has the consequence that the focus of supervision can be qualitatively different at succeeding stages. It is helpful for both supervisors and supervisees to be aware that this kind of developmental sequence can take place, and to adjust their behaviour and expectations accordingly.

Throughout this account of the supervision process, it can be observed that the quality of the relationship between supervisor and supervisee is of paramount importance (Shohet and Wilmot, 1991). Charny (1986: 20) has written that 'the greatest possibilities of growth in supervision . . . [lie] in tapping candidly just what is going on in the heart, mind and body of a therapist in relation to a given case.' He adds that, for him, the most valuable question in supervision is: 'what about this case really worries me?' To undertake this kind of open exploration of self in relation to the client requires the same degree of emotional safety and the same 'core conditions' that are offered to clients. As in counselling, the freedom to choose an appropriate helper is valuable, as is the freedom to terminate. The sensitivity to relationship issues that is found in much effective supervision can also lead to the danger of straying over the boundary which separates supervision from actual therapy. The role of supervision in counsellor training and ongoing development is, therefore, closely linked to issues of how and when to structure counsellor personal therapy or work on self.

Training and supervision in counselling: some conclusions

The development of theory and research into the practice of counselling and psychotherapy has not been matched by equivalent critical attention to the problems of training and supervision. Few studies have been carried out on the evaluation of the effects of training programmes. Major questions remain unanswered concerning methods of addressing ethical and cross-cultural perspectives in training. The implications for training of the movement towards integrationist and eclectic approaches are only beginning to be addressed. The relevance for counselling practice of research training or the adoption of a 'scientist-practitioner' model has not been fully investigated. There are few courses for training trainers and supervisors. The specific training and supervision needs of non-professional or volunteer counsellors have not been assessed. There is, therefore, room for a great deal of additional theory and research in this area.

On the other hand, it is possible to assert with some confidence that the core elements of counsellor training and education are known. Competent counsellors are able to make use of accurate self-awareness, knowledge of theoretical models and a range of counselling skills.

Topics for reflection and discussion

1 How would you organize the initial selection of people who wish to participate in counsellor training? In your view, what are the most important qualities of

the person who has the potential to be an effective counsellor? How can these qualities be reliably assessed?

2 Do you agree with those who would insist on personal therapy as a requirement for all those in training as counsellors? Should non-professional counsellors, who may be seeing only two or three clients each week, also receive personal therapy?

3 Compare the relative strengths and weaknesses of integrationist/eclectic and 'single theory' approaches to counsellor training.

4 It is generally accepted that counselling courses should contain inputs in the three areas of theory, practical skills, and work on self. In your view, what is the ideal balance between these elements?

5 How do you know whether someone is a competent counsellor?

REFERENCES

Abramowitz, S. I. and Murray, J. (1983) Race effects in psychotherapy. In J. Murray and P. R. Abramson (eds) *Bias in Psychotherapy*. New York: Praeger.

Agazarian, Y. and Peters, R. (1981) *The Visible and Invisible Group: Two Perspectives on Group Psychotherapy and Group Process*. London: Tavistock/Routledge.

Albee, G. W. (1977) The Protestant ethic, sex and psychotherapy. *American Psychologist* 32: 150–61.

Alexander, F. and French, T. M. (1946) *Psychoanalytic Therapy: Principles and Applications*. New York: Ronald Press.

Allen, L. (1990) A client's experience of failure. In D. Mearns and W. Dryden (eds) *Experiences of Counselling in Action*. London: Sage.

Alloy, L. B. and Abramson, L. Y. (1982) Learned helplessness, depression and the illusion of control. *Journal of Personality and Social Psychology* 42: 1114–26.

American Association for Counseling and Development (1988) *Ethical Standards*. Alexandria, VA: AACD.

Anderson, W. (ed.) (1977) *Therapy and the Arts: Tools of Consciousness*. New York: Harper and Row.

Andrews, J. D. W. (1991) *The Active Self in Psychotherapy: An Integration of Therapeutic Styles*. Boston: Allyn and Bacon.

Angus, L. E. and Rennie, D. L. (1988) Therapist participation in metaphor generation: collaborative and noncollaborative styles. *Psychotherapy* 25: 552–60.

Angus, L. E. and Rennie, D. L. (1989) Envisioning the representational world: the client's experience of metaphoric expressiveness in psychotherapy. *Psychotherapy* 26: 373–9.

Antze, P. (1976) The role of ideologies in peer psychotherapy organizations. *Journal of Applied Behavioral Science* 12: 323–46.

Aronson, T. A. (1989) A critical review of psychotherapeutic treatments of the borderline personality: historical trends and future directions. *Journal of Nervous and Mental Disease* 177: 511–28.

Arsenian, J. and Arsenian, J. M. (1948) Tough and easy cultures: a conceptual analysis. *Psychiatry* 11: 377–85.

Atkinson, D. R. (1985) Research on cross-cultural counseling and psychotherapy: a review and update of reviews. In P. Pedersen (ed.) *Handbook of Cross-Cultural Counseling and Psychotherapy*. New York: Praeger.

Austin, K. M., Moline, M. E. and Williams, G. T. (1990) *Confronting Malpractice: Legal and Ethical Dilemmas in Psychotherapy*. London: Sage.

Aveline, M. O. (1986) Personal themes from training groups for health care professionals. *British Journal of Medical Psychology* 59: 325–35.

Aveline, M. (1990) Developing a new NHS psychotherapy service and training scheme in the provinces. *British Journal of Psychotherapy* 6: 312–23.

Aveline, M. and Dryden, W. (eds) (1988) *Group Therapy in Britain.* Milton Keynes: Open University Press.

Ayllon, T. and Azrin, N. H. (1965) The measurement and reinforcement of behavior of psychotics. *Journal of the Experimental Analysis of Behavior* 8: 357–83.

Ayllon, T. and Azrin, N. H. (1968) *The Token Economy*. New York: Appleton Century Crofts.

Bachelor, A. (1988) How clients perceive therapist empathy: a content analysis of 'received' empathy. *Psychotherapy* 25: 227–40.

Badaines, A. (1988) Psychodrama. In J. Rowan and W. Dryden (eds) *Innovative Therapy in Britain*. Milton Keynes: Open University Press.

Bakan, D. (1966) *Against Method*. New York: Basic Books.

Bakan, D. (1976) Politics and American psychology. In K. Riegel (ed.) *Psychology: Theoretical-Historical Perspectives*. New York: Springer.

Baker, S. B., Daniels, T. G. and Greeley, A. T. (1990) Systematic training of graduate-level counselors: narrative and meta-analytic reviews of three programmes. *Counseling Psychologist* 18: 355–421.

Baldwin, M. (ed.) (1987) *The Use of Self in Therapy*. New York: Haworth Press.

Bandura, A. (1971) Psychotherapy based upon modeling principles. In A. E. Bergin and S. L. Garfield (eds) *Handbook of Psychotherapy and Behavior Change: An Empirical Analysis*. New York: Wiley.

Bandura, A. (1977) *Social Learning Theory*. Englewood Cliffs, NJ: Prentice-Hall.

Barker, P. (1992) *Basic Family Therapy,* 3rd edn. Oxford: Blackwell.

Barkham, M. (1989) Brief prescriptive therapy in two-plus-one sessions: initial cases from the clinic. *Behavioural Psychotherapy* 17: 161–75.

Barkham, M. (1992) Research on integrative and eclectic therapy. In W. Dryden (ed.) *Integrative and Eclectic Therapy: A Handbook*. Buckingham: Open University Press.

Barkham, M. and Shapiro, D. A. (1989) Towards resolving the problem of waiting lists: psychotherapy in two-plus-one sessions. *Clinical Psychology Forum* 23: 15–18.

Barkham, M. and Shapiro, D. A. (1990a) Brief psychotherapeutic interventions for job-related distress: a pilot study of prescriptive and exploratory therapy. *Counselling Psychology Quarterly* 3: 133–47.

Barkham, M. and Shapiro, D.A. (1990b) Exploratory therapy in two-plus-one sessions: a research model for studying the process of change. In G. Lietaer, J. Rombauts and R. Van Balen (eds) *Client-Centered and Experiential Psychotherapy in the Nineties*. Leuven: Leuven University Press.

Barlow, D. H. and Hersen, M. (1986) *Single Case Experimental Designs: Strategies for Studying Behavior Change,* 2nd edn. New York: Pergamon.

Barlow, D. H., Hayes, S. C. and Nelson, R. O. (1984) *The Scientist Practitioner: Research and Accountability in Clinical and Educational Settings*. New York: Pergamon.

Barrett-Lennard, G. T. (1962) Dimensions of therapist response as causal factors in therapeutic change. *Psychological Monographs* 76 (Whole Number 562).

Barrett-Lennard, G. T. (1979) The client-centered system unfolding. In F. J. Turner (ed.) *Social Work Treatment: Interlocking Theoretical Approaches,* 2nd edn. New York: Free Press.

Barrett-Lennard, G. T. (1981) The empathy cycle – refinement of a nuclear concept. *Journal of Counseling Psychology* 28: 91–100.

Barrett-Lennard, G. T. (1986) The Relationship Inventory now: issues and advances in theory, method and use. In L. S. Greenberg and W. M. Pinsof (eds) *The Psychotherapeutic Process: A Research Handbook.* New York: Guilford.

Bates, C. M. and Brodsky, A. M. (1989) *Sex in the Therapy Hour: A Case of Professional Incest.* London: Guilford Press.

Battye, R. (1991) On being a trainee. In W. Dryden and B. Thorne (eds) *Training and Supervision for Counselling in Action.* London: Sage.

Bauer, G. and Kobos, J. (1987) *Brief Therapy: Short-Term Psychodynamic Intervention.* New York: Jason Aronson.

Bayer, R. (1987) *Homosexuality and American Psychiatry: The Politics of Diagnosis,* 2nd edn. Princeton, NJ: Princeton University Press.

Beauchamp, T. L. and Childress, J. F. (1979) *Principles of Biomedical Ethics.* Oxford: Oxford University Press.

Beck, A. (1976) *Cognitive Therapy and the Emotional Disorders.* Harmondsworth: Penguin.

Beck, A. and Weishaar, M. (1989) Cognitive therapy. In A. Freeman, K. M. Simon, L. E. Beutler and H. Arkowitz (eds) *Comprehensive Handbook of Cognitive Therapy.* New York: Plenum Press.

Beck, A. Y., Rush, A. G., Shaw, B. F. and Emery, G. (1979) *Cognitive Therapy of Depression.* New York: Guilford.

Beidel, D. C. and Turner, S. M. (1986) A critique of the theoretical bases of cognitive-behavioral theories and therapy. *Clinical Psychology Review* 6: 177–97.

Bennis, W. and Shepard, H. (1956) A theory of group development. *Human Relations* 9: 415–57.

Bennun, I. (1985) Unilateral marital therapy. In W. Dryden (ed.) *Marital Therapy in Britain, Volume 2.* London: Harper and Row.

Berger, M. (1983) Toward maximising the utility of consumer satisfaction as an outcome. In M. J. Lambert, E. R. Christensen and S. S. DeJulio (eds) *The Assessment of Psychotherapy Outcome.* New York: Wiley.

Bergin, A. E. (1980) Psychotherapy and religious values. *Journal of Consulting and Clinical Psychology* 48: 95–105.

Bergin, A. E. and Jensen, J. P. (1990) Religiosity of psychotherapists: a national survey. *Psychotherapy* 27: 3–7.

Bergner, R. M. and Staggs, J. (1987) The positive therapeutic relationship as accreditation. *Psychotherapy* 24: 315–20.

Berman, J. S. and Norton, N. C. (1985) Does professional training make a therapist more effective? *Psychological Bulletin* 98: 401–7.

Berne, E. (1975) *What Do You Say After You Say Hello? The Psychology of Human Destiny.* London: Corgi.

Bernstein, B. (1972) Social class, language and socialization. In P. P. Giglioli (ed.) *Language and Social Context.* Harmondsworth: Penguin.

Berven, N. L. (1987) Improving evaluation in counselor training and credentialing through standardized simulations. In B. A. Edelstein and E. S. Berler (eds) *Evaluation and Accountability in Clinical Training.* New York: Plenum Press.

Berven, N. and Scofield, M. (1980) Evaluation of professional competence through standardised simulations: a review. *Rehabilitation Counseling Bulletin* 179: 178–202.

Bettelheim, B. (1983) *Freud and Man's Soul.* London: Chatto and Windus.

Beutler, L. (1983) *Eclectic Psychotherapy: A Systematic Approach.* New York: Pergamon.

Beutler, L. E. and Crago, M. (eds) (1991) *Psychotherapy Research: An International Review of Programmatic Studies*. Washington, DC: American Psychological Association.

Beutler, L. E., Crago, M. and Arizmendi, T. G. (1986) Therapist variables in psychotherapy process and outcome. In S. L. Garfield and A. E. Bergin (eds) *Handbook of Psychotherapy and Behavior Change*, 3rd edn. New York: Wiley.

Beutler, L. E. *et al.* (1987) Training integrative/eclectic psychotherapists II. *Journal of Integrative and Eclectic Psychotherapy* 6: 296–332.

Binswanger, L. (1963) *Being-in-the-World*. New York: Basic Books.

Bion, W. (1961) *Experiences in Groups*. London: Tavistock.

Blackwell, R. T., Galassi, J. P., Galassi, M. D. and Watson, T. E. (1985) Are cognitive assessment methods equal? A comparison of think aloud and thought listing. *Cognitive Therapy and Research* 9: 399–413.

Bloch, S., Crouch, E. and Reibstein, J. (1981) Therapeutic factors in group psychotherapy. *Archives of General Psychiatry* 38: 519–26.

Boadella, D. (1988) Biosynthesis. In J. Rowan and W. Dryden (eds) *Innovative Therapy in Britain*. Milton Keynes: Open University Press.

Bohart, A. C. (1990) Psychotherapy integration from a client-centered perspective. In G. Lietaer, J. Rombauts and R. Van Balen (eds) *Client-Centered and Experiential Therapy in the Nineties*. Leuven: Leuven University Press.

Bolger, A. W. (1985) Training and research in counselling. *British Journal of Guidance and Counselling* 13: 112–24.

Bolger, A. W. (1989) Research and evaluation in counselling. In W. Dryden, D. Charles-Edwards and R. Woolfe (eds) *Handbook of Counselling in Britain*. London: Routledge.

Bond, T. (1989) Towards defining the role of counselling skills. *Counselling* 69 (August) 24–6.

Bond, T. (1992) Ethical issues in counselling in education. *British Journal of Guidance and Counselling* 20: 51–63.

Boorstein, S. (ed.) (1986) *Transpersonal Psychotherapy*. Palo Alto, CA: Science and Behavior Books.

Bordin, E. S. (1979) The generalizability of the psychoanalytic concept of working alliance. *Psychotherapy: Theory, Research and Practice* 16: 252–60.

Boss, M. (1957) *Psychoanalysis and Daseinanalysis*. New York: Basic Books.

Bourguignon, E. (1979) *Psychological Anthropology: An Introduction to Human Nature and Cultural Differences*. New York: Holt, Rinehart and Winston.

Bowlby, J. (1969) *Attachment*. London: Hogarth.

Bowlby, J. (1973) *Separation, Anxiety and Anger*. London: Hogarth.

Bowlby, J. (1980) *Loss, Sadness and Depression*. London: Hogarth.

Bowlby, J. (1988) *A Secure Base: Clinical Applications of Attachment Theory*. London: Routledge.

Bowling, A. (1991) *Measuring Health: A Review of Quality of Life Scales*. Milton Keynes: Open University Press.

Boy, A. V. and Pine, G. J. (1980) Avoiding counselor burnout through role renewal. *Personnel and Guidance Journal* 59: 161–3.

Boy, A. V. and Pine, G. J. (1982) *Client-Centered Counseling: A Renewal*. Boston: Allyn and Bacon.

Bozarth, J. D. (1984) Beyond reflection: emergent modes of empathy. In R. F. Levant and J. M. Shlien (eds) *Client-centered Therapy and the Person-Centered Approach: New Directions in Theory, Research and Practice*. New York: Praeger.

Brammer, L., Shostrom, E. and Abrego, P. J. (1989) *Therapeutic Psychology: Fundamentals of Counseling and Psychotherapy*. Englewood Cliffs, NJ: Prentice-Hall.

Braude, M. (ed.) (1987) *Women, Power and Therapy*. New York: Haworth Press.

Bray, D. W. (1982) The assessment center and the study of lives. *American Psychologist* 37: 180-9.

Brazier, D. (1991) *A Guide to Psychodrama*. London: Association for Humanistic Psychology in Britain.

Breger, L. and McGaugh, J. (1965) Critique and reformulation of 'learning-theory' approaches. *Psychological Bulletin* 63: 338-58.

Brightman, B. K. (1984) Narcissistic issues in the training experience of the psychotherapist. *International Journal of Psychoanalytic Psychotherapy* 10: 293-371.

British Association for Counselling (1977) *Counselling News No. 16*. Rugby: BAC.

British Association for Counselling (1984) *Code of Ethics and Practice for Counsellors*. Rugby: BAC.

British Association for Counselling (1992) *16th Annual Report 1991/92*. Rugby: BAC.

Brodsky, A. M. and Holroyd, J. (1975) Report on the task force on sex bias and sex-role stereotyping in psychotherapeutic practice. *American Psychologist* 30: 1169-75.

Bromley, E. (1983) Social class issues in psychotherapy. In D. Pilgrim (ed.) *Psychology and Psychotherapy: Current Issues and Trends*. London: Routledge.

Broverman, I. *et al.* (1970) Sex-role stereotypes and clinical judgements of mental health. *Journal of Consulting and Clinical Psychology* 34: 1-7.

Buckley, P., Karasu, T. B. and Charles, E. (1981) Psychotherapists view their personal therapy. *Psychotherapy: Theory, Research and Practice* 18: 299-305.

Budman, S. and Gurman, A. (1988) *Theory and Practice of Brief Psychotherapy*. London: Hutchinson.

Bugental, J. (1976) *The Search for Existential Identity*. San Francisco: Jossey-Bass.

Buhrke, R. A., Ben-Ezra, L. A., Hurley, M. E. and Ruprecht, L. J. (1992) Content analysis and methodological critique of articles concerning lesbian and gay male issues in counseling journals. *Journal of Counseling Psychology* 39: 91-9.

Burks, H. M. and Stefflre, B. (1979) *Theories of Counseling*, 3rd edn. New York: McGraw-Hill.

Burton, A. (1970) The adoration of the patient and its disillusionment. *American Journal of Psychoanalysis* 29: 194-204.

Carkhuff, R. (1969) *Helping and Human Relations, Vol. 2*. New York: Holt, Rinehart and Winston.

Carroll, M. (1988) Counselling supervision: the British context. *Counselling Psychology Quarterly* 1: 387-96.

Carvalho, R. (1990) Psychodynamic therapy: the Jungian approach. In W. Dryden (ed.) *Individual Therapy: A Handbook*. Milton Keynes: Open University Press.

Casement, P. (1985) *On Listening to the Patient*. London: Tavistock.

Casement, P. (1990) *Further Learning from the Patient: The Analytic Space and Process*. London: Tavistock/Routledge.

Cash, R. W. (1984) The Human Resources Development model. In D. Larson (ed.) *Teaching Psychological Skills: Models for Giving Psychology Away*. Monterey, CA: Brooks/Cole.

Cashdan, S. (1988) *Object Relations Therapy: Using the Relationship*. New York: W. W. Norton.

Charny, I. W. (1986) What do therapists worry about? a tool for experiential supervision. In F. W. Kaslow (ed.) *Supervision and Training: Models, Dilemmas and Challenges*. New York: Haworth Press.

Cherniss, C. and Krantz, D. L. (1983) The ideological community as an antidote to burnout in the human services. In B. A. Farber (ed.) *Stress and Burnout in the Human Service Professions*. New York: Pergamon.

Chesler, P. (1972) *Women and Madness*. New York: Doubleday.

Chester, R. (1985) Shaping the future: from marriage movement to service agency. *Marriage Guidance* (Autumn) 5–15.

Chevron, E. and Rounsaville, B. (1983) Evaluating the clinical skills of psychotherapists. *Archives of General Psychiatry* 40: 1129–32.

Chodorow, N. (1978) *The Reproduction of Mothering*. Berkeley, CA: University of California Press.

Clarkson, P. (1989) *Gestalt Counselling in Action*. London: Sage.

Clarkson, P. (1991) *Transactional Analysis Psychotherapy: An Integrated Approach*. London: Tavistock/Routledge.

Clarkson, P. (1992) Systematic integrative psychotherapy training. In W. Dryden (ed.) *Integrative and Eclectic Therapy: A Handbook*. Buckingham: Open University Press.

Clarkson, P. and Gilbert, M. (1990) Transactional Analysis. In W. Dryden (ed.) *Individual Therapy: A Handbook*. Milton Keynes: Open University Press.

Clarkson, P. and Gilbert, M. (1991) The training of counsellor trainers and supervisors. In W. Dryden and B. Thorne (eds) *Training and Supervision for Counselling in Action*. London: Sage.

Clulow, C. and Mattinson, J. (1989) *Marriage Inside Out: Understanding Problems of Intimacy*. Harmondsworth: Penguin.

Cochrane, R. (1983) *The Social Creation of Mental Illness*. London: Longman.

Cohen, L. H., Sargent, M. H. and Sechrest, L. B. (1986) Use of psychotherapy research by professional psychologists. *American Psychologist* 41: 198–206.

Coleman, E. (1982) *Developmental Stages of the Coming Out Process*. New York: Haworth.

Coleman, E. (ed.) (1988) *Psychotherapy with Homosexual Men and Women: Integrated Identity Approaches for Clinical Practice*. New York: Haworth Press.

Collier, H. V. (1987) The differing self: women as psychotherapists. *Journal of Psychotherapy and the Family* 3: 53–60.

Coltart, N. E. C. (1986) 'Slouching towards Bethlehem' . . . or thinking the unthinkable in psychoanalysis. In G. Kohon (ed.) *The British School of Psychoanalysis: the Independent Tradition*. London: Free Association.

Combs, A. W. (1986) What makes a good helper? *Person-Centered Review* 1: 51–61.

Combs, A. W. (1989) *A Theory of Therapy: Guidelines for Counseling Practice*. London: Sage.

Combs, A. W. and Soper, D. W. (1963) Perceptual organization of effective counselors. *Journal of Counseling Psychology* 10: 222–6.

Conrad, P. (1981) On the medicalization of deviance and social control. In D. Ingleby (ed.) *Critical Psychiatry: The Politics of Mental Health*. Harmondsworth: Penguin.

Cooter, R. (1981) Phrenology and the British alienists: 1825–1845. In A. Scull (ed.) *Mad-houses, Mad-doctors and Madmen*. Pennsylvania: University of Pennsylvania Press.

Corey, G. (1990) *Theory and Practice of Group Counseling*. San Francisco: Brooks/Cole.

Corey, G., Corey, M. and Callanan, P. (1988) *Issues and Ethics in the Helping Professions*, 3rd edn. Pacific Grove, CA: Brooks/Cole.

Corsini, R. J. and Wedding, D. (eds) (1989) *Current Psychotherapies* 4th edn. Itasca, IL: F. E. Peacock.

Craighead, L. W., McNamara, K. and Horan, J. J. (1984) Perspectives on self-help and bibliography: you are what you read. In S. D. Brown and R. W. Lent (eds) *Handbook of Counseling Psychology*. New York: Wiley.

Cramer, D. (1992) *Personality and Psychotherapy: Theory, Practice and Research*. Buckingham: Open University Press.

Crandall, R. and Allen, R. (1981) The organizational context of helping relationships. In T. A. Wills (ed.) *Basic Processes in Helping Relationships*. New York: Academic Press.

Crits-Christoph, P., Cooper, A. and Luborsky, L. (1988) The accuracy of therapists' interpretations and the outcome of dynamic psychotherapy. *Journal of Consulting and Clinical Psychology* 56: 490–5.

Crits-Christoph, P. *et al.* (1991) Meta-analysis of therapist effects in psychotherapy outcome studies. *Psychotherapy Research* 1: 81–91.

Crouch, A. (1992) The competent counsellor. *Self and Society* 20: 22–5.

Cullen, C. (1988) Applied behaviour analysis: contemporary and prospective agenda. In G. Davey and C. Cullen (eds) *Human Operant Conditioning and Behaviour Modification*. London: Wiley.

Cullen, C. (1991) Radical behaviourism and its influence on clinical therapies. *Behavioural Psychotherapy* 19: 47–58.

Culley, S. (1992) Counselling skills: an integrative framework. In W. Dryden (ed.) *Integrative and Eclectic Therapy: A Handbook*. Buckingham: Open University Press.

Dalley, T. (ed.) (1984) *Art as Therapy: An Introduction to the Use of Art as a Therapeutic Technique*. London: Routledge.

Dalley, T. and Case, C. (1992) *The Handbook of Art Therapy*. London: Tavistock/Routledge.

d'Ardenne, P. and Mahtani, A. (1989) *Transcultural Counseling in Action*. London: Sage.

Davanloo, H. (ed.) (1980) *Short-term Psychodynamic Psychotherapy*. New York: Jason Aronson.

Davis, J. (1989) Issues in the evaluation of counsellors by supervisors. *Counselling* 69 (August) 31–7.

Delfin, P. E. (1978) Components of effective telephone intervention: a critical incidents analysis. *Crisis Intervention* 9: 50–68.

DeWaele, J. P. and Harré, R. (1976) The personality of individuals. In R. Harré (ed.) *Personality*. Oxford: Blackwell.

Dobson, K. S. (ed.) (1988) *Handbook of Cognitive Behavioural Therapies*. London: Routledge.

Dryden, W. (1984) Issues in the eclectic practice of individual therapy. In W. Dryden (ed.) *Individual Therapy in Britain*. London: Harper and Row.

Dryden, W. (ed.) (1985a) *Therapists' Dilemmas*. London: Harper and Row.

Dryden, W. (ed.) (1985b) *Marital Therapy in Britain Volume 1: Context and Therapeutic Approaches*. London: Harper and Row.

Dryden, W. (1991) *A Dialogue with John Norcross: Toward Integration*. Milton Keynes: Open University Press.

Dryden, W. (ed.) (1992) *Integrative and Eclectic Therapy: A Handbook*. Buckingham: Open University Press.

Dryden, W. and Barkham, M. (1990) The two-plus-one model: a dialogue. *Counselling Psychology Review* 5: 5–18.

Dryden, W. and Feltham, C. (1992) *Brief Counselling: A Practical Guide for Beginning Practitioners*. Buckingham: Open University Press.

Dryden, W. and Golden, W.L. (1986) *Cognitive–Behavioural Approaches to Psychotherapy*. Milton Keynes: Open University Press.

Dryden, W. and Spurling, L. (eds) (1989) *On Becoming a Psychotherapist*. London: Tavistock/Routledge.

Dryden, W. and Thorne, B. (1991) Approaches to the training of counsellors. In W. Dryden and B. Thorne (eds) *Training and Supervision for Counselling in Action*. London: Sage.

Dryden, W. and Trower, P. (eds) (1988) *Developments in Cognitive Psychotherapy*. London: Sage.

Dryden, W., Charles-Edwards, D. and Woolfe, R. (eds) (1989) *Handbook of Counselling in Britain*. London: Tavistock/Routledge.

Durlak, J. A. (1979) Comparative effectiveness of paraprofessional and professional helpers. *Psychological Bulletin* 86: 80–92.

Durlak, J. A. (1981) Evaluating comparative studies of paraprofessional and professional helpers: a reply to Nietzel and Fisher. *Psychological Bulletin* 89: 566–9.

Durre, L. (1980) Comparing romantic and therapeutic relationships. In K. S. Pope (ed.) *On Love and Loving: Psychological Perspectives on the Nature and Experience of Romantic Love*. San Francisco: Jossey-Bass.

Dusay, J. M. and Dusay, K.M. (1989) Transactional Analysis. In R. J. Corsini and D. Wedding (eds) *Current Psychotherapies*, 4th edn. Itasca, IL: F. E. Peacock.

Dworkin, S.H. and Gutierrez, F. (1989) Introduction to special issue. Counselors be aware: clients come in every size, shape, color and sexual orientation. *Journal of Counseling and Development* 68: 6–8.

Edelwich, J. and Brodsky, A. (1991) *Sexual Dilemmas for the Helping Professional*, 2nd edn. New York: Brunner/Mazel.

Egan, G. (1984) People in systems: a comprehensive model for psychosocial education and training. In D. Larson (ed.) *Teaching Psychological Skills: Models for Giving Psychology Away*. Monterey, CA: Brooks/Cole.

Egan, G. (1986) *The Skilled Helper: A Systematic Approach to Effective Helping*, 3rd edn. Belmont, CA: Brooks/Cole.

Egan, G. (1990) *The Skilled Helper: A Systematic Approach to Effective Helping*, 4th edn. Belmont, CA Brooks/Cole.

Ekstein, R. and Wallenstein, R. S. (1958) *The Teaching and Learning of Psychotherapy*, New York: International Universities Press.

Ellenberger, H. F. (1970) *The Discovery of the Unconscious: The History and Evolution of Dynamic Psychiatry*. London: Allen Lane.

Elliott, R. (1983) 'That in your hands . . .': a comprehensive process analysis of a significant event in psychotherapy. *Psychiatry* 46: 113–29.

Elliott, R. (1984) A discovery-oriented approach to significant change events in psychotherapy: Interpersonal Process Recall and Comprehensive Process Analysis. In L. N. Rice and L. S. Greenberg (eds) *Patterns of Change: Intensive Analysis of Psychotherapy Process*. New York: Guilford Press.

Elliott, R. (1986) Interpersonal Process Recall (IPR) as a psychotherapy process research method. In L. S. Greenberg and W. M. Pinsof (eds) *The Psychotherapeutic Process: A Research Handbook*. New York: Guilford Press.

Ellis, A. (1962) *Reason and Emotion in Psychotherapy*. New York: Lyle Stuart.

Ellis, A. (1973) *Humanistic Psychotherapy*. New York: McGraw-Hill.

Ellis, A. (1980) Psychotherapy and atheistic values: a response to A. E. Bergin's 'Psychotherapy and religious values'. *Journal of Consulting and Clinical Psychology* 48: 635–9.

Ellis, A. (1989) The history of cognition in psychotherapy. In A. Freeman, K. M. Simon, L. E. Beutler and H. Arkowitz (eds) *Comprehensive Handbook of Cognitive Therapy*. New York: Plenum Press.

Emrick, C. (1981) Nonprofessional peers as therapeutic agents. In M. H. Bean and N. E. Zinberg (eds) *Dynamic Approaches to the Understanding and Treatment of Alcoholism*. New York: Free Press.

Erikson, E. (1950) *Childhood and Society*. New York: W. W. Norton.

Eskapa, R. (1992) Multimodal therapy. In W. Dryden (ed.) *Integrative and Eclectic Therapy: A Handbook*. Buckingham: Open University Press.

Eysenck, H. J. (1952) The effects of psychotherapy: an evaluation. *Journal of Consulting Psychology* 16: 319–24.

Eysenck, H. J. (1970) A mish-mash of theories. *International Journal of Psychiatry* 9: 140–6.

Farber, B. A. (ed.) (1983a) *Stress and Burnout in the Human Service Professions*. New York: Pergamon.

Farber, B. A. (1983b) Dysfunctional aspects of the psychotherapeutic role. In B. A. Farber (ed.) *Stress and Burnout in the Human Service Professions*. New York: Pergamon.

Farber, B. A. and Heifetz, L. J. (1981) The satisfactions and stresses of psychotherapeutic work: a factor analytic study. *Professional Psychology* 12: 621–30.

Farber, B. A. and Heifetz, L. J. (1982) The process and dimensions of burnout in psychotherapists. *Professional Psychology* 13: 293–301.

Farson, R. (1978) The technology of humanism. *Journal of Humanistic Psychology* 18: 5–35.

Feild, H. S. and Gatewood, R. (1976) The paraprofessional and the organization: some problems of mutual adjustment. *Personnel and Guidance Journal* 55: 181–5.

Fiedler, F. E. (1950) A comparison of psychoanalytic, nondirective and Adlerian therapeutic relationships. *Journal of Consulting Psychology* 14: 436–45.

Fine, R. (1988) *Troubled Men: The Psychology, Emotional Conflicts and Therapy of Men*. San Franciso: Jossey-Bass.

Firth, J., Shapiro, D. A. and Parry, G. (1986) The impact of research on the practice of psychotherapy. *British Journal of Psychotherapy* 2: 169–79.

Fitz, R. and Cada, L. (1975) The recovery of religious life. *Review for Religious* 34: 690–718.

Fordham, M. (1986) *Jungian Psychotherapy*. London: Karnac.

Forsyth, D. R. (1990) *Group Dynamics*, 2nd edn. Pacific Grove, CA: Brooks/Cole.

Foskett, J. and Jacobs, M. (1989) Pastoral counselling. In W. Dryden, D. Charles-Edwards and R. Woolfe (eds) *Handbook of Counselling in Britain*. London: Tavistock/Routledge.

Foskett, J. and Lyall, D. (1988) *Helping the Helpers*. London: SPCK.

Foucault, M. (1967) *Madness and Civilization: A History of Insanity in the Age of Reason*. London: Tavistock.

Frank, J. D. (1973) *Persuasion and Healing: A Comparative Study of Psychotherapy*. Baltimore: Johns Hopkins Press.

Frank, J. D. (1974) Psychotherapy: the restoration of morale. *American Journal of Psychiatry* 131: 272–4.

Frazier, P. A. and Cohen, B. B. (1992) Research on the sexual victimization of women: implications for counselor training. *Counseling Psychologist* 20: 141–58.

Freeman, A. and Simon, K. M. (1989) Cognitive therapy of anxiety. In A. Freeman, K. M. Simon, L. E. Beutler and H. Arkowitz (eds) *Comprehensive Handbook of Cognitive Therapy*. New York: Plenum Press.

Freeman, A., Simon, K. M., Beutler, L. E. and Arkowitz, H. (eds) (1989) *Comprehensive Handbook of Cognitive Therapy*. New York: Plenum Press.

Freeman, C. and Tyrer, P. (eds) (1989) *Research Methods in Psychiatry: A Beginner's Guide*. London: Gaskell.

Freeman, D. R. (1990) *Couples in Conflict: Inside the Consulting Room*. Milton Keynes: Open University Press.

Freud, S. (1901/1979) The case of Dora. *Pelican Freud Library Vol. 8: Case Histories I*. Harmondsworth: Penguin.

Freud, S. (1905/1977) Three essays on the theory of sexuality. *Pelican Freud Library Vol. 7: On Sexuality.* Harmondsworth: Penguin.

Freud, S. (1909/1979) Notes upon a case of obsessional neurosis (the 'Rat Man'). *Pelican Freud Library Vol. 9: Case Histories II.* Harmondsworth: Penguin.

Freud, S. (1910/1979) Psychoanalytic notes on an autobiographical account of a case of paranoia (Dementia Paranoides) (Schreber). *Pelican Freud Library Vol. 9: Case Histories II.* Harmondsworth: Penguin.

Freud, S. (1917/1973) *Introductory Lecture on Psychoanalysis.* Harmondsworth: Penguin.

Freud, S. (1924/1977) The dissolution of the Oedipus complex. *Pelican Freud Library Vol. 7: On Sexuality.* Harmondsworth: Penguin.

Freud, S. (1933/1973) *New Introductory Lectures on Psycho-Analysis.* Harmondsworth: Penguin.

Freudenberger, H. J. (1974) Staff burn-out. *Journal of Social Issues* 30: 159–65.

Friedman, D. and Kaslow, N. J. (1986) The development of professional identity in psychotherapists: six stages in the supervision process. In F. W. Kaslow (ed.) *Supervision and Training: Models, Dilemmas and Challenges.* New York: Haworth Press.

Friedman, M. (1982) Psychotherapy and the human image. In P. W. Sharkey (ed.) *Philosophy, Religion and Psychotherapy: Essays in the Philosophical Foundations of Psychotherapy.* Washington: University Press of America.

Fulero, S. M. (1988) Tarasoff: 10 year later. *Professional Psychology: Research and Practice.* 19: 184–90.

Garfield, S. (1982) Eclecticism and integration in psychotherapy. *Behavior Therapy* 13: 610–23.

Garfield, S. L. (1986) Research on client variables in psychotherapy. In S. L. Garfield and A. E. Bergin (eds) *Handbook of Psychotherapy and Behavior Change.* 3rd edn. London: Wiley.

Garfield, S. L. and Bergin, A. E. (1971) Personal therapy, outcome and some therapist variables. *Psychotherapy* 8: 251–3.

Garfield, S. L. and Bergin, A. E. (eds) (1986) *Handbook of Psychotherapy and Behavior Change,* 3rd edn. New York: Wiley.

Garfield, S. and Kurtz, R. (1974) A survey of clinical psychologists: characteristics, activities and orientations. *The Clinical Psychologist* 28: 7–10.

Garfield, S. and Kurtz, R. (1977) A study of eclectic views. *Journal of Consulting and Clinical Psychology* 45: 78–83.

Gay, P. (1988) *Freud: A Life for our Times.* London: Dent.

Geertz, C. (1973) *The Interpretation of Cultures.* New York: Basic Books.

Gelso, C. J. and Fassinger, R. E. (1990) Counseling psychology: theory and research on interventions. *Annual Review of Psychology* 41: 355–86.

Gendlin, E. T. (1962) *Experiencing and the Creation of Meaning.* New York: Free Press.

Gendlin, E. T. (1964) A theory of personality change. In P. Worchel and D. Byrne (eds) *Personality Change.* New York: Wiley.

Gendlin, E. T. (1966) Experiential explication and truth. *Journal of Existentialism* 6: 131–46.

Gendlin, E. T. (1969) Focusing. *Psychotherapy* 6: 4–15.

Gendlin, E. T. (1973) Experiential psychotherapy. In R. Corsini (ed.) *Current Psychotherapies.* Itasca IL: Peacock.

Gendlin, E. T. (1974) Client-centered and experiential psychotherapy. In D. A. Wexler and L. N. Rice (eds) *Innovations in Client-Centered Therapy.* New York: Wiley.

Gendlin, E. T. (1978) *Focusing.* New York: Bantam Books.

Gendlin, E. T (1984a) The client's client: the edge of awareness. In R. F. Levant and

J. M. Shlien (eds) *Client-Centered Therapy and the Person-Centered Approach: New Directions in Theory, Research and Practice*. New York: Praeger.

Gendlin, E. T. (1984b) The politics of giving therapy away. In D. G. Larson (ed.) *Teaching Psychological Skills: Models for Giving Psychology Away*. Monterey, CA: Brooks/Cole.

Gendlin, E. T. (1984c) Imagery, body and space in focusing. In A. A. Sheikh (ed.) *Imagination and Healing*. New York: Baywood.

Gendlin, E. T. (1990) The small steps of the therapy process: how they come and how to help them come. In G. Lietaer, J. Rombauts and R. Van Balen (eds) *Client-Centered and Experiential Therapy in the Nineties*. Leuven: Leuven University Press.

Gilligan, C. (1982) *In a Different Voice*. Cambridge, MA: Harvard University Press.

Glaser, B. G. (1978) *Theoretical Sensitivity: Advances in the Methodology of Grounded Theory*. Mill Valley, CA: The Sociology Press.

Glaser, B. G. and Strauss, A. (1967) *The Discovery of Grounded Theory*. Chicago: Aldine.

Glasgow, R. E. and Rosen, G. M. (1978) Behavioral bibliotherapy: a review of self-help behavior therapy manuals. *Psychological Bulletin* 85: 1–23.

Goldberg, C. (1988) *On Being a Psychotherapist: The Journey of the Healer*. New York: Gardner Press.

Goldberg, E. M. and Morrison, S. C. (1963) Schizophrenia and social class. *British Journal of Psychiatry* 109: 785–802.

Goldfried, M. R. (1982) On the history of therapeutic integration. *Behavior Therapy* 13: 572–93.

Goldfried, M. R., Greenberg, L. S. and Marmar, C. (1990) Individual psychotherapy: process and outcome. *Annual Review of Psychotherapy* 41: 659–88.

Gomes-Schwartz, B. and Schwartz, J. M. (1978) Psychotherapy process variables distinguishing the 'inherently helpful' person from the professional psychotherapist. *Journal of Consulting and Clinical Psychology* 46: 196–7.

Good, D. A. and Watts, F. N. (1989) Qualitative research. In G. Parry and F. N. Watts (eds) (1989) *Behavioural and Mental Health Research: A Handbook of Skills and Methods*. London: Lawrence Erlbaum.

Goodman, G. (1984) SASHA tapes: a new approach to enhancing human communication. In D. Larson (ed.) *Teaching Psychological Skills: Models for Giving Psychology Away*. Monterey, CA: Brooks/Cole.

Gordon-Brown, I. and Somers, B. (1988) Transpersonal psychotherapy. In J. Rowan and W. Dryden (eds) *Innovative Therapy in Britain*. Milton Keynes: Open University Press.

Graham, H. (1990) *Time, Energy and the Psychology of Healing*. London: Jessica Kingsley.

Greenberg, I. (ed.) (1974) *Psychodrama: Theory and Therapy*. London: Souvenir Press.

Greenberg, J. R. and Mitchell, S. A. (1983) *Object Relations in Psychoanalytic Theory*. Cambridge, MA: Harvard University Press.

Greenberg, L. S. (1984a) A task analysis of intrapersonal conflict resolution. In L. N. Rice and L. S. Greenberg (eds) *Patterns of Change: Intensive Analysis of Psychotherapy Process*. New York: Guilford Press.

Greenberg, L. S. (1984b) Task analysis: the general approach. In L. N. Rice and L. S. Greenberg (eds) *Patterns of Change: Intensive Analysis of Psychotherapy Process*. New York: Guilford Press.

Greenberg, L. S. and Johnson, S. (1988) *Emotionally Focused Therapy for Couples*. New York: Guilford Press.

Greenberg, L. S. and Pinsof, W. M. (eds) (1986) *The Psychotherapeutic Process: A Research Handbook*. New York: Guilford Press.

Greening, T. C. (1977) The uses of autobiography. In W. Anderson (ed.) *Therapy and the Arts: Tools of Consciousness*. New York: Harper and Row.

Grencavage, L. M. and Norcross, J. C. (1990) Where are the commonalities among the therapeutic common factors? *Professional Psychology: Research and Practice* 21: 372–8.

Gronbjerg, K. A. (1992) Nonprofit human service organizations: funding strategies and patterns of adaptation. In Y. Hasenfeld (ed.) *Human Services as Complex Organizations*. London: Sage.

Grumet, G. W. (1979) Telephone therapy: a review and case report. *American Journal of Orthopsychiatry* 49: 574–84.

Guggenbuhl-Craig, A. (1971) *Power in the Helping Professions*. Dallas: Spring Publications.

Gustafson, J. P. (1986) *The Complex Secret of Brief Psychotherapy*. New York: W. W. Norton.

Gutierrez, L. M. (1992) Empowering ethnic minorities in the twenty-first century: the role of human service organizations. In Y. Hasenfeld (ed.) *Human Services as Complex Organizations*. London: Sage.

Haaga, D. A. and Davison, G. C. (1986) Cognitive change methods. In A. Kanfer and A. Goldstein (eds) *Helping People Change*, 3rd edn. New York: Pergamon.

Hackman, J. and Walton, R. (1986) Leading groups in organisations. In P. Goodman (ed.) *Designing Effective Work Groups*. San Francisco: Jossey-Bass.

Halgin, R. P. (1985) Teaching integration of psychotherapy models to beginning therapists. *Psychotherapy* 22: 555–63.

Hall, A. S. and Fradkin, H. R. (1992) Affirming gay men's mental health: counseling with a new attitude. *Journal of Mental Health Counseling* 14: 362–74.

Halmos, P. (1965) *The Faith of the Counsellors*. London: Constable.

Handy, C. (1990) *Voluntary Organisations*. Harmondsworth: Penguin.

Hanley, I. and Gilhooley, M. (eds) (1986) *Psychological Therapies for the Elderly*. London: Croom Helm.

Hardy, J. (1987) *Psychology with a Soul: Psychosynthesis in Evolutionary Context*. London: Routledge and Kegan Paul.

Hardy, J. and Whitmore, D. (1988) Psychosynthesis. In J. Rowan and W. Dryden (eds) *Innovative Therapy in Britain*. Milton Keynes: Open University Press.

Hare, E. (1962) Masturbatory insanity: the history of an idea. *Journal of Mental Science* 108: 1–25.

Harrison, D. K. (1975) Race as a counselor-client variable in counseling and psychotherapy: a review of the research. *Counseling Psychologist* 5: 124–33.

Harrison, J. (1987) Counseling gay men. In M. Scher, M. Stevens, G. Good and G. A. Eichenfield (eds) *Handbook of Counseling and Psychotherapy with Men*. London: Sage.

Hart, J. T. and Tomlinson, T. M. (eds) (1970) *New Directions in Client-Centered Therapy*. Boston: Houghton Mifflin.

Harway, M. (1979) Training counselors. *Counseling Psychologist* 8: 8–10.

Hasenfeld, Y. (1992) The nature of human service organisations. In Y. Hasenfeld (ed.) *Human Services as Complex Organizations*. London: Sage.

Hattie, J. A., Sharpley, C. F. and Rogers, H. J. (1984) Comparative effectiveness of professional and paraprofessional helpers. *Psychological Bulletin* 95: 534–41.

Hawkins, P. and Shohet, R. (1989) *Supervision in the Helping Professions: An Individual, Group and Organizational Approach*. Milton Keynes: Open University Press.

Hawkins, P. and Shohet, R. (1991) Approaches to the supervision of counsellors. In W. Dryden and B. Thorne (eds) *Training and Supervision for Counselling in Action*. London: Sage.

Heimann, P. (1950) On countertransference. *International Journal of Psycho-Analysis* 31: 81–4.

Hellman, I. D. and Morrison, T. L. (1987) Practice setting and type of caseload as factors in psychotherapist stress. *Psychotherapy* 24: 427–33.

Henry, W. E. (1966) Some observations on the lives of healers. *Human Development* 9: 47–56.

Henry, W. E. (1977) Personal and social identities of psychotherapists. In A. S. Gurman and A. M. Razin (eds) *Effective Psychotherapy: A Handbook of Research.* Oxford: Pergamon.

Henry, W. E., Sims, J. H. and Spray, S. L. (1971) *The Fifth Profession.* San Francisco: Jossey-Bass.

Heppner, P. P., Kivlighan, D. M. Jr and Wampold, B. E. (1992) *Research Design in Counseling.* Belmont, CA: Wadsworth.

Hess, A. K. (ed.) (1980) *Psychotherapy Supervision: Theory, Research and Practice.* New York: Wiley.

Hill, C. E. (1989) *Therapist Techniques and Client Outcomes: Eight Cases of Brief Psychotherapy.* London: Sage.

Hirschhorn, L. (1978) The stalemated agency: a theoretical perspective and a practical proposal. *Administration in Social Work* 2: 425–38.

Hobson, R. E. (1985) *Forms of Feeling: The Heart of Psychotherapy.* London: Tavistock.

Holdstock, L. (1990) Can client-centered therapy transcend its monocultual roots? In G. Lietaer, J. Rombauts and R. Van Balen (eds) *Client-Centered and Experiential Therapy in the Nineties.* Leuven: Leuven University Press.

Holland, R. (1977) *Self and Social Context.* London: Macmillan.

Holland, S. (1979) The development of an action and counselling service in a deprived urban area. In M. Meacher (ed.) *New Methods of Mental Health Care.* London: Pergamon.

Holland, S. (1990) Psychotherapy, oppression and social action: gender, race and class in black women's depression. In R. J. Perelberg and A. C. Miller (eds) *Gender and Power in Families.* London: Tavistock/Routledge.

Hollon, S. D. and Kendall, P. C. (1981) *In vivo* assessment techniques for cognitive-behavioral processes. In P. C. Kendall and S. D. Hollon (eds) *Assessment Strategies for Cognitive-Behavioral Interventions.* New York: Academic Press.

Holroyd, J. C. and Brodsky, A. (1977) Psychologists' attitudes and practices regarding erotic and nonerotic physical contact with patients. *American Psychologist* 32: 843–9.

Holtzman, B. L. (1984) Who's the therapist here? Dynamics underlying therapist-client sexual relations. *Smith College Studies in Social Work* 54: 204–24

Hooper, D. and Dryden, W. (eds) (1991) *Couple Therapy: A Handbook.* Milton Keynes: Open University Press.

Hosking, D. and Morley, I. (1991) *A Social Psychology of Organizing: People, Processes and Contexts.* Englewood Cliffs, NJ: Prentice-Hall.

Houston, G. (1990) *Supervision and Counselling.* London: The Rochester Foundation.

Howard, K. I., Kopta, S. M., Krause, M. S. and Orlinsky, D. E. (1986) The dose-effect relationship in psychotherapy. *American Psychologist* 41: 159–64.

Howell, E. (1981) Women: from Freud to the present. In E. Howell and M. Bayes (eds) *Women and Mental Health.* New York: Basic Books.

Howell, E. and Bayes, M. (eds) (1981) *Women and Mental Health.* New York: Basic Books.

Hurvitz, N. (1967) Marital problems following psychotherapy with one spouse. *Journal of Consulting Psychology* 31: 38–47.

Inskipp, F. and Johns, H. (1984) Developmental eclecticism: Egan's skills model of helping. In W. Dryden (ed.) *Individual Therapy in Britain.* Milton Keynes: Open University Press.

Ivey, A. E. and Galvin, M. (1984) Microcounseling: a metamodel for counseling, therapy, business and medical interviews. In D. Larson (ed.) *Teaching Psychological Skills: Models for Giving Psychology Away*. Monterey, CA: Brooks/Cole.

Ivey, A. E, Ivey, M. B. and Simek-Downing, L. (1987) *Counseling and Psychotherapy: Integrating Skills, Theory and Practice*, 2nd edn. Englewood Cliffs, NJ: Prentice-Hall.

Jacobs, M. (1986) *The Presenting Past*. Milton Keynes: Open University Press.

Jacobs, M. (1988) *Psychodynamic Counselling in Action*. London: Sage.

James, M. and Jongeward, D. (1971) *Born to Win: Transactional Analysis with Gestalt Experiments*. Reading, MA: Addison-Wesley.

James, W. (1890) *Principles of Psychology*. New York: Holt.

Jeske, J. O. (1984) Varieties of approaches to psychotherapy: options for the Christian therapist. *Journal of Psychology and Theology* 12: 260–9.

Johnson, W. B. and Ridley, C. R. (1992) Sources of gain in Christian counseling and psychotherapy. *Counseling Psychologist* 20: 159–75.

Jones, E. (1951) *Essays in Applied Psychoanalysis, Vol. II*. London: Hogarth Press.

Jones, E. (1955) *Life and Work of Sigmund Freud, Vol. 2*. London: Hogarth Press.

Jung, C. G. (1963) *Memories, Dreams, Reflections* (edited by A. Jaffe). New York: Pantheon Books.

Jung, C. G. (1964) *Man and His Symbols*. New York: Doubleday.

Jupp, J. J. and Shaul, V. (1991) Burn-out in student counsellors. *Counselling Psychology Quarterly* 4: 157–67.

Kachele, H. (1992) Narration and observation in psychotherapy research: reporting on a 20 year long journey. *Psychotherapy Research* 2: 1–15.

Kagan, N. (1984) Interpersonal Process Recall: basic methods and recent research. In D. Larson (ed.) *Teaching Psychological Skills: Models for Giving Psychology Away*. Monterey, CA: Brooks/Cole.

Kagan, N. and Kagan, H. (1990) IPR – A validated model for the 1990s and beyond. *Counseling Psychologist* 18: 436–40.

Kagan, N., Krathwohl, D. R. and Miller, R. (1963) Stimulated recall in therapy using videotape – a case study. *Journal of Counseling Psychology* 10: 237–43.

Kanfer, A. and Goldstein, A. (eds) (1986) *Helping People Change*, 3rd edn. New York: Pergamon.

Kaplan, A. G. (1987) Reflections on gender and psychotherapy. In M. Braude (ed.) *Women, Power and Therapy*. New York: Haworth Press.

Karasu, T. B. (1986) The specificity against nonspecificity dilemma: toward identifying therapeutic change agents. *American Journal of Psychiatry* 143: 687–95.

Kareem, J. and Littlewood, R. (1992) *Intercultural Therapy*. Oxford: Blackwell.

Karlsruher, A. E. (1974) The nonprofessional as psychotherapeutic agent. *American Journal of Community Psychology* 2: 61–77.

Kaslow, F. W. (1986) Supervision, consultation and staff training – creative teaching/learning processes in the mental health profession. In F. W. Kaslow (ed.) *Supervision and Training: Models, Dilemmas and Challenges*. New York: Haworth Press.

Katz, D. and Kahn, R. I. (1978) *The Social Psychology of Organizations*, 2nd edn. New York: Wiley.

Kaufmann, Y. (1989) Analytical Psychotherapy. In R. J. Corsini and D. Wedding (eds) *Current Psychotherapies*, 4th edn. Itasca, IL: F. E. Peacock.

Kazdin, A. E. (1978) *History of Behavior Modification: Experimental Foundations of Contemporary Research*. Baltimore: University Park Press.

Kelly, T. A. (1989) The role of values in psychotherapy: a critical review of process and outcome effects. *Clinical Psychology Review* 10: 171–86.

Kendall, P. C. and Hollon, S. D. (1981) Assessing self-referent speech: methods in the measurement of self-statements. In P. C. Kendall and S. D. Hollon (eds) *Assessment Strategies for Cognitive-Behavioral Interventions*. New York: Academic Press.

Kernberg, O. F. (1975) *Borderline Conditions and Pathological Narcissism*. New York: Aronson.

Kernberg, O. F. (1976) *Object Relations Theory and Clinical Psychoanalysis*. New York: Jason Aronson.

Kernberg, O. F. (1984) *Severe Personality Disorders: Psychotherapeutic Strategies*. New Haven, C T: Yale University Press.

Kirsch, I. (1978) Demonology and the rise of science: an example of the misperception of historical data. *Journal of the History of the Behavioral Sciences* 14: 149–57.

Kirschenbaum, H. (1979) *On Becoming Carl Rogers*. New York: Dell.

Kirschenbaum, H. and Henderson, V. L. (eds) (1990) *Carl Rogers: Dialogues*. London: Constable.

Kitchener, K. S. (1984) Intuition, critical evaluation and ethical principles: the foundation for ethical decisions in counseling psychology. *Counseling Psychologist* 12: 43–55.

Klein, J. (1987) *Our Need for Others and its Roots in Infancy*. London: Tavistock.

Klein, M. H., Mathieu-Coughlan, P. and Kiesler, D. J. (1986) The Experiencing Scales. In L. S. Greenberg and W. M. Pinsof (eds) *The Psychotherapeutic Process: A Research Handbook*. New York: Guilford Press.

Klemp, G. and McClelland, D. (1986) What characterizes intelligent functioning among senior managers? In R. Sternberg and R. Wagner (eds) *Practical Intelligence: The Nature and Origins of Competence in the Everyday World*. Cambridge: Cambridge University Press.

Knight, B. (1986) *Psychotherapy with Older Adults*. London: Sage.

Koffka, K. (1935) *Principles of Gestalt Psychology*. New York: Harcourt, Brace.

Kohler, W. (1929) *Gestalt Psychology*. New York: Liveright.

Kohon, G. (ed.) (1986) *The British School of Psychoanalysis: The Independent Tradition*. London: Free Association Books.

Kohut, H. (1971) *The Analysis of the Self*. London: Hogarth.

Kohut, H. (1977) *The Restoration of the Self*. Madison, CT: International Universities Press.

Koltko, M. E. (1990) How religious beliefs affect psychotherapy: the example of Mormonism. *Psychotherapy* 27: 132–41.

Kopp, S. (1972) *If You Meet the Buddha on the Road, Kill Him!* Palo Alto, CA: Science and Behavior Books.

Kopp, S. (1974) *The Hanged Man*. Palo Alto, CA: Science and Behavior Books.

Kottler, J. (1988) *The Imperfect Therapist*. San Francisco: Jossey-Bass.

Kovacs, A. L. (1976) The emotional hazards of teaching psychotherapy. *Psychotherapy* 13: 321–34.

Kovel, J. (1981) The American mental health industry. In D. Ingleby (ed.) *Critical Psychiatry: The Politics of Mental Health*. Harmondsworth: Penguin.

Kuehnel, J. and Liberman, P. (1986) Behavior modification. In I. Kutush and A. Wolf (eds) *A Psychotherapist's Casebook*. San Francisco: Jossey-Bass.

Kuhn, T. S. (1962) *The Structure of Scientific Revolutions*. Chicago: University of Chicago Press.

Kurtz, R. and Grummon, D. (1972) Different approaches to the measurement of therapist empathy and their relationship to therapy outcomes. *Journal of Consulting and Clinical Psychology* 39: 106–15.

LaFramboise, T. D. and Foster, S. L. (1992) Cross-cultural training: scientist-practitioner model and methods. *Counseling Psychologist* 20: 472–89.

Lago, C. and Thompson, J. (1989) Counselling and race. In W. Dryden, D. Charles-Edwards and R. Woolfe (eds) *Handbook of Counselling in Britain*. London: Tavistock/Routledge.

Laing, R. D. (1960) *The Divided Self*. Harmondsworth: Penguin.

Laing, R. D. (1961) *Self and Others*. Harmondsworth: Penguin.

Lakin, M. (1988) *Ethical Issues in the Psychotherapies*. New York: Oxford University Press.

Lambert, M. J., Christensen, E. R. and DeJulio, S. S. (eds) (1983) *The Assessment of Psychotherapy Outcome*. New York: Wiley.

Larson, D. (ed.) (1984) *Teaching Psychological Skills: Models for Giving Psychology Away*. Monterey, CA: Brooks/Cole.

Larson, L. M. *et al.* (1992) Development and validation of the counseling self-estimate inventory. *Journal of Counseling Psychology* 39: 105–20.

Lazarus, A. A. (1989a) *The Practice of Multimodal Therapy*. Baltimore: Johns Hopkins University Press.

Lazarus, A. A. (1989b) Multimodal therapy. In R. J. Corsini and D. Wedding (eds) *Current Psychotherapies*, 4th edn. Itasca, IL: F. E. Peacock.

Lener, R. (1972) *Therapy in the Ghetto*. New York: Wiley.

Lester, D. (1974) The unique qualities of telephone therapy. *Psychotherapy* 11: 219–21.

Levant, R. F. and Shlien, J. M. (eds) (1984) *Client-Centered Therapy and the Person-Centered Approach: New Directions in Theory, Research and Practice*. New York: Praeger.

Lewinsohn, P. M., Steinmetz, J. L., Larson, D. W. and Franklin, J. (1981) Depression related cognitions: antecedent or consequences? *Journal of Abnormal Psychology* 90: 213–19.

Lewis, J., Clark, D. and Morgan, D. (1992) *Whom God Hath Joined Together: The Work of Marriage Guidance*. London: Routledge.

Lieberman, M., Yalom, I. and Miles, M. (1973) *Encounter Groups: First Facts*. New York: Basic Books.

Lietaer, G. (1984) Unconditional positive regard: a controversial basic attitude in client-centered therapy. In R. F. Levant and J. M. Shlien (eds) *Client-Centered Therapy and the Person-Centered Approach: New Directions in Theory, Research and Practice*. New York: Praeger.

Lietaer, G. (1990) The client-centered approach after the Wisconsin project: a personal view on its evolution. In G. Lietaer, J. Rombauts and R. Van Balen (eds) *Client-Centered and Experiential Therapy in the Nineties*. Leuven: Leuven University Press.

Lietaer, G., Rombauts, J. and Van Balen, R. (eds) (1990) *Client-Centered and Experiential Therapy in the Nineties*. Leuven: Leuven University Press.

Linden, J., Stone, S. and Shertzer, B. (1965) Development and evaluation of an inventory for rating counseling. *Personnel and Guidance Journal* 44: 267–76.

Lipkin, S. (1948) The client evaluates nondirective therapy. *Journal of Consulting Psychology* 12: 137–46.

Llewelyn, S. and Hume, W. (1979) The patient's view of therapy. *British Journal of Medical Psychology* 52: 29–36.

Llewelyn, S. and Osborn, K. (1983) Women as clients and therapists. In D. Pilgrim (ed.) *Psychology and Psychotherapy: Current Trends and Issues*. London: Routledge.

Locke, A. (1971) Is behavior therapy 'behavioristic'? *Psychological Bulletin* 76: 318–27.

Lomas, P. (1981) *The Case for a Personal Psychotherapy*. Oxford: Oxford University Press.

Lomas, P. (1987) *The Limits of Interpretation: What's Wrong with Psychoanalysis*. Harmondsworth: Penguin.

Lopez, S. R., Lopez, A. A. and Fong, K. T. (1991) Mexican Americans' initial preferences for counselors: the role of ethnic factors. *Journal of Counseling Psychology* 38: 487–96.

Lorion, R. P. and Felner, R. D. (1986) Research on psychotherapy with the disadvantaged. In S. L. Garfield and A. E. Bergin (eds) *Handbook of Psychotherapy and Behavior Change*, 3rd edn. London: Wiley.

Luborsky, L., Crits-Christoph, P. and Mellon, J. (1986) Advent of objective measures of the transference concept. *Journal of Consulting and Clinical Psychology* 54: 39–47.

Luborsky, L., Singer, B. and Luborsky, L. (1975) Comparative studies of psychotherapies: is it true that 'everyone has one and all must have prizes'? *Archives of General Psychiatry* 32: 995–1008.

McCarley, T. (1975) The psychotherapist's search for self-renewal. *American Journal of Psychiatry* 132: 221–4.

McConnaughy, E. A. (1987) The person of the therapist in therapeutic practice. *Psychotherapy* 24: 303–14.

McGrath, G. and Lowson, K. (1986) Assessing the benefits of psychotherapy: the economic approach. *British Journal of Psychiatry* 150: 65–71.

Mack, J. (1981) Alcoholism, AA and the governance of self. In M. H. Bean and N. E. Zinberg (eds) *Dynamic Approaches to the Understanding and Treatment of Alcoholism*. New York: Free Press.

McKinney, F. (1976) Free writing as therapy. *Psychotherapy* 13: 183–7.

McLeod, J. (1984) Group process as drama. *Small Group Behavior* 15: 319–32.

McLeod, J. (1990) The client's experience of counselling: a review of the research literature. In D. Mearns and W. Dryden (eds) *Experiences of Counselling in Action*. London: Sage.

McNeill, B. W. and Worthen, V. (1989) The parallel process in psychotherapy supervision. *Professional Psychology: Research and Practice* 20: 329–33.

McNeill, J. T. (1951) *A History of the Cure of Souls*. New York: Harper and Row.

Macquarrie, J. (1972) *Existentialism*. Harmondsworth: Penguin.

Mahler, M. S. (1968) *On Human Symbiosis and the Vicissitudes of Individuation: Infantile Psychosis*. New York: International Universities Press.

Mahler, M. S., Pine, F. and Bergman, A. (1975) *The Psychological Birth of the Human Infant*. New York: Basic Books.

Mahrer, A. (1989) *The Integration of Psychotherapies: A Guide for Practicing Therapists*. New York: Human Sciences Press.

Mahrer, A. R. *et al.* (1987) Good and very good moments in psychotherapy: content, distribution and facilitation. *Psychotherapy* 24: 7–14.

Mair, M. (1989) *Between Psychology and Psychotherapy: A Poetics Of Experience*. London: Routledge.

Malan, D. H. (1976) *The Frontiers of Brief Psychotherapy*. New York: Plenum.

Malan, D. H. (1979) *Individual Psychotherapy and the Science of Psychodynamics*. London: Butterworths.

Malony, H. N. (1983) God-talk in psychotherapy. In H. N. Malony (ed.) *Wholeness and Holiness*. Grand Rapids, MI: Baker.

Maluccio, A. (1979) *Learning from Clients: Interpersonal Helping as Viewed by Clients and Social Workers*. New York: The Free Press.

Mangen, S. (1988) Assessing cost-effectiveness. In F. N. Watts (ed.) *New Developments in Clinical Psychology, Vol. II*. Chichester: Wiley.

Mann, D. (1989) Incest: the father and the male therapist. *British Journal of Psychotherapy* 6: 143–53.

Mann, J. (1973) *Time-limited Psychotherapy*. Cambridge, MA: Harvard University Press.

Manning, N. (1989) *The Therapeutic Community Movement: Charisma and Routinization*. London: Routledge.

Marineau, R. F. (1989) *Jacob Levy Moreno 1889–1974: Father of Psychodrama, Sociometry and Group Psychotherapy*. London: Tavistock/Routledge.

Marlatt, G. A. and Gordon, J. R. (eds) (1985) *Relapse Prevention: Maintenance Strategies in the Treatment of Addictive Behaviors*. New York: Guilford Press.

Marmor, J. (1953) The feeling of superiority: an occupational hazard in the practice of psychotherapy. *American Journal of Psychiatry* 110: 370–6.

Marmor, J. and Woods, S. M (eds) (1980) *The Interface Between the Psychodynamic and Behavioral Therapies*. New York: Plenum.

Marston, A. R. (1984) What makes therapists run? A model for the analysis of motivational styles. *Psychotherapy* 21: 456–9.

Martin, J., Slemon, A. G., Hiebert, B., Hallberg, E. T. and Cummings, A. L. (1989) Conceptualizations of novice and experienced counselors. *Journal of Counseling Psychology* 36: 395–400.

Maslach, C. and Jackson, S. E. (1984) Burnout in organisational settings. In S. Oskamp (ed.) *Applied Social Psychology Annual 5: Applications in Organizational Settings*. London: Sage.

Masson, J. M. (1984) *The Assault on Truth: Freud's Suppression of the Seduction Theory*. New York: Farrar, Strauss and Giroux.

Masson, J. (1988) *Against Therapy: Emotional Tyranny and the Myth of Psychological Healing*. Glasgow: Collins.

Masson, J. (1992) The tyranny of psychotherapy. In W. Dryden and C. Feltham (eds) *Psychotherapy and its Discontents*. Buckingham: Open University Press.

Mathieu-Coughlan, P. and Klein, M. H. (1984) Experiential psychotherapy: key events in client-therapist interaction. In L. N. Rice and L. S. Greenberg (eds) *Patterns of Change: Intensive Analysis of Psychotherapy Process*. New York: Guilford Press.

Maultsby, M. C. (1971) Systematic written homework in psychotherapy. *Psychotherapy* 8: 195–8.

Maxwell, R. J. (1984) Quality assessment in health. *British Medical Journal* 288: 1470–2.

May, R. (1950) *The Meaning of Anxiety*. New York: W. W. Norton.

May, R., Angel, E. and Ellenberger, H. (1958) *Existence: A New Dimension in Psychology and Psychiatry*. New York: Basic Books.

Meadow, A. (1964) Client-centered therapy and the American ethos. *International Journal of Social Psychiatry* 10: 246–60.

Mearns, D. and Thorne, B. (1988) *Person-Centred Counselling in Action*. London: Sage.

Meichenbaum, D. (1977) *Cognitive-Behavior Modification: An Integrative Approach*. New York: Plenum.

Meichenbaum, D. (1985) *Stress Innoculation Training*. New York: Pergamon.

Meichenbaum, D. (1986) Cognitive-behavior modification. In A. Kanfer and A. Goldstein (eds) *Helping People Change*, 3rd edn. New York: Pergamon.

Meltzer, J. D. (1978) A semiotic approach to suitability for psychotherapy. *Psychiatry* 41: 360–76.

Menzies, I. (1959) A case-study in the functioning of social systems as a defence against anxiety: a report on a study of the nursing service of a general hospital. *Human Relations* 13: 95–121.

Miller, A. (1987) *The Drama of Being a Child and the Search for the True Self*. London: Virago.

Miller, D. J. and Thelen, M. H. (1987) Confidentiality in psychotherapy: history, issues and research. *Psychotherapy* 24: 704–11.

Miller, J. B. (1976) *Toward a New Psychology of Women*. Harmondsworth: Penguin.

Miller, J. B. (1987) Women and power. In M. Braude (ed.) *Women, Power and Therapy*. New York: Haworth Press.

Mischel, W. (1968) *Personality and Assessment*. New York: Wiley.

Mitchell, J. (1974) *Psychoanalysis and Feminism: A Radical Reassessment of Freudian Psychoanalysis*. London: Allen Lane.

Moore, J. (1991) On being a supervisee. In W. Dryden and B. Thorne (eds) *Training and Supervision for Counselling in Action*. London: Sage.

Morley, S. (1989) Single case research. In G. Parry and F. N. Watts (eds) (1989) *Behavioural and Mental Health Research: A Handbook of Skills and Methods*. London: Lawrence Erlbaum.

Morrow-Bradley, C. and Elliott, R. (1986) Utilization of psychotherapy research by practicing psychotherapists. *American Psychologist* 41: 188–97.

Moyers, J. C. (1990) Religious issues in the psychotherapy of former Fundamentalists. *Psychotherapy* 27: 42–5.

Murray, H. A. (1938) *Explorations in Personality: A Clinical and Experimental Study of Fifty Men of College Age*. New York: Oxford University Press.

Myrick, R. and Kelly, F. (1971) A scale for evaluating practicum students in counseling and supervision. *Counselor Education and Supervision* 10: 330–6.

Neimeyer, G. and Resnikoff, A. (1982) Qualitative strategies in counseling research. *Counseling Psychologist* 10: 75–85.

Nelson, R. O. (1981) Realistic dependent measures for clinical use. *Journal of Consulting and Clinical Psychology* 49: 168–82.

Nelson, S. H. and Torrey, E. F. (1973) The religious functions of psychiatry. *American Journal of Orthopsychiatry* 43: 362–7.

Neugebauer, R. (1978) Treatment of the mentally ill in medieval and early modern England: a reappraisal. *Journal of the History of the Behavioral Sciences* 14: 158–69.

Neugebauer, R. (1979) Early and modern theories of mental illness. *Archives of General Psychiatry* 36: 477–83.

Nietzel, M. T. and Fisher, S. G. (1981) Effectiveness of professional and paraprofessional helpers: a comment on Durlak. *Psychological Bulletin* 89: 555–65.

Norcross, J. (ed.) (1986) *Handbook of Eclectic Psychotherapy*. New York: Brunner/Mazel.

Norcross, J. C. and Aranowitz, H. (1992) The evolution and current status of psychotherapy integration. In W. Dryden (ed.) *Integrative and Eclectic Therapy: A Handbook*. Buckingham: Open University Press.

Norcross, J. C. and Grencavage, L. M. (1989) Eclecticism and integration in counselling and psychotherapy: major themes and obstacles. *British Journal of Guidance and Counselling* 17: 215–47.

Norcross, J. C. and Guy, J. D. (1989) Ten therapists: the process of becoming and being. In W. Dryden and L. Spurling (eds) *On Becoming a Psychotherapist*. London: Tavistock/Routledge.

Norcross, J. C., Strausser, D. J. and Faltus, F. J. (1988a) The therapist's therapist. *American Journal of Psychotherapy* 42: 53–66.

Norcross, J. C., Strausser, D. J. and Missar, C. D. (1988b) The processes and outcomes of psychotherapists' personal treatment experiences. *Psychotherapy* 25: 36–43.

Norcross, J. C. *et al.* (1986) Training integrative/eclectic psychotherapists. *International Journal of Eclectic Psychotherapy* 5: 71–103.

Oatley, K. (1980) Theories of personal learning in groups. In P. B. Smith (ed.) *Small Groups and Personal Change*. London: Methuen.

Oatley, K. (1984) *Selves in Relation: An Introduction to Psychotherapy and Groups*. London: Methuen.

Ogles, B. M., Lambert, M. J. and Craig, D. E. (1991) Comparison of self-help books for coping with loss: expectations and attributions. *Journal of Counseling Psychology* 38: 387–93.

Omer, H. and Dar, R. (1992) Changing trends in three decades of psychotherapy research: the flight from theory into pragmatics. *Journal of Consulting and Clinical Psychology* 60: 88–93.

Omer, H. and London, P. (1988) Metamorphosis in psychotherapy: end of the systems era. *Psychotherapy* 25: 171–84.

Orleans, C. T. *et al.* (1991) Self-help quitting smoking interventions: effects of self-help manuals, social support instructions and telephone counselling. *Journal of Consulting and Clinical Psychology* 59: 439–48.

Osipow, S. H. and Reed, R. A. (1987) Training and evaluation in counseling psychology. In B. A. Edelstein and E. S. Berler (eds) *Evaluation and Accountability in Clinical Training*. New York: Plenum Press.

Ossip-Klein, D. J. *et al.* (1991) Effects of a smokers' hotline: results of a ten-county self-help trial. *Journal of Consulting and Clinical Psychology* 59: 325–32.

O'Sullivan, K. R. and Dryden, W. (1990) A survey of clinical psychologists in the South East Thames Region: activities, role and theoretical orientation. *Clinical Psychology Forum* 29: 21–6.

Paolino, T. and McCrady, B. (eds) (1978) *Marriage and Marital Therapy: Psychoanalytic, Behavioral and Systems Theory Perspectives*. New York: Brunner/Mazel.

Parlett, M. and Page, F. (1990) Gestalt Therapy. In W. Dryden (ed.) *Individual Therapy: A Handbook*. Milton Keynes: Open University Press.

Parloff, M. B. (1986) Frank's 'common elements' in psychotherapy: nonspecific factors and placebos. *American Journal of Orthopsychiatry* 56: 521–30.

Parry, G. (1992) Improving psychotherapy services: applications of research, audit and evaluation. *British Journal of Clinical Psychology* 31: 3–19.

Parry, G. and Watts, F. N. (eds) (1989) *Behavioural and Mental Health Research: A Handbook of Skills and Methods*. London: Lawrence Erlbaum.

Passons, W. R. (1975) *Gestalt Approaches to Counselling*. New York: Holt, Rinehart and Winston.

Pates, A. and Knasel, E. (1989) Assessment of counselling skills development: the learning record. *British Journal of Guidance and Counselling* 17: 121–32.

Patterson, C. H. (1984) Empathy, warmth and genuineness in psychotherapy: a review of reviews. *Psychotherapy* 21: 431–8.

Patterson, C. H. (1989) Eclecticism in psychotherapy: is integration possible? *Psychotherapy* 26: 157–61.

Paul, G. L. (1967) Strategy of outcome research in psychotherapy. *Journal of Consulting Psychology* 31: 109–18.

Peake, T. (1988) *Brief Psychotherapies: Changing Frames of Mind*. London: Sage.

Peck, M. S. (1978) *The Road Less Traveled: A New Psychology of Love, Traditional Values and Spiritual Growth*. New York: Simon and Schuster.

Pedersen, P. (ed.) (1985) *Handbook of Cross-Cultural Counseling and Psychotherapy*. New York: Praeger.

Peebles, M. J. (1980) Personal therapy and ability to display empathy, warmth and genuineness in therapy. *Psychotherapy* 17: 252–62.

Perls, F. S. (1947) *Ego, Hunger and Aggression*. London: Allen and Unwin.

Perls, F. S. (1969) *Gestalt Therapy Verbatim*. Lafayette, CA: Real People Press.

Perls, F. S. (1973) *The Gestalt Approach and Eye-Witness to Therapy*. Ben Lomond, CA: Science and Behavior Books.

Perls, F. S., Hefferline, R. F. and Goodman, P. (1951) *Gestalt Therapy: Excitement and Growth in the Human Personality*. New York: Julian Press.

Phillips, J. P. N. (1986) Shapiro Personal Questionnaire and generalized personal questionnaire techniques: a repeated measures individualized outcome measurement. In L. S. Greenberg and W. M. Pinsof (eds) *The Psychotherapeutic Process: A Research Handbook*. New York: Guilford Press.

Pilgrim, D. (1990) British psychotherapy in context. In W. Dryden (ed.) *Individual Therapy: A Handbook*. Milton Keynes: Open University Press.

Pilgrim, D. (1992) Psychotherapy and political evasions. In W. Dryden and C. Feltham (eds) *Psychotherapy and Its Discontents*. Buckingham: Open University Press.

Pines, A. (1981) Helpers' motivation and the burnout syndrome. In T. A. Wills (ed.) *Basic Processes in Helping Relationships*. New York: Academic Press.

Pines, M. (ed.) (1983) *The Evolution of Group Analysis*. London: Tavistock/Routledge.

Piper, W. E. (1988) Psychotherapy research in the 1980s: defining areas of consensus and controversy. *Hospital and Community Psychiatry* 39: 1055–63.

Polanyi, M. (1958) *Personal Knowledge*. London: Routledge.

Ponterotto, J. G. (1988) Racial/ethnic minority research in the *Journal of Counseling Psychology*: a content analysis and methodological critique. *Journal of Counseling Psychology* 35: 410–18.

Pope, K. S. (1986) New trends in malpractice cases and trends in APA's liability insurance. *Independent Practitioner* 6: 23–6.

Pope, K. S. (1991) Dual relationships in psychotherapy. *Ethics and Behavior* 1: 21–34.

Pope, K. S. and Bouhoutsos, J. C. (1986) *Sexual Intimacy between Therapists and Patients*. New York: Praeger.

Pope, K. S., Keith-Speigel, P. and Tabachnick, B. G. (1986) Sexual attraction to clients: the human therapist and the (sometimes) inhuman training system. *American Psychologist* 41: 147–58.

Pope, K. S., Levenson, H. and Schover, L. R. (1979) Sexual intimacy in psychology training: results and implications of a national survey. *American Psychologist* 34: 682–9.

Porter, R. (ed.) (1985) *The Anatomy of Madness, Vols. 1 and 2*. London: Tavistock.

Prince, R. (1980) Variations in psychotherapeutic procedures. In H. C. Triandis and J. G. Draguns (eds) *Handbook of Cross-Cultural Psychopathology Volume 6*. Boston: Allyn and Bacon.

Prochaska, J. O. and DiClemente, C. C. (1982) Transtheoretical therapy: toward a more integrative model of change. *Psychotherapy* 19: 276–88.

Prochaska, J. and Norcross, J. (1983) Contemporary psychotherapists: a national survey of characteristics, practices, orientations and attitudes. *Psychotherapy* 20: 161–73.

Progoff, I. (1975) *At a Journal Workshop*. New York: Dialogue House.

Propst, L. R., Ostrom, R., Watkins, P., Dean, T. and Mashburn, D. (1992) Comparative efficacy of religious and nonreligious cognitive-behavioral therapy for the treatment of clinical depression in religious individuals. *Journal of Consulting and Clinical Psychology* 60: 94–103.

Purton, C. (1991) Selection and assessment in counsellor training courses. In W. Dryden and B. Thorne (eds) *Training and Supervision for Counselling in Action*. London: Sage.

Rabin, A. I., Aronoff, J., Barclay, A. and Zucker, R. (eds) (1981) *Further Explorations in Personality*. New York: Wiley.

Rabin, A. I., Zucker, R. A., Emmons, R. A. and Frank, S. (eds) (1990) *Studying Persons and Lives*. New York: Springer.

Ramaswami, S. and Sheikh, A. A. (1989) Buddhist psychology: implications for healing. In A. A. Sheikh and K. S. Sheikh (eds) *Eastern and Western Approaches to Healing: Ancient Wisdom and Modern Knowledge*. New York: Wiley.

Ramirez, M. III (1991) *Psychotherapy and Counseling with Minorities: A Cognitive Approach to Individual and Cultural Differences*. Oxford: Pergamon Press.

Rapaport, D. and Gill, M. (1959) The points of view and assumptions of meta-psychology. *International Journal of Psycho-Analysis* 40: 153–62.

Rayner, E. (1990) *The Independent Mind in British Psychoanalysis*. London: Free Association Books.

Rennie, D. L. (1990) Toward a representation of the client's experience of the psychotherapy hour. In G. Lietaer, J. Rombauts and R. Van Balen (eds) *Client-Centered and Experiential Therapy in the Nineties*. Leuven: University of Leuven Press.

Rennie, D. L. (1992) Qualitative analysis of the client's experience of psychotherapy: the unfolding of reflexivity. In S. Toukmanian and D. Rennie (eds) *Psychotherapy Process Research*. London: Sage.

Rennie, D. L., Phillips, J. R. and Quartaro, J. K. (1988) Grounded theory: a promising approach for conceptualization in psychology? *Canadian Psychology* 29: 139–50.

Rice, L. N. (1974) The evocative function of the therapist. In D. A. Wexler and L. N. Rice (eds) *Innovations in Client-Centered Therapy*. New York: Wiley.

Rice, L. N. (1984) Client tasks in client-centered therapy, in R. F. Levant and J. M. Shlien (eds) *Client-Centered Therapy and the Person-Centered Approach: New Directions in Theory, Research and Practice*. New York: Praeger.

Rice, L. N. and Greenberg, L. S. (eds) (1984a) *Patterns of Change: Intensive Analysis of Psychotherapy Process*. New York: Guilford Press.

Rice, L. N. and Greenberg, L. S. (1984b) The new research paradigm. In L. N. Rice and L. S. Greenberg (eds) *Patterns of Change: Intensive Analysis of Psychotherapy Process*. New York: Guilford Press.

Rice, L. N. and Kerr, G. P. (1986) Measures of client and therapist voice quality. In L. S. Greenberg and W. M. Pinsof (eds) *The Psychotherapeutic Process: A Research Handbook*. New York: Guilford Press.

Rice, L. N. and Saperia, E. (1984) Task analysis of the resolution of problematic reactions. In L. N. Rice and L. S. Greenberg (eds) *Patterns of Change: Intensive Analysis of Psychotherapy Process*. New York: Guilford.

Riesman, D., Glazer, N. and Denny, R. (1950) *The Lonely Crowd*. New Haven, CT: Yale University Press.

Rippere, V. and Williams, R. (eds) (1985) *Wounded Healers: Mental Health Workers' Experiences of Depression*. New York: Wiley.

Robbins, S. P. (1991) *Organizational Behavior*, 3rd edn. Englewood Cliffs, NJ: Prentice-Hall.

Roberts, J. and Pines, M. (eds) (1991) *The Practice of Group Analysis*. London: Tavistock/Routledge.

Robinson, D. (1980) Self-help health groups. In P. B. Smith (ed.) *Small Groups and Personal Change*. London: Methuen.

Rogers, C. R. (1942) *Counseling and Psychotherapy*. Boston: Houghton Mifflin.

Rogers, C. R. (1951) *Client-Centered Therapy*. Boston: Houghton Mifflin.

Rogers, C. R. (1957) The necessary and sufficient conditions of therapeutic personality change. *Journal of Consulting Psychology* 21: 95–103.

Rogers, C. R. (1961) *On Becoming a Person*. Boston: Houghton Mifflin.

Rogers, C. R. (1963) The concept of the fully functioning person. *Psychotherapy: Theory, Research and Practice* 1: 17–26.

Rogers, C. R. (1968) Interpersonal relationships: USA 2000. *Journal of Applied Behavioral Science* 4: 265–80.

Rogers, C. R. (1975) Empathic: an unappreciated way of being. *Counseling Psychologist* 5: 2–10.

Rogers, C. R. (1978) *Carl Rogers on Personal Power: Inner Strength and its Revolutionary Impact*. London: Constable.

Rogers, C. R. (1980) *A Way of Being*. Boston: Houghton Mifflin.

Rogers, C. R. and Dymond, R. F. (eds) (1954) *Psychotherapy and Personality Change*. Chicago: University of Chicago Press.

Rogers, C. R., Gendlin, E. T., Kiesler, D. J. and Truax, C. B. (eds) (1967) *The Therapeutic Relationship and its Impact: A Study of Psychotherapy with Schizophrenics*. Madison: University of Wisconsin Press.

Rogers, C. R. and Stevens, B. (eds) (1968) *Person to Person: The Problem of Being Human*. Lafayette, CA: Real People Press.

Rogler, L. H., Malgady, R. G., Costantino, G. and Blumenthal, R. (1987) What do culturally sensitive mental health services mean? The case of Hispanics. *American Psychologist* 42: 565–70.

Rokeach, M. (1973) *The Nature of Human Values*. New York: The Free Press.

Rosen, G. M. (1987) Self-help treatment books and the commercialization of psychotherapy. *American Psychologist* 42: 46–51

Rosenbaum, M. (1974) Continuation of psychotherapy by 'long distance' telephone. *International Journal of Psychoanalytic Psychotherapy* 3: 483–95.

Rosewater, L. B. and Walker, L. E. A. (eds) (1985) *Handbook of Feminist Therapy: Women's Issues in Psychotherapy*. New York: Springer.

Rothman, D. (1971) *The Discovery of the Asylum: Social Order and Disorder in the New Republic*. Boston: Little Brown.

Rowan, J. (1992a) *The Transpersonal: Psychotherapy and Counselling*. London: Routledge.

Rowan, J. (1992b) *Breakthroughs and Integration in Psychotherapy*. London: Whurr.

Rowan, J. and Dryden, W. (eds) (1988) *Innovative Therapy in Britain*. Milton Keynes: Open University Press.

Rutter, P. (1989) *Sex in the Forbidden Zone*. London: Mandala.

Rycroft, C. (1966) Causes and meaning. In C. Rycroft (ed.) *Psychoanalysis Observed*. London: Constable.

Rycroft, C. (1985) *Psychoanalysis and Beyond*. London: Chatto and Windus.

Ryle, A. (1978) A common language for the psychotherapies? *British Journal of Psychiatry* 132: 585–94.

Ryle, A. (1987) Cognitive psychology as a common language for psychotherapy. *Journal of Integrative and Eclectic Psychotherapy* 6: 191–212.

Ryle, A. (1990) *Cognitive-Analytic Therapy: Active Participation in Change: A New Integration in Brief Psychotherapy*. Chichester: Wiley.

Ryle, A. and Cowmeadow, P. (1992) Cognitive-analytic therapy (CAT). In W. Dryden (ed.) *Integrative and Eclectic Therapy: A Handbook*. Buckingham: Open University Press.

Sachs, J. (1983) Negative factors in brief psychotherapy: an empirical assessment. *Journal of Consulting and Clinical Psychology* 51: 557–64.

Salmon, P. (1991) Psychotherapy and the wider world. *The Psychologist* 2: 50–1.

Sampson, H. and Weiss, J. (1986) Testing hypotheses: the approach of the Mount Zion Psychotherapy Research Group. In L. S. Greenberg and W. M. Pinsof (eds) *The Psychotherapeutic Process: A Research Handbook*. New York: Guilford Press.

Sattler, J. M. (1977) The effects of therapist-client racial similarity. In A. S. Gurman and A. M. Razin (eds) *Effective Psychotherapy: A Review of Research*. New York: Pergamon.

Sayers, J. (1991) *Mothering Psychoanalysis: Helene Deutsch, Karen Horney, Anna Freud and Melanie Klein*. Harmondsworth: Penguin.

Scarf, M. (1987) *Intimate Partners*. New York: Century.

Scheff, T. (1974) The labeling theory of mental illness. *American Sociological Review* 39: 444–52.

Scher, M., Stevens, M., Good, G. and Eichenfield, G. A. (eds) (1987) *Handbook of Counseling and Psychotherapy with Men*. New York: Sage.

Schiff, J. L., Schiff, A. W. *et al.* (1975) *Cathexis Reader: Transactional Analysis Treatment of Psychosis*. New York: Harper and Row.

Scofield, M. and Yoxheimer, L. (1983) Psychometric issues in the assessment of clinical competencies. *Journal of Counseling Psychology* 30: 413–20.

Scogin, F., Bynum, J., Stephens, G. and Calhoon, S. (1990) Efficacy of self-administered treatment programmes: meta-analytic review. *Professional Psychology: Research and Practice* 21: 42–7.

Scull, A. (1975) From madness to mental illness: medical men as moral entrepreneurs. *European Journal of Sociology* 16: 218–61.

Scull, A. (1979) *Museums of Madness: The Social Organization of Insanity in Nineteenth Century England*. London: Allen Lane.

Scull, A. (1981a) Moral treatment reconsidered: some sociological comments on an episode in the history of British psychiatry. In A. Scull (ed.) *Mad-houses, Mad-doctors and Madmen*. Pennsylvania: University of Pennsylvania Press.

Scull, A. (ed.) (1981b) *Mad-houses, Mad-doctors and Madmen*. Pennsylvania: University of Pennsylvania Press.

Scull, A. (1989) *Social Order/Disorder: Anglo-American Psychiatry in Historical Perspective*. London: Routledge.

Scully, R. (1983) The work-setting support group: a means of preventing burnout. In B. A. Farber (ed.) *Stress and Burnout in the Human Service Professions*. New York: Pergamon.

Searles, H. (1975) The patient as therapist to his analyst. In R. C. Givaccini (ed.) *Tactics and Techniques in Psychoanalytic Treatment, Vol II*. New York: Jason Aronson.

Seeman, J. (1949) A study of the process of nondirective therapy. *Journal of Consulting Psychology* 13: 157–68.

Segal, H. (1964) *Introduction to the Work of Melanie Klein*. London: Hogarth.

Segal, J. (1985) *Phantasy in Everyday Life: A Psychoanalytical Approach to Understanding Ourselves*. Harmondsworth: Penguin.

Segal, J. (1992) *Melanie Klein*. London: Sage.

Seligman, M. E. P. (1975) *Helplessness*. San Francisco: Freeman.

Shafranske, E. P. and Malony, H. N. (1990) Clinical psychologists' religious and spiritual orientations and their practice of psychotherapy. *Psychotherapy* 27: 72–9.

Sharaf, M. R. and Levinson, D. J. (1964) The quest for omnipotence in professional training. *Psychiatry* 27: 135–49.

Shaw, B. and Dobson, K. (1988) Competency judgements in the training and evaluation of psychotherapists. *Journal of Consulting and Clinical Psychology* 56: 666–72.

Sheikh, A. A. and Sheikh, K. S. (eds) (1989) *Eastern and Western Approaches to Healing: Ancient Wisdom and Modern Knowledge*. New York: Wiley.

Shepard, M. (1975) *Fritz*. New York: Bantam Books.

Shohet, R. and Wilmot, J. (1991) The key issue in the supervision of counsellors: the supervisory relationship. In W. Dryden and B. Thorne (eds) *Training and Supervision for Counselling in Action*. London: Sage.

Shotter, J. (1975) *Images of Man in Psychological Research*. London: Methuen.

Showalter, E. (1985) *The Female Malady: Women, Madness and English Culture, 1830–1980*. New York: Pantheon Books.

Sifneos, P. E. (1979) *Short-term Dynamic Psychotherapy*. New York: Plenum.

Silberschatz, G., Fretter, P. B. and Curtis, J. T. (1986) How do interpretations influence the process of psychotherapy? *Journal of Consulting and Clinical Psychology* 54: 646–52.

Skinner, B. F. (1953) *Science and Human Behavior*. New York: Macmillan.

Skynner, R. and Cleese, J. (1983) *Families and How to Survive Them*. London: Methuen.

Slaikeu, K. A. and Willis, M. A. (1978) Caller feedback on counselor performance in telephone crisis intervention: a follow-up study. *Crisis Intervention* 9: 42–9.

Sloane, R. B., Staples, F. R., Cristol, A. H., Yorkson, N. J. and Whipple, K. (1975) *Psychotherapy Versus Behavior Therapy*. Cambridge, MA: Harvard University Press.

Smail, D. (1978) *Psychotherapy: A Personal Approach*. London: Dent.

Smail, D. (1984) *Illusion and Reality: The Meaning of Anxiety*. London: Dent.

Smail, D. (1991) Towards a radical environmentalist psychology of help. *The Psychologist* 2: 61–5.

Smith, M., Glass, G. and Miller, T. (1980) *The Benefits of Psychotherapy*. Baltimore: Johns Hopkins Press.

Snyder, W. U. (1945) An investigation of the nature of non-directive psycho-therapy. *Journal of Genetic Psychology* 13: 193–223.

Sollod, R. N. (1978) Carl Rogers and the origins of client-centered therapy. *Professional Psychology* 9: 93–104.

Sollod, R. N. (1982) Non-scientific sources of psychotherapeutic approaches. In P. W. Sharkey (ed.) *Philosophy, Religion and Psychotherapy: Essays in the Philosophical Foundations of Psychotherapy*. Washington: University Press of America.

Southgate, J. and Randall, R. (1978) *The Barefoot Psychoanalyst: An Illustrated Manual of Self-Help Therapy*. London: Association of Karen Horney Psychoanalytic Counsellors.

Southwell, C. (1988) The Gerda Boyson method: Biodynamic Therapy. In J. Rowan and W. Dryden (eds) *Innovative Therapy in Britain*. Milton Keynes: Open University Press.

Spanos, I. (1978) Witchcraft in histories of psychiatry: a critical analysis and alternative conceptualisation. *Psychological Bulletin* 85: 417–39.

Spurling, L. and Dryden, D. (1989) The self and the therapeutic domain. In W. Dryden and L. Spurling (eds) *On Becoming a Psychotherapist*. London: Tavistock/Routledge.

Stadler, H. A. (1986) Making hard choices: clarifying controversial ethical issues. *Counseling and Human Development* 19: 1–10.

Starker, S. (1988) Do-it-yourself therapy: the prescription of self-help books by psychologists. *Psychotherapy* 25: 142–6.

Steenbarger, B. N. (1992) Toward science-practice integration in brief counseling and therapy. *Counseling Psychologist* 20: 403–50.

Stein, D. M. and Lambert, M. J. (1984) Telephone counseling and crisis intervention: a review. *American Journal of Community Psychology* 12: 101–26.

Steiner, C. (1970) *Games Alcoholics Play*. New York: Grove Press.

Steiner, C. (1971) *Scripts People Live*. New York: Grove Press.

Stern, E. M. (ed.) (1985) *Psychotherapy and the Religiously Committed Patient*. New York: Haworth.

Stevenson, J. F. and Norcross, J. C. (1987) Current status of training evaluation in clinical psychology. In B. A. Edelstein and E. S. Berler (eds) *Evaluation and Accountability in Clinical Training*. New York: Plenum Press.

Stiles, W. B. (1991) Longitudinal study of assimilation in exploratory psychotherapy. *Psychotherapy* 28: 195–206.

Stiles, W. B., Elliott, R., Llewelyn, S. P., Firth-Cozens, J. A., Margison, F. R., Shapiro, D. A. and Hardy, G. (1990) Assimilation of problematic experiences in psychotherapy. *Psychotherapy* 27: 411–20.

Stiles, W. B., Meshot, C. M., Anderson, T. M. and Sloan, W. W. (1992) Assimilation of problematic experiences: the case of John Jones. *Psychotherapy Research* 2: 81–101.

Stiles, W. B. and Shapiro, D. A. (1989) Abuse of the drug metaphor in psychotherapy process-outcome research. *Clinical Psychology Review* 9: 521–43.

Stock, W. (1988) Propping up the phallocracy: a feminist critique of sex therapy and research. In E. Cole and E. D. Rothblum (eds) *Women and Sex Therapy: Closing the Circle of Sexual Knowledge*. New York: Harrington Park Press.

Stoltenberg, C. D. and Delworth, U. (1987) *Supervising Counselors and Therapists*. San Francisco: Jossey-Bass.

Street, E. and Dryden, W. (eds) (1988) *Family Therapy in Britain*. Milton Keynes: Open University Press.

Strupp, H. (1978) The therapist's theoretical orientation: an overrated variable. *Psychotherapy* 15: 314–17.

Strupp, H. H. (1980a) Success and Failure in time-limited psychotherapy. A systematic comparison of two cases: comparison 1. *Archives of General Psychiatry* 37: 595–603.

Strupp, H. H. (1980b) Success and failure in time-limited psychotherapy. A systematic comparison of two cases: comparison 2. *Archives of General Psychiatry* 37: 708–16.

Strupp, H. H. (1980c) Success and failure in time-limited therapy: with special reference to the performance of the lay counselor. *Archives of General Psychiatry* 37: 831–41.

Strupp, H. H. (1980d) Success and failure in time-limited psychotherapy. Further evidence: comparison 4. *Archives of General Psychiatry* 37: 947–54.

Strupp, H. H. (1986) The nonspecific hypothesis of therapeutic effectiveness: a current assessment. *American Journal of Orthopsychiatry* 56: 513–20.

Strupp, H. H. and Hadley, S. W. (1979) Specific vs nonspecific factors in psychotherapy: a controlled study of outcome. *Archives of General Psychiatry* 36: 1125–36.

Sue, D. W. (1981) *Counseling the Culturally Different: Theory and Practice*. London: Wiley.

Sue, S. *et al.* (1991) Community mental health services for ethnic minority groups: a test of the cultural responsiveness hypothesis. *Journal of Consulting and Clinical Psychology* 59: 533–40.

Sugarman, L. (1992) Ethical issues in counselling at work. *British Journal of Guidance and Counselling* 20: 64–74.

Sutich, A. J. (1986) Transpersonal psychotherapy: history and definition. In S. Boorstein (ed.) *Transpersonal Psychotherapy*. Palo Alto, CA: Science and Behavior Books.

Suzuki, D. T., Fromm, E. and de Martino, R. (eds) (1970) *Zen Buddhism and Psychoanalysis*. New York: Harper and Row.

Symington, N. (1983) The analyst's act of freedom as an agent of therapeutic change. *International Review of Psycho-Analysis* 10: 83–91.

Szasz, T. S. (1971) *The Manufacture of Madness: A Comparative Study of the Inquisition and the Mental Health Movement*. London: Routledge and Kegan Paul.

Szasz, T. S. (1974) *The Ethics of Psycho-Analysis: The Theory and Method of Autonomous Psychotherapy*. London: Routledge and Kegan Paul.

Tausch, R. (1990) The supplementation of client-centered communication therapy with other valid therapeutic methods: a client-centered necessity. In G. Lietaer, J. Rombauts and R. Van Balen (eds) *Client-Centered and Experiential Therapy in the Nineties*. Leuven: Leuven University Press.

Taylor, M. (1990) Fantasy or reality? the problem with psychoanalytic interpretation in psychotherapy with women. In E. Burman (ed.) *Feminists on Psychological Practice*. London: Sage.

Taylor, M. (1991) How psychoanalytic thinking lost its way in the hands of men: the case for feminist psychotherapy. *British Journal of Guidance and Counselling* 19: 93–103.

Taylor, V. (1983) The future of feminism in the 1980s: a social movement analysis. In L. Richardson and V. Taylor (eds) *Feminist Frontiers: Rethinking Sex, Gender and Society*. Reading, MA: Addison-Wesley.

Thoresen, C. and Mahoney, M. (1974) *Behavioral Self-Control*. New York: Holt, Rinehart and Winston.

Thorne, B. (1985) Interview with Brian Thorne. In W. Dryden (ed.) *Therapists' Dilemmas*. London: Harper and Row.

Thorne, B. (1987) Beyond the core conditions. In W. Dryden (ed.) *Key Cases in Psychotherapy*. London: Croom Helm.

Thorne, B. (1991) *Person-Centred Counselling: Therapeutic and Spiritual Dimensions*. London: Whurr.

Thorne, B. (1992) *Carl Rogers*. London: Sage.

Thorne, B. and Dryden, W. (1991) Key issues in the training of counsellors. In W. Dryden and B. Thorne (eds) *Training and Supervision for Counselling in Action*. London: Sage.

Tiefer, L. (1988) A feminist critique of the sexual dysfunction nomenclature. In E. Cole and E. D. Rothblum (eds) *Women and Sex Therapy: Closing the Circle of Sexual Knowledge*. New York: Harrington Park Press.

Timms, N. and Blampied, A. (1985) *Intervention in Marriage: The Experience of Counsellors and their Clients*. University of Sheffield: Joint Unit for Social Services Research.

Tolman, E. C. (1948) Cognitive maps in rats and men. *Psychological Review* 55: 189–208.

Toukmanian, S., Capelle, R. and Rennie, D. (1978) Counsellor trainee awareness of evaluative criteria: a neglected variable. *Canadian Counselor* 12: 177–83.

Towbin, A. P. (1978) The confiding relationship: a new paradigm. *Psychotherapy* 15: 333–43.

Trower, P., Bryant, M. and Argyle, M. (1978) *Social Skills and Mental Health*. London: Tavistock.

Truax, C. B. (1966) Reinforcement and nonreinforcement in Rogerian psychotherapy. *Journal of Abnormal Psychology* 71: 1–9.

Truax, C. B. and Carkhuff, R. R. (1967) *Toward Effective Counseling and Psychotherapy*. Chicago: Aldine.

Tyler, J. and Weaver, S. (1981) Evaluating the clinical supervisee: a survey of practice in graduate training programmes. *Professional Psychology* 12: 434–7.

Tyndall, N. (1985) The work and impact of the National Marriage Guidance Council. In W. Dryden (ed.) *Marital Therapy in Britain, Vol. 1*. London: Harper and Row.

Van Balen, R. (1990) The therapeutic relationship according to Carl Rogers: only a climate? a dialogue? or both? In G. Lietaer, J. Rombauts and R. Van Balen (eds) *Client-Centered and Experiential Therapy in the Nineties*. Leuven: Leuven University Press.

Van Belle, H. A. (1990) Rogers' later move toward mysticism: implications for client-centered therapy. In G. Lietaer, J. Rombauts and R. Van Balen (eds) *Client-Centered and Experiential Therapy in the Nineties*. Leuven: Leuven University Press.

Van De Riet, V., Korb, M. P. and Gorrell, J. J. (1980) *Gestalt Therapy: An Introduction*. New York: Pergamon.

Van Deurzen-Smith, E. (1988) *Existential Counselling in Practice*. London: Sage.

Van Hoose, W. H. and Kottler, J. A. (1985) *Ethical and Legal Issues in Counseling and Psychotherapy*, 2nd edn. San Francisco: Jossey-Bass.

Wade, P. and Bernstein, B. L. (1991) Cultural sensitivity training and counselors' race: effects on black female clients' perceptions and attrition. *Journal of Counseling Psychology* 38: 9–15.

Wallace, A. F. C. (1958) Dreams and the wishes of the soul: a type of psychoanalytic theory among the seventeenth century Iroquois. *American Anthropologist* 60: 234–48.

Waller, D. and Gilroy, A. (eds) (1992) *Art Therapy: A Handbook*. Buckingham: Open University Press.

Walls, G. B. (1980) Values and psychotherapy: a comment on 'Psychotherapy and Religious Values'. *Journal of Consulting and Clinical Psychology* 48: 640–2.

Wanigaratne, S., Wallace, W., Pullin, J., Keaney, F. and Farmer, R. (1990) *Relapse Prevention for Addictive Behaviours: A Manual for Therapists*. Oxford: Blackwell.

Ward, C. A. (ed.) (1989) *Altered States of Consciousness and Mental Health: A Cross-cultural Perspective*. London: Sage.

Warnath, C. F. and Shelton, J. L. (1976) The ultimate disappointment: the burned-out counselor. *Personnel and Guidance Journal* 55: 172–5.

Watson, G. (1940) Areas of agreement in psychotherapy. *American Journal of Orthopsychiatry* 10: 698–709.

Watson, J. B. (1919) *Psychology from the Standpoint of a Behaviorist*. Philadelphia: J. B. Lippincott.

Watson, N. (1984) The empirical status of Rogers's hypotheses of the necessary and sufficient conditions for effective psychotherapy. In R. F. Levant and J. M. Shlien (eds) *Client-Centered Therapy and the Person-Centered Approach: New Directions in Theory, Research and Practice*. New York: Praeger.

Wexler, D. A. and Rice, L. N. (eds) (1974) *Innovations in Client-Centered Therapy*. New York: Wiley.

Whitaker, D. (1985) *Using Groups to Help People*. London: Tavistock/Routledge.

Whiteley, J. M. (1984) A historical perspective on the development of counseling psychology as a profession. In S. D. Brown and R. W. Lent (eds) *Handbook of Counseling Psychology*. New York: Wiley.

Whiteley, J. M., Sprinthall, N. A., Mosher, R. L. and Donaghy, R. T. (1967) Selection and evaluation of counselor effectiveness. *Journal of Counseling Psychology* 14: 226–34.

Whitfield, G. (1988) Bioenergetics. In J. Rowan and W. Dryden (eds) *Innovative Therapy in Britain*. Milton Keynes: Open University Press.

Whitman, R. and Stock, D. (1958) The group focal conflict. *Psychiatry* 21: 267–76.

Wills, T. A. (1982) Nonspecific factors in helping relationships. In T. A. Wills (ed.) *Basic Processes in Helping Relationships*. New York: Academic Press.

Winnicott, D. W. (1958) *Collected Papers: Through Paediatrics to Psychoanalysis*. London: Hogarth.

Winnicott, D. W. (1964) *The Child, the Family and the Outside World*. Harmondsworth: Penguin.

Winnicott, D. W. (1965) *The Maturational Process and the Facilitating Environment*. London: Hogarth.

Winnicott, D. W. (1971) *Playing and Reality*. London: Hogarth.

Wise, E. A. (1988) Issues in psychotherapy with EAP clients. *Psychotherapy* 25: 415–19.

Wittmer, J. and Lister, J. L. (1971) The Graduate Record Examination, 16PF questionnaire, and counseling effectiveness. *Counselor Education and Supervision* 10: 293.

Wollheim, R. (1971) *Freud*. London: Fontana.

Wolpe, J. (1958) *Psychotherapy by Reciprocal Inhibition*. Stanford, CA: Stanford University Press.

Wolpe, J. (1978) Cognition and causation in human behavior and its therapy. *American Psychologist* 33: 437–6.

Woody, R. H. (1989) *Business Success in Mental Health Practice: Modern Marketing, Management and Legal Strategies*. San Francisco: Jossey-Bass.

Woolfe, R. (1983) Counselling in a world of crisis: towards a sociology of counselling. *International Journal for the Advancement of Counselling* 6: 167–76.

Worell, J. (1981) New directions in counseling women. In E. Howell and M. Bayes (eds) *Women and Mental Health*. New York: Basic Books.

Yalom, I. (1975) *Theory and Practice of Group Psychotherapy*. New York: Basic Books.

Yalom, I. D. (1980) *Existential Psychotherapy*. New York: Basic Books.

Yalom, I. (1986) *Theory and Practice of Group Psychotherapy*, 3rd edn. New York: Basic Books.

Yalom, I. D. (1989) *Love's Executioner and Other Tales of Psychotherapy*. Harmondsworth: Penguin.

Yontef, G. M. and Simkin, J. S. (1989) Gestalt Therapy. In R. J. Corsini and D. Wedding (eds) *Current Psychotherapies*, 4th edn. Itasca, IL: F. E. Peacock.

Young, H. S. (1988) Practising RET with Bible-Belt Christians. In W. Dryden and P. Trower (eds) *Developments in Rational-Emotive Therapy*. Milton Keynes: Open University Press.

Young, R. (1989) Helpful behaviors in the crisis center call. *Journal of Community Psychology* 17: 70-7.

Zajonc, R. (1980) Feeling and thinking: preferences need no inferences. *American Psychologist* 35: 151-75.

INDEX

DARING TO BE MYSELF
A CASE STUDY IN RATIONAL-EMOTIVE THERAPY
Windy Dryden and Joseph Yankura

This book is unique in the field of psychotherapy in the substantial use it makes of actual dialogue between therapist and client. It is the first book to take an in-depth look at the experience of rational-emotive therapy, exploring a single case as sessions unfold over time. The book traces closely the developing therapeutic work between Sarah and Dr Windy Dryden, and uses substantial transcript material to illustrate the therapist's interventions and the client's response. The sessions are contextualized by background information on client, therapist and therapeutic techniques; and also by post-therapy feedback from both Sarah and Windy Dryden. The book provides both a unique insight into the actual processes of psychotherapy and a fascinating story of how Sarah finally 'dared to be herself'.

'. . . an outstanding document that is rare in the entire annals of psychotherapy'.

Albert Ellis

'How often do we have the opportunity to observe an effective and innovative therapy in action? Dr Dryden makes therapy come alive by demonstrating the precise clinical choice-points and counselling strategies that were employed session-by-session. Thus, students, practitioners and teachers of counselling and therapy have the chance of learning from poignant response-couplets and compelling choice-points throughout.'   Arnold Lazarus

Contents
Background information: therapist and client – The basic theory and techniques of rational-emotive therapy – The initial session – The early sessions: teaching self-importance; teaching other-acceptance; learning how to cope with adverse circumstances – The middle sessions: review of progress on original presenting problems; troubleshooting and identification of additional problem areas; anticipating termination – The later sessions: dealing with approval anxiety; exposing one's humanness; treatment's end – The follow-up session – The post-therapy interviews – References – Index.

192pp   0 335 09341 8 (Paperback)

BRIEF COUNSELLING
A PRACTICAL GUIDE FOR BEGINNING PRACTITIONERS

Windy Dryden and Colin Feltham

This very practical book is designed to help beginner counsellors and therapists to examine and improve their work. It is addressed to those practitioners who choose, or are obliged to work within a brief contact; and to all those who recognize the reality that counselling and therapy often turn out to be much briefer than their popular image might suggest. The ideas in the book are culled from the authors' own experiences as seasoned practitioners of brief counselling as well as from their work as supervisors and trainers of counsellors. They address the kind of questions frequently asked by trainee and beginner counsellors, and provide guidelines rather than injunctions. They do not assume that any particular counselling orientation is more fitting for brief counselling than any other, and they give various examples of how practitioners from different schools might regard particular issues. They provide helpful hints from a broad perspective and an invaluable resource for fine-tuning the work of counsellors and therapists.

Contents
Part I: Orienting the client to counselling – Part II: Assessing the client's concerns – Part III: Initiating change – Part IV: Encouraging change through homework – Part V: Counselling in the middle phase – Part VI: Ending counselling – Afterword – Appendices – References – Index.

240pp   0 335 09972 6 (Paperback)

SURVIVING SECRETS
THE EXPERIENCE OF ABUSE FOR THE CHILD,
THE ADULT AND THE HELPER

Moira Walker

In recent years considerable attention has been paid to the subject of abuse in childhood. Less attention has been paid to what happens to the vast number of women and men who have reached adulthood with this experience haunting them. Moira Walker overviews the experience and its implications, dealing with physical, sexual and psychological abuse. An essential part of the content is based on interviews with survivors of child abuse, voicing their views on the effects of the experience and the effectiveness of the help offered. At the same time, *Surviving Secrets* seeks to understand the context in which abuse takes place, the society which itself contains and sustains abuse at various levels. It is a moving account of the experience and effects of childhood abuse, and a handbook for all those in the caring professions, in voluntary organizations and elsewhere who are helping survivors of abuse.

Contents
Introduction – A web of secrets: generations of abuse – Adults reflect: the child's experience – Childhood abuse: the adult's experience – Sharing secrets: the child's and the adult's experience – The development of Multiple Personality Disorder – Stages in the process of counselling and therapy – Particular issues in the process of therapy – Issues for the helper – References – Index.

224pp   0 335 09763 4 (Paperback)   0 335 09764 2 (Hardback)

INSIGHT AND EXPERIENCE
A MANUAL OF TRAINING IN THE TECHNIQUE AND THEORY OF PSYCHODYNAMIC COUNSELLING AND THERAPY

Michael Jacobs

This is a series of original and practical exercises for tutors, trainers and supervisors to use with counsellors; and for student counsellors who have experienced the exercises to use for revision of their learning. It is designed to promote some of the more advanced skills used in counselling and therapy, and to further an understanding of many of the issues and concepts which underlie a psychodynamic approach. It charts a developmental course, firstly in terms of the counsellor's own development and secondly in terms of the individual client's life cycle. The exercises illustrate the interplay between client and therapist, past and present, reality and fantasy, and give insight into the constituent elements that contribute to the development of people's relationships, attitudes, preconceptions and beliefs. For each exercise there is a clearly argued rationale for its use; details of the necessary materials, methodology, duration, instructions and debriefing; and the author's own contextualizing and concluding comments.

This is an experiential training manual for psychodynamically informed individual counselling and, as we have come to expect from Michael Jacobs, it is packed with a wealth of illustrative case material, insights, knowledge and experience.

Contents
Preconceptions: revising basic skills – The facilitating environment: further skills – Working in and working with groups – Insight and experience – Trust and dependency – Authority and autonomy – Co-operation and competition – Experiencing adolescence – The ages of adulthood – Some issues in adult life – Loss and death – Drawing together: The Evil Man – Notes to chapters – Bibliography – Indexes of exercises and subjects.

240pp   0 335 09791 X (Paperback)   0 335 09792 8 (Hardback)